GO GREYHOUND, GO!

Go Greyhound, Go!

A Journey Through Sixties America

Paul Watkins

Illustrations by the author

FORMAT BOOKS

For Millie
The New American

Published by
Format Books
23 Jeffreys Street
London NW1 9PS
www.formatbooks.com

A catalogue record for this book is available
from the British Library

ISBN 978-0-903372-20-6

Printed and bound by CPI Group (UK) Ltd, Croydon CR0 4YY

Cover design and illustrations by the author

Contents

Foreword

The idea was fanciful, impractical, romantic. To see America on six dollars a day.

Could it be done? Even after a diligent course of Arthur Frommer I wasn't sure. All I had were the hopes that had lasted through three months of planning. Plus, three essential items. A book of traveller's cheques to guard my currency. A book of Greyhound Bus tickets, pre-paid, guaranteeing me non-stop travel for three months. And a stamp in my passport, admitting me as an immigrant to the United States.

This was the trump card. I'd got it holding my left arm out for a blood test and my right arm up in the air, swearing to uphold the constitution of the United States. Taking me at my word the US Embassy officials had presented me with a large yellow envelope, containing all my personal data, which I was required to hand over to the immigration authorities on arrival in New York. In return for this I would receive an alien registration card, sent to a forwarding address in Texas, which would identify me as an immigrant. The object of all this formality was simple. If the daily budget showed signs of strain I could use the card to get employment.

But if one thing made it all physically possible it was that little book of tokens, each worth a single journey over any distance and making an entire continent (Canada was included) open to twentieth-century explorers. The mainspring of the idea was a full-page ad in a travel magazine inviting readers to 'Travel a New World – See the U.S.A'. A challenging proposition, coupled with a panoramic shot of the Grand Canyon with a group of spellbound sightseers. Enough to bait the hook of the main copy, a brief treatise on the wonders of America which culminated in a line of bold type proclaiming '99 days of travel for only £35'. To promote bookings the Greyhound Bus Company, together with its competitor Continental Trailways, had provided the biggest travel bargain of the century. A book of tickets costing 99 dollars, which covered the holder for 99 days of unlimited travel on their buses.

The challenge was irresistible. After three years working in a London office I'd developed a chronic fever to get out into the world. Three months seemed a fair amount of time to satisfy my migratory instincts and to get to know America.

And the six-dollar budget? If my calculations were wrong, it could evaporate. My immigrant's visa, entitling me to work? As good as the next tomato crop in California. Unpredictable events? Hurricanes in Florida, earthquakes in San Francisco, blizzards in the Rockies... All potential hazards, like getting lost in the desert or being mauled by a grizzly bear. My hopes of survival, I felt sure, lay with those kindred spirits along the way who were looking out for me.

Publisher's comment: please note that with some amendments the text of this book is that of the original version written in the 1960s.

New York, 1965

Put Me Down on Bleecker Street

'*May I have your attention, please. The 2.30am Baltimore Express is now loading at Gate Seven...*'

The Tannoy echoed through the frozen concourse of New York's Greyhound Bus Depot. The man sitting next to me in the waiting room did the math. 'Three more hours we got, till the Philadelphia,' he muttered. Like me, he was spending the night.

Could I possibly survive three more hours in the New York Port Authority Bus Terminal, among that happy crowd of down-and-outs, furlough boys and rucksack zombies?

By that Monday dawn we'd all lost a weekend.

'*... It was tough on Bougainville. Y'had to keep up with the tanks, even with the mud up to your goddam knees...*'

If sleep was possible then the drawling monotone of the Pacific War veteran behind me would have lulled me into it. But the hardness of the wooden bench defied even the droop of an eyelid.

The seat divisions, screwed in at eighteen-inch intervals, demanded a single upright posture. In their war against the dossing multitudes, the Port Authority had invented an effective strategy to keep everyone awake. This was no consolation to a weary traveller – and in my case one who'd been spoiled by two nights on a YMCA mattress and five in a cosy transatlantic cabin...

The only gain from spending a night in the bus depot was a saving of four dollars (YMCA), and the promise of a dawn ride southwards on the Great American Freeway. Such considerations would set the course of the next three months.

From the journey ahead my thoughts reverted to the arrival in New York, two days ago. At the outset it had been traumatic.

Hastening to the Sports Deck of the great Cunarder (RMS *Queen Elizabeth*) I had hacked my shin on the gangway. Catching my breath, I wished I'd shown some moderation the night before, to keep a clear head – and eye – for that first glimpse of the famous skyline.

As it was, I'd been a victim of fate. Chosen randomly as a guest at the Purser's Table during the voyage, and on the final night an invitee to drinks in his cabin, I'd been inveigled by the Assistant Purser (female) into drinking more gin and tonics than were good for me. Sleeping it off had not been an option when this lady had further induced me to join her in the Garden Lounge for the Elimination Dance, a contest in which partners had to freeze when the music stopped (same rules as Musical Chairs but without the benefit of sitting down). In my semi-paralytic state I'd found myself immobile, and fully dependent on the support of my partner, thus guaranteeing our statue-like stance at the critical moment. The prize for my efforts was a propelling pencil with a miniature *Queen Elizabeth* floating in the cap. As a dutiful employee of Cunard Lines my partner had forsaken any prize, no doubt grateful enough to be relieved of my inert body.

The breeze on the Sports Deck cleared my head just enough for me to absorb my first lesson in scale. The world's largest passenger liner passing *under* a road bridge.

The recently opened Verrazano Narrows Bridge was the world's largest suspension span. Stretching over the harbour entrance it was like a vast steel bow, the triumphal arch of the New World. If the bridge was an eye-opener, it was nothing compared to what followed. Coasting through the Narrows we soon had our first haze-shrouded view of the Manhattan skyline. An image that more than any other symbolized America.

My feelings on approaching it were, I like to think, akin to those of earlier arrivals, beholding their promised land for the first time. Between them and me, of course, there was a measurable distance. They the 'huddled masses, yearning to breathe free' and me the tourist archetype with rucksack and Rolleiflex.

I could assure myself that I would have a better reception than my historical predecessors. After a gruelling transatlantic voyage, endured by many of them on open decks, those wretched but resolutely hopeful people had suffered the pain and ignominy of Ellis Island.

The notorious immigration depot they'd called 'The Isle of Tears' had closed its doors only eleven years previously, after sixty-two years as America's human sorting house. In the early 1900s there might have been as many as 15,000 potential immigrants a day queuing at its gates, seeing their hopes of a new life either confirmed or denied. The lucky ones who passed the examination by doctors and immigration inspectors would step finally on the mainland shore with a landing card and a singing heart: the unlucky ones would be turned around, their fate sealed by a chalk mark.

We passed too far from the Statue of Liberty to appreciate its size or significance. To my straining eyes, which had anticipated more, it was merely a sunlit figurine on a pedestal, raising an arm more in supplication than welcome. Was it really 300 feet tall?

Emerging from the haze, Manhattan was stupendous. The great aerial city, its skyscrapers like towers of quartz shimmering in the morning sun, was no longer a photo in the *National Geographic* or a cigarette ad, but the real thing. It was like a giant pinnacled mountain, rising from the sea. As we drew near it was possible to distinguish the individual buildings of the Financial District, the cluster at the tip of the peninsula: but where was the Empire State? Such was the scale of the city that I was unable to see the world's tallest building – located little more than a mile from the waterfront – until we were almost parallel and I could spy it between the other looming giants.

The great Queen moved slowly up the Hudson, her sirens saluting the mighty ranks of concrete and stone. Then under the guidance of the tug-boats she drew us gently into the city.

First impressions on stepping ashore at a new destination are often bewildering. Pier 92, New York Harbour, was no exception. The Cunard Line customs hall was vast, enclosing most of the pier. A flurry of anxious passengers queued to clear their baggage under the watchful gaze of customs officials and police.

As I surrendered my visa, their view of me as the latest recruit to the Great Society was not declared – but I was happy enough to receive the scribbled chalk mark on my rucksack.

At first sight New York's enchantment took a dive. Leaving the Customs Hall I entered a street which despite the '*Bienvenue*' sign looked singularly unwelcoming. A clothing store, a bar-cum-diner, a filling station, a few advertisement hoardings and a distant view of a gasometer. An endless line of parked yellow cabs. Hesitating, I retrieved the *National Geographic* tourist map from my rucksack.

'Keep movin', buddy!'

What first looked like an equestrian statue, towering above me, turned into a mounted policeman, booted and spurred, a nightstick hanging at his side. The horse shifted towards me and I backed away. This was my first encounter with a New York icon: others would follow.

On paper Manhattan looked easy to navigate. The streets were laid out in a giant trellis-work, with only the odd creeper – such as Broadway – cutting across at an angle. The numbering was systematic, the streets working in sequence from south to north and the avenues from east to west. The buildings were numbered according to their block, the area between the horizontal and vertical. Hippodamus may have got there first, in the days of ancient Greece, but it was a system that worked.

The Sloane House YMCA, at 356 West 34th Street, was its own grid reference. From the West Side Highway it lay three blocks east and twenty blocks south. Hefting the rucksack onto my shoulders I took the first step into the unknown.

'Wanna ride, pal?'

A yellow cab swung into the kerb, blocking my way. My plan to walk twenty blocks suddenly faded.

The driver second-guessed me. 'Sloane House 'Y'?'

In a cab, Manhattan was not so easy. The streets were one-way, limiting the options, and the lights at each block reduced the traffic to a fume-choked crawl. The street signs, set at right angles at each intersection, were the only clue to our place on the grid.

South of 42nd Street we hit the traffic peculiar to the Garment District: coat hangers on wheels that wove an adroit passage through vehicles and pedestrians alike, apparently self-propelled and with an unerring sense of direction. I had to look twice to spot the pair of scampering legs amidst the coats and dresses. Clothing, I understood, was a major industry here. Second only to construction.

Craning my head out of the cab I tried to glimpse the top storeys of the giants that enclosed us. Glazed pillars of commerce, vying for a foothold on the slender thoroughfare dividing them. Some thrust forward at their lower levels, using every square inch of allotted space before reluctantly stepping back their storeys: others achieved their supremacy more economically by shooting tall straight towers out of spacious plazas. One way or another they were obeying the New York City laws which related the amount of floor space you squeezed out of your site to the amount of daylight that the little people were getting below.

The cab driver's commentary, which had been running since we started, brought me back to earth.

'If you ask me, friend, the city's goin' down the tubes. Got an election for mayor in November, but it ain't gonna make no difference. Look at the state of the streets. Garbage, traffic jams, carbon monoxide. Take a deep breath an' feel lousy. Any driver from outside should pay a dollar toll. Or take the subway. I'd make 'em pay more for that, too. Fifteen cents? Make it twenty-five, make it self-supporting. But don't get me wrong, I'm just sayin' somethin' simple. If you're one of the seven and a half million folks who wanna live in the greatest city in the world you should pay for it. Your money's gonna make the place better after all. Or should do, if they spend it right. But those guys in City Hall, what do they do? Here we are, like I said, in the greatest city in the world, an' we got the country's worst air pollution, worst water pollution, worst housin', worst crime. An' traffic? You know what they say about gettin' to the East Side? You're either born there or you come on the *Queen Elizabeth...*'

The New York cab driver, I knew, was part of the city's folklore. The trouble was, they knew it too.

Somewhere, I'd read that there were three different types. The best were the ones who spoke English and had a good knowledge of the city. Then there were those, less strongly recommended, who spoke only Polish and required detailed directions for any location beyond 42nd Street. Finally there were the ones who knew the five boroughs backwards but would have been happier working for Blueline Sightseeing or the *Wall Street Journal*. My driver clearly belonged in the third category.

We'd turned into Ninth Avenue, a canyon of concrete and steel. 'We got disputes in this city. Power companies, transportation, newspapers... *Look to the left, three blocks, that's the Rockefeller. Radio City, you wanna go there...* Trouble today is automation. Automation means fewer jobs. It's the cause of all the major strikes right now. Joke is, it's automation that's gonna make strikes obsolete. Bell, Con-Ed, those push-button plants can run themselves. We don't need operators no more, to put through a call, switch on the power... If the city could clean up its act it could run itself, we wouldn't need them hacks in City Hall no more. *Hey, we're on 42nd! Times Square two blocks east, Grand Central five...*'

The core of the Big Apple: my heart pounded anew. My driver too was on a high. 'They want a new mayor? I'll take the job. For starters I'd make every vehicle illegal 'ceptin' fire department, ambulances and NYPD. Yeah, an' taxis – yellow cabs, not them goddam gypsies... *Here y'are, buddy, 34th Street an' the Sloane House 'Y'. Further down, Penn Station, Macy's, Empire State...*'

Like the huddled masses who'd preceded me I'd come to America as an immigrant. A beardless youth of twenty-seven (we were late developers in those days), I hailed from the Thames-side town of East Molesey, which would have been just another amorphous suburb of London had it not been for its location near Hampton Court Palace, a gem of England's Tudor heritage viewed from the capital as 'a good day's outing'. My ancestry, which like that of most non-genealogists consisted of only two generations, included grandfathers who would have been defined as 'trade' and lived in other discreet Surrey towns, and grandmothers different enough to write stories (father's side) and be French (mother's side) and die young; and parents whose devotion to the middle-class work ethic (banking and book-keeping) put them firmly on the side of respectability.

In the manner of any other conventionally reared and only notionally rebellious individual I had taken a long time to make my move, inhibited by the usual institutional experiences. Sensations of jostling in musty corridors, squeezing onto hard wooden benches and shivering on frozen football fields had conditioned me to the mortification of the flesh that came with a public-school education. Similar experiences on parade grounds and night exercises prolonged my painful subservience through two years of National Service.

Discovering myself enabled, by the liberated and subversive Sixties, to do something different, I'd sailed away one summer morning to a new land and – theoretically – a new life.

Viewed from the lobby, the barrack-block of Sloane House YMCA was a long way from Ellis Island. But for all that it had the undeniable feeling of a clearing station. At $3.50 a night the 1,500-room 'Y' was the inevitable entry point to the United States for all those budget-conscious young men who couldn't quite manage the $7 they charged at the 2,500-room New Yorker. And although there were no awkward questions or peering under the tongue there was a definite induction procedure. Practically, it involved nothing more rigorous than presenting a passport and YHA card and paying a dollar deposit on a key, but these were just formalities. By crossing the threshold into that great battery sleeper, collecting-point for the world's starry-eyed youth, I was doing so much more. I was becoming a member of a dynamic and demanding new society with its own exemplary set of rules.

'Welcome to New York!'

My greeter was a smartly dressed Spanish American, with crinkle-cut hair and a crucifix lapel pin. He stood proprietorially beside a display board headed 'News 'n' Cues'. Holding my gaze, he shook my hand. 'I hope your stay here is a rewarding one.'

'News 'n' Cues' made it clear that Christianity was a Good Thing, with a Fellowship Bible Breakfast laid on for 8.30am to be led by the Reverend Lombardo Estrada, Second Vice President of the Southern Baptist Convention (was it he?). A second notice declared that the next priority was a Healthy Body. 'Help Yourself to Fitness, the 'Y''s Way' it said, inviting guests to obtain a free pass at the desk for the benefits of the steam room, gymnasium and sun deck. Less demanding therapies in the Northeast Lounge included chess, checkers, Scrabble and 'kibitzing', a peculiarly Yiddish pastime which I understood did not involve taking part in anything but merely commenting on the performance of others.

Tours of the Statue of Liberty and the New York Stock Exchange were the major outdoor attractions. Those inclined to stop home could settle down for some TV pro-football: at 2.30pm they could watch the New York Jets playing the Kansas City Chiefs. And those still unsure about what constituted the American Way of Life could attend the Sunday Variety Program which included a showing of the feature film *Task Force* with Gary Cooper, Jane Wyatt and Walter Brennan.

My own choice for a first-night frolic was to go for an essential New York experience: coffee and doughnuts in Times Square. To accompany me on this adventure I found two companions, staying at the 'Y', who had come over with me on the same voyage. Both were teachers: Leslie, an American who had been on a teacher's exchange scheme at a school in High Barnet, London, and was now returning to his home in Chicago, and Michael, an Englishman who was on a similar scheme, travelling to a school in California. Surprisingly, he seemed to know more about New York than Leslie. 'Let's go to Broadway,' he suggested.

Back in the street it was night time and the opaque walls of the skyscrapers had transformed into checkerboards of light. A tantalising image of the city that made it like nowhere else on earth.

Nine blocks north and one east I realised my visions of bright lights and razzamatazz in Times Square, the foyer of the theatre district. To be honest, the square itself was rather disappointing, being more of a triangle than anything – a thin overloaded wedge of neon driven into the showbiz heart. Its two most interesting features were the tower of the NYC Information Centre, with its elaborate illuminated newscaster spelling out the latest triumph of the New York Yankees, and a memorable advertisement for a famous cigarette brand that had as its centrepiece a huge face with a hole in the mouth that emitted irregular puffs of smoke. Was this the real Virginia?

The next two or three blocks consisted of a dazzling succession of theatres, bars, cinemas, hotels and restaurants, all blazing their invitations like a row of carnival sideshows. Sadly, the price of everything from a milk-shake to a ticket for *The Sound of Music* lay in the realm of fantasy. Having Michael convert everything into pounds, shillings and pence didn't help. Instead we allowed ourselves to be carried along on the Broadway tide.

This was where the melting pot simmered. The faces that flowed past us were universal: African American, Latin American, Chinese, Indian. Distinctive types perhaps, but then shake up all those Europeans, offspring of generations of Ellis Islanders, and you were in a guessing game, trying to identify the descendants of Irish, Swedish, Dutch, Russian, Polish, French, German etc. or – from the sunny Mediterranean – Spanish, Italian and Greek. Add to the mix a sprinkling of Catholic, Protestant, Mormon, Muslim and Mennonite: what bound all these ingredients to make an American?

Soon the crowded sidewalks had combined with the light show and high percentage humidity to overwhelm us. In the middle of July, the midtown stroll had become a quest for somewhere cool to sit out the evening.

Eventually we found a place just short of Central Park, an air-conditioned 'Dunkin' Donuts' bar that promised refuge. After the muggy warmth of the street the opening door was like a waft of the Arctic, the refrigerated air seductively embracing us. For an Englishman, the natural order of things was surely reversed when instead of passing from a chilly exterior to a warm inside he found himself escaping from a sweltering street to a cool haven of soda fountains and canned music.

The American coffee, served with cream, maintained its worldwide reputation. Likewise the doughnuts, which came in an epic variety, some jam-filled, some chocolate-covered, some nut-sprinkled.

'I think you're going to like America,' said Michael, and Leslie nodded in agreement, his lips sealed by a goo of jam.

After Leslie's departure for Chicago, Michael and I had another evening together. While we were in New York Michael insisted that I take a stroll with him around Greenwich Village. This was the other Manhattan, of bijou streets and squares, of beatnik hangouts, arts and crafts and risqué theatre. It lay twenty blocks to the south of the 'Y', in an area roughly the size of London's Chelsea.

The folk figure who drove our taxi was fully adjusted to his role, with a peaked cap and a cigar stub jammed in the corner of his mouth. This one, like the cabbie who'd taken me to the 'Y', didn't ask us where we wanted to go but just put us down in Bleecker Street, on the corner of MacDougal. This was the heart of the Village, as defined by the tourist agencies.

But if we had set out to find the key to the Village we would probably never have found it. On my own I would quickly have lost myself in the back streets, the maze of alleys that hid their tales under the shroud of folklore.

The Village's origins were in the early eighteenth century when a handful of New Yorkers, threatened by yellow fever, had fled their original settlement at the foot of the peninsula to start a new village on a tobacco plantation to the north. Any trace of this village had long since disappeared, and it was perhaps more profitable to summon up the ghosts of the famous American writers, born in the nineteenth century – Henry James, Theodore Dreiser, Eugene O'Neill – who had lived in, and (in the case of James) immortalised the place. Their perceptive gaze had, I reflected, touched upon the more mellow buildings, some of which could be a century old and were now celebrated as 'characteristic' – two or three-storey walk-ups with an iron crochet of fire escapes and drainpipes clinging to their façades. Not very beautiful, but their 'character' was undeniable when compared with the modern-day excesses elsewhere.

At street level they invited us in: restaurants, coffeehouses, craft shops, antique markets and bookshops. This section of the Village was the tourist honeypot with few visible natives, the bohemian types that we imagined as the authentic Greenwich Villagers. Fleeing the bustle we went in search of the latter in what appeared to be the genuine heart of the place, where the night spots and bars coalesced into a more interesting hybrid. These were the dives that were their true habitat.

Here, standing in the doorways, were the shock troops in the war against convention. Their shoulder-length hair topped by dusty bowlers, their thigh-deep sweaters hanging over patchwork jeans. Their bare feet kneading the soil of the old plantations. Beatnik commissionaires mumbling their psalms in praise of a good time coming.

Spotting a sign that read 'The Four Winds' I nudged Michael. 'That's where Bob Dylan used to play.'

Michael looked as if he might have been interested, had he known who Bob Dylan was. 'Why don't we try it?' he said.

We paused cautiously at the entrance, listening to the strange dirge-like sounds from within. The last of the tobacco planters, defying assimilation to the end, moved towards us. Stroking his beard, to show us he had no quarrel with nature – nor for that matter anything else – the doorman beckoned us in. 'We've got the greatest, man...'

Where Satan beckoned, we could only follow. The famous coffeehouse had a long cavernous interior with a scattering of tables and benches and a two-foot high stage at one end. The only illumination came from the fitful candlelight on the tables, and a spotlight suspended over the stage, playing weakly on a bearded guitar-player. Wedging ourselves on a bench next to some enraptured, long-haired groupies we settled in for the great folkloric experience.

A bar girl wandered over with a bill of fare. Studying it by the flame of the candle Michael said, 'Is that all you have – coffee or coke?'

With a drawn-out sigh that said *'Here we go again'*, the girl pointed to a tattered notice on the wall. 'Yuh see what is says there? "This premises not licensed for the sale of or consumption of alcoholic liquor". Police regulations – ain't nothin' we can do 'bout it. The only way we use alc'ol is for *cookin'* – get me? Now, what's it gonna be?'

Michael smiled knowingly. 'A rum and coke, please.'

I nodded my concurrence. Was that what the doorman had meant by 'the greatest'? The greatest fiddle in Greenwich Village? The freest interpretation of the culinary art?

While we waited for our drinks The Four Winds offered us a choice of entertainment. We had plenty to choose from, like counting the spots of candlewax on the tablecloth or the cigarette butts in the ashtrays. Or, more interestingly, comparing the lipstick smears on the used glasses for matching shades. When this palled we could follow the progress of the bar girl, whose duties had been temporarily suspended by the doorman. Otherwise, as a last resort, there was the singer, a mournful Woody Guthrie impersonator who held his guitar like a dead child, lamenting the interment of Lazarus.

Unexpectedly he paused to make an announcement. 'Ladies and gentlemen,' he intoned, 'I hope you appreciate that if I didn't have to eat periodically, music would be my first love. As it is, whenever I catch sight of the hole in this here guitar I'm reminded of the one in my stomach. That hamburger I didn't have for lunch. Folks, you're lookin' at the original victim of New York City licensing law. That notice up there says that professional performers ain't permitted in this joint, which means that you can play all night if you want, so long as you don't take any money. But of course if there's any well-wishers willin' to part with a dime or two, I won't turn down a contribution, an' you'll find the little tin box just inside the door. So, to misquote the great William Shakespeare, if 'music be the love of food' I'll play on, in anticipation that all you good people will leave a donation for the burger on your way out.'

With that he resumed his gentle dirge, bowing his head over the guitar. When our drinks eventually arrived (rum-laced cokes at a dollar-fifty each) we disposed of them as slowly as possible and then made for the door. Here we were waylaid by Monsieur Gauguin, proffering a tin box for our gratuity. Michael donated a dime and I wished him goodnight and that was the end of our night out in Greenwich Village.

Philadelphia

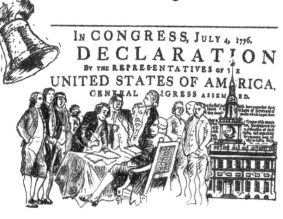

The Pursuit of Happiness

'*May I have your attention, please. The 5.30am Greyhound for Philadelphia is now loading at Gate Thirty...*'

The Liberty Bell. The Declaration of Independence. John Hancock's signature. The Stars and Stripes of Betsy Ross. My first destination after New York irresistibly beckoned.

Ignoring the forty-five-pound weight on my back I took the steps to the lower concourse two at a time. Heading the line at Gate Thirty I was the first on the bus, handing my ticket to the grey-uniformed driver. Dumping my rucksack on one of the seats at the back I slipped in beside it with a sigh of relief and settled down for the bus journey of a lifetime.

The thirty-odd people who followed me onto the bus were easily lost in the spacious interior, swallowed by the high-backed seats. Through my window I saw headlights flickering on the streamlined aluminium bodies of the other buses, manoeuvring skilfully in and out of their bays. On the side of each I saw a lithe, bounding greyhound, symbol of tireless vigour, that would be my spur and companion through 12,000 miles of American freeway.

'Hi, folks, and welcome aboard. This is your driver, Phil Oakes. Twenty years' safe drivin' an' five on probation for violatin' the traffic code. This coach is non-stop, scheduled to arrive at Philadelphia 7.30am.'

In a few minutes we were leaving Manhattan and the City of New York via the main western exit, the Lincoln Tunnel, passing under the Hudson River to New Jersey. Other than that no record exists of this stage of the journey as I was asleep long before we were half-way through the tunnel.

I awoke to a vague swishing sound and ultra violet light filtering through my eyelids. It was dawn and we were somewhere on the New Jersey Turnpike, driving at a steady fifty through open countryside. After the walls of stone and concrete which for two days had closed my vision, such openness and greenness seemed strangely fanciful, especially through the blue-tinted glass of the bus windows. This had the effect of intensifying the green of the foliage, an appropriate backdrop for 'The Garden State'. This was one of the more seductive nicknames given to an American state, but I couldn't help remembering a less enchanting epithet: 'The Armpit of the East'. Bestowed by a citizen of Pennsylvania, of course.

As we headed south, thoughts of increasing humidity ran through my mind. I'd read somewhere that during the summer months in Washington African ambassadors got hardship money and ice-cream was served with drinking straws. I was not, of course, going to believe those stories.

But how much, ultimately, would I have to believe? After two days in New York – which we all knew was not America – it was still a land of myth and marvel, in which handsome, tall-in-the saddle heroes galloped into sunsets.

The pieces of the puzzle still had to be assembled, those second-hand references – albeit related to our own culture – that made up the average Englishman's image of America. Putting serious literature to one side, we relied on films, advertisements, comic-books and travel guides to instruct us in both the glorious and the trivial, presenting their material in such a way that we could never tell the difference. Which had the greatest significance to the average American – Gettysburg or the OK Corral? The Metropolitan Opera House or a drive-in cinema? The Painted Desert or a parking lot? Right now these were hardly questions I could ask, let alone answer.

The first lesson had to be history. This, and the clockwise direction, had determined my route. Down the eastern seaboard I would visit Philadelphia, Washington and Charleston, all cities that had made their contribution to the political evolution of America. The southern states, with New Orleans as the focus of the colonial period, were the next objective, and then Texas with its Lone Stardom and Spanish missions. Following the wagon-trains westwards I would discover the terrain through which those pioneers had driven, forging the new nation's western frontiers. At this point the marks of man would give way to landscape, with the forests and canyons of Utah and Arizona and the deserts and mountains of Nevada and California. Returning eastwards, I would gaze upon the natural miracles of the Yellowstone National Park and the Rockies. From the Midwest my route would take me via the Great Lakes and Niagara full-circle back to the tap-root of the American heritage, the historic city of Boston, Massachusetts.

But if the places were important, then so were the people. To help me on my way I'd arranged to meet a variety of Americans, some of whom I knew, others who were only names. The latter were mostly contributors to the magazine which had employed me – writers or photographers on natural history projects. Among them were a marine biologist in Florida and a lady in New York (reserved for my return journey) who kept a jungle cat in her apartment. To all these people I'd addressed the hope that in view of their association with the magazine they would not object to my calling on them during the trip.

Apart from my string-pulling I was lucky enough to have one or two ready-made personal links. Among them were a friend and a relative of a widely travelled uncle and – more significantly – a group of four American students whom I had met recently on holiday. Second-year students at Stanford University, California, they'd been taking a break from the university's campus in Florence to visit one of my favourite Sicilian resorts, Taormina. Exchange of addresses had led to further meetings with one of them in London, a bright-eyed sophomore by the name of Elizabeth Mendell. Employing my considerable charm I had persuaded Elizabeth (through the good offices of her father) to sponsor my visit (a technicality that did not involve funds unless I fell by the wayside) and provide a forwarding address for my alien registration card. Happily the Mendells were up for a visit from an itinerant Englishman and conveniently resided on my route in the city of Houston, Texas.

A tollbooth marked the end of the freeway into Philadelphia, and we were soon crossing the Benjamin Franklin Bridge on the Delaware River, which swept us into the heart of the city. At the scheduled time of 7.30am we pulled into the bus depot – an impressive performance by our four-legged – or should I say six-wheeled – friend. Leaving the bus I spotted the sign over the driver's seat: 'Your Operator Phil Oakes: Safe, Reliable and Courteous'. The man himself, standing at the step to acknowledge his passengers, had the pose of an airline steward at the end of a flight.

With the intention of continuing to Washington before dark I had a whole day to lavish on Philadelphia. Leaving my rucksack in a locker I headed for the Hospitality Center, where I loaded up with maps and guides on the city.

After the three-hour journey the lure of breakfast in the neighbouring Post House was strong. The cult of the American breakfast was enshrined in this coast-to-coast institution, which must have contributed more than any other eating place to the joy and obesity of the nation. From the panoramic menu, a much hallowed Declaration of Indulgence that needed only the verification of John Hancock's signature, one could choose Waffles with Crispy Bacon, Hot Cakes with Whipped Butter and Molasses, Fluffy Blueberry Pancakes with Blueberry Sauce and Lots of Whipped Butter or – the all-time favourite – Two Eggs (any style) with Hash Brown Potatoes, Buttered Toast and Jelly.

Before ordering the Two Eggs, I needed to remember an important US culinary refinement. If you preferred your fried egg unflipped it was 'Sunny Side Up' or for flipped, 'Over and Easy' (or 'Medium' or 'Hard' if you wanted the yolk to disappear).

A generous cup of Post House Coffee helped me through the guides and brochures, giving me a decent overview of the history of Philadelphia and the United States (the two being more or less synonymous). In 1682 the Quaker William Penn was here with a charter to found a British colony which he called Philadelphia ('brotherly love') the principle of which was sustained, pretty well, until the outbreak of the War of Independence a century later.

It was in Philadelphia, of course, that the historic Declaration of Independence was signed, and later the Constitution which had framed the guiding principles of democratic government.

The actions of those early Congressmen, endorsing with their quill pens the documents that had changed the course of world history, had taken place in the Assembly Room of the Old State House, now known as Independence Hall, that stood at the heart of the two-square-mile area of Penn's original 'greene country towne'. This remnant of the old city was now just a carefully preserved corner of a booming industrial metropolis of 130 square miles, its precise location only discernible with the aid of a large-scale street map. The city of the colonial and revolutionary period lay close to the west bank of the Delaware River and there, in an area six blocks square, the Dream of America was enshrined.

A ten-cent bus ride took me to the Independence National Historical Park. Alighting at Chestnut Street I admired the classical red brick and stone buildings on its south side, aware that I was standing on America's most historic square mile. Directly in front of me was a modest two-storey building with a white wedding-cake tower topped by a belfry and steeple: Independence Hall. After the overpowering sense of scale that I had so far experienced in the United States, it was difficult to allow for the passage of 220 years and contemplate a building of human proportions.

Passing through a flanking arcade I found a more familiar view of the Hall on the other side. In a stately square, crossed by wide flagstone walks bordered by sedate elm trees, I caught an imaginary glimpse of history.

The bell of the old State House was ringing beneath its cupola, calling the delegates to Assembly. Crossing the State House yard in answer to the summons were several figures in cutaway coats and breeches, converging on the central door. The founding fathers of a new nation, intent on drafting their heroic declaration that would put an end to British rule in the Colonies and establish a great democratic confederation. Among them perhaps the very men whose task it was to inscribe that declaration on paper: John Adams, Thomas Jefferson, Benjamin Franklin, John Hancock. Their memorial was in their words:

> We hold these truths to be self-evident, that all men are created equal, that they are endowed by their Creator with certain inalienable rights, that among these are Life, Liberty and the Pursuit of Happiness. That to secure these rights, Governments are instituted among Men, deriving their just powers from the consent of the governed...

I rubbed my eyes, wondering if it might be possible that those eighteenth-century nation builders had returned to the twentieth, to see what they'd created. As appreciative posterity, in the shape of a sun-hatted tourist in Bermuda shorts hung with camera accessories, crossed my line of vision, I concluded they had not.

As a finely restored piece of colonial administrative architecture, Independence Hall was not only a memorial to those great men but to the City Council, the Daughters of the American Revolution, the National Park Service and the other bodies who'd worked to preserve it. Their diligent work could be seen again inside in the crisp décor of the rooms, tastefully painted and furnished in the revolutionary style. Most interesting, of course, was the Assembly Room, the scene of the birth of the American nation (1776) and the meeting-place of her first Congress. Matched to the period were the carefully arranged tables and chairs at which the founding fathers had sat, and on the Speaker's table stood the silver inkstand used for the signing of the famous Declaration. (This required refilling for the majestic signature of the President of Congress, John Hancock.)

Behind the Speaker's chair a full-length portrait of George Washington commanded the proceedings (a fanciful concept as the great man was not actually present at the signing, being at the time with his troops in New York). Looking at that masterful military figure, posed with his left hand on a cannon barrel and right hand on his hip, with his legs nonchalantly crossed, it was hard to believe that this was the same man who on hearing his name put forward at a meeting of Congress for the job of General and Commander-in-Chief of the Army had modestly withdrawn from the chamber until his appointment by unanimous vote was declared. The same man, too, who before his election some years later as the first President of the United States had expressed a whimsical preference for retirement to his plantation in Virginia.

In the charge of a crisply uniformed ranger of the National Park Service, my tourist group was conducted to the adjacent Congress Hall, where we were treated to a recited history of the meetings of the new nation's representatives that had taken place here after the inauguration of the Republic. This was the formative period, from 1790 to 1800, dominated by Washington's presidency, when Philadelphia had been the capital city of the United States before the transfer of the federal government to the city that bore his name.

This substantial helping of history required at least a tot of folklore to help it down. We duly proceeded to the tower of Independence Hall, wherein we discovered America's greatest patriotic symbol.

Looking at the old cracked bell that was as close to the heart of the nation as the star-spangled banner itself, I couldn't help wondering what all the fuss was about. The Liberty Bell, they called it, the original of all those little bells that kept cropping up on postage stamps, fifty-cent pieces and advertisements for US Bonds. If size were any measure of fame, then the 2,000lbs of cast metal proclaimed by our guide, even though comprising a short ton (American), were hardly eligible for competition with the Tsar Kolokol bell in Moscow at 200 tons or our own Big Ben, weighing in at a modest 13.5 tons.

But perhaps it was unfair, even in America, to make this kind of comparison. There was, after all, another more significant feature of the Liberty Bell. Running from its lower edge for two-thirds of its depth was the nation's most admired, most venerated and most photographed crack after the Grand Canyon. A testimonial to the workmanship of Mr Thomas Lester's foundry in Whitechapel, London, whose bell had apparently succumbed to the very first stroke of the clapper. This surely gave the lie to any claim that might be made for the superiority of British manufacture. But hang on a moment, what were those two names on the side of the bell, just above the crack? Pass and Stow – weren't they the 'Two ingenious workmen of Philadelphia' who in 1753 had recast the bell to restore it to its original uncracked splendour? Fortunate indeed that these proud craftsmen had not lived to regret the inclusion of their names on their handiwork. Eighty years later, tolling for a Chief Justice's funeral procession, the bell had cracked again. Accorded a peremptory, though no doubt honourable retirement, it had hung for a while in mute and peaceful obscurity inside the tower, until that fateful day that it had been recognised as Part of the American Heritage. Thereafter, displayed in many different ways and many different places, it had done overtime as the nation's most popular *memento gloriae*. Its travels had taken it all over America. Wherever it had gone, the citizens had flocked to see and touch it, with all the devotion of pilgrims in pursuit of a holy relic. None of this, of course, had done anything to improve the damage, and only when a permanent crack-up was threatened was the bell taken off active service and given a permanent resting place in Independence Hall.

Leaving Independence Square with my fifty-cent copy of the Declaration, I ventured into the neighbouring streets to discover the tucked-away gems of brick and mortar whose very survival in twentieth-century America seemed a miracle. Any romantic Englishman travelling to Philadelphia in search of the decayed remains of King George's province would, I imagined, feel somewhat let down. Even after seeing the reconditioned heritage of Independence Square they would be astonished by the pristine appearance of the other historic buildings. Carpenters' Hall (meeting place of the First Continental Congress in 1774 and birthplace of the Commonwealth of Pennsylvania), Christ Church (founded in 1695 as a Church of England parish church and subsequently the mother church of the American Episcopalians), and the Friends Meeting House (built in the early nineteenth century on a site deeded to the city in 1701 by the Quaker William Penn) wore their well-honed antiquity with pride. Nearby was the early eighteenth-century Elfreth's Alley, the oldest residential street in America, which was a glimpse of London's Chelsea, and round the corner from here the Betsy Ross House.

This was the home of the industrious seamstress who in 1777 had made the first flag of the United States. Behind the shiny white shutters of her front parlour I found the flag trade still booming, with wall-to-wall displays of star-spangled banners (none of them stitched by hand, sadly) which were walking – or should it be flying – out of the shop.

My sightseeing bug was yet to be satisfied. Taking the free bus to Fairmount Park in the north-west of the city I jumped off at Logan Circle to visit Philadelphia's Natural History Museum, and from there continued to the Franklin Institute Science Museum. This museum, a huge colonnaded memorial to Philadelphia's greatest citizen, looked impressive; but as I didn't see myself getting around it in less than an afternoon I kept my admiration for the exterior.

At the ground floor level I spotted a circular yellow plaque. Assuming that it was another of the historic site markers with which the city abounded, I was disconcerted to see that it was the sign for a fall-out shelter. On a building dedicated to science, in the city of Brotherly Love.

Washington

National Treasures

At 3.30pm my four-legged friend left Philadelphia for Washington, heading south along the Delaware River. To get the full benefit of the panoramic windscreen I sat in the front seat. From this vantage point I had the added bonus of the driver's remarks to his passengers, sometimes relayed over the PA system, more often shouted over his shoulder. He seemed anxious to impress on his charges that they were on a non-stop run to Baltimore, Maryland, of two hours and twenty minutes, and that they should therefore take note of the 'restroom' located at the rear of the coach. A tiny cubicle with a red light over the door showed an imaginative use of America's greatest euphemism, which extended from the basic facilities of the Greyhound Bus Depot (wash-basin, urinal) to the marbled halls of the luxury hotels.

A day of intense sightseeing in Philadelphia preceded by an early morning departure from New York had a predictable effect and in a short time I dozed off, lulled by a relentlessly smooth 60mph. When I picked up the journey again we were crossing a broad mud-brown river dotted with cargo vessels. The signs told me that this was the Susquehanna, a river that flowed from the Appalachian Mountains to the Chesapeake Bay, one of America's most heavily industrialized regions. We were in Maryland, a state numbered proudly among the original Thirteen of the Revolution.

After the bay area the countryside was much like New Jersey's – uniformly lush and green. Then, as we drove into Baltimore, it disappeared again in the built-up congestion of the great seaport. Emerging from the Baltimore Harbour Tunnel on the far side of the city I saw the debris that was the customary aftermath of industrial growth: intermittent rubbish tips, scrap yards and car breakers' yards. In the yard of an 'Auto Demolition Expert' I was thrilled to observe one of those incredible car-crushing machines in operation, thrusting its claw into a pile of wrecks like a huge voracious crab and tugging out a four-wheeled morsel for transmission to the maw of the crusher. At a single crunch, Oldsmobiles were reduced to the size of a large suitcase. The towering pyramids of compressed vehicles said all that was needed about the paradigm of the consumer society.

As we entered Washington Parkway the scenery was transformed into stretches of wooded parkland, a pleasant introduction to Washington, District of Columbia. Capital of the United States and some would say of the Free World.

The city of the Capitol, the White House and the Pentagon. The city of symbols, built on the dynamic of power. The classic setting for the political dramas that held the whole world – more or less – in thrall. Since my first consumption of newspapers and radio I could claim to be as zealous a spectator as any, and now that I was at the very place where it all happened there was one thought in my mind. How much more would I see at a closer range?

A couple of days in the Big Apple had left me with the question of whether New York was America. Now, driving through the streets of the nation's capital, I had a similar question. Was *Washington* America? At this stage of my journey I could not venture an opinion, but on one point I could pronounce: Washington was not New York. In place of the pre-cast concrete and curtain walls of Manhattan's buildings there was self-conscious, classical conformity. In place of the tall apartments, modish bow-windowed houses. Two cities, 250 miles apart, that might have been on different continents.

The Greyhound pulled into the Downtown Bus Depot at 6.50pm, another perfect piece of timing. As I left the air-conditioned interior the warmth of the streets embraced me like a python, snatching my breath. Within a minute I was sweating. It was my introduction to a Washington summer.

At only five blocks' distance, the hike to the Washington YMCA was less challenging than that of New York. And although there were more diagonals (such as Pennsylvania and Massachusetts Avenues) the grid system was very much in play, the north-south streets signed with numbers and the east-west streets with letters. '17th and G' was my reference to the 'Y'.

In the heat of the dusk the rucksack weighed heavily on my shoulders and my limbs felt strangely clogged as I hurried across the intersections on New York Avenue. At the junction with Pennsylvania Avenue I enjoyed the anticipated view of a large stately building with a colonnaded portico and sweeping lawns, set back from the road beyond iron railings. The guards at the entrance gate confirmed that this was the world's most famous residence.

Given its proximity to the street the White House seemed strangely approachable. Its classical charm was enhanced by a gently gushing fountain and a gathering of squirrels that hopped around on the grass beneath the dark graceful trees. Shedding my rucksack for a few minutes I took a break and absorbed the picture, sitting on the low railing wall. My gaze wandered expectantly towards the great entrance portico, but there was no sign of life. It was a vain hope, and I should have known better than to imagine that on this hot, muggy evening Mr Lyndon Baines Johnson would wish to be anywhere but inside his nice air-conditioned office. Picking up my rucksack I stumbled on to my own less splendid pad on G Street.

In the city of national remembrance I decided that my first objective should be the Washington Monument, that great white needle, 555 feet high, which was the dominant feature of the city's skyline and forever in the background in shots of the Mall and other views. Properly this giant obelisk belonged on a launch pad at Cape Kennedy, but I couldn't imagine its mid-eighteenth-century builders had the space age in mind. Their only concern had been to produce a fitting memorial to the country's first president, dramatically conveyed in gleaming white marble.

Mounting the crest supporting the monument I gazed at the towering column above me, at the long queue for the elevator at its base, and at the notice by the entrance suggesting the alternative climb of 900 steps to the top. My conclusion: a view too far.

Near to noon on my first day in Washington, the temperature had soared beyond 80°. In a quest for cool drinks and shade I spotted a restaurant pavilion, which doubled as a first-aid tent for the Monument climbers. Inside I beheld a mouth-watering display of crushed-ice drinks, ready-poured in paper cups. There were 'eats', too. Joining the queue at the counter I purchased a half-smoke (a breed of hot dog with an extra-big sausage) and the largest size I could get in one of the crushed-ice drinks, orange-flavoured. The sausage was only half-cooked – hence the name? – but filled a gap. The crushed ice, deliciously cold, had a glorious flavour: I could have poured it down my throat forever.

Returning to the Monument I surveyed the view from the vantage point of its hill. To the east lay the immense green stretch of the Mall, culminating in the airy white cathedral of the Capitol building. To the north the Federal Triangle, with its massive complex of administrative buildings, and next to it the White House, gleaming through a shroud of trees. To the south, through more trees, a glimpse of the tidal basin that served as a reservoir of the river that marked the eastern boundary of Washington DC, the Potomac. To the east, delicately mirrored in a long, rectangular reflecting pool, were the beautiful Grecian columns of the Lincoln Memorial, gracefully terminating the Mall at its junction with the West Potomac Park. Thus I beheld the 'magnificent distances' that were Washington's special feature, unique among American cities. The creation, dare I say, of a Frenchman.

If a city could take its genesis from its architect, then Pierre Charles l'Enfant would have been Washington's founding father. The city would have been French, complete with its own *Assemblée Nationale* (Capitol) and *Champs Elysées* (Mall). And no doubt the French would have fought for, and probably lost, their colony, leaving them only with the dubious legacy of a *Relation Spéciale*.

My foray on the first 'distance' was a walk to the Lincoln Memorial, bearing with me a mental image of the great man enthroned in his marble hall. Surveying a world of miracles and misdeeds with a stern, fatherly eye.

Approaching the memorial, I was impressed by its classical detail. Not an exact facsimile of the Parthenon (I counted the columns) but certainly a tribute to that great temple of Greece's Golden Age, with its splendid Doric order. With the relentless file of tourists mounting its stairway it even had its own Panathenaic procession.

These pilgrims were not however bearing libation bowls but Leica 4.5s, pointing them in every direction with cries of 'Stand over by the column', or 'Start walking up the steps', or 'Get one inside of me and Abe'. I hurried up the steps ahead of the horde.

Inside the memorial chamber it was different. I could conjure up a new sense of time and space which excluded the hushed voices, the click of camera shutters. Under the steadfast gaze of the great seated figure I could pause for a moment and believe in the power of one man to command a nation.

I studied the inscribed stone tablets, one on either side of the chamber, which bore the words of Lincoln's two most famous speeches. The first, on the south wall, was of the Gettysburg Address, the short speech of dedication made on the great Civil War battlefield that had become a National Cemetery. The last lines were, of course, the most memorable: '... we here highly resolve that these dead shall not have died in vain – that this nation under God shall have a new birth of freedom – and that government of the people, for the people, by the people shall not perish from the earth'. The second, equally historic speech was commemorated on the north wall. This was the President's Second Inaugural Address, delivered on his return to office at the end of the Civil War. Again, the stirring last lines rang through the passages of history: 'With malice toward none, with charity for all... let us strive on to finish the work we are in to bind up the nation's wounds...'

Returning to the centre of the chamber I contemplated once more the great man who in four years – the last of his life – had made himself immortal. I read the tablet above his head: 'In this temple, as in the hearts of the people for whom he saved the Union, the memory of Abraham Lincoln is enshrined forever' and considered the question that always occurred to me when confronted by the effigies of the famous. Was it the individual, or the moment, that had created the legend?

In 1861, in his lesser known First Inaugural Address, Lincoln had declared himself unopposed to slavery in those states where it already existed, and opposed only to its extension to other states. His primary concern at that point had been to salvage the Union by any means – including appeasement of the South. A year later, however, he saw the necessity of abandoning conciliation for a committed anti-slavery line. Here, at an uncertain stage of the war, was a cause that would unite the North against the South and attract the sympathy of nations that might otherwise have supported the latter. The Emancipation Proclamation, promising the liberation of three and a half million slaves in the South, gave the Union its strongest weapon. A crusade which eventually carried them to decisive victory over the Confederacy. At this point Lincoln had shown his true greatness. Instead of giving way to the voices that clamoured for the punishment of the defeated South by removal of their privileges as former member states of the Union, he had agreed without condition to the readmission of any state that applied for it, and the right of its representatives to sit in Congress. For the second time, 'Honest Abe' had chosen conciliation, but this time the choice was motivated not by politics but humanity. Looking again at the far-seeing eyes, set deep under the firm, jutting brows, I could see that this had been the lodestar of Abraham Lincoln.

From the sanctuary of the memorial I returned to the cloudless glare outside and the chatter of the tourists. On the other side of the monument I discovered a striking view of the Potomac River with the spanner arm of the Arlington Memorial Bridge right below me, the sun glinting on the slowly moving traffic. At the far end lay a steep, tree-covered hill, which I recognised as the next day's destination. The Arlington National Cemetery was a long hike across the bridge and I made a note to take my salt tablets.

A fan was whirring close to my ear and I lay in its cooling breeze for quite a while before I remembered where I was. At $4 a night the 'Y' had priced me out and after a good swim in their pool the day before I'd transferred to a cheaper place three blocks along the street. For three dollars, though, air conditioning had been a wishful thought, and after looking in every corner of my room for the switch I'd been obliged to come to terms with the fan on the bedside table. It was this that was now humming noisily in my ear, recalling me to consciousness after a night of near suffocation. I couldn't be sure if I was still reliving that glorious dip in the pool, but throughout the night I'd had the weird sensation of swimming, my limbs thrashing about under the mangled sheets. Eventually the bed had turned into a swamp and I was trying to escape, only to find that I was sinking deeper. Lying there breathless in a pool of sweat I was glad I'd woken up in time.

In the blaze of light from the partially open curtains I looked at my watch. Quarter to eleven. I did a rapid vault into the shower, sluicing myself with the tepid water. Swamp or no swamp, this was a poor start to my second day in Washington.

Going downstairs to hand in my key I found the reception clerk, a middle-aged black woman, engaged in an altercation with a middle-aged white man. The guy was pestering her, and could he please leave her alone? Pretending not to listen I held back and examined the drab lobby, with its cracked linoleum and nicotine-stained ceiling. Lingering only briefly on the fly-paper hanging from the light, and the cigarette butts crushed in the ashtrays.

Under the reception clerk's tirade her adversary finally backed out of the lobby and into the street. She then turned to me, her anger unspent. I hoped that what she saw was not another white man but a neutral tourist guest at whom she could direct her diatribe.

'Iffen these whites wanna stick to their own kind, I reckon they oughta leave us black folks be. But they just follow us aroun' – you know?' Her eyes hardened. 'There's that white feller, lives down the block. Yesterday when I went out he just tagged onto me. Whenever I looked roun' he was there, right behind me, like some stray dog. I ask myself: "Why don't he go home an' water his grass or somethin'? I don't want nothin' to do with his kind." But this feller, he don't know better than to hang aroun' watchin' for me all day. Was a time when street crawlers like him just came out at

night-time, when their wives were out playin' bridge or somethin'
– but they don't seem to care 'bout that no more. You white folks
might call it *integration* –'

That appeared to be the end of my neutrality. I gave her my
key, and a dime for the newspaper on the counter.

The headline read: '*Seventeen Killed in Riots. Hundreds Hurt.
Fire Loss $100 Million*'. The picture below showed a street scene
in the black district of Watts, Los Angeles, with armed National
Guardsmen silhouetted against a background of fire and smoke.
This was the latest in a series of riots against police nationwide,
sparked by the arrest of black protesters.

Although the riot was on the other side of America it felt, in
that unquiet moment in the lobby of a downtown Washington
hotel, that it might be exploding in the street outside.

The reception clerk said, 'That's a lotta black people got killed
yesterday. But they got a sheriff's deputy – you read that?'

Arlington, I knew, was huge, its 639 acres the last resting place
of more than 400,000 American dead of the past century, from the
Civil War to the current conflict in Vietnam. The endless rows of
white headstones, reminiscent of those on the First World War
battlefields of France, began to appear beyond the screen of trees
as I passed through the Memorial Gate and started the climb to
Arlington House.

The mansion that stood at the summit had its own history to
contribute. The Grecian-style villa that dominated the site was
a monument to a strange anomaly. Originally the home of the
Confederate General Robert E. Lee, it had been appropriated by the
Union during the Civil War and its grounds designated as a national
military cemetery. At the outbreak of the war Lee had opted for
his home state of Virginia – and the losing side. This honourable
decision had reflected much credit on Lee and it was appropriate
that the dead of both sides, Union and Confederate, were buried at
Arlington. When a man's loyalties were dictated solely by his birthplace, the differences between the sides seemed strangely remote.

For a while I stood on the front lawn of the house, taking in one
of the finest panoramas of Pierre L'Enfant's vision. From this point,
south of the Potomac, the conurbation to the north was lost in the

haze and it was a city of green and white, the trees billowing amidst the monuments. Though distant, the landmarks of the Lincoln Memorial, the Washington Monument, the Jefferson Memorial and the Capitol were plain to the eye. I was glad that L'Enfant, whose grave lay on the slope below the house, could enjoy the view that he had created.

Since the Civil War, the dead of many other conflicts had been added to the Arlington roll. Among the thousands of ordinary servicemen many were unknown, but some had been destined for lasting glory. On the way to the Tomb of the Unknowns I spotted the gravestone of Major Glenn Miller, who had volunteered to join the US military to entertain the troops in 1942. Miller had his own 'big band' orchestra, creating legendary hits such as 'In the Mood' and 'Tuxedo Junction'. Sadly, on a flight from England to France in 1944, Miller's plane had been lost in the English Channel. Miller's contribution to wartime morale had been enormous, and it was touching to see the scattering of pebbles – votive offerings from a new generation of admirers – at the foot of his stone.

The focal point of Arlington was an elaborate complex which included the Memorial Amphitheater and the Tomb of the Unknown Soldier, Sailor and Marine of World Wars I and II and the Korean War. For me – and the other expectant visitors – the curiosity of the monument lay not so much in the memorial itself but in the activity surrounding it.

Performing the Honor Guard ritual was a smart young cadet from a military academy, in peaked cap and sunglasses, marching up and down a strip of carpet in front of the tomb. Somewhere I had read that this was known as 'walking the mat'. The finesse of the guard's movements was keenly observed by the crowd, gathered with their cameras behind a restraining circle of rope. The peak of their attention was clearly focused on the moment when, on reaching the end of the strip, the cadet turned, his heels swivelling like a ballet dancer's and his feet sliding silently together at the end of the movement. After a pause of twenty-one seconds, the patrol was resumed in the opposite direction. Ten hushed minutes went by before I realised from the way that people were glancing at their watches that something was about to happen. A clock on a nearby chapel struck the hour and two more guards appeared, marching out onto the dais. One, carrying a rifle, was identical to the first; the other a burly top sergeant without a rifle who was even smarter than the other two, his uniform apparently stitched to his skin with every crease honed to a knife-edge. Like the other guards he wore white gloves.

Dressing on to the first guard the sergeant and the relief marched with him along the strip with the same precision, all three of them coming to an abrupt halt in line with the tomb. With immaculate co-ordination they turned to face the tomb and saluted it, the two cadets presenting arms as the sergeant's gloved hand arched in a brisk salute. The ceremony completed, the guards continued their patrol to the end of the strip, where the second guard changed places with the first, who then marched off with the sergeant.

The Changing of the Guard at the Tomb of the Unknowns had taken less than three minutes, but for the spectators it was obviously the high spot they'd been waiting for. In their own synchronised movement they dispersed from the dais, leaving the solitary guard to continue his vigil alone.

Presidents too had the honour of being interred at Arlington. With the guidance of a map I found my way to a more recent grave that was now the object of worldwide pilgrimage. In 1963, three days after his assassination in Dallas, Texas, the remains of President John F. Kennedy had been buried at a site that the president himself had approved. Before a permanent tomb could be constructed it had been necessary to create a temporary gravesite, which I discovered near a walkway on the hillside below Arlington House.

The arrangement of the site was simplicity itself. Enclosed by a white picket fence there were three graves, with Kennedy's at the centre flanked by his two children (a son who had died in infancy and a stillborn daughter). Although the children had headstones taken from their original grave sites, Kennedy's burial place was marked by a modest mound of pine branches masking the burner of an eternal flame. Laid upon the mound were JFK's service caps and military insignia. As the holder of a Purple Heart, the war-hero president had a double qualification for Arlington.

After a good sluice in a fountain I made my way back across the Potomac to the Jefferson Memorial. Located on a promontory overlooking the river's Tidal Basin, the memorial presented a refreshing image: the chaste marble columns, curved architrave and sunlit dome clearly reflected in the placid water. Within stood the bronze figure of Thomas Jefferson, the man whose words, written two centuries ago, pledging the commitment of himself and his fellow representatives to the ideals of 'life, liberty and the pursuit of happiness' had lived on in the minds of successive generations of Americans.

As in the Lincoln Memorial, the historic words were inscribed on panels on the walls of Jefferson's memorial chamber. A lasting tribute to the author of the Declaration of Independence. Other well chosen extracts from his writings were there, revealing more of his philosophy. Thoughts on education, religious freedom and constitutional government. On the latter, one was reminded of Jefferson's realistic interpretation of the Constitution, which he had regarded not as an inviolable set of conditions but a framework only, which could be stretched to accommodate new political exercises. The most celebrated example, of course, was the 1803 Louisiana Purchase. Here was the biggest deal in real estate ever made, or likely to be made, by a US president: 823,000 square miles for $15 million. For this sum Jefferson had more than doubled the size of the United States, adding to its resources the land that was to be moulded into such rich farming states as Missouri, Iowa, Kansas and Nebraska. In addition Jefferson had effected by the acquisition the removal of an aggressive foreign power – France – from the west bank of the Mississippi, thereby opening up a new frontier for westward expansion. All this for the price by today's values of ninety-two Manhattan acres.

At the time the purchase could hardly have had the significance that it acquired in later years, when the US frontier had been pushed beyond the Rockies and the full potential of the country was realised. To Jefferson, striving to forge a new country in the face of enemies, it had been a vital transaction, to prevent the containment of his country by a foreign nation. An extension of the purposes of that great document for which he had wished, above all his achievements, to be remembered.

Standing inside the latter-day Pantheon, with its coffered ceiling, white marble walls and colonnaded portico, I was intrigued by the date of its dedication, given in the National Park Service leaflet as April, 1943. By comparison the Lincoln Memorial – completed in 1922 – was an ancient monument. This laid a startling emphasis on the greenness of American history and the incredible rapidity of her growth from a forested wilderness to the front-runner of industrial and scientific nations. When Jefferson died, Lincoln was fifteen, and when Lincoln died Theodore Roosevelt was playing with toy soldiers a long way from Cuba. When Roosevelt died, Kennedy was two years old. This made me realise a vital truth about America. While the histories of other nations were on the bookshelves, hers was still being written.

From Jefferson's hallowed temple it was a natural progression to Washington's Acropolis – and home of the original Declaration of Independence. The tiered flights of steps to the Capitol reminded me of the processional approach to a great cathedral (St Paul's came to mind with its matching dome), but once inside the sense of sanctity quickly faded.

I found myself with about 300 other people in a vast circular hall. This was the Rotunda, which lay under the great Capitol dome. Stretching round it was a rope barrier which restricted the human flow. At the other side of the hall the visitors were herded into groups of forty or so by uniformed female guides who addressed them with confident authority. To the inexpectant ear the combination of their three or four voices in the echo-chamber of the Rotunda, competing for their audience's attention, was unnerving.

My own guide, a smartly uniformed Doris Day, spent a few seconds describing the frescoes of the Rotunda before sweeping us into the Statuary Hall. To add to the confusion, this chamber was filled not only with tourists but with a large number of statues, positioned within its colonnades. Almost every public figure in American history was represented, from George Washington to Will Rogers, and for the benefit of the children the game was to call out as many famous names as possible before being ushered elsewhere by the guide. For my own part, I must admit to a certain discomfort in the presence of so many giants of history. Under their stern and watchful gaze I wondered how the day-to-day machinations of the powerful were conducted. It must have been difficult for anyone to hatch a plot with Washington standing behind them, or dismember a rival within earshot of Abraham Lincoln. I could only conclude that the intrigues of *Advise and Consent* had been drawn from more private corridors.

With implacable briskness our guide introduced us successively to the House of Representatives and the Senate, explaining in her best cheerleader voice America's system of government, the powers of the legislative branch and the procedure of each chamber. Sitting amidst her hushed audience in the back row of the Senate gallery I looked down at the semi-circle of desks on the floor of the chamber, scattered with sheets of paper, and fancied myself not in the Upper House of the United States Congress but in a university lecture theatre. The academic layout of the chamber was emphasised by the Speaker's platform and the facing rows of desks radiating from it. The majority party, it seemed, had no way of exhibiting their advantage, and a visitor not knowing the personalities would have difficulty telling one side from the other. On such a stage Gladstone would have foundered and Disraeli expired. Churchill, I was sure, would never have made an entrance.

A prearranged meeting with Michael, who was taking a break in Washington on his way to California, took us to a restaurant on Connecticut Avenue, where for a dollar-ten we enjoyed a typical American dinner (half a chicken, farm-bred, milk-fed). The bar downstairs, we discovered, had a pleasantly pubby atmosphere, with draught beer, warming pans and honky-tonk piano to put us in the mood. Spotting our English nationality from half-a-mile, the pianist coerced us into a lusty rendering of old favourites, including *I've Got a Lovely Bunch of Coconuts*, in which we led the assembled company. For my personal benefit ('Where you from, pardner?') the canny performer segued into *Maybe It's Because I'm a Londoner*.

His name was Tom and his command of the English pub song was phenomenal. Eventually Michael and I were up on the stage with him, before a spellbound (mystified?) audience of locals who must have thought that they were witnessing some momentous folk revival by the last of its surviving exponents.

We got plenty of fun out of the evening, but not as much, it appeared, as Tom. When the bar closed he offered to drive us back to our hotels, and all the way down Connecticut told us what a swell time he'd had. He insisted on a return match the following evening.

Next day I was back in a queue. Along with the rest of the world I entered the White House by a side door, commencing a slow procession along the ground floor corridor. The minimal ventilation here was provided by electric fans, whose draught reached only those at close range: the rest of us slowly melted. Relief came when the guard ushered us up the stairs to the Entrance Hall on the first floor (State Floor). From here we entered the East Room, used for White House receptions, which was blissfully air conditioned. Breathing deeply I looked around me. The coolness of the room was enhanced by its classical décor and elegant, imposing chandeliers, their glittering lights reflected on the waxed surface of the floor.

The stewardship of America's First Ladies (most famously Jacqueline Kennedy, who had commissioned her own French designer) had created a White House as close as possible to the original, the product of successive renovations that began after 1814, when the British Redcoats in a last retaliatory fling had left it a blackened ruin.

While the East Room had spoken of formal receptions and social functions the adjacent Green Room, decorated and furnished in the style of an eighteenth-century parlour, spoke more of fireside chats with visiting dignitaries and corporation chiefs, the conversation subdued, perhaps, to match the soft tone of the green silk damask lining the walls. Adding to the solemn charm of the room were portraits of two soldier-presidents whose lives came at either end of the White House's span of history: George Washington and Dwight D. Eisenhower.

The next room offered the immediate appeal of its oval shape, royal blue carpet and drapes, and the superb view from its bow window of the White House Lawn, the Ellipse and the Washington Monument beyond. This was the Blue Room, used for the formal reception of visiting officials of state. A pause at this point would have been welcome, but the White House guards maintained a smart trot as we continued to a third colour-themed room, a state parlour named the Red Room. What was in fact a small dining room looked like the stage set for a Regency drama. Bright fuchsia silk adorned the walls, and the Empire-style armchairs were sedately arranged, as though awaiting the actors' entrance.

Vibrant green, blue and red were followed by an antidote of white and gold in the State Dining Room. Used for major diplomatic events, the décor of this room evoked the grand manner with its classical panelling, moulded ceiling and banqueting table decorated by an elaborate centrepiece in bronze and gold. It was inevitable that one of the throng should ask if this was where the President had his breakfast every morning. To our universal disappointment the guard replied that it was not. The president, he said, lived on the second floor and had his own facilities. His office, too – the famous Oval Office – was in the West Wing and sadly was not part of the tour.

Twilight brought me back, hotfoot, to Tom's bar on Connecticut. Michael, sensibly, had made his excuses, keen to get his head down before his westward trek. With a fresh repertoire of tap-room ditties coursing through my brain I settled at the same table as the previous evening and ordered a beer. Tom, already exercising on the piano, played me in with *Knees Up Mother Brown*.

After last night's triumph my reprise fell a little flat. Deprived of Michael's vocal and moral support I muffed the songs I only half-remembered. Exhausting his Cockney playlist, Tom resorted to his own brand of blues and hill-billy, which became more and more syncopated as the bottles stacked up on the piano. Support became more personal as his groupies crowded round the piano, among them a tipsy woman who seemed more interested in Tom than his music.

As the evening wore on the crowd thinned out, and by the time the lights were flicking on and off only Tom and I were left, dutifully singing both of our national anthems. For some reason the woman had disappeared, perhaps at his own request. He came over, absently running a comb through his sideburns.

'Paul, I like your singin', real well.' His eyes were starry as he sat beside me, gazing at the space above my head, and I guessed we'd had about the same amount to drink. His gratitude seemed genuine though, and I mumbled something about having no special gift.

'It's sure been nice to make your acquaintance, Paul. Sorry your friend couldn't make it. It's been a good long time since we had any English boys down here.'

He got up unsteadily and straightened his tie. His appearance, I could see, was important to Tom, who sported not only coiffured sideburns but a blow-wave. The details of his outfit too, had been closely observed, with mother-of-pearl buttons on his jacket and waistcoat. Though he must have known it was midnight he made a great display of examining his watch, a silver-braceleted affair that dropped down when he shook his wrist.

'How 'bout you an' me goin' on to Sam's Place, Paul? They got a bar stays open 'til two am.'

I wasn't sure whether I agreed to the idea, but found myself outside nonetheless as Tom led me to his car, a monster eight-cylinder coupe complete with driver.

Tom squeezed in between me and the driver. 'You'll like Sam's Place. It's *gay* –'

The gum-chewing youth at the wheel gave me a quick searching glance and then drove at speed up Connecticut Avenue. We pulled up shortly in a tangle of neon and I followed Tom past a couple of nodding bouncers into an ill-lit bar-cum-disco. A handful of shadowy figures were sitting at tables and side booths in an atmosphere that was decidedly downbeat.

We took a table and ordered drinks. Tom offered me a cigar, which I declined, and said conspiratorially: 'I come here most nights, just for the company. I know most of the people here. You might think their way of life is different than other folks, but that's their choice. They know how to live, Paul, 'cause they've figured it out. They don't care too much about social convention an' all –'

A dime dropped into the juke box and suddenly the place was flooded with a pink light, illuminating some of the crowd. The boys, attired in smart leather and jeans, sat in a separate booth to the girls, who wore diamante tops. As the music vibrated they moved out onto the floor.

All except one girl in lamé tights and a bolero who walked over to us in a measured sort of way. She had heavy make-up and in the weird light her bouffant hair-do looked like candy floss. Tom got up to take her hand and kissed it rather ostentatiously before turning to me with a vulpine smile.

'Paul, I'd like you to meet Marlene. Marlene, this is Paul.'

I bowed from the waist, even more ostentatiously, and Marlene winked at me through blue mascara lashes. Then she held out her hand.

I was impressed by the strength of her grip. Then Tom said: 'Brace yourself, Paul. Marlene is a boy.'

I wanted to say something clever, like she was the prettiest boy I ever saw, but somehow the words wouldn't come. I just shrugged, as though I was meeting transvestites all the time and it was becoming a drag.

Tom took my hand so we formed a kind of fairy circle on the dance floor. 'Marlene, would you do a number for Paul?'

At that Marlene laughed, a high-pitched scream that turned all heads in our direction. 'She's got a real purty voice,' said Tom, '... just like a girl's.'

A quiver of mascara and a shake of candy floss deflected the compliment. 'Some other time, honey.'

I couldn't help admiring the rapid swivel of the heels, the faultless steerage of the hips, as Marlene teetered away. As we sat down again a titter spread among the nearby tables.

Tom didn't want to leave it there. 'You ought to get to know someone like Marlene, Paul. You'd be dynamite together. You don't wanna make too much of the costume – that's just part of the scene. There's a coupla others over there dress like girls, but they're just two of the fellers – you know, *gay* people.' He paused for a moment, an earnest expression in his eyes. 'Maybe I should tell you about myself, Paul. You should know that I'm *gay*, too.'

I nodded, in a way that I hope suggested that I understood, rather than that I knew.

'My home state's Florida,' he continued. 'Don't know if I was born there or nothin', but I got foster parents down Okeechobee. Growin' sugar cane. I got a plantation down there someplace, but I ain't never seen it. Ain't been that way five, six years. Don't reckon they approve of my lifestyle, so no call to make the trip. Anyhow, I got a good thing goin' here, Paul.'

A long-haired person, more determinately male, approached our table. He saluted Tom with his hand raised, palm outwards. He examined me with curiosity. 'Who's your boyfriend, Tom?'

Glancing a little diffidently from the newcomer to me Tom said, 'Paul, this is Rusty. Rusty, this is Paul. Paul's from England. He's straight, but you'll like him.'

Rusty's interest seemed to wane a little, like a candle flame in a draught. Repeating his salute he wandered off. From his manner I guessed that 'straight' was opposite in meaning to 'gay'. It was interesting, learning the language.

Someone had chosen Charlie Parker and the mood of the dancing slowed to the tremulous notes of his saxophone. I noticed Rusty in the middle of the crowd, his hands splayed outwards as he gyrated around a girl in cutaway Bermudas. They got closer and closer, their ecstatic movements owing nothing to Charlie P but an apology. When I pointed at them Tom said: 'They make a nice couple. Rusty's queer as a three-dollar bill, but it's OK. She's a lesbian.'

I had to think about that for a moment, but didn't get very far. Not while Tom was there to confuse me a little more.

'I guess you don't know too much about gay people, Paul. You oughta hang around a few days, and get the picture. Maybe you could get somethin' goin' for yourself. Now, you take a set-up like mine – that's the kinda deal you wanna fix. I got a couple real nice relationships goin', with people I met right here on the Avenue. You recall that lady in the other bar, at the piano? That's Jay, she lives with me. Then there's Jimmy, our driver. He's a Junior Naval Officer in the Pentagon.'

The dimes ran out and the dancers began to unwind. Taking its cue from the juke box the pink glow faded, giving the whole scene the end-of-reel effect of a silent movie. Tom got up, yawning. Offering me a lift to my hotel he suggested we go first to his apartment for a nightcap. I realised I couldn't accept one offer without the other.

On the way out of Sam's Place we passed the bouncers, who responded to our 'goodnights' with a nod and a flexing of their shoulder pads. When I quietly enquired about their precise function, Tom said they were there to check everyone was appropriately dressed. Presumably Jimmy the driver, who patiently awaited us, was excluded because of his T shirt. Maybe he should have worn his naval uniform.

The moments of that evening pickled overnight in my brain as I lay comatose in a sweaty bed back at the hotel. I had recollections of Tom at his piano, chanting *Swanee River*, Marlene sashaying in a pink haze, Rusty erotically twirling. Then the drive to Tom's place, two floors of a rambling house in Foggy Bottom where a smell of cannabis and old sofas had predominated. And inside, the floor show put on by the occupants, Jimmy down to socks and underpants playing a guitar, and the fabulous Jay in a night gown singing along. Vaguest of all the memories was the final one, sitting on the front step with Tom and drinking a farewell Coke and mutually agreeing that he shouldn't make his life any more complicated.

Charleston

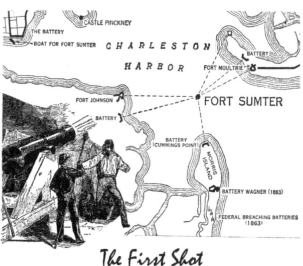

The First Shot

'Talk to me, sweetheart.'

I stared blankly at the Joe Louis look-alike who stood before me, serving tongs poised. The chef's hat, adding generously to his height, gave him some authority.

'Roast brisket, please.'

The Adventurer's Inn had welcomed me off the bus from Washington, at the downtown depot in Charleston. After the overnight journey I was ready for the sliced-beef sandwich, skilfully loaded on to my paper plate. My 'thank you' went unheeded as the *Brown Bomber transferred his charm to another customer.

Shunted along by the queue I added a coleslaw salad, a layer cake and a coffee to my tray. A simple meal, practising my avowed economy. When the girl at the till rang up $1.50 I was nonplussed.

'Excuse me, but aren't you adding ten cents somewhere?'

'Uh-uh.' Giving me a long tired look she pointed at my layer cake. 'That's *á la mode* you got there.'

---

* Nickname of Louis, who was world heavyweight champion 1937-49

Sure enough there was a dab of ice cream on the cake. Had I chosen to add that in a moment of weakness? Happily the reprimand was assuaged by a further temptation. By the checkout there was a stainless steel dispenser, displaying a choice assortment of pickles and sauces for no extra charge. With shameless abandon I helped myself to about half-a-dozen paper cups containing apple jelly, diced gherkins, shredded carrot, chopped beetroot, French mayonnaise and relish of different kinds – redemption in part for my earlier restraint.

With the addition of a cellophane bag of plastic eating utensils I had the complete meal kit. Perching at a counter, I settled down to the serious business of deconstructing American fast-food packaging.

My first task was to extricate the sandwich from its envelope of tissue paper. Then to separate the hygienically wrapped knife, fork and spoon. Next to strip the top from the little cellophane pack and squeeze the mustard on to the contents of the sandwich. This done, to scoop out the apple jelly, diced gherkins and other relishes from their containers onto the paper plate. Finally to sweeten my coffee by taking one of the teaspoon-size packets of sugar from the bowl on the counter, slitting the corner to release the contents, pouring the sugar into my paper cupful of coffee and then, having removed its protective tissue sleeve, stirring it with the plastic spill provided for the purpose.

I don't remember much about the meal, but getting through the paperwork brought its own satisfaction. In the old days, we used to just munch on a bone.

Maybe I'm moving ahead a little, without giving an account of my last day in Washington and the overnight run to Charleston. Suffice it to say that with a late departure in prospect I had a leisurely finale in Washington, allocated to the pursuit of an essential project.

This was part of the natural history reporting that I have already mentioned. Although the Smithsonian had beckoned me with its amazing stuffed specimens I was more interested in their live counterparts, notably a couple of household names residing in the Washington Zoo. Here I had booked 'interviews' with its two most famous inmates, Smokey the Bear and Ham the Chimpanzee.

As a cub, Smokey had been rescued from a forest fire in New Mexico in 1950, and consequently became the inspiration for the character of the same name created by the US Forest Service as a symbol of fire prevention. The rather wistful-looking brown bear that I encountered at the zoo had long since recovered from his burns and – despite the adulation of his young admirers – looked as disgruntled as any other wild animal in a cage.

In the primates' section I was presented to the other animal celebrity, an elderly chimpanzee called Ham who in 1961 had become – no doubt through no wish of his own – the first creature in the higher order of mammals to travel in space. For his services to science this celebrated 'chimponaut', who had survived speeds of up to 5800mph, altitudes of up to 157 miles and gravitational pulls of up to 18G, had been granted an honourable retirement in the Federal Zoo. In 1962 his human successor, John Glenn, became the first astronaut to orbit the earth.

Glenn was rewarded with a seat in the US Senate. Ham's reward was an apple.

After my zoo visit, and doubting my ability to survive another day of Washington's monuments, temperature and strange society, I had decided to move on. Unseen by the Washington Press Corps, I had slipped out of the hotel and headed off to the bus depot. Here I had booked my passage to Charleston, South Carolina, via Richmond, Virginia.

This journey would take me from the capital of the Union to the capital of the Confederacy, and then to its heart. It was in Charleston, in April 1861, that the recognised first shot of the Civil War had been fired, an appropriate event in the state which had been the strongest advocate of slavery and the first to secede from the Union. From Richmond to Charleston lay a distance of 430 miles. No problem for a Greyhound, but quite a stretch of terrain, a century ago, to carry on a war.

At Richmond I was directed onto another bus which would take me through to Charleston with a rest-stop at Raleigh in North Carolina. Climbing aboard I was disconcerted to see that all the seats were taken, except for one at the front next to an elderly black woman that was largely covered by her belongings. Having no desire to stand, at least until Raleigh, I made my claim by putting my rucksack in the baggage compartment above her seat. It seemed however that the woman, busy ferreting around for something in her tangle of baskets and packages, had not noticed me.

'You found it yet, lady?' The bus driver had just come aboard, looking impatiently at the woman.

At the sound of his voice she threw her arms in the air, addressing a soulful entreaty to the roof of the bus. 'Glory, glory – you hear that man talkin'? He's askin' if Ah found it, Lord!'

Frenziedly, she returned to her rummaging. I looked enquiringly at the driver, but all he seemed able to do was stand there, pushing his cap further and further to the back of his head. Hesitantly, I offered to help the woman find whatever she'd lost, only to be met by a wail and an eruption of paper bags. Again, I turned to the driver. 'Her ticket?'

He nodded. 'Yeah, and if she don't find it soon, she's gonna leave the bus – or I go on vacation.'

At this the woman wailed more loudly, upending her basket on her lap so that the contents spilled everywhere. 'You cain't turn *me* off, feller! Ah bin waitin' three hours for this bus – three hours, d'yuh hear? Ah knows my rights, same as anybody!' A murmur of approval came from the rest of the passengers, who obviously saw an application of leniency as the quickest way of getting the show on the road.

The driver, however, did not see it that way. 'No ticket, no ride, lady.'

The woman stared at him. 'Lan' sakes! Just listen to the man! Talkin' like he was runnin' the company or somethin'. Mister, you wanna see there ain't no holes in your pockets, else them dimes'll be rollin' out, all over the place. Well, that's right, ain't it? You're sure worried about them dimes, ain't yuh? Huh! Let me tell you somethin', Mr Bus Driver. Ah've got a yearnin' for *my* dimes, just the same as you. An' when I done paid my fare, Ah ain't buyin' no more tickets for your buses. Lord, have mercy! You ain't turnin' me off this bus, no sir. Nobody ain't turnin' me off, nobody! You're gonna have to wrap me in a sheet first, an' carry me to the Bellevue Cemet-airy –'

It was the voice of the Deep South, the voice of persecution. By stages the woman had worked herself into a tantrum, and her voice tailed off into a kind of keening sound. Her arms were like the wings of a butterfly, fluttering at her sides. Like her ticket she was beyond recall, and she knew exactly what she was doing.

The murmur from the other passengers had become more vocal and the driver was looking confused, clearly trying to recall the instructions in his courtesy training manual which dealt with this kind of situation. Finally, with a heave of his shoulders, he capitulated. 'OK, lady, so you paid for your ticket. That's all I wanted to know. Now, how about makin' a bit of room on that seat for the gentleman?'

With a conciliatory snort my travelling companion gathered her belongings on to her lap and settled down, to the accompaniment of a sigh of relief from the rest of the bus. Taking my seat I blessed the memory of Rosa Parks, the black civil rights campaigner who ten years ago had sat in the whites-only section of a segregated bus in Montgomery, Alabama and whose subsequent arrest and trial had led to a bus boycott and a successful campaign for the desegregation of public transport. Now I was sitting next to a latter-day Rosa who had asserted her own rights with a positive result. Whether she had paid for her ticket, no-one would ever know.

'We are now leaving Richmond. This coach is due at Charleston, South Carolina, at 8.15 tomorrow morning. Your first rest-stop will be at Raleigh, North Carolina, at 1am.'

Hoping to sleep until that stage of the journey I was disappointed. Three things kept me awake. First the discomfort of my long legs, wrapped around Rosa's baskets. Then the good lady herself, who though otherwise at peace with the world had sorted her paper bags and unwrapped her provisions for the night. Main item on her menu was chicken bones, which she commenced to suck and crunch in her teeth with atavistic relish. Had these combined irritants failed, a third experience would have been enough to keep my eyes open all the way to Raleigh.

At a road junction we crawled to a halt at a disturbing scene:

a shattered, overturned car, with flames leaping from it into the darkness. Reflected in their light the terrified face of a black man in a blood-stained shirt – the driver? A motorcycle policeman, newly arrived on the scene, waved us on. Even in a situation like this the 'keep moving' rule of the freeway prevailed.

Half an hour later relief was manifest in the driver's voice as he pulled into the Raleigh rest stop. 'While we're here,' he announced, 'this beautiful vehicle is gonna have a hose-down, so I want y'all to make yourselves nice-lookin' too.' With that he brought out his comb, adroitly parting his hair as he steered into the parking bay. Even my travelling companion was tickled by his humour – but this, of course, was where she got off the bus.

Following the driver's recommendation I had a good clean-up in the depot restroom and a coffee in the Post House Cafeteria. Revitalised for the next stage of the journey I returned to the bay and was the first aboard when the bus returned, glistening, from the cleaning shed. This time I was relieved to have a spare seat beside me and enjoyed the additional luxury of a pillow, provided by the man who brought a pile of them onto the bus before departure to distribute among the passengers. Comfort assured I could settle down to a free night's accommodation, courtesy of the Greyhound Corporation.

Six hours later the sunlight was playing on my eyelids and I slowly opened them to behold a new vision. This was the South, an image that magically recalled the one Harriet Beecher Stowe had created for me in childhood. Plantations of cotton and tobacco, with the occasional view of an owner's mansion or, closer to the road, clusters of frame houses very much in the 'Uncle Tom' tradition. On the raised porches of these houses the figures of families, descendants of the slaves who had originally worked the plantations, coming out to enjoy the first rays of the sun. The picture had a dream-like quality, like the one I had seen a few days before in New Jersey, but this time it was not the impression of waking to a contrasting landscape but to one that was totally foreign to my eyes.

Trees and ferns abounded, a tropical luxuriance that I had not anticipated this side of Florida. And everywhere a strange growth flourished: the trailing hanks of Spanish moss hanging from the trees or anything that would support them. As we swept beneath them, the telegraph wires unreeled like stretches of bunting, and the eaves of the houses that we passed were dressed in harmony, as for some mystic celebration. The whole effect was of a setting for a fairy tale, the moving, silver tendrils the work of a wand waving over an enchanted forest.

Soon the driver was announcing our arrival at Charleston, a busy seaport city that like NewYork's Manhattan lay on a finger-shaped peninsula, bounded by a river on either side and forming a harbour protected by scattered islands. But here, of course, the similarity ended. In place of modern skyscrapers there were three- or four-storey buildings that wore for the most part an air of quiet retirement, with here or there a church or meeting house that belonged to the old world. These buildings, some of them pre-dating the Revolution, were of great historical interest, but I suspected authentic survivals were rare and needed careful tracking down.

Like Philadelphia and Boston, Charleston had the proud (shared) title of 'America's Most Historic City'. Her record in this connection must be taken seriously, for not only was she settled by the English as far back as 1670 (Charles' Towne) but became within a hundred years America's leading port. In 1748 the country's first export, cotton – seven whole bags of it – was shipped from here to England, and in the latter half of the century Charleston could claim that her maritime trade exceeded even that of her great northern rival, Boston.

But it was not for commerce alone that Charleston had earned her place in the history books. The curtain-raiser of the American Revolution had been the hauling down of the British flag here in 1775, and the Revolution's first decisive victory had been gained at Fort Moultrie in the harbour, when a British landing was strongly repulsed a year later. In more peaceful times, Charleston had introduced the first drug store, the first artificially-produced ice and the first fireproof building (defences against summer temperatures?) and given a rousing send-off to the first US steam locomotive to run with passenger and freight cars, in 1830.

Back in the throes of political conflict, Charleston had again answered the call of destiny, not only by her arguments for secession (which from the heart of the Southern slave trade were forceful) but by the action of that fateful day in April 1861, when Confederate batteries had opened fire on a tiny fortified island in the middle of the harbour garrisoned by Union forces. The first shot in an exchange that was to continue up and down the country like a wind-driven holocaust for four years.

For all the appearance of ruin and destruction that it nowadays presented, Fort Sumter could be fairly described as Charleston's Capitol, Independence Hall and Empire State Building rolled into one. Although its tourist potential was not fully recognised until 1948, when it was accorded the status of a National Monument, it was unquestionably the most popular historical shrine of the south-east United States. Part of its attraction was due, perhaps, to the thrilling boat trip from Charleston Harbor of three miles or so which was the only means of reaching the island. My own experience of this trip made it one of the most indelible memories of my American journey.

The boat departed at 2.30 in the afternoon, which gave me all the time I needed to fix a 'Y' and check the layout of the city. The morning bore the promise of another sultry day, but at noon the sky clouded over and as I walked south to the Municipal Yacht Basin there was a sharp drop in the temperature. Very soon I began to feel the strength of the Atlantic breeze, and then the first drops of rain. With the wariness of my breed I had taken the precaution of packing a plastic mac in my small pack, but without seriously considering that I might have to use it. My premonitions were however strong and I donned the mac, moments before a rainstorm of torrential proportions swept over me.

The downpour persisted all the way to the Yacht Basin where I made a hasty beeline for a placard saying 'Fort Sumter Harbor Tours'. With some misgivings I noticed that the sightseers gathered at the ticket office were all heavily shrouded in oilskin capes and leggings. My ticket purchased, I followed them onto the jetty and up a precariously tossing gangplank to the Gray Line Tour boat that awaited us, the *Major Anderson*. Clinging awkwardly to the rail as she lurched beneath me I trusted she would show the same intrepid qualities as her namesake, Sumter's 1861 Union commander.

In doughty defiance of the rough water the boat cast off and headed out to the harbour mouth, the rain lashing her decks. Although the observation deck was under cover, the rain and sea spray drove in under the canopy and after a few minutes the less intrepid retreated below. I stood firm, gripping hard on the forward rail while the salty wind stung my face and purged my lungs.

As we curved outwards from the tip of Charleston's battery I peered at the harbour mouth through the mist of rain, trying vainly to decipher the shape of Fort Sumter and its opposing headlands. Under the leaden sky even the horizon was invisible, and I found my earlier exhilaration tinged with apprehension.

When the sky was at its darkest the first stab of lightning came, slicing through the void. Extinguished by the sea it was followed by another and then another; whiplash traceries of light. The thunder followed, a reverberating wall of sound that began with a crescendo and ended with a murmur. To my impressionable ears it seemed that the sound came not from above but from either side of me, a fragmented cannonade bursting from the invisible shores that flanked the tiny distant island. To my eyes the lightning was the flash of the gunfire, the heaving vessel beneath me not a tour boat but the supply ship *Star of the West*, dispatched by the North to succour the beleaguered island and now bombarded by the Confederate guns.

That was how it had started. A few days after South Carolina's secession the commander of Charleston's Federal garrison, anticipating an immediate takeover by rebel forces, had moved his men overnight from Fort Moultrie on the east side of the harbour to the refuge of Fort Sumter, about a mile from the nearest point of land. What might have appeared a retreat was in fact a judicious manoeuvre. Recognising his best defence as the sea, Major Robert Anderson had taken the only course open to him short of surrender. Following his departure, the rebels had occupied Fort Moultrie.

The next move in this hazardous chess game had been the dispatch by the North of a supply ship, to carry provisions and reinforcements to their menaced outpost. On arrival in the harbour the unarmed *Star of the West* had promptly been sent packing by the Southern shore batteries, whereupon it became apparent that Sumter would have to be relieved by other means.

With a four-month supply of provisions time had been on Anderson's side. But by April 11 these were running low and Lincoln's promise of supplies had not been fulfilled. Anderson's reply to Confederate demands for his evacuation of Sumter had been dictated by the circumstances. Yes, he would evacuate, but not before April 15, when his supplies would be exhausted. A rider to this was that no contrary instructions – or indeed, supply ships – should have reached Sumter from the North before the Union deadline.

Reinforcements were, in fact, on their way from New York. Realising that further delay might bring an indefinite prolongation of the siege, the Confederates had rejected the Union commander's reply and precipitated the first act of war by announcing their impending bombardment of Sumter. In the early hours of April 12, a shell fired from a mortar at Fort Johnson, on the west side of the harbour, had burst almost directly over Sumter to signal the beginning of the attack.

The honour – or dishonour – of firing the first shot of the actual bombardment and of the Civil War had gone to a man of Virginia, Edmund Ruffin. From the battery at Cummings Point he had fired a cannon directed at Fort Sumter, a scant mile to the north across the mouth of the harbour. By daybreak forty-three guns were firing at Sumter from the batteries at Cummings Point, Fort Johnson and Fort Moultrie, a three-sided bombardment that would last until 2pm the following day.

As we approached the fortress island the storm relented. In an astonishing silence, broken only by the wash of the sea against our bow, we glided in towards the grey, huddled shape that was emerging from the mist. In my imagination the firing had ceased and we were now a boat of the Confederacy, carrying a white flag and an offer of truce to the exhausted defenders.

For thirty-four hours Anderson had maintained a stout resistance, answering the enemy gunfire with his own cannon. But it had not been an equal exchange. Shortage of ammunition had reduced his firepower to six guns on the first day, and eventually his capitulation had been forced by the sheer weight of the rebel bombardment. On April 13 surrender terms had been agreed and a day later the Federal garrison had evacuated Sumter, happily without serious casualties. On April 15 President Lincoln had issued his historic proclamation: a call for 75,000 volunteers from the northern states 'to cause the laws to be duly executed.' The Civil War had begun.

From that date until the end of the war Fort Sumter had been a powder keg set beside a furnace, which though touched by the flames had never exploded, remaining a threat and a provocation until the fire had died away. In 1863 it had been the Confederates' turn to hold the fort, against a Federal navy whose blockade of the Atlantic coast was being effectively countered by the protection Sumter gave to Charleston harbour. On another violent April day a force of nine armoured ships had steamed towards the fort and for two hours had peppered it with shells, only to withdraw in bad shape after the combined riposte of their target and its supporting shore batteries. Shortly afterwards a different kind of operation had been mounted: a sea and land assault on Morris Island to the south which had acquired some commanding ground for the Federals. Gun emplacements were set up and in a short time the first Union bombardment proceeded, the start of a determined effort to breech Sumter's walls. The latter, buttressed by the defenders with bales of cotton and sand, had for a time withstood the enemy shells, but the concentration of the attack had eventually reduced them to ruins. The spirit of the rebel defenders, however, had remained intact, surviving a further four months' pounding by the Union artillery. A pause in December had been followed by renewed bombardments in the summer of the following year, but their effect had been minimal and the siege had tailed off into a desultory exchange between Sumter, supported by Confederate batteries at Fort Moultrie and other points, and the enemy guns on Morris Island. This had been maintained until the next year, 1865, and might have gone on longer had not events on a larger scale taken a hand.

The Napoleonic figure of the Union general, William T. Sherman, was turning northwards. His scorched earth campaign had already cut a swathe through Georgia to the south, and at his impending approach the Confederate troops had withdrawn from Charleston, leaving Sumter's commander to evacuate his garrison. The date was February 17, 1865. In less than two months the American Civil War was over.

After all this, what remained of Fort Sumter? An undistinguished ruin, partially restored for the tourist but conveying nonetheless an air of bleak desolation. Walking along the jetty where the Gray Line boat had moored I surveyed the mist-wrapped walls that rose from the shoal, the gun ports gaping out like pigeon holes. At the sally port we were met by a chilled- looking park ranger who was happy to welcome his own twentieth-century relief force.

The walking tour of the ruined interior of the fort was thorough, starting with the gun rooms at ground level and then progressing to the topmost tier of the fortification. From here it was possible to pick out the shapes of the surrounding islands and headlands. The mist blurred their outlines and I could guess how close they must have looked on a fine spring day, with the sunlight glinting on the enemy's batteries. The ranger, who may have had his own fanciful moments, proceeded to give us a graphic reconstruction of the scene on the morning of the first rebel bombardment, when the guns of three batteries had been hurling shot at Sumter and the garrison's defence had depended on only six cannon, firing intermittently. His account of the defenders' plight had us all enthralled, from the moment when the shell of the signal mortar had burst over the fort to the drama on the second day when the barracks had erupted into flames and the hard-pressed Federals had been forced to surrender.

As he spoke the wind whipped our shoulders and the sense of an apocalypse swept through me, so that I saw in the dark sea, shell-torn masonry and menacing encircling headlands that very picture of a hundred years ago, when the peace of a whole continent had resided momentarily in the actions of a single artilleryman, gazing apprehensively at his target across a short stretch of water. Here, indeed, was the real thrill of Sumter. The experience – even without the bonus of celestial stage effects – of a seminal incident in history.

From the short-lived Federal defence of one and a half days, our guide went on to describe the twenty-two-month Confederate defence – at sufficient length to confirm his own loyalties. Recalling the amazing fortitude of the Confederate garrison I felt that I should share these sentiments. But as I looked around me at the grim, windswept ruin, so forlorn in its isolation, I knew that my personal sympathies lay with the small defending force that had evacuated the island. Major Anderson had clearly recognised the limitations of the place.

Main street, Charleston was Meeting Street. It ran straight from north to south with a kink at the end where it approached the East Bay area. At this point it abounded with curiosities: old colonial and ante-bellum buildings crammed to their eaves with the folklore of the South.

In the Old Market Hall, at the centre of the City Market area, I discovered a remarkable museum of Civil War memorabilia. As one might expect in a museum run by the Daughters of the Confederacy, the exhibits showed a distinctly Southern bias. Arranged, captioned and encased with great reverence, it was only a pity that they had not been better preserved from the ravages of time. Everything bore a faded, rescued-from-the-battlefield look, to such an extent that I had to separate the glorious from the trivial by reading the captions. A striking similarity, for example, could be noted between a pair of rebel drawers and the last Confederate flag to fly over Fort Sumter.

Although the instruments of war – flintlocks, pistols, mortar and cannon shells – were accorded their place, the emphasis of the collection was on personal mementos. A child's dress of the period, embroidered in wool. A handkerchief of Sea Island cotton, woven in Lancashire and sold at a bazaar held by Southern sympathisers in Liverpool. A soldier's toilet case. The uniform and sash of a captain of the South Carolina Volunteers, killed in action at Petersburg, Virginia. Part of a pair of suspenders, woven by a Confederate woman for her soldier sweetheart.

Other items of this kind revealed the sacrifices endured by the women of South Carolina during the Federal blockade, deprived of the luxuries that the non-manufacturing South had customarily imported. Two pairs of shoes made from the canvas awning of a store, one worn by the mistress and the other by her cook. A pair of hand-knitted gloves, the last resort of a Miss St Clair of Greenville after the supply of kid and other fine materials had run out. Despite the less than comely appearance of this accessory, such enterprise had been deemed to the lady's credit.

My tour of the museum left me with two contradictory conclusions. Either that the Confederacy was the only side in the war, or the only one to come out of it with any glory. A typical example of Union infamy was contained in the caption to an exhibit that had been presented to the museum by the granddaughters of a Mrs Harris Simons of Charleston. The exhibit was an Order of Protection given to Mrs Simons by the Union General Sherman, during his occupation of the town. When she had shown the order to the guard detailed to protect her, his response had been to laugh at her and say, 'The General knows this is not worth the paper it is written on. We all have our orders: the town is to be burned'.

In another case I saw the testament of two Confederate soldiers who had died in a Union prison camp on Hart's Island, New York. No mention of the Confederate prison camp at Andersonville, Georgia from which Union captives had emerged like living skeletons. The first shot in a war that had cost 750,000 lives had been fired close to here, but I felt like reminding those proud ladies of the Charleston Chapter who had created this exhibit that the last shot had been fired as well, a long time ago.

Three blocks from the museum, at No 6 Chalmers Street, I found another curiosity. This was the Old Slave Mart Museum, which as the name suggested was an office of one of the city's numerous slave auctioneers before the war put an end to the business. Its interest lay not so much in the quality of the exhibits as in their association.

Of the relics here I can say very little, except that they were even sadder than those in the Civil War Museum. They were the implements of the oppressed and spoke only of hardship and privation. They might have been made a thousand years ago. A rice mortar and pestle, *circa* 1830, used for breaking and rubbing the hulls of the grain. A copper pot made by a plantation blacksmith, used for cooking rice and hominy. A wooden hoe, a rusted scythe, a copper sugar dipper, an oak-split basket, a piggin used for washing grist.

The instruments of bondage were also on display. An auctioneer's booth, made of oak, and a copy of a handbill of 1852 advertising a sale to be held at the Mart. Under the heading 'A Prime Gang of 25 Negroes, Accustomed to the Culture of Sea Island Cotton and Rice', were listed the names of the enslaved, grouped in families. In the next column their ages, and details of their 'capacity'. The first few names were:

1. Aleck, 33, Carpenter.
2. Mary Ann, 31, Field Hand, Prime.
3. Louisa, 10.

Further on came Daniel, 45, Field Hand, Not Prime, and James, 13, who was recorded as 'Slight Defect in Knee from Broken Leg'.

In spite of all this a strange loyalty between slavers and some of the enslaved became apparent. From a dedication in a pamphlet ('Slave Days') I learned that the Old Slave Mart Museum was 'Dedicated to the Memory of the Loyal Faithful Negroes who, During and After the War Between the States Remained Faithful to Their Former Owners. Who Nursed the Sick and Wounded Soldiers Returning to the Ruins of their Homes, and Protected the Widows and Fatherless during the *Carpetbagger Days'. Thus were the virtues of service extolled. There was no mention, however, of the other slaves, the great majority of whom had 'betrayed' their former owners by gratefully accepting emancipation.

In the foreword of the same pamphlet the dedication was extended to the followers of the black educator Booker T. Washington, whose policy in the early years of the twentieth century had been to cultivate among his people a feeling of self-help and racial integrity. On the more significant issue of their relationship to white authority however, the words of the man who had been born a slave in the era of 'Uncle Tom's Cabin' must be recalled. In 1912, addressing a delegation of white university professors, he had pronounced: 'We are trying to instil in the Negro mind that if education does not make the Negro humble, simple, and of service to the community, then it will not be encouraged'.

Booker T. may have had his followers (he reached his apotheosis on a 1909 Virginia Railway speaking tour), but the people that he sought to represent were invariably his victims, the butt-end of the patronage and prejudice that his words inadvertently inspired. For them, of course, it was no new experience. Their role as victims

---

* Northerners who came to exploit the Southern States after the Civil War.

had commenced in 1619 when their ancestors had arrived in the first slave ships. These people were the beginning of a flourishing trade between America, Europe and Africa that was to evolve as a model of the 'vicious circle'. Molasses and sugar, the products of slave labour in the West Indies, were shipped to New England for conversion into rum. This in turn was shipped to Africa, where it was offered to the tribal chiefs in payment for the captives of their tribes who had been selected for the slave markets of the West Indies and the American continent. The slaves of the New World were thus working for the enslavement of their fellows in the Old, an irony that was to be repeated in the post-Civil War years in the misguided actions of those who were arguing so vociferously for their civil rights.

Here again the black men and women had become the victims, not of the slave-masters of the South but of the liberators of the North, the radical Republicans who had uprooted with a righteous and vindictive tug the entire slave-based economy of the South. And who by failing to introduce an effective new system had squandered the honourable intentions of their late President. The newly-freed slaves, given the promise of unimagined opportunities, had not known how to exploit it. Urged on by the cohorts from the North – government administrators, industrialists and carpetbaggers – they had fallen in behind the Republican banner and accepted appointments in the Southern state legislature.

As former field hands promoted to government office, the Bench and the police force, they had been putty in the hands of the people who put them there, open to graft and manipulation. Among other devices they had been made unwitting executors of the punitive tax laws used by the Northerners to carry out wholesale confiscation of Southern property. Deprived of their slaves and wealth the former plantation owners had been easy prey for the ever-rapacious carpetbaggers, whose eager claws had fallen on whatever remained of their land, crops and timber. All this had done little to endear the Southerners to the political regime imposed by the North, and its element of emancipated black men – however much a façade – was an open provocation. What else, when the sons and daughters of Dixie had looked north and seen not a single one of those ex-slaves in elective office?

With such a record it was surprising that Reconstruction – the incongruous name of this period – had lasted as long as it did. In South Carolina it had taken eleven years to shake off carpetbagger rule and the perceived threat of black ascendancy. The weapon employed to achieve this end had been a double-edged sword. One edge the Democratic Party, which after its pledge to end Reconstruction had become the point of convergence for Southern white voters. The other the Ku Klux Klan, organised initially for the single purpose of keeping the other voters – the Republican blacks – away from the polls. The methods of this society of sub-humans are well known.

After Reconstruction had come Redemption, a period in which the Southern whites had endeavoured to regain their political power and racial supremacy. A bargain with the North, bringing the withdrawal of Federal troops from the South, had left the way clear for a crusade of repression and terrorism against the black population, starting with a poll tax and voting restrictions and continuing into the twentieth century with lynchings and segregation. The latter, maintained in spirit to this day despite the efforts of the reformers (Frederick Douglass through to Martin Luther King) and the Civil Rights legislation of the 1950s and '60s, had been the ineradicable aftermath of that historical backlash.

In the wake of King's 'I Have a Dream' speech there had to be hope that white prejudice against ten per cent of the US population, so strongly rooted in the past, would eventually decline as humanity advanced. This seemed something of a vain hope, however, in the context of the Old Slave Mart Museum. The author of 'Slave Days' insisted that the crime against the Negro was not in bringing him to America as a slave but in freeing him without having taught him to be self-supporting. The same Miriam Bellangee Wilson, who had 'gathered the factual information' for the pamphlet, was sufficiently confident in her theories to include a quotation of her own on the title page:

'God has a place for every man regardless of race or color.'

Miami and the Keys

Sharks and Sea Urchins

The journey down to Miami was one of the longest 'hops'. Six hundred miles of coast-hugging highway that would take me to the South beyond the South, the sub-tropical tip of the country which was the state of Florida.

What did I know about Florida? Nothing, except that of all the states that made the claim, it was perhaps the most *different* part of the USA. It had swamps and alligators, sugar cane and sunken treasure. Hurricanes galore and the largest population of Cubans outside Cuba. Its differences meant that it could never be counted as part of America's Deep South, whose history it shared, but a tenuous appendage, coerced by geography into its past alignments. Today, like California, it stood on its own and acted paradoxically as a magnet to the crowd.

The farther south I travelled, the greater the differences, most notable in the variety of people who climbed on the bus. The accents were interesting. From Washington southwards they had run up the scale and now, in South Carolina and Georgia, were approaching their highest pitch. If I hadn't already 'studied' the language I would have been at a loss to comprehend the sing-song voices that carolled around me. But my recollections of *Lord Ashley Cooper's Dictionary of Charlestonese* were strong.

Ain't	Sister of one of your parents
Beckon	Meat from a pig
Cane chew	Can't you?
Des Moines	They belong to me
Gate	Obtain, persuade
Gay-yet	Opening in a fence
Hail	Abode of Civil Rights campaigners, and William Tecumseh Sherman
Hell	Small mountain
Lack	Enjoy, like
Mine eyes	Salad Dressing
Minuet	You and I have dined

All of which is terribly useful for strangers wishing to express themselves with phrases such as 'Cane chew gate your ain't to open the gay-yet?' or 'I lack mine eyes with beckon'.

There are few more entertaining ways of passing a bus journey than listening to fellow passengers' scrambled version of your language and trying to pick up the thread of the conversation. This I did for much of the ride through Georgia, getting my dialogues either second-hand from the seat behind or in front, or first-hand from the person who sat next to me.

My first companion was a young man of about eighteen, in the company of four others, who won my immediate sympathy by announcing that he and his friends were conscripts on their way to a 'boot camp' near Savannah, Georgia. After Savannah his place was taken by a night nurse from an old ladies' home, on her way to visit a son in New Orleans. This was for a vacation, and when she produced a thermos and sandwiches I had to remind myself that the distance between Savannah and New Orleans is about the same as London to Marseille. On the long run to Jacksonville, Florida, she proved a congenial companion, proffering at intervals a basketful of the fruit that for many connoisseurs – even non-

Georgians – was the supreme example of its kind. I refer, of course, to the Georgia peach, an experience in succulence that no-one passing this way can afford to miss.

Later on I was charmed and amused by a little girl with tightly-plaited hair who was sitting in front of me. Under her arm she clutched a Beatles record, and in a tremulous voice was chanting one of their latest hits. When she heard my English voice she jumped up and peered over the back of her seat at me, her eyes struck with awe.

'Have yo' bin to Liverpool?'

Awkwardly I said 'no', but before her disappointment became too great added that I had however seen Paul McCartney, climbing into a taxi in Park Lane. This was enough to assure me a steady supply of peppermint-flavoured bubble gum as far as Jacksonville, Florida.

I took a four-hour break there, part of an elaborate plan to reach Miami in daylight. On the Miami bus my hope for a snooze was dispelled by a crushing weight on my right shoulder and a friendly slap on my knee as a large black man, weighing at least twenty stone, slid like an avalanche into the seat beside me.

'Ah'm goin' to Ma-ami. You goin' to Ma-ami?' I gave him a bruised nod, to which he replied by grasping my hand, as though this was enough to establish a relationship. 'Ah'm a ph'tographer. You a ph'tographer?'

With the Rolleiflex sitting on my lap I could not deny it. Seeing my camera the man emitted a sound resembling a purr and hauled up a large square case containing a quantity of photographic equipment. At the sight of the Leica camera, zoom lenses, filters, flash equipment and exposure meters I could not fake any detachment: rather I listened to him with green-eyed wonder as he told me he was planning to take some pictures of his family at Coral Gables that weekend. My Rollei, in its battered leather case, slipped slowly between my knees.

Most of the passengers on this bus were black, though not all possessing the affluence of my companion. One, in fact, who kept patrolling the gangway, had all the appearance of a chancer. For some time after the Greyhound's departure I was puzzled as to why this man was continually wandering up and down the bus.

The answer eventually came from the man himself, who on one of his migrations leaned confidentially over my companion.

'Hey, buddy – you read?'

My companion said, 'sure' and the other one passed him a note. 'You read that, buddy.'

The fat man studied the note for a moment and then cleared his throat to read the message. *'Ah lack you. But Ah'm married with a three-week-ol' chile, an' I don' wanna fool aroun' wid you.'*

He looked at the other man to see his reaction, only to be presented with a pencil.

'Write me an answer, buddy.'

Leica Man was nonplussed. 'What you wan' me to say?'

The chancer rolled his eyes and tipped his hat. Shrugged his shoulders and yanked his lapels. 'Words of love, man... Words of love...'

My companion dug the pencil into his brow, working it round like a screwdriver. Finally, with a grunt of inspiration, he turned the paper over and wrote on the back: *'I like you too. Why don't you and me get together?'*

Taking the note the other man studied it with a kind of eager incomprehension, then disappeared with it to the object of his desire at the back of the bus.

After the four-hour pause in Jacksonville, I had to ask myself, come the dawn, why I had created the delay. My vision of a golden sun breaking the horizon to illumine a pearl-coloured beach, fanned by gently bowing palm trees, was dispelled by the sight that met my waking eyes. For golden sun, I read neon. For horizon the outline of advertisement hoardings. For beach the endless vista of a road flanked by petrol stations, doughnut bars, motels and food stores. One element of my dream survived, but not in its original form. The palm trees, inseparable from my picture of tropical bliss, had here been adapted to a new environment. Set neatly between lamp standards and traffic signs, they had become part of the urban scene.

Imagining that we were somewhere on the outskirts of Greater Miami I nudged my companion. 'Is this Miami by any chance?'

He grunted. 'Ma-ami?' Sleepily, he peered at his watch. 'We ain't there for two-three hours, yet.'

Bewilderedly I unfolded my map, looking to see if there was a built-up area to the north of Miami. Most of the place names, I discovered, were something 'Beach', which seemed implausible on a stretch of road which so far had not offered a single glimpse of the sea. After another half-hour in which the blue horizon eluded me I realised that we were running on an inland parkway, non-stop to the city of Miami, and that the rapturous view of the fabled Palm Beach was nowhere to be seen. Only the endless hotels, apartment houses and drive-in stores that owed their existence to a far distant stretch of ocean. In addition the holiday residences – multi-coloured clapboard or cement buildings – which were the homing boxes of the northern migrants coming to winter in the sun.

Anyone with a buck to burn was, it seemed, welcome, and I searched hard for a building that was not exclusively dedicated to their interests. The nearest I could get was a mission hall, with the sign 'Salvation and Healing Tent Revival, Conducted by Rev N. Froman', but that was more than compromised by the flanking signs: 'Robin Hood Inn – Eat, Drink and be Merrie' and 'Mom's Kitchen for Best Burgers'.

At the end of it all, or more precisely at the end of another hundred miles, we passed under a huge climactic sign that came like the long-awaited finale to a tiring extravaganza. It said 'Welcome to Miami, Sun Capital of America'. With a spasm of relief I approached the threshold of my dream.

The Miami 'Y' was easy to find, a block or two from the downtown bus depot. After checking in I attended to the primary object of my visit to Florida. A telephone call to Lower Matecumbe Key.

Eighty miles south of Miami, this was one of the chain of islands hanging from the hook of the peninsula. Miraculously the voice that answered belonged to the man I'd written to, several weeks ago.

'Robert Schroeder here... That you, Paul? We've been waiting for you! When are you coming out to see us?'

Even though I'd arrived in Miami on the appointed day I was impressed that Robert was expecting me. It was my first personal welcome to America, and it made me feel less of a stranger. The delights of the Florida Keys lay tantalisingly before me.

We agreed on Sunday. Before ringing off he said, 'I'll look out a snorkel for you.'

The exclusiveness of Miami Beach lay first in its situation. Like the Lido at Venice it was a sandbar, running parallel to the shore and only approachable by causeways running across the lagoon end of Biscayne Bay. Connecting the centre of Downtown Miami with the Beach, Venetian Causeway was about three miles long, and as the bus swept along it I fantasised about being conveyed over shimmering water to a sea-girt paradise. On the bridge of islands supporting the causeway a profusion of sea grape and oleander brought a touch of the exotic, and the palm trees had reverted to their natural setting.

At the end of the causeway, however, I was bluntly reminded of the other aspect of the Beach's exclusiveness. There, in all their pride and pomp, stood the hotels. Vast balconied blocks, jostling for a purchase on the Elysian sand-pile and proclaiming their triumph with every storey thrust towards the sun. The Bel Mar, The Algiers, The Wafford Beach, The Seville. One hundred dollars a day peak season, the price including free TV, iced water and – if you happened to have booked an upper floor – a free view of Miami Beach.

Leaving the bus on the main boulevard I searched for a way through the concrete barricade. At one intersection I turned between two hotels, each forming a block. Passing beneath their towering, canopied walls I arrived eventually on a promenade, to gaze at the vision so long denied me. The blue Atlantic, glowing through feathery palm trees.

Breaking into a run, my feet soon left tarmac and were scudding through sand. As I ran through the circling palms the beach opened out before me, a dazzling, irresistible expanse. Spared that dismal caution so essential on a stony English beach, I threw myself down on the sand close to the sea and peeled off to embrace the sun.

Despite the strong trade wind that blew in from the Atlantic the UV waves were soon burning my skin. In my swimming trunks I felt like a white beach marker, keeping the ships from running ashore. I had no need to be self-conscious, however, as it was midday and there were few others on the beach apart from a

Charles Atlas figure roasting on a sunbed a few yards away. His bare-skinned anonymity gave me the reassurance that although this hedonist might be in oil, metal or paper cups and worth a cool million dollars he was still pretty much like me. Except perhaps for the cigar and month-old tan.

With a day to spare before my trip to the Keys, and with the choice of a 'Thousand Pleasures', I had but one firmly fixed in my mind. In a booming holiday resort so closely linked to the sea it would have been unthinkable to miss the Miami Seaquarium.

Located on Virginia Key to the south of Miami Beach the Seaquarium, along with its neighbouring Institute of Marine Sciences, was one of America's greatest centres of oceanographic study. It was also, using a more commercial description, one of the animal kingdom's greatest presentations, with all the thrills, action and spectacle of the ocean depths brought before the public gaze.

To get to the Seaquarium I took a bus along the Rickenbacker, the southernmost causeway that connected the city to the Virginia and Biscayne Keys. The bus was pretty crowded and I had to strap-hang all the way, an experience that brought me my first close-up of the people of Miami.

Even by the broad measure of the melting pot my companions were interesting. Small-statured types, with dark hair and complexions and talking the Spanish of the descendants of Ponce de Leon. My historical knowledge did a quick flip, from a sixteenth-century explorer to a twentieth-century revolution. Sixty miles to the south of Florida lay the island of Cuba, whose revolution had so recently rocked the world. Not all Cubans, I recalled, had admired its aims. Most of those who had fled had found their way to Florida, and specifically to the city of Miami. Looking at the nicotine-stained and barely legible notice inside the bus which read 'No Fumar' I guessed that a few of their compatriots had been here to welcome them.

The setting of Miami Seaquarium was well chosen. A green island embraced by Gulf Stream waters, stocked with fish and sea animals of every kind. A treasure trove of marine life to supply the tanks, pools and channels of the aquarium. The Seaquarium was, in fact, the ocean transported to land, offering a glimpse to us surface creatures of the preserves of the underwater explorer.

In the vast central tank was a sight that plunged me breathlessly into the world of Jacques Cousteau. Through one of the viewing windows in the side of the tank I beheld creatures that I'd never seen before, other than in the pages of the *National Geographic* magazine. A moray eel, fang-jawed and slithery and six feet long. A sting-ray, scudding across the sandy floor on its flap-like pectoral fins. A sawfish, probing the bottom with its sharp file-shaped bill. Passing on to the next window I was met by a startling sight. The implacable stare of a giant bass whose head filled the whole window, as grey and immobile as a boulder. I was grateful at that moment for the sheet of glass that separated us.

As I worked my way around the tank, gazing into its interior, I allowed my eyes to adjust to its eerie greenish glow. With a diameter of eighty feet and a depth of seventeen I could not see to the other side or to the surface. With a graceful flurry, more familiar shapes came into view. Circling the tank, the sun-dappled water reflected on their pale, sleek forms, the dolphins seemed to be searching for something.

An unexpected creature soon arrived on the scene. This one was amphibious and wearing an orange helmet emitting a froth of fine bubbles. In front of him, the diver held a wire basket from which he dispensed handfuls of fish to the converging dolphins. The antics of the playful cetaceans could not have helped him in his task. No sooner had one of these wily creatures plucked a fish from his hand than it would shoot behind him and flip round to his other side – to all appearances a newly arrived and unfed customer. The diver, however, who must have known his dolphins pretty well, was not so easily led. With a dogged attention to fair play he rebuffed the queue jumpers, keeping as even a distribution as the melee would allow. When the dolphins' craft turned to knavery, however, there was little he could do. One particularly greedy individual, determined to have more than its share, made the most of its opportunity when – in an unguarded moment – the diver paused to feed a green turtle that had been hovering rather forlornly at the edge of the fray. In this brief distracted moment the dolphin did a nosedive into the basket, grabbing a mouthful of fish before the diver could shut the lid.

From the outdoor viewing platform, above the tank, I had a

different view of the dolphin knockabout. With the circular tank as their arena they were performing a dazzling repertoire of acrobatic tricks, guided by an athletic young trainer poised on a feeding platform. He, too, had a basket of fish and although the dolphins had the same motivation as below they had to work much harder in front of the crowd. Two of their cleverest feats, receiving ecstatic applause, showed their gymnastic versatility. The first was a backwards 'walk' through the water, performed by a dolphin that propelled itself in reverse – and standing upright – across the width of the tank, to catch a fish thrown by the trainer. The second was a leap in which one of the larger dolphins cleared the surface by twenty feet, shooting out of the water like a sleek grey missile to pluck a fish from the trainer's hand.

Poised on his perch above the platform, the trainer gave this last trick a twist that convincingly disproved the theory that dolphins have poor eyesight. Putting a cigarette in his mouth he leant forward, hands behind his back, and let the dolphin leap up and take it from his lips. The applause was tumultuous – but the dolphin wasn't satisfied. If further proof of cetacean intelligence was needed, then it was demonstrated by the animal's follow-up leap, to claim its proper reward.

Bottlenose dolphins, I was aware, had a brain-size greater than that of humans. If the behaviour I was witnessing was not evidence enough, then their broad smiles would have said it all.

From the slapstick world of the dolphins I retired to the more tranquil environment of the Tropical Reef Tank. This was smaller than the main tank, and contained a striking conglomeration of rock and coral, transplanted from the sea floor off the Florida coast. Around it, in their rainbow-hued multitudes, flitted the fish of the reefs, their feathery bodies briefly translucent as they caught the shafts of sunlight lancing the water. Their variety was so bewildering and their movements so quick that I gave up any attempt to pick out individual species and just gorged on the whole effect, marvelling at the interplay of their delicate colours. In anticipation of my visit to the Keys, however, I had to work on the taxonomy, and to this end made a tour of a series of separate small tanks containing species located by habitat and concisely labelled.

Their names, inspired by their colour, appearance or behavioural characteristics, gave an indication of their variety. Also, given these characteristics, their doubtful compatibility.

Assuming that most of these fish were found in the same region – from the Florida coast to the West Indies – there had to be some social problems. How, for example, was it possible for an Ocellated Frogfish to live in any kind of harmony with a Spotted Scorpionfish? Or a Mutton Snapper with a Porkfish Grunt? How did you integrate a Puddingwife and a Ladyfish, a Bigeye Scad and a Damselfish, or a Hogchoker and a Hogfish? Or, come to think of it, a Soapfish and a Black Angel? Perhaps the Tobaccofish and the Southern Puffer had found the answer, but I couldn't be sure, as they were in separate tanks.

Demonstrated in one of the tanks was an example of symbiosis that I found sadly unconvincing. The occupants were a clownfish and a type of sea anemone, which according to the label were supposed to work together in a kind of feeding partnership. The role of the brightly coloured clownfish was, apparently, to attract other fish to within range of the anemone's tentacles, where they would be rapidly paralysed by the anemone's stinging cells. Its own protection being assured by a mucus that effectively disarmed the anemone, the clownfish was offered in return for its services a peaceful life beyond the reach of all predators. Unfortunately, in this demonstration, the partnership was not working out too well. The clownfish, caught in the anemone's tentacles, was slowly being engorged.

I had yet to see the Seaquarium's most startling exhibit, 'the only one of its kind anywhere in the world'. This was the Shark Channel, home of a score or more of these creatures whose notoriety had generated an expectant gathering. The channel took the form of a moat, 750 feet long, through which a million gallons of salt water was kept constantly flowing as a vehicle for the sharks. Positioning myself on a bridge spanning the channel I looked down at its swirling currents, but could see nothing of the inhabitants. The water was muddily opaque, and the sharks might well have passed beneath me, in search of – what? If they were hungry, then anything, I felt sure, would have been acceptable, from a bag of popcorn to a vertiginous tourist. I gripped the rail of the bridge a little tighter and waited for something to happen.

To give the audience some relief – and value for money – I guessed that the suspense could not be maintained forever. A dramatic climax had to be provided, which while not necessarily involving the sacrifice of a human being had at least to contain some element of the gruesome and spectacular. The Seaquarium's answer was Feeding Time.

On one of the plankwalks bridging the channel a member of the staff appeared, dangling the carcass of a large fish on the end of a rope. After briefly trailing it in the water he tied it to the rail of the plankwalk so that it hung, half-submerged, in the channel.

After a nerve-wracking pause the black triangular fins broke the surface of the water and sliced towards the target. Within seconds the water round the carcass was turned into a boiling, bloody froth which contained, at the roughest estimate, half-a-dozen sharks. In the midst of this maelstrom I tried to decipher their shapes, but all I got was the fleeting glimpse of a fin, tail, snout or jaw. Before I could get my camera focused on the spot their slashing teeth had ripped away the fish and they were gone, leaving only the frayed piece of rope hanging from the rail. For a moment I stared numbly at it, thinking about paper plates and foil dispensers and how such things were really quite civilised.

Next morning I took the Greyhound out of Miami on the unfailing US1, the highway that I had followed for most of the journey south and which, from the state of Maine in New England, ran all the way to Key West. Across the hundred-mile chain of the Keys it was more of a causeway than a road, running between the islands on huge bridges that reached up to seven miles long on some stretches. My own destination was about a third of the way along the chain at Islamorada, on Upper Matecumbe Key, where I was due at noon to meet the Schroeders.

Leaving the World's Playground behind us the bus passed through the quieter reaches of Coral Gables. Unlike Miami, with its large tourist population, Coral Gables was an exclusively residential area. Or more accurately a residentially exclusive area. Although it lay on the outskirts of a city, Coral Gables would never answer to the name of suburb. With its luxurious, sun-orientated houses and carefully nurtured gardens it had its own distinct personality, rather like Hollywood's Beverly Hills. But the history of the Gables was very much the history of Miami. Both were born of the same boom period of the 1920s when the sun-seekers, duped by the ballyhoo of the planners and real estate people, had barrelled down from the north to invest in the area. The biggest prize had been a piece, however small, of Coral Gables – the nearest thing to Paradise for every chilled Chicagoan or necrotic New Yorker.

From Coral Gables and the equally exclusive Coconut Grove the road sped on through more estates, some – as the signboards proclaimed – currently in development. Further on, however, the natural scenery reasserted itself. This was the tropical vegetation, much of it West Indian in origin, that was typical of the tip of the peninsula. Even in this natural environment, however, no opportunities were missed. Outside a town called Goulds I saw a sign that read 'Monkey Jungle – Where Humans are Caged and Monkeys Run Wild'.

Further south lay Homestead, a market town in the centre of an area, once waterlogged and infertile, which by a tenacious campaign of land improvement had been turned into productive farmland. But even with all the devices of man – drainage, fertilization, artificial soil production – such a transformation would have been impossible without the immeasurable bonus of Florida's climate. Year-round sunshine which, coupled with the natural humidity of the terrain, ensured a high crop yield for the winter vegetables that supplied much of America.

Without denying this the label of progress it was fortunate that not all the southern part of Florida had been reclaimed. Thanks to the efforts of the conservationists, who had witnessed the inroads being made by such development into rare communities of plant and animal life, an area of two and a half million acres of natural wilderness was designated in 1947 as a National Park, to save it from eventual disappearance. By this act a unique habitat – the Everglades – was preserved.

Even in a land as diverse as the US, the flora and fauna of the Everglades was exceptional. Among the birds, the waders were probably the most spectacular: heron, spoonbill, ibis, flamingo and pelican. The mammals, though less seen, were hiding out in limited numbers: cougar, bobcat, raccoon, muskrat, opossum. Other more prolific denizens of the sloughs and marshes were the reptiles: crocodile, alligator, snake and lizard. Of these, the American Crocodile, found exclusively in Florida, was perhaps the most successful, with an increasing population threatened only by road traffic accidents.

Although the road did not enter the park it skirted the mangroves that lay on its fringe: dense, fleshy-leaved plants with high aerial roots like spiders' legs. Salt-resistant, they grew close to the shore, and I guessed that we would soon be in sight of the ocean. Their thickets were so dense that I could see little of the landscape of the park, the 'river of grass' with its freshwater sloughs and sawgrass extending mile after mile across the foot of the peninsula. Switching on the PA system, the driver had something to say about the current state of the park, which was suffering from Florida's worst drought for years. 'Sloughs all dried up, this year. Ain't no fish in 'em, ain't no birds. Bad time for seein' the Glades, right now.'

After all I'd read about the beauty of the Everglades it was dismal news. I could see that the absence of fish would deter the waders, and make life very hard for the other water creatures that depended on them for food. On the stretch of road that ran along the park boundary to the Keys the only visible wildlife was a cormorant and two or three egrets, sheltering in the mangroves.

The road swung east and the sea lay before us, a dazzling arc of blue contained by a long, bow-shaped island that I realised with a hop and a skip of my heart was Key Largo, the first of the long thin archipelago known as the Florida Keys. Crossing a mile-long bridge we drove into Largo and then turned south again, to commence US1's last fling before it reached its final destination at Key West.

There can be few road trips to match the run down the Keys on a summer's day. The world's longest over-water highway, the road itself was an experience, straight and white with the gleaming line of the water pipe snaking beside it. The sky almost overpowering, its blueness exalted to a rare intensity by the sun. The sea, glimpsed in varying expanses on either side of the road and then full vision in the breath-taking plunge from island to island. I could only

wish, in the air-conditioned interior of the bus, that I was sitting at
the wheel of the Buick convertible that had just overtaken us. Or at
the side of the sun-tanned blonde driving it.

In no time at all we had reached Islamorada, the small
settlement north of Lower Matecumbe Key. As I stepped out of the
bus a broad figure strode forward to greet me.

'Hi Paul, welcome to the Keys! I'm Bob Schroeder and this is
Jean.'

From the beefy, sweat-shirted Schroeder my gaze switched to
his wife, a lively, corn-haired woman in Bermudas. As we shook
hands she gave a relieved laugh. 'Well, you're OK. We were
expecting a bowler hat and pin-stripes!'

Taking my rucksack Bob dropped it in the back of his car. As
we climbed in he said, 'Glad you could make it, Paul. I was getting
to wonder who to take out in the boat this afternoon.'

In a few minutes we were on Lower Matecumbe Key and
pulling in at the Schroeders' bungalow. I immediately savoured
the scene. Palm trees in the garden, an upturned dinghy in the
drive. A creek at the back, another boat or two, a whiff of the Gulf
Stream waters. Diving gear stacked against a wall, swim-suits
hanging up to dry, a pair of discarded flippers on the lawn. As
natural a setting for a marine biologist as one could imagine. With
the white warmth of the sun on my arms and face I wondered how
it was possible for anyone to have any other kind of occupation.

The bungalow was sun-proofed and very cool inside and we
had lunch from the ice-box, the Schroeders talking all the while
with great animation about their life on the Keys. The fish-out-of-
water feeling that had engulfed me on arrival rapidly diminished
as I listened to them; two people absorbed in an exciting field of
activity that offered endless challenges and no declared frontier.
Schroeder was a post-graduate student of Miami University
working at the university's Institute of Marine Science on various
projects involving the study of marine life off the coast of Florida.
His current research, on which he'd been engaged for the past three
years, was into a virtually unexplored and little considered aspect
of the underwater world, the pursuit of which – in my opinion at
least – required more than average courage. Robert Schroeder's
speciality was the study of the life of the coral reef – *at night*.

His purpose was to record by observation and, where possible, by photography, the varied phenomena that darkness brought to the reef. The activity of the coral itself, which fed only at night, was an obvious subject for study. Then there were the peculiar colour adaptations of the fish and the striking differences between their daytime and nocturnal activities. To record all this, Schroeder and two colleagues made regular night dives from a boat anchored five miles to the west of the Keys, over a part of the great reef extending from Key Largo in the north into the Gulf of Mexico 200 miles to the south-west. With their Aqua-Lung diving gear they were able to descend to a depth of five fathoms and with their special under-water cameras, equipped with electronic flash, to photograph the denizens of the deep. Having seen some of Schroeder's photographs in a *National Geographic* article I could testify to their brilliance.

Up to the point of joining him in his nocturnal dives, Jean Schroeder shared enthusiastically in her husband's activities. A valuable extension of his researches lay in her own studies of marine parasites – an unusual interest which involved, among other things, the close examination of the sponges that Bob brought home in his bucket.

They were both keen to have me stay, for as long as I liked, on Lower Matecumbe. In the process of politely saying how much I would love to, but couldn't, I was secretly questioning whether my schedule couldn't be stretched a little. And that was before I went out on the reef.

As soon as lunch was done Bob was on his feet and presenting the challenge. 'What do you say we go look at some fish?'

Seeing that he already had his face-mask, snorkel and flippers tucked under his arm I could hardly demur. Only Jean held back for a moment, giving me a quick uneasy glance. 'You're not taking him out to – ?'

'India Reef,' said Bob. 'We'll just poke around for a bit.'

Jean seemed happy with that and within a few minutes we were in Bob's outboard and heading into Florida Bay. The way lay through a series of narrow inlets, deeply banked with marsh grasses, which made for some exciting manoeuvring, the boat sweeping round the tight corners with some finely controlled steering by Bob. In the bay itself – the area between the Keys and the foot of the peninsula – there lay a number of coral islands, rising from a seabed that in reality was a tract of submerged plateau, covered by only a few feet of water that marked the increase in the sea level over a period of many thousand years.

Anchoring off one of the islands Bob and I donned skin-diving gear and slipped over the side, leaving Jean to watch our efforts from the boat. This was my first attempt at skin-diving, but once I had adjusted myself to breathing through the snorkel I discovered all the rare pleasures that it had to offer. Effortlessly floating in the warm, buoyant water I used my flippers to propel me through the shallows, inspecting with the aid of my perspex mask the glorious underwater world of the coral reef. Although the water was only three or four feet deep it was filled with a breathtaking throng of creatures that I had never imagined seeing outside the tropical tank of the Seaquarium. Flitting around in the coral panorama were fish of every shape, size and colour, from the large multi-hued angel fish to the tiny blue-striped neon gobies. Surgeon fishes, trailed by their attendant wrasses, were much in evidence, as were the comical parrot fishes with their iridescent bodies and beaks, which they used for scraping food from the coral. Some fish, I noticed, were less active than others. The striped grunts, for example, hovered in lazy indifference to the frenetic movements of the neon gobies, darting in and out of the coral like tiny slivers of light. Swimming alongside me, Bob offered the explanation.

'The grunts and snappers are night foragers, but the gobies earn their living by day, picking parasites off the larger fish. Look at the way they flick around the coral, looking for customers. Come night, though, they'll be nestling down into the coral, and it'll be the turn of the grunts to take off and get supplies. As with mammals, you get your day hunters and your night hunters, and half the fun of this game is working out the difference. There's a lot of fish for instance, that you practically never see in the daytime. Like the cardinals. They spend the day tucked away in the coral and only come out to feed at night. Even then they're not easy to spot. They change their colour, from red to white.'

From this I could begin to appreciate the real significance of the reef. Not just as a structure, built up over millions of years from the deposits of tiny animals, but as an environment on which countless marine species depended for their existence. Swimming through the scenery of the reef I could liken it to a tropical landscape, the waving sea fans its trees and the coral its mountains, covered with a brilliant vegetation of sponges and algae. Within these mountains lay a complex of caves, crevices and indentations in which myriad creatures could shelter from the vigorous currents and tides and the pursuit of predators. Plant and animal substances adhering to the reef were the staple diet of many of its inhabitants, and those that were carnivorous and foraged beyond the reef could always return to its shelter for rest after their forays. Between the many organisms that shared the reef there was a remarkable community relationship that demonstrated their interdependence: 'You pick my teeth, and I'll save you from your enemy's.'

Looking down at the sandy bottom I was baffled to see a pair of eyes staring up at me. Nothing else until an agitated movement revealed the shape of a stingray settling into its camouflage of sand. A glimpse of its whip-like, poison-secreting tail was enough to galvanise my flippers into action and to put a respectable distance between us. But in avoiding one peril, I swam straight into another. Coming up against a ledge of coral I put out a fending hand, only to withdraw it again with a gasp of pain. Looking at my hand I saw three sharp spines, sticking from my forefinger. Hastily I brushed them off, which was about the worst thing I could do. The spines broke, leaving their tips embedded in my skin.

Seeing my difficulties, Bob swam over to inspect the wound. '*Trichometra*,' he observed, as though the name alone were enough to reassure me. 'Nobody's a skin diver 'til they've been christened by that darn thing.'

He was talking about the sea urchin, a tiny spined creature found everywhere on the coral. Glad that I had made the grade I sucked my finger. 'What do I have to do to become a Scuba diver?'

For a couple of hours we continued our exploration of the reef shallows, Bob working alongside me with a specimen jar into which he scooped things from the reef and the coral rubble. Although he had probably been to the same spot a dozen times he went about his task with complete absorption, sifting and examining the material like a prospector. His enthusiasm, I guessed, was based on the simple theory that you could never stop learning about the reef.

Eventually though we did stop, when Jean remembered with a yell of distress a cocktail party that we'd been invited to. The party was being given by a neighbour of the Schroeders who had organised a get-together of the naturalist fraternity. As we motored back to the bungalow it occurred to me that this was my chance to try on the formal attire that I'd brought with me to America for just such an occasion.

The items in the ensemble had been specially chosen to withstand the rigours of rucksack travel: a white nylon drip-dry shirt, a folded lightweight jacket and a pair of slim-fitting terylene trousers. The only snag was that my idea of cocktail attire did not accord with the Schroeders'. When I joined them Bob was wearing Bermudas and a short-sleeved tropical shirt and Jean a sun-top frock. Apparently a cocktail convention of the Keys.

Their neighbour's house, a little way along the Key, provided an ideal setting for an outdoor gathering. For sheer poetry it would have been difficult to beat the view from the back lawn, which sloped gently to the sun-glazed water of the Florida Bay. Straining my eyes I could see islands, as far as the horizon. The sunset was only half-an-hour away.

In addition to the trays of Daiquiri and ginger the company offered its own special stimulus, including two characters whose names were synonymous with wildlife conservation in America. Alexander Sprunt IV was such a name, and one not easily forgotten. He was Research Director of the National Audubon Society, known throughout the world for its work in bird conservation. The other man was Dr Archie Carr, a professor of zoology at the University of Florida, an expert on sea turtles whose current concern was the conservation of the green turtles nesting at Tortuguero on the coast of Costa Rica.

The survival of these turtles was being endangered by the local egg collectors, who were nowadays waiting on the beach for the turtles to arrive, baskets at the ready. No sooner had the poor creatures made their laborious way up the beach to dig a hole in the sand and deliver their clutch of eggs than the raiders would descend and grab the fruits of their labour – perhaps a hundred eggs in each clutch. Carr's method of protection was to beat the raiders at their own game by retrieving the eggs from the sand before anyone else could get to them and then transferring them to fenced hatcheries, where they could incubate in peace. Then, when the baby turtles had been hatched, they were taken out to sea and released – far enough from the shore to escape the host of predators that normally awaited them. In this way they secured a dual start in life. Unlike their fellows, the majority of whom ended up either as a *specialité de la maison* or a shark's snack, they stood a fair chance of becoming adult turtles.

Bob was very enthusiastic about the venture and it transpired that he and Jean were going to join Carr at Tortuguero in two weeks' time to do an article on the rescue operation for the *National Geographic*. This was roughly the time of the turtles' breeding season, and they hoped to be on the spot when the turtles came ashore, to photograph them burying their eggs. It sounded like an exciting project, in support of a cause that seemed supremely worthwhile. When Jean suggested that I might like to come along I was inclined to take her seriously.

After lobster thermador and iced tea – a gastronomic vagary that seemed to work on this occasion – we gathered our chairs in a semi-circle on the lawn to gaze at the dipping sun and the impasto of scarlet that surrounded it in the darkening sky. Here was the sunset of one's most heady imaginings, complete with palm tree silhouettes and rippled reflections in the darkening sea. The gentle vision of a twilight Florida. The sun had scarcely vanished when Dr Carr, in a supremely matter-of-fact way, suggested that we might like to see a film he had brought with him of some Ridley turtles, going up on a beach in East Mexico.

From the murmurs of astonishment and acclaim that greeted the suggestion it appeared that this film was unique, the sort that nature photographers and turtle enthusiasts would crawl on hands and knees halfway round the world to catch on their cameras. It had, in fact, been taken purely by chance, in 1947, by a Mexican amateur who had happened to be in the right place at the right time with a movie camera. The uniqueness of the film lay in its record of an event rarely seen by man: the breeding operations of the Ridley turtle on the Atlantic shore of Mexico. To reduce the chances of this event being observed by human beings it was known to occur on but a single day in a two-month period once a year, at any point along a ninety-mile stretch of isolated coastline.

A cine-projector and screen were rapidly assembled and for ten minutes or so we were treated to the spectacle of a colony of these turtles – at least a hundred strong – making their way up the beach to lay their eggs. The film was very pink and jerky and could not claim any quality outside its uniqueness. For its audience, however, it was the work of an Eisenstein.

Did you know that Flipper was more than one dolphin? I only learnt this the following day, when Bob and Jean took me down to Grassy Key. This was the home of Santini's Porpoise Training School, the ultimate academy for all dolphins with aspirations to celluloid stardom. Here they were put through their paces by a team of highly qualified trainers, whose job was to coach them to a standard of proficiency in a variety of manoeuvres.

Following the route around the training lagoon we saw dolphins playing basketball, jumping through hoops, towing boatloads of children and leaping for fish. Each dolphin appeared to have one trick as its speciality, repeating it untiringly until the trainer moved on to the next performer. Between them they mounted an impressive repertoire, and when I learned that some of them were understudies to Flipper I could only ask, with all the wholesome innocence of a twenty-seven-year-old, if there was any chance of seeing that world-famous cetacean, star of the eponymous film and TV series. To my dismay I learned that Flipper – the original – was not on public display but resting in a private lake in the Seaquarium.

Apart from dolphins and fish I should mention, however briefly, the other preoccupations of the Keys. Sunken treasure and hurricanes.

Sunken treasure, spoken of elsewhere in the language of make-believe, was here a reality. For the tourist it provided an endless source of speculation; to the boatman an enduring source of profit. The latter, while conducting the former to a likely spot a few miles offshore, must have constantly blessed the ill winds that centuries ago had blown the great Spanish cargo vessels onto the shoals and reefs of the Keys, depositing thereon the riches from their holds. And watching their Scuba-clad charges slip over the side in search of mythical doubloons, the same twentieth-century treasure hunt tour operators must have congratulated themselves on continuing so profitably in the tradition of the war-like Calusa Indians, an indigenous Floridian tribe who way back in colonial times had done the original treasure hunting.

Less in the realm of make-believe was the hurricane. Scourge of the gulf and peninsula regions, and a continuing cause of speculation and despair for their inhabitants. The question was either about the effect of last year's hurricane, the effect of the current one, or the possible effect of the next one. From this I assumed that hurricanes were annual visitations, as predictable as tourists. Some expectation of their arrival would certainly reduce their impact, but like most freaks of nature they worked by stealth. They were most likely to strike during the warm, wet season, which meant any time in the summer and autumn. Sweeping up from the tropics they gathered energy from the moist, oceanic air, and by the time they reached the coastline had customarily built up a speed of over 150mph. The havoc created, however, was not only from the force of the wind but from the waves piled up by the storm. These could raise the ocean level six feet or more, swamping low-lying beaches and islands and anything standing on them. The Keys – which as a former coral reef were barely above sea level – were particularly vulnerable.

On the way back to Lower Matecumbe, Bob made his own evaluation, both of hurricanes and sunken treasure. Passing a succession of colossal signs promoting 'Boat Trips to Treasure Ship Reefs' and 'Exhibitions of Sunken Treasure' he said laconically, 'They reckon sunken treasure's the only good thing to come out of a hurricane. I say, the only good ever comes out of a hurricane is when it blows down those damn billboards.'

That afternoon we went out in the boat again, this time without Jean. When Bob told her that he was taking me to Alligator Reef I got the impression that this was the idea that had made her nervous earlier. In the boat, heading out to the open sea, Bob put me in the picture.

'Jean gets kind of anxious about me taking people to the reef.

It gets a bit rough at times, but there'd be no point taking anyone in those conditions.'

He turned the boat into the waves, and I grabbed at the rail as we chopped with a great *thwack* through a breaker and plunged heavily into the trough behind it. The wind was up, corrugating the sea, and I could feel the spray prickling through my T-shirt. With the next wave my grip tightened as the outboard lifted clear out of the water before it flopped down again. I glanced at Bob with his wind-in-the-teeth grin, and wondered what it was like when it was 'rough'.

A second later he answered my unvoiced question by pointing to a distant lighthouse, about five miles from the shore. 'See that? Alligator Reef Lighthouse. One time, during a hurricane, I've seen waves break over the top of it.'

He steered an unswerving course for the light.

'There's a big reef out there, thirty feet down. Big ship went down on that reef, the *Alligator*. That's how it got the name. We do our night dives over there.'

My heart gave a bound, in no way related to the switchback frenzies of the outboard. Alligator Reef was the last resting place of the USS *Alligator*, a merchantman which ran aground here in 1822, while tracking slave ships sent out from the African coast. Reaching the lighthouse we circled round it, looking for a spot to anchor.

Gazing down into the water I could see the bottom quite clearly, at a depth of five fathoms. At one point Bob leant over the side, showing me an outline on the sandy floor that marked out the shape of a ship's hull. 'The *Alligator*'s ballast,' he said. 'All that's left of her.'

Our first glimpse of coral reef fish was a school of grunts, passing sedately beneath the boat. Bob dropped anchor and I saw the edge of the reef, palely illuminated by the deeply-reaching sunlight. A succession of shapes flittered through the shadow of the coral, too vague to identify. As I stripped down to my trunks an unpleasant thought occurred to me, which I felt obliged to mention. 'Do you get any – *sharks* in this area?'

With one leg over the side of the boat, Bob paused, looking as though he'd never seriously considered the question. 'Not really. You get the odd hammerhead.'

'H-hammer-h-head?'

With a splash Bob had disappeared and I saw him striking down through the water towards the reef, his flippered feet working like pistons. With only a snorkel he needed all the time he could get, and I wondered why he had encumbered himself with the long aluminium pole that he bore, lance-like, in his right hand. In a couple of minutes he came up for breath and waved the thing vigorously at me before ducking back into the water. Realising that he wanted me to join him I gripped the mouthpiece of my snorkel between my teeth, tightened my face mask and plunged rather inexpertly into the sea. I must have gone down about three feet when both my mask and mouth filled with water and I was forced to grope my way blindly to the surface again. Recovering my breath, I voted against further experiment and remained flotsam-like on the surface, contenting myself with an aerial view of Bob's tutorial. The word 'hammerhead' was still stinging my ears and I stayed close to the boat, gyrating rhythmically in the water to maintain a 360° surveillance.

After ten minutes Bob swam up behind me, looking a bit disgruntled. 'Fish must've gone into hiding. Nothing down there, 'cept a few gobies.' Grabbing the side of the boat he hauled himself out of the water, and with unheroic speed I clambered up after him. When we were dry and Bob had hauled in the anchor for the return trip I pointed, almost as an afterthought, at the mysterious aluminium pole. 'What's that for?'

He picked it up, weighing it gently in his hand. 'A bangstick.'

In response to my baffled gaze he added, 'Contains a Magnum .357 cartridge, fired by jamming the end against the target. Kills by concussion as well as bullet. Haven't had to use it so far.'

I nodded, while noting that he hadn't given me one.

Schedules were made to be broken and I stretched mine to spend another day with the Schroeders. A blissful day of poking around in the shallows, eating crayfish and basking in the sun. At the end of it I met Bob's night-diving companion, Walter Starck II, who also lived in the Keys. The talk was mainly about the trip to Costa Rica and I knew I would have to tear myself away pretty soon before I volunteered my services as a turtle-egg conservator.

The Schroeders, who had their flight and injections to fix, offered to drive me into Miami that evening. Before we left Bob led me to the creek, saying he had something to show me.

Bending over the edge of the jetty he lifted a large water-logged box from the creek that contained, amid a quantity of seaweed, three young turtles.

'My contribution to the conservation programme,' he said. 'When they're fully grown I'll let them go.'

It was a nice thought, to end three perfect days.

New Orleans

Slow Drags, Fast Tunes

On the bus the next day I felt like an overdone steak. Stuck to the griddle of my seat through moist layers of clothing. And my skin burning as three days' exposure to the Florida sun took its toll.

The New Orleans Express was not routed, as I had hoped, along the west coast of Florida but north again to Jacksonville on the same interminable stretch of US1 that had brought me into Miami. Not until Jacksonville would we join US90, the route to the west.

Sad to say that in the first half-hour of the journey, to add to my physical discomfort, the Greyhound's air-conditioning system broke down. Everyone had to open their window, to allow some circulation of air. Winding mine down about an inch, to admit a minimum of dust and petrol fumes, I settled down to an uncomfortable journey, erasing from my mind the knowledge that it would take a good twenty-four hours to get to New Orleans.

At Jacksonville, after only a third of the journey, I was ready to turn in my ticket. Nobody had told me that the ninety-nine dollars included sauna.

In the few minutes allocated to the rest stop a shower was

impossible and I had to content myself with the cooling effect of three fruit juices. In the soft drinks department, these juices were the nearest thing to value in the States, coming at ten cents a glass and with a choice of flavours including pineapple, prune, tomato and orange. Along with Scotch, root-beer, coffee and Coke, they were America's national beverage, consumed at any hour of the day. Their popularity, strangely, was explained more by the nation's eating than drinking habits. What sensitive American could face their blueberry pancakes, grilled ham, waffles and jelly in the morning without first imbibing that sweet, purgatory mouthwash?

Nothing was done about the air conditioner at Jacksonville and for the next twelve hours I remained in a semi-liquid state, my body immersed in sweat and my mind in visions of the next cooling drink. Unhappily there were only two rest stops in this period and nothing to fill the gaps but fitful sleep and dreams of relief. At Tallahassee it was crushed ice and at Pensacola a can of orange juice, my farewell toast to Florida.

Sometime in the early hours of the following morning we crossed the state line into 'Historic Alabama, Heart of Dixie'. Despite the Confederate flag emblazoned on the sign I felt that I had turned the corner of my journey and was heading west, away from the settlers' land towards the explorers'. For a while the road ran through plantations of young pine, tinged pink with a rising sun that offered the quiet hint of another sweltering day. Then, dramatically, it sprang out on to the causeway spanning Mobile Bay, the spearhead of sea that cut deep into the Gulf coastline, forming a natural harbour for the seaport of Mobile, Alabama.

At Mobile our transfer to another bus – with air conditioning – was like a reprieve from a life sentence. It offered us a chance to cool down for the run into New Orleans.

In the final four hours of the journey we passed from Alabama into Mississippi, and by a coastal route into the state of Louisiana. This, as my 'Early America' map told me, was the tail-end of the great territory of French Louisiana ('La Louisiane') forged by the explorer de la Salle and named in honour of King Louis XIV in 1682. In its entirety, the original territory had extended from the

Gulf of Mexico to the Canadian border and from the Mississippi to the Rockies, an area of over 800,000 square miles.

The acquisition of that piece of land in 1803 by the United States – which at a price tag of 15 million dollars (eighteen dollars per square mile) would surely be acknowledged by Madison Avenue as America's Best Buy – had achieved two great things for the country.

First it had doubled its size, and second it had removed a dangerous neighbour and the continuing prospect of foreign control of the Mississippi River and the port of New Orleans, so vital to the development of the new territories. Today New Orleans occupied much the same position, as the principal outlet for the wealth of the Mississippi basin. Added to that, retaining the flavour of its 250-year history.

With the explorations of La Salle in the seventeenth century the French had staked their claim to the territory, to be followed in 1763 by the Spanish, taking advantage of France's defeat in the Seven Years' War. In 1800, with Napoleon at the helm and dreaming of a New World Empire, France had returned to the scene, prising her old territory from the weakened grip of the Spanish and reoccupying 'La Nouvelle Orleans'. Three years later, however, after her military debacle in the West Indies, France was ready to talk business with the US, in more than generous terms.

The city of New Orleans had been the best part of the investment. The growth of the cotton industry, the arrival of the Mississippi steamboats and the influx of migrants from the east had generated a new dynamic for the city, replacing the old Bourbon gentility with the vitality of an independent country. But I knew that one quarter of the old city had survived – too celebrated to suffer the architectural dereliction that had occurred elsewhere. This was the 'Vieux Carré', an area of graceful eighteenth and nineteenth-century buildings abutting the Mississippi waterfront.

It would be wrong, however, to suggest that the quarter owed its fame solely to its exquisite ironwork balconies. The French and Spanish had left another legacy, their cuisine. And if the Cajun/ Creole *jambalaya* and *gumbo* were not enough to satisfy you, there was always the birth of jazz.

Following my arrival in New Orleans I paused only briefly at one of the hotels on Canal Street. Sadly I was unable to deposit my rucksack, which had disappeared somewhere in the Mobile bus depot. This apocalyptic event had occurred because of the change of buses, when the rucksack, instead of being transferred with me to the new bus, remained in the hold of the old one, which had been withdrawn from service to fix the air-conditioning. The rucksack, I was reassured, would eventually catch up with me in the New Orleans depot.

In the meantime, before recovering my worldly goods, I had a few hours to kill in New Orleans. Unfortunately it was the middle of the afternoon, which was not a good time to visit the Vieux Carré: a bit like touring Soho, Montmartre or Greenwich Village in daylight. I found myself standing instead on a kerbside in Canal Street, the central spoke of downtown New Orleans, which ran down to the Mississippi River. The broad busy thoroughfare did not make an easy walk and I soon turned eastwards.

In a short while I was following a sidewalk of lacework shadows. Looking up, I saw the finely-wrought balconies, intertwined with flowers, and realised that I had unwittingly made my way into a corner of the old quarter. I paused, gazing down a street of three-storied, gabled buildings that belonged in another time, another place. Balconies and arcades that shielded them with intricate filigree. Potted palms that decayed in their forgotten corners, basket plants that draped their façades with random tendrils. Shuttered, shaded windows. Street lamps that spoke of Nineties' night-times, kerbside carriage posts ornamented with horses' heads, grilled doorways that masked their invitations.

Only the parked cars and neon signs impaired the illusion of a graceful past, in which one could recreate the images of frock coats and finery, flowers tossed from balconies, suggestive glances from the shade of a parasol. The sound of horse's hooves just then could not have been more appropriate and with a thrill of curiosity I turned to see a carriage with a fringed canopy coming up the street, pulled by a horse in a frayed sun hat and driven by a man in a topper. Instead of the crinolined Southern belle, however, it bore a T-shirted tourist.

My wanderings brought me to Jackson Square, a short step from the riverside. From here I caught a glimpse of a muddy barge-laden stretch of water that left my vision of America's greatest waterway sadly unfulfilled. Returning to the square I browsed around its most interesting features, mainly of the Spanish period. On the east and west sides of the square were the magnificent porticoed Pontalba apartment houses, held to be the oldest buildings of their kind in America. On the north side, facing the river, stood the Gabildo, the meeting-place of the Spanish colonial government, and the triple-spired Roman Catholic church of St Louis. The latter, dedicated in 1794, was referred to in my guide as America's oldest cathedral.

Rearing up in the centre of the square was the equestrian statue of General – later President – Andrew Jackson, a soldier-politician whose reputation as a warmonger, despite his democratic cred-entials, was unexcelled in American history. 'The Union Must and Will be Preserved' were his most famous words, engraved on the base of the statue. One could hardly think of a better epitaph for the man who had effectively annihilated the Creek nation, wiped the floor with the British at the Battle of New Orleans (1815) and chased the Spanish and the Seminole Indians out of Florida.

Submitting to the spell of the Vieux Carré I ventured north to Bourbon Street. From what I knew of this street, its daytime character carried little hint of its night. The one or two bars that were open offered little temptation, nor did the extinct neon of its strip and jazz clubs. I felt like standing there for a few hours, just to watch it all come to life.

Wandering through the heat-stifled streets of the Quarter, I had a sense of their decadence that emanated not only from the peeling stucco and rusted ironwork of the buildings but from the context of their setting: a modern nation that for all its colonial roots was gradually consigning the relics of its European past to oblivion. Like the palazzi of Venice the old houses gave the impression of sinking slowly into the substance that had borne them up. They too were built on mud, the vast swamp of the Mississippi estuary.

North of the Quarter I was reminded of this fact by an encounter inside the walls of the St Louis Cemetery. The cemetery, located in Basin Street, was not an obvious tourist attraction, but the story goes beyond that.

In 1928 this somewhat hangdog street, the main street of Storyville, the old red-light district of New Orleans, had been the inspiration for a famous Dixieland song, *The Basin Street Blues*, which – once Louis Armstrong had played it on his trumpet – gave the place a whole new character.

Inside the cemetery I was enthralled by the metropolis of stone and marble vaults and sarcophagi. In one of the narrow alleyways between the tombs I asked an elderly black gentleman who looked well integrated with his surroundings if this was the method by which all New Orleans' citizens were laid to rest. Scratching his chin for a moment he said he didn't know about any modern ideas, but in the old days it was a straight choice between above and below ground, which meant either a stone coffin or a wooden one with holes in it.

Returning to the bus depot I had an almost tearful reunion with my rucksack. A quick check revealed that none of my precious film – or anything else – was missing, and I should acknowledge that this was the only occasion – in 12,000 miles of Greyhound travel – that my four-legged friend had lost his footing.

Back in the hotel I made ready for my night in the Quarter. A good work-out with my battery razor and the application of a sponge to my jacket and trousers brought me back to a state of decency. To get the full effect I searched around the room for a mirror. After discovering that there were none in the usual places (walls, back of door, washstand, inside of cupboard) I realised with dismay that this refinement had been overlooked. Checking the tariff on the back of the door I reassured myself that I was paying only $2.50 for the room. At a dollar a night less than the 'Y', the omission didn't loom so large.

It was very hot in the room and I went over to open the window. To my astonishment, when I pulled the curtains, I discovered a mirror. Combing my hair in the reflection I concluded that the missing refinement in the room was, in fact, a window. Looking up at the naked light bulb above the washstand I recalled that it had been shining when I had first entered the room at midday. Shifting my gaze to the fan that whirred like an aircraft propeller on the ceiling I wondered how in heaven's name I was going to get through the night.

In the corridor outside it was very dark and I made for a sliver of light that turned out to be an exit. My room being on the first floor there was a flight of steps outside with a handrail. Gripping the rail and treading on the first step I was terrified to find myself suddenly dropping downwards. I couldn't see what was happening and it seemed as if the steps had disconnected with the building and were falling away under my weight. Clinging like a petrified bat to the rail I tensed myself for the impact, which came with a bone-shaking *clang* as the steps hit the pavement. Gingerly I descended, realising that I must have climbed out on a type of burglar-proof fire escape. When I reached the bottom I made sure to jump clear as the steps, relieved of my weight, swung up again.

Although this was hardly the most shattering experience of my trip, I had to mark it down as Lesson Number One on the facilities available in American hotels. For $2.50 a night, not only windows but stairs could be a luxury.

The Quarter at night was everything I'd anticipated. Full of noise and light, the essence of a past that it could neither live up to nor live down. Strip shows and jazz clubs, pizza bars and art galleries, restaurants and dives. Gaiety and blues, haute cuisine and bar-top, culture and corn. The native soil of the night people, whose chosen hours were given to its pleasures.

On either side of Bourbon Street I was flashed by the neon snares, whose invitations resided more in the comic strip than the striptease. 'TNT Red, the Atomic Kitten' sounded more as if she should be coming out once a week rather than nightly, along with 'Sextana, the Devil's Dancer', 'Jade the Jewel of the Orient' and 'The Fabulous Tempeste Storm'.

Every second or third door that I passed swung open at a well-timed moment, allowing me a fleeting glimpse of temptation. The doorman who controlled the glimpse added his own verbal inducement, a parrot phrase that came out something like: 'hottest show in town', 'biggest – in town' or 'watch the little lady take her wrappers off'. A further catch for the unwary were the signs that announced 'No Cover Charge or Minimum', with no mention of the price of the drinks. Having heard somewhere that the cost of a small beer in one of these places was around two dollars I decided to stay on the outside. In no sense, however, was I frustrated. The thrust of successive doormen's feet against the swing doors was enough for me to build up a satisfying composite picture as I walked past. A raucous soundtrack, a spot-lit stage behind a bar. An arched back, a sequinned bosom, a bare convulsive thigh. I got quite tired, walking up and down.

A hot buttered corn on the cob with French fries put me back on my feet and I headed for Dixieland Hall, where the old-time New Orleans jazz bands could be heard for a small donation. Although I could never claim to be a follower of jazz, the chance to hear it played in its birthplace – by bands that included a few of its original exponents – was one that I'd have been dumb to miss.

The invitation to join Blanche Thomas, 'Queen of the Blues', was all I needed to make my 'donation' and follow the seductive rhythm into Dixieland Hall. Through a crowded bar I elbowed my way into a smoke-filled room and took a seat at the back. The New Orleans Jazz Band was tuning up and I could sense the readiness of the audience. The performers – five black and one Latino – were all in their seventies. In jazz terms, old enough to have been in at the birth.

A sign over the piano gave the rate for Traditional Requests: Slow Drags, One Dollar; Fast Tunes, Two Dollars; 'The Saints', Five Dollars. Without any prompting from the audience the band went into its warmer, *The Bourbon Street Parade*.

Even the fervent atmosphere in the room could not have prepared me for the response. The opening bars, followed by the combined fanfare of trumpet, trombone and clarinet, were almost lost in a frenzy of cheering, clapping and foot-thumping – the applause of the faithful. Led by the clarinettist, a rotund, pouch-cheeked veteran, the band marched Indian file up the aisle, playing as they went. Inevitably the bass-player brought up the rear, negotiating the instrument across the floor in some miraculous feat of strength as he strummed his accompaniment. Turning around at the back of the hall the players marched triumphantly back to their places, finishing the number in a further spontaneous round of applause.

The favourites followed, catching the audience's mood. A boisterous rendering of *Tiger Rag*, a melancholy *Wabash Blues* and a lilting *Georgia Brown*. This was the real thing, performed by the real people.

It had started with the work chants of the cotton fields, the church hymns, the marching bands. And continued in the saloons and dance halls of Storyville, a notorious area of the city which now survived only in name.

The seeds of the new music had dispersed when a bill from Congress condemned it as a threat to the morale of the US Navy. Lumped in with the operators of brothels, drinking dens and gambling parlours, the only sin of the jazz men had been earning a living. Deprived of this legitimacy they had migrated in their hundreds to pastures new, most notably St Louis and Chicago, where the mood was right for a revolutionary kind of music. Thus it was, in the pre-1920s, that jazz had begun its transformation. From a folk music, wrapped in the shrouds of southern tradition, to a national cult that had eventually swept the world.

In that crowded hall the old songs of New Orleans were being revived, not only for the aficionados but for the musicians themselves, old timers who were doing what they knew best and enjoying every moment of it. And that, clearly, was the essence of the audience's response. Not just listening but sharing the rapture of the players, conveyed in every lingering, nostalgic note.

In the confined space there was no escaping the sound, which vibrated through the bare floorboards and the legs of my chair so that my whole body became an integral part of the rhythm. Apart from a tap dance routine and some throaty blues from the star turn, Blanche Thomas, the old-timers held the stage throughout, bringing it all back from 1917. At the end of it all, cheered on by an ecstatic audience, they repeated their procession through the hall, playing themselves out with undiminished gusto. For them, I suppose, it had been an evening of relaxation.

That night I got little sleep on account of the aircraft propeller. This was the contraption fixed to the ceiling over my bed that whirred continuously in the darkness directly above my head. The unhappy truth was that although I had the power to switch it off I did not have the inclination, knowing that within a few minutes of doing so I would be lying in a lake of sweat. An alternative option was to move the bed, but this proved impossible in the narrow space it occupied between the wall and cupboard. I was caught, ultimately, between two conflicting forces. On the one hand my compelling desire for sleep and on the other an irrational fear of the thing that spun around above me.

Lying there in a state of tortured alertness I could imagine all sorts of terrors. The propeller, breaking loose from its fixture, slicing downwards. Or dropping gradually on its flex like that scary device in Edgar Allan Poe's *The Pit and the Pendulum*, getting nearer the bed with each revolution. Or stopping altogether, and leaving me to suffocate in the airless, windowless room...

When I drifted into sleep eventually it was the second speculation that became the nightmare. The bedclothes, it seemed, were knotted around me so that I couldn't move, and the blades of the propeller were descending, in a direct line with my head. Snapping back into consciousness I stared up into the darkness, listening with stretched ears to the humming of the propeller. It was, I imagined, already much closer. Leaping out of bed I fumbled for the cord of the fan and with a sharp tug switched it off.

I woke up, still in darkness, at 11.30am. A frenetic knocking on the door was accompanied by a shrill voice telling me that it was time I vacated my room. Switching on the light I tumbled out of bed, put my head under the tap and searched anxiously for my diary to see what day it was. To my alarm I discovered that I was due in Houston, Texas, the following morning.

Bemusedly I sorted through maps, mileage charts and bus timetables, trying to make sense of distance and time. The Texan border, I discovered, was 300 miles west of New Orleans, and Houston ninety miles further on, which made it a journey of about nine hours.

My date in Houston was with Elizabeth Mendell, the girl I'd met on holiday the previous year in Sicily touring with her fellow students from Stanford University. From the ruins of ancient Syracuse it would be a quantum leap to the twentieth century metropolis of Houston, Texas, where she was currently vacationing with her family. I was keen not only to re-unite with Elizabeth but to meet her father, Wilbert Mendell, who had generously (sight unseen) agreed to bail me out in any emergency and to offer an open-ended invitation to stay at the Mendell home. The prospect of such hospitality was, to a soiled and weary Greyhounder, extremely cheering. Also the notion of making the next stage of my journey with someone I knew at the end of it.

The 8.45pm Greyhound seemed the best choice, particularly as it offered – in place of aircraft propellers and reduced oxygen – the more familiar limitations of its own overnight accommodation. Packing my rucksack I fled the Pit and headed up Canal Street to the bus depot.

Dumping my trappings in a locker I went south again to the Quarter, where I spent the afternoon at the street corners, camera at the ready, waiting for the picturesque carriages with their straw-hatted mules. These were my farewell shots of the Old World, before I plunged into the raw wonders of Texas.

With a 5.40am arrival scheduled for Houston I sought sleep reparations on the Greyhound. The inside seats were all taken, but choosing an outer one next to a man comfortably settled with a copy of *Playboy* I bedded down, zipping myself into my sleeping bag and tipping back the seat. No sooner were we underway, however, than my companion asked me to excuse him as he needed the restroom. Making way for him, I found myself tottering down the aisle like a competitor in a sack-race, my legs trapped in the sleeping bag. Fortunately he got out at the next stop and I was able to grab the sanctuary of the inner seat.

In this refuge I slept, miraculously, for the rest of the journey. So deeply that I only vaguely heard the crack of six-guns and the whoosh of arrows as we crossed the border into Texas.

The fantasy seemed to fit with my first image of Texas, which was significantly larger than life. In the dawning light of day I saw a landscape – man-made and otherwise – that was on a different scale to anything I had seen before, with the road like a runway driving across the limitless flatlands. The Lone Star State, I was aware, was three times the size of Britain, which could fit comfortably inside its northern panhandle. After Alaska – whose admission to the Union six years previously was still disputed down here – Texas was by far the largest state in the US, beating California by a cool 100,000 square miles. In terms of population it had to tilt its Stetson to its west coast rival, but could claim more millionaires to the square mile than any other state.

Where Texas scored, for sure, was in the output of two of

America's most important natural products, cotton and petroleum. Here in South Texas the cotton harvest was in full swing, with the bale-loaded trucks rumbling along the highway, and as far as the eye could see the oil pumps dotting the plain, their beaked heads dipping on their lever arms like praying mantises.

The state's apotheosis came with the establishment of NASA's Manned Spacecraft Centre in Houston, in 1963. This was where the astronauts of the future were trained and the spaceflight programme planned. 'Mission Control Houston' was a by-word for the space age: the Lone Star had acquired a galaxy. The mushrooming city of Houston itself, however, owed less to science and more to its status as oil capital. Wedges of newly-built skyscrapers, squaring off the view as we drove into the city, were the product of an immense natural resource.

Thinking that a dawn call to the Mendells might be a little indiscreet, I waited a few hours after my arrival at the bus depot for what I judged to be the right moment. I was delighted when I caught breakfast time in the Mendell household and Elizabeth herself picked up. Thankfully I'd got the day right as well, and everyone was expecting me. Her father, who was coming into Houston, would collect me in an hour. I could stay for as long as I liked in the family home, which was just on the outskirts of town. It was the beginning of my personal experience of that local phenomenon which was a reward for any journey – Texan hospitality.

Houston

The Eighth Wonder

The Texan welcome to a stranger is a lesson for the British to take home. Forget about polite handshakes, nods, and formal introductions. In Texas 'formality' is a dirty word, the only way to treat people being as if you'd known them all your life. When Mr Mendell pulled up outside the bus depot it was 'Hi, Paul – Wilbert T. Mendell – climb inside' and I was immediately sinking into contour-cushioned, air-conditioned luxury and whisking out along the boulevard to the downtown exit.

At the Mendell home – a sedate, white-painted mansion – we parked up behind five other cars. When I asked if there were other guests Wilbert T. shook his head. 'Don't think so, they're all ours.'

Ushered into the house by my host I was immediately surrounded by Mendells and Mendell dogs. Elizabeth was in the front line, introducing her mother, two sisters Sarah and Barbara, brothers John and Chris and a rather preppy-looking, square-shouldered youth who stood slightly apart from the rest. Was this Elizabeth's boyfriend from college? To show the infectiousness of Texan goodwill, even Marsden Blois III pumped my hand. And he was Californian.

'Paul, you look as if you've just got off a Greyhound,' said Elizabeth. 'I guess you could use a shower and fresh clothes.'

Only too aware of my crumpled appearance I was happy to be shown into my room. When I came out of the shower I was surprised to discover that the dirty clothing I'd tipped from my rucksack had been quietly removed. Later I learned that the house included among its facilities a laundry, staffed by two house servants, that was fully geared to tackle such emergencies. In the face of such organisation I could only surrender gratefully to the practicality of my hosts.

In the evening the Mendells had a barbecue in their garden, with the steaks 'char-broiled' on a special brick-built grill. No inventory of the Texan way of doing things could omit steaks, which over here were carved in inch-thick slices. After chewing doggedly through mine for ten minutes I was confounded by having a second hunk, just as big, forked onto my plate, with the instruction to cut myself another piece whenever I wanted it. Helplessly I stared at the Mendell girls, sawing away enthusiastically with the plates perched on their knees.

'You must be hungry after that long journey, Paul.'

Next day the welcome programme began in earnest, with a visit to the 'Eighth Wonder of the World'.

When I first heard this epithet applied to a domed sports arena that had just been opened south of the city I couldn't help thinking that Texas, for all its achievements, was getting things a little out of proportion. Elizabeth and Marsden, driving with me out of Houston on the South Loop Freeway, insisted that I must have heard about the Astrodome, even in England.

'It's been in the news for years,' Elizabeth told me. 'How much publicity do you think it needed to raise thirty-one million dollars?'

I gulped. 'Is that what it cost?'

'The largest indoor arena on the planet,' Marsden intoned. 'The world's first air-conditioned, domed, all-purpose stadium. Seats 66,000. Used for baseball, football, circuses, conventions, big fights, Billy Graham –'

Billy it was who had dubbed it the 'Eighth Wonder', hyperbole being essential to the world of evangelism. Hearing this, I was prepared to be impressed. When we finally drove into the stadium car park, in sight of the huge glazed dome, I knew what to expect. The first trial by scale.

Seeing the sizeable queue at the entrance gates I asked Elizabeth what event was currently showing.

She shrugged. 'Nothing. They've come to see the Astrodome.'

As we walked up the ramp leading to the first seating level we were met by our guide, a youth of high-school age wearing an Astrodome blazer. Leading us and a ready-made group into the auditorium he requested that we take our seats and admire the surroundings. Looking up at the interior of the dome, 200 feet above the arena, I could only obey the command and gape.

The dome consisted of a self-supporting steel framework that carried a cast acrylic roof of thousands of oblong skylights to a span of 640 feet; a masterwork of engineering. The arena invited comparisons with a more famous structure of ancient times whose function had been much the same. There were, however, differences, which the guide was happy to point out.

The Roman Colosseum, we learned, had laid on some pretty spectacular shows that had entailed a certain amount of carnage and human suffering. Happily this element was missing from the Astrodome presentations, and even the latest attraction – bullfighting – was entirely bloodless. Another point that the Astrodome scored over its ancient rival was in the shape of its arena, not confined to an oval but adaptable to the needs of the event. By rolling up the turf and moving the front stands along steel rails, the diamond shape of a baseball pitch could be transformed into the rectangle of a football field. Other conversions were for rodeos, circuses and bullfights, when the turf was removed completely, or for concerts and conventions, when the carpets were rolled out. Among all the possibilities, however, there was no mention of full-scale naval battles. One up to the Colosseum.

The seats were filling up and to reach everyone the guide had to pitch his voice – by the sound of it, only recently broken – to a height that was as much a strain for his audience as for him. Dramatically he pointed at one of the great air coolers suspended above us from the roof of the stadium. Here, would the visitors please note, was the most important difference of all. Like no other sports arena in the world, the Astrodome was fully air-conditioned.

'Every single minute,' he proclaimed, 'Two hundred and fifty thousand cubic feet of fresh air is drawn into the stadium. This air is conditioned by electronic filters and activated charcoal odour removers. Two point three million cubic feet of air is in constant circulation, the hot air and smoke drawn out through the roof. Whatever the weather's doing outside, the Astrodome guarantees a steady seventy-two degrees. How's that for playing it cool?'

Before the murmur of amazement had subsided the guide was pitching in again with more facts and figures on the dome, a recital of well-rehearsed superlatives that left me wondering if there were any records left to beat. The scoreboard, for example, was the world's largest, measuring 474 feet long by four storeys high. Electronically operated, it was also the most elaborate, expensive and extraordinary construction of its kind. For two million dollars, you got more than just the score, you had a sideshow. Adverts, animated cartoons, comments on the game and even – when the home team scored – electronic *fireworks*...

After this it came as a surprise to learn that the price of a seat in the Astrodome could run as low as $1.50. But there were, of course, a number of seats available to those who could afford more realistic prices, like $18,000 for a year's rental of a box at the top of the stadium.

Here the Astrodome's clientele was presented with the summit of social aspiration. Most of the boxes, Elizabeth told me, had gone to corporations on five-year leases, for the entertainment of staff and clients. And the others? I couldn't resist the picture of the lone cattle baron, nibbling popcorn in the isolated splendour of his thirty-seat private box and wondering if it would be more relaxing to watch the game on TV.

For his $18,000, of course, he had the choice. At the back of each 'Skybox' was a private apartment, consisting of an anteroom with an ensuite bathroom and kitchenette, a bar, refrigerator, telephone and closed-circuit TV. On the latter, tenants of the Skybox could watch the game while mixing a cocktail, making a telephone call or cleaning their teeth.

'Additionally,' the guide declared, his voice reaching a higher and more exultant note, 'all Skybox holders are members of the Skydome Club, where they enjoy exclusive dining with Japanese waitresses and their own personally-monogrammed silver spatula.'

At this point we quietly withdrew to consider our next move. When I suggested the bar, the other two looked a little uncertain. 'There isn't one,' said Elizabeth. 'Only the Astrodome Club, and you have to be a member.' Marsden checked the guide. 'Must be worth it,' he said, 'it's got the longest bar in the world.'

For the rest of the day, after our departure from the 'Eighth Wonder', our heads were drumming with facts. After essential further information on restroom facilities and hurricane resistance, we were left with one conclusion. That we should see some baseball.

Conveniently, Elizabeth's father had some tickets for a game that evening, the Houston Astros versus the Los Angeles Dodgers. To make it a proper outing we called first at a seafood restaurant near the freeway where the *plat du jour* was fried red snapper – a far but tasty cry from the coral reef – and then on to the Astrodome. With the help of a guide – this one a 'hostess' in a gold lamé suit – we made our way to our seats, located strategically over the home plate.

Those anticipating a dissertation on the finer points of baseball will be disappointed. I must make it clear from the outset that the ignorance accompanying me to my seat remained with me until the end. Some simple facts were known to me, like the 'home plate' being where the striker stood, the 'pitcher' being the bowler and the 'home run' being equivalent to a 'rounder' in our own English game. After nine innings' worth of the finer points, however (the inscrutable technicalities of scoring) the mysteries of the game remained as infinite as ever.

Am I being fair? In the context of the Astrodome no event could be completely dull. A degree of fascination came not only from witnessing a sporting event – normally held in the open – under a vast celestial dome, but from the details that marked it out from other spectator experiences. The first thing I noticed was the way that the smoke from the audience's cigarettes rose in thin vertical streamers, disappearing almost immediately into the purified atmosphere of the stadium. Then – a further symbol of purity – the lush greenness of the *Bermuda grass, 'tested and selected for its ability to flourish under artificial conditions'.

Finally, the most impressive detail of all. Hardly a detail, though, when it dominated every event at the Astrodome from beginning to end. The first moment that we became aware of the scoreboard was when the music started and the lamps flashed out, in huge capital letters, the traditional Texan greeting: 'HOWDY!' From then on we were treated to an electronic sideshow of announcements, advertisements, animated cartoons and critical comments on the game.

For the serious sports addict the scoreboard must have been a bit of an intrusion, a distraction from any finer appreciation of the game. For the rest, however – myself included – it provided a necessary element of light relief. The start of the game, for instance, was very slow, with the home team – the 'Astros' – very much on the defensive. The scoreboard, being unashamedly partisan, began to exert its influence, flashing up the instruction 'Go, go, go' which the audience chanted in unison. When at last an Astro striker made a run for first base the scoreboard leapt into action. A cartoon of a cowboy on a galloping horse appeared, blowing a trumpet which was amplified stereophonically through the stadium. At the same time, responding to the accompanying caption, the crowd yelled 'Charge!'

Having heard the guide tell us earlier about the fantastic forty-two-second display, complete with ricocheting bullets, snaking lassos, snorting bulls and fireworks that greeted a home run, I asked Elizabeth what the chances were of my witnessing the event. She shrugged. 'Depends what shape the Dodgers are in.'

As it turned out they were in pretty good shape, or good enough to keep the Astros pinned down. The Dodgers, in fact, were the first team to score a home run, an event marked by the scoreboard with a cartoon of a spluttering firework, fading out with a '*Phffft*...'

Despite its repetitiveness the repertoire of the scoreboard

---

* Retrospective note: this natural grass, deprived of direct sunlight, had turned brown and eventually succumbed after being sprayed with green dye. This resulted in the introduction of the man-made 'Astroturf', now used in parks and sports stadia throughout the world.

invariably struck the right note with an audience eagerly awaiting the next wry comment on the game. One of the regular cartoons, which came up whenever the pitcher was changed, was 'Pitcher Gone to Shower' which showed a little Magoo-like figure walking into a cubicle, operating the shower and disappearing in a rapidly-rising tide of water. Another opportunity that the scoreboard never missed would be the moment, in the middle of an innings, when the visiting team interrupted the game for a strategy conference. While the Dodgers went into a huddle in the middle of the pitch the jests came thick and fast: 'How are the wife and kids?' – 'No use praying for rain, fellers' and 'Who forgot his Right Guard?'

The art of mass communication, for which the Americans have a special genius, was demonstrated most spectacularly during the interval before the seventh innings. At this point the scoreboard announced, in letters that stretched and contracted with kinetic persuasiveness, 'SEVENTH INNINGS STRETCH'. The audience, acting almost by reflex, rose in a body and for a moment I thought I was going to hear *The Star-Spangled Banner*. Instead I was conscious of the seismic cracking of bones as arms were stretched and shoulders flexed, and respiratory gasps as waistbands were tugged and garters hitched. The straining of unused muscles as press-ups were performed on seat-backs, popcorn bags recovered from the floor. It was the spectacle of an organised society gone mad; 50,000 people combining in one giant orgasmic movement. I wondered what effect it might have had on the Astrodome's unique air-conditioning system if, at the same time as stretching, every one of those 50,000 happened to yawn...

Two more innings and the game was over, and to my enduring disappointment I realised that I had missed the ultimate experience of the scoreboard going wild for forty-two seconds. Though manfully holding the Dodgers at 0-1 for eight innings the Astros had never come near a home run themselves and in the last innings took too many chances in going for one. They finished up 0-3, a defeat that the scoreboard accepted with as much grace as possible, considering that it had been denied its moment of glory. Its last comment, as the two teams made their exit, was a model of restraint:

'They wuz lucky.'

As a technological marvel the Astrodome was a mighty elaboration of a national obsession. Like the central heating of northern climes, Texas air-conditioning had become an essential support of human life, without which a large number of her citizens would be expiring daily on the sidewalks. To avoid this happening a cool environment was maintained through much of the day. From an air-conditioned home the average middle-class Texan would practise a quick sprint into an air-conditioned car and a drive to an air-conditioned office or supermarket. After this they would return home, then go out to an air-conditioned restaurant, movie theatre or bowling alley. There were of course gaps, encountered in crossing streets or entering backyards, but these areas were designated as 'natural' zones, primarily, I understood, for the benefit of visiting strangers who needed to maintain their output of sweat and intake of carbon monoxide.

It was, altogether, a different Texas to the one I'd conceived. No camp fires, round-ups, rolling prairies, dust storms. Just a Great Indoors, which I guess offered its own kind of spectacle.

On a smaller scale than the Astrodome experience, but considerably more entertaining, was the Lamar High School Orientation Day. This was an annual event, celebrated by most schools in America, in which the year's intake of new students was introduced. The traditional ceremony involved a welcoming address from the principal and other staff members and a salute from the school band and accompanying cheerleaders. Mrs Mendell, who took me to the event, was this year particularly enthusiastic as her youngest daughter, Barbara, was one of the team. Although I didn't know the exact function of a cheerleader, I guessed from the hint of pride in Mrs Mendell's voice that her daughter was a key figure in the ceremony.

The welcome was staged in the school's main assembly hall, with the new students gathered in strength and the school band, resplendent in fancily-embroidered uniforms, grouped below the stage. From our seats in the gallery Mrs Mendell and I watched the principal and four or five teachers arrive on the stage, to the accompaniment of a rousing march from the band. They were followed by the head pupils and when they had all taken their seats the principal stood up to make the opening speech.

Briefly but warmly he welcomed his new protégés, saying that although it was a lot of fun at Lamar everyone was expected to do their bit and work for the greater success of the school, which meant students pulling their weight at lessons as well as games. The sports instructor then got up and said much the same thing (with an emphasis on the games) and the message was devoutly echoed by the rest of the staff, enthusing about the challenges that lay ahead for the new students. The only discordant note was struck by the last-but-one speaker, a tough crew-cut character in Army serge who carried over his arm a set of badge-emblazoned jerkins. With a steely eye on his audience he said:

'You might think from lookin' at me I'm a clothes dealer, so I'd better put you straight. I'm the commander of the cadet corps, and these here are rifle jackets. We got a great record for shootin' in the corps, and I'm lookin' to all you new fellers comin' to Lamar to maintain it. One of these jackets belongs to the best shot in the school, and that feller's got somethin' to talk about.' He paused, targeting his hard, slowly-sweeping gaze on the male component of the audience. 'I want these jackets filled...'

The grit of the veteran gave way to the geniality of youth in the shape of the head girl, a preppy little brunette who wound up the welcome with a chatty sermon about how much she and her fellow students owed Lamar. Embracing her audience with the familiar Southern 'y'all', she added, 'Y'all gonna know it's 'cause Mirabeau B. Lamar's the greatest.'

Rising to the cue the band launched into the school song. Along with the cheerleaders, who now came onto the stage to replace the speakers, it was a stirring antidote to any flagging spirits in the audience. Banners were unfurled to reveal the words of the song, and the function of the cheerleaders – three boys and three girls including the euphoric Barbara – was similarly revealed as they paraded to the front of the stage to exhort the audience to join in the singing.

'Fight Lamar for ever, we'll see you through
We'll defend your honour, always and so true –'

The verve and energy of the six teenagers was astonishing. Dressed in matching red and white outfits – the boys in slacks and the girls in tennis skirts and waving pom-poms of red ribbon – they went through a punishing routine of high kicks and handstands, pausing only to snatch up megaphones and yell encouragement at the audience. When the chorus had been sung enough times for the newcomers to remember it the cheerleaders plunged into their finale, a series of acrobatics ending with a rousing cheer for the school in which everyone joined, shaking the hall to its foundations.

Elated by her daughter's performance, Mrs Mendell asked me what I had thought of the ceremony, and how it compared with the way we did it back in England. For a moment, remembering the staid ritual of an English prep school speech day, with the head master holding the stage for an eternity with a recitation of aphorisms, Latin quotations and premeditated pauses for laughter and applause, I was at a loss for a reply. All I could say, without committing myself to an appraisal of the different educational systems, was that it had been quite unlike anything *we'd* ever done at school.

The climax of my stay with the Mendells was a three-day visit to their weekend home, situated 200 miles north-west and about seventy miles from Austin, the state capital. This was their retreat, in the summer months, from the heat and traffic of the city. The setting was idyllic, but if I hadn't actually done the journey I would never have believed it was deep in the heart of Texas. The skies were blue and the sun was bright, but for the rest it was a cool Scandinavian scene, with a log-built chalet and lake, a fringing belt of shady trees, and lush grass to the water's edge. It was all so quiet, fresh and green that my first reaction, arriving in one of the family cars, had been to glance skywards. To my relief there were no air coolers – no cast acrylic dome above our heads. Jumping out of the car and onto the lawn, I discovered that this too was real. The only artificial element was the lake, and this didn't matter too much when you could do all those marvellous things in it.

The choice was limitless. At the jetty a small fleet was gathered that offered every variety of boating activity, from a 90mph motorboat to a canoe. The tiny 'Sailfish' sailing boats were special fun, and by the end of my visit I had become quite skilled in handling them. I could not, unfortunately, say the same for the water skis, which reduced me rapidly to despair. In the process of my repeated efforts to get 'up' and stay 'up' I came to resemble that peculiarly English type of ninny whose bulldog determination to succeed brought increased disaster. During one attempt – the last – I carried this determination to an extreme which, though testifying to my indomitable Anglo-Saxon spirit, said little for my good sense. Having failed to draw my knees up to my chest in the prescribed style for starting I was pulled along by the motorboat with my head under the water, a hopeless predicament which I did little to relieve by clinging persistently to the grip-bar. Assuming from the tautness of the rope that I was still trying to get out of the water the driver of the motorboat had spontaneously increased his speed, with the result that I was dragged behind it like a piece of flotsam, unable to do anything but hang on and pray that by some miracle I would achieve the correct posture. Only when the skis had been sucked off my feet and my arms all but wrenched from their sockets did I release the bar and signal my defeat.

Swimming back to the jetty with my skis I was met by the youngest member of the family. A bespectacled twelve-year-old, Chris had apparently been watching my progress with great interest through his binoculars.

'You get up, Paul?'

I dropped my skis on the jetty like the two halves of a broken lance. Looking out across the lake I saw the athletic figure of Marsden Blois III skimming across the water in a clean silver spray. I shook the water out of my ears and shrugged. There must be some other way of proving one's manhood.

I found it at the end of my stay, when I appeared once more before the family in full marching order. Standing by John Mendell's car (he was taking me to Austin on his way back to the University of Texas) I was surrounded again by admiring Mendells. A natural response – or so I liked to think – to any individual who could seriously consider trekking across America with a forty-five-pound pack when there were so many more straightforward and comfortable ways of getting round the country.

With grateful thanks for their hospitality I took my leave of the Mendells. Happily, as far as Elizabeth was concerned, my farewell was *au revoir*. A few days after my departure she too would be heading west, to Stanford University, where we would meet up again on the California leg of my journey. In the meantime she gave me a parting treat, a memento of Mendell generosity. A giant bag of pecan and chocolate chip cookies.

San Antonio, Mexico and the Borderlands

'Remember the Alamo!'

From Austin I travelled south the same day to San Antonio. Once a Spanish mission and now the second city of Texas, San Antonio nurtured in its dusty heart the West's most famous legend.

Here was an outpost of American history that excited the same responses in the national breast as Bunker Hill, and in the Texan breast as the glimpse of the ubiquitous flag with the single star. For Texans, the Lone Star and the Alamo were jointly symbolic of the most glorious period of their history, the ten years of their independence.

It had started with the modest stone-built church of San Antonio de Valero, founded by the Franciscan order during the eighteenth-century Spanish rule, that had later served as a fortress, the Alamo, for alternating Mexican and Texan garrisons during the war against the Santa Anna dictatorship. In 1836 the stronghold had been garrisoned by 180 supporters of the Texas cause under the command of Colonel Travis: a hard core of patriots standing in defiance of the gathering Mexican forces. Included in this number were two names that stirred story-book memories, strangely implausible as characters in a real-life drama. Davy Crockett from Tennessee, riding in with seventeen men and a determination to fight for Texas, and Jim Bowie of the famous knife who was ready to give his life in the same cause.

And that, spectacularly, was what they had done. For ten days the tiny garrison had held out against 3,000 Mexicans, with dwindling hopes of relief. Then, on the night before the final attack, Travis had made his appeal to the defenders that was to become as much a part of the Alamo's fabric as its crumbling, shell-shattered walls.

Restored as a museum of the siege, the mission church's gloomy interior was laden with tragedy. In its charged atmosphere I was able to picture the scene of that final evening. Travis the commander, unsheathing his sword and cutting a line in the earth, with the offer of glory to every man who would cross the line to join him. The united movement, save for one dissident, of men accepting their responsibility and fate. The pain-wracked cry, from a room in the barracks, of the ailing Jim Bowie – stricken with typhoid pneumonia – for one of his comrades to come and carry his cot over the line.

The dawn light of the next day had shown a broken fortress, the scaling ladders of the Mexicans hanging from its walls, the bodies of defenders and attackers lying inside the church and barracks and around the gun emplacements. The heroes were there, revealed to the dictator's triumphant gaze: Crockett in the church doorway, Bowie in his cot, Travis lying across his cannon. As a final act of revenge Santa Anna had ordered their bodies, and those of the other defenders, to be burned.

Retribution came six weeks later when General Sam Houston, future President of the Republic of Texas, had led his army against the Mexican dictator on the battlefield of San Jacinto, to the ringing cry of 'Remember the Alamo!' An act of grim retaliation that within eighteen minutes saw the Mexicans routed, Santa Anna captured and the war ended. In that decisive victory the Republic was born, a lone star shining proudly for the next ten years.

Wandering outside in the grounds of the mission, peacefully

landscaped with walks and flowerbeds, I came to an inescapable destination: the souvenir shop. Lone Star flags, facsimile Declarations of Independence, portraits of Houston and Travis, miniature Alamos and postcards dedicated to the 'Shrine of Texas Liberty' came with a piece of territory devoutly owned, or at least managed, by the Daughters of the Republic of Texas.

For all the emphasis, both spoken and written, on the glorious era of the Texan Republic, I found myself more magnetically drawn towards the period that preceded it by a hundred years. Old San Antonio was a Spanish town, with vestiges of the era that could be detected in La Villita, an 'historic district' with some authentic Spanish-Mexican houses detectable among the ubiquitous art and craft stores.

Other buildings that might have given this area more authenticity had been removed stone by stone to a museum north of the city and reconstructed in its grounds. Fortunately they'd resisted this temptation, further west, with the Spanish Governor's Palace, a unique adobe construction with three-foot thick walls and an interior that recaptured the domestic setting of an eighteenth-century Spanish aristocrat.

In marked contrast to the simple flagstone floors, open fireplaces and heavy-beamed doorways were the antique chandeliers in the dining-room and the elaborately-carved tester-bed in the bedroom. Stylish, but not at all self-conscious, was the little pebble-mosaiced patio at the back of the palace, a walled refuge of great charm with a water-lily fountain at its centre and a profusion of bougainvillea, banana and other tropical plants around its walls. One feature of San Antonio, discovered in my walk from La Villita to the palace, gave it an unusual appeal. It was one of the few non-coastal cities in America to have a river running through its centre. This river, the San Antonio, flowed from north to south, making a lariat loop through La Villita. Thirteen bridges spanned the loop, and on either side of the river I saw stone walks bordered by flowers and trees. With such a setting the associations were compelling, particularly for the Municipal Information Bureau. Apart from being 'The Alamo City', San Antonio was the 'Venice of the Prairies'. From where I paused a moment, to watch a Texan in a straw hat punt a gondola downstream, I could almost hear the Bridge of Sighs.

In addition to the Alamo, San Antonio was famous for its four other Spanish missions, all built in the first half of the eighteenth century. Grouped together at the city's southern limits they could be visited in the space of an afternoon, taking a Gray Line bus tour from the Alamo. The most impressive of these unpretentious buildings was the Mission San Jose, a National Historic Site. Outwardly it seemed very modest, a small, single-towered church in an enclosure of other buildings. But closer inspection brought the reward of unexpected charm and detail, an echo of the artistic culture of the nation whose missionaries had created it.

Established by the Franciscans in 1720, San Jose became the home of American Indians of various tribes, who in return for their living quarters performed tasks for the mission and received Christian teaching. They also became skilled in other ways, helping with carvings on the church façade and the wall paintings inside. Unhappily the mission was abandoned in the middle of the nineteenth century and much of this work obliterated. Some of the buildings, including part of the church, were allowed to decay and collapse, and it was not until the 1920s that anything was done to restore them.

After a look at the workers' quarters – ingeniously built together to form the enclosing walls of the mission – I went to the church to admire the sculpture on the façade and tower, carved so expertly by those native hands. On the east side of the church I discovered the detail that was my most cherished encounter with the Old World in the New – the Rose Window. It was very small, barely an opening, but framed by a delightful piece of stone carving that featured the acanthus leaves and garlands of the Baroque style. Included in the garlands were tiny roses that had presumably given the window its name. On Santiago de Compostela's cathedral such a detail would have been lost: here in America it was the finest piece of ornamentation from the Spanish colonial period.

Despite the tourist pilgrimages that he conducted every day, the golden years of Spanish history did not overly impress the Gray Line bus driver, a hard-jawed man who looked a bit like John Wayne without the Davy Crockett hat. If I'd harboured any doubts about Texan supremacy he was the man to dispel them.

As he turned the bus around to return to the city he reminded his passengers about the most important period of American history, which had begun somewhere around 1836 and ended in 1845. 'That, folks, was when the Union joined Texas.'

With the Lone Star – or should I say the Greyhound schedule – faithfully guiding me, I continued my journey westwards out of San Antonio. The time was 4.30pm, the destination El Paso, Texas, a town tucked into the westernmost corner of the state where it wedged into New Mexico to the north and Old Mexico to the south. The distance was 560 miles and the road time twelve hours, which meant I would be travelling on a sleeper's ticket again, to save my dollars. The Greyhound was one of the Scenicruiser type, with upper deck and panoramic vision. Thinking about the landscape I would miss in the darkness I hoped I hadn't made a false economy.

With prickly pear, mesquite and other desert plants and shrubs in evidence I began to feel the pull of the south-west. That wild, vast and empty region of America that for most travellers, even in modern times, was the land beyond the frontier. Waking up from a long sleep between the rest stops of Del Rio and Fort Stockton I looked out on a ghostly, moonlit stretch of sand and realised that we were crossing one of the arid plateau lands that marked the end of the Great Plains and the beginning of the Rocky Mountains.

The Rockies! I could hardly wait for daylight.

Sadly, the dawn brought the familiar view of concrete and neon, and the kind of building-block architecture that had come to typify the modern American city. This was El Paso, 'The Pass', an urban agglomeration that one could only imagine had been created to fill the gap in the Rockies that had bestowed its name. Its main feature, in fact, was its situation, south of the tongue of the San Andreas range in the Rocky Mountain chain and north of the Rio Grande and the Mexican border. Across the river, however, there was the prospect of another culture in Juarez, the Mexican border city.

As I got out of the bus – a little unsteadily after the twelve-hour stint – I discovered that El Paso had its saving grace. For the first time since New York I could feel some air between my shirt and skin, evidence of a final escape from the humidity of the east.

From now on I would be enjoying the more pleasant dry heat of the desert country.

The El Paso YMCA was another reprieve, in my experience the cleanest and best-appointed of its kind. Resisting the temptation of a very comfortable-looking bed I had a hot shower and laundry session and then a relaxed and hearty breakfast of crispy bacon and waffles in the canteen. With the prospect of another country to explore, I felt the need for sustenance.

In reality it was all too easy. A five-minute trip across the Rio Grande, on a ten-cent tram. The only hardship was having to stand sandwiched between two animated Mexican men, who alternately embraced and shouted at one another. The tram was very crowded and it was fortunate that there were no formalities involved in crossing the border, other than a cursory check of shopping bags by a tired-looking Customs man on the other side. Once across the bridge I squirmed my way through the tightly packed bodies of my fellow passengers and at the first stop jumped out onto Mexican soil.

To my dismay this action proved no more than a figure of speech. There was a gentle squelching underfoot and when I looked down I saw my trousers caked in mud. Bewilderedly I picked my way out of the water, wondering how it could happen that after crossing half a continent without a glimpse of a puddle I should have to cross the border into Mexico to step into one. Glancing down the street I saw that this was a pretty inevitable experience, as the puddle stretched as far as I could see and was only one of several that transformed the area into a network of small canals. On either side of the street lay piles of earth and uprooted water pipes, which though explaining the puddles raised certain maintenance questions, unresolved by the total absence of labourers. At ten in the morning it seemed an odd time for a siesta.

'Taxi, *señor?*'

At a guess it was ten or twenty seconds since I had descended from the tram. Time enough, it seemed, for Mexican enterprise to assert itself. Without a local map and stuck in an alien street leading into the unknown, I was in the taxi driver's hands. As I followed him to his cab – parked in a side street – I remembered the strategy, recommended in the guide books, about agreeing the fare beforehand. The only problem here was my total ignorance of the city of Juarez, and the distances involved in reaching the points of interest. When the Mexican suggested the cathedral for seventy-five cents there was little I could do but agree.

My misgivings about the fare were balanced by the length of our route to the destination, which took us through a network of streets that became increasingly congested as we neared the city centre. Trams (for the citizens) and taxis (for the tourists) were competing for space with motor cycles, scooters and bicycles, navigating the succession of road and building works. The object of all drivers, it seemed, was to get past these barriers before the traffic coming the other way, which depended on having the room to manoeuvre and being faster on the accelerator. The result was typically a face-to-face, bumper-to-bumper deadlock, coupled with a predictably histrionic exchange that did little to assist the traffic flow and came to an end only when the primary aggressor surrendered to the orchestra of car horns and put his vehicle in reverse.

Eventually we reached the cathedral square. Getting out of the taxi I thanked the driver for my deliverance and handed him a dollar bill. My gratitude was liberally interpreted and I received, in change, a peso and an apology. 'I'm sorry, *señor*. No American money.'

With the equivalent of eight cents in my pocket and the prospect of meeting other Mexicans unable to offer change for a dollar bill, the possibilities of Juarez seemed limited. The cathedral, which I had hoped would be interesting, was in fact rather dull, mixing modern construction with traditional style. I was left to wander aimlessly through the surrounding streets.

No longer viewed from the immunity of a vehicle, these streets were even less attractive, exposing me to the immediate personal hazards of death-wish driving and the yawning kerbside craters that threatened to engulf me the moment that I took an unwary step from the sidewalk. In another sense, too, it was an alien prospect, with many of the buildings only half-finished, the rusted iron spokes jabbing like nails from their reinforced concrete pillars. The older buildings – by which I can only refer to those not actually in the process of construction – were uniformly shabby, their stucco crumbling and paintwork faded. The telegraph wires threaded between them were like spiders' webs after a storm, trailing in great tangled loops from their poles. As on the north side of the river the neon predominated, taking the shape of whatever it was trying to sell. The most popular symbol was a bottle, representing Juarez' main source of income from the US. *'Vinos e licores'* was the most ubiquitous sign, and in case there was any doubt about its meaning, another sign – juxtaposed to the fitfully winking bottle – announced 'Wholesale Liquor Store'. In other signs the two languages were skilfully integrated, as in *'Super Farmacia'* and *'Pantalones Billy the Kid'*. Juarez might have been the largest border town in Mexico, but it was still the poor man's El Paso.

By chance I found myself back at the river, somewhere between the two international bridges (one southbound, one northbound). Another precious dollar was spent in a riverside *cantina*, which offered me a rare T-bone steak with radishes and hot chilli sauce.

The taste of Mexican chilli became my indelible memory of the country, a mouthful of molten lava that burned its way from my tongue to the back of my throat, taking off the roof of my mouth in transit. No amount of cool *cerveza*, willingly supplied by the aproned proprietor, could calm its fiery pungency.

To add to my discomfort the *cantina* was the first eating-place I'd visited on my trip that did not have the benefit of air-conditioning. Even with the doors and windows open and a couple of fans going it was above 90° in the room. The effect, in combination with the chilli, was a continuous warm trickle of sweat down my front, back and legs.

The Wurlitzer Stereophonic in the corner of the *cantina* was a further torment. Pounding out the latest beat tune from across the border it imposed a jerky rhythm on my whole digestive system so that my stomach, fired by the chilli, began to react like an overheated car engine. At any moment I felt I might seize up.

The proprietor came over, his face wreathed in the smile of hospitality. 'You like the chilli, *señor?*'

My reply was lost in the Wurlitzer beat. Discreetly I offered alms to the two scraggy-looking cats that were waiting under the table.

Outside the *cantina* I stared across the grey-brown trickle of the Rio Grande at the shimmering skyscrapers of El Paso and wondered how a couple of hundred yards could make such a difference. Eager to get a view on this – however superficial – I made the decision to cross back into El Paso. And from there take a Gray Line Bus Tour into Mexico.

Re-entry into the US was rather more controlled than the exit. The footbridge carried a toll (one cent), and there were floodlights and barbed wire fences on either side. On the American side there was a customs shed and immigration officials. All of which seemed a bit superfluous when at any point you could walk across the dried-up river bed.

The Gray Line offices were in the bus depot building, and with a ticket for the Juarez Afternoon Tour I joined the queue at the pick-up point outside. The coach was over half an hour late and the driver did not immediately win us over by introducing himself as 'the late Gene Taylor'. Suspecting that we had a wag on our hands, I wondered if the ticket cost would prove worthwhile.

Before we started the driver, who doubled as a tour guide, looked us over carefully, reassuring himself as to the nature of his payload. 'Welcome to the Juarez tour, folks. Juarez, Old Mexico.' The words were uttered with a kind of deadly languor, suggesting that he'd done the tour more times than he cared to recall. 'Juarez is the fourth largest city in Mexico, and the largest on the border with the United States. That kinda makes it a large city, but right now is a pretty good time to visit. Most of the Mexicans have left, they're working in El Paso.'

A titter went round the coach and I gave the other passengers an anxious scrutiny. Like Mr Taylor I was reassured that there were no Mexicans on board.

As we crossed the international bridge and were waved on encouragingly by Mexican customs, he went on, 'You may like to know, folks, how many Mexicans come across the river every day. No fewer than 23,000, all got jobs in America.' He drove slowly past the forsaken road works, the piles of earth. 'Maybe that's why they've got a labour shortage over here.'

We clung to our seats as the coach lurched into a pothole, an unexpected jolt for anyone who hadn't watched our driver steer into it. With a patient sigh and a shrug of his shoulders he eased the wheels clear.

'"*Mañana*" is a Mexican word,' he said. 'It's also a Mexican philosophy.'

We had just turned into one of the main streets of the city: on either side, as he pointed out, was the evidence of this philosophy. 'Take a look at those buildings. After five years of construction they've just about made it to the first floor. How's that for progress? It's quite interesting you know, the way they tackle their building projects over here. They start with just enough money for the ground floor and by the time they've finished that, they hope they've got some more for the one above. If they haven't, well, they can always rent out the ground floor and sooner or later they'll have enough money to carry on. In Mexico "*mañana*" means "tomorrow", folks.'

Of all attitudes, cynicism is one of the least endearing. But in many respects naivety is even worse. At the Plaza Monumental bull ring our driver announced that from this point a Mexican guide would be taking over the tour. My relief at this news turned to incredulity as a thickset, moustachioed individual leapt aboard and introduced himself as 'Raffaelo, Citizen of Juarez'.

Welcoming us to his city he expressed the hope that we would enjoy our brief visit and sample to the full the many and varied pleasures and amenities that we would find at our disposal. 'The bull ring that we are to visit, the Plaza Monumental, is the most comfortable in the world,' he proclaimed. 'The bull fights that we have here are the very most spectacular, to rival those of the famous arenas in Mexico City, Madrid and Sevilla.'

At his invitation we followed him from the coach into the bull ring. Not having seen the inside of a bull ring before, I was unable to endorse Raffaello's civic pride. On the face of it the Plaza Monumental was rather ordinary, with tiers of plain wooden seats encircling a dusty arena and a backdrop of flimsy advertisement hoardings at the top, interspersed with floodlights. Over the entrances to the arena were such signs as '*Toriles*' and '*Picadores*', but these seemed a bit fanciful when the only hint of a *corrida* was in the antics of a pair of trainee matadors in a corner of the arena, one brandishing a cape and the other a pair of horns.

From the bull ring we proceeded to the centre of the city, driving through many of the streets that I had first endured that morning in the taxi. In the driving seat, steering a skilful course through the shambles of traffic and roadworks, our erstwhile guide maintained a discreet silence. Not so Raffaelo, who was clearly out to impress.

'On either side of the street,' he said, 'you can see the great progress of our city. In Juarez, building is our first priority, to meet the demands of our growing population. Our country today plans to support a total of 400 millions, ten times the present number of forty millions. Here in Juarez, the fourth largest city in Mexico, we are going ahead with our plans to double the population to one million in ten years. For these people we are building a new city.'

Hearing this proud statement I tried to catch a glimpse of Mr Gene Taylor's face in the driving mirror, but this became impossible as the coach rode a further assault course of potholes. After a visit to the cathedral, which I'd already seen, and the more interesting Church of the Mission of Guadalupe – built in 1659 – we drove out of the city into the residential area. To my now critical eye this appeared as another custom-built suburb on the American pattern. Bungalows of various shapes and sizes, enclosed by stone walls decked out with potted plants and creepers. All looking like miniature *haciendas*. To Raffaelo, of course, they were the latest thing. 'The property of the upper class,' he told us proudly.

The property of the lower class, which we viewed next, received slightly less comment. A shanty town of adobe, spread over a limitless plain of scorched earth. This was the city beyond the suburb, not a feature of the tourist itinerary but a glimpse of the other Mexico that was there to haunt the dreamers.

The attraction that had brought us out of the city to this spot was a museum of Mexican primitive art. It was an extraordinary place, not so much by virtue of its exhibits as by the way in which they were displayed. Here I refer to the remarkable concept of the museum buildings themselves, whose spectacular design added so much to the pleasure of the visitor.

A building that particularly impressed me was one shaped rather like a lampshade, windowless and with the light coming through the open top and falling on the great stone objects spaced around its circumference. Most dramatic of these was a giant Toltec warrior column about thirteen feet high that had been placed directly in the centre of the floor, the overhead light throwing its blunt features into stark relief. The effect of this image on my sun-dazed eyes, entering this nebulous space, was electrifying. I felt as the Toltec pilgrims must have felt, a thousand years ago, confronting the statue-pillars as they approached their sanctuary. This was a museum doing its job, exhibiting a culture not only through image but experience. Was this something the Mexicans could teach the folk across the border?

From ancient cultures we were transported to modern industry. In a nearby factory we witnessed the art of glass-blowing, a popular tourist attraction that was also a big money-spinner for Juarez. After watching the technique of the craft demonstrated by a number of perspiring, vigorously exhaling glass-blowers we were smoothly conveyed from the furnace by a smiling *señora* who led us into the cooler and more familiar environment of the gift shop.

The invitation to browse did not immediately excite me. Surrounding us was an array of intricately modelled glass novelties that could be found in any market-place in any corner of the world: representations of animals from coy chihuahuas to mettlesome *toros* and eccentrically shaped glasses, bottles, jugs, carafes and vases. I would not wish, however, to make myself an arbiter of taste. The coach party from El Paso was in its element.

For all its popularity glass-blowing was not Juarez' major industry. Its biggest draw – after cheap spirits – was easy divorce. A business which Raffaelo warmly commended. '*Señores y señoras*, you will know that Juarez is the divorce capital of the world. We arrange here approximately 18,000 divorces every year which is more than fifty every day of the week including Sundays. To obtain a divorce requires two hundred and fifty dollars and the signatures of the Consul General of the United States and the Municipal President.'

I pictured the two dignitaries, pens strapped to their enfeebled hands, signing away fifty marriages a day. For $250 a shot they might not find it too difficult. The service was, of course, specifically for American citizens who couldn't get a divorce as quickly or as easily elsewhere. With pride Raffaelo added: 'The famous band leader Artie Shaw has been here nine times.'

With one billion dollars to beat (the impressive figure of last year's tourist spending in Mexico) we were hustled off the bus in Juarez' main shopping street and given half an hour's 'free time'. In this time we were expected to spend as much as possible of the hundred dollars granted for the purpose by the United States. With liquor stores advertising gin at $3.50 a quart and brandy at $2.30 this was hardly a challenge, particularly for those who had the notion of selling it over the border at a reasonable profit. Before the idea took too firm a hold I saw the notice in the window of a store advertising 'Juarez Whiskey'. The limit of spirits that could be taken back into the United States, it said, was a gallon – and only once in every thirty-one days. Shrugging my shoulders I went into the next shop, where I bought a postcard and a flag of Mexico for sixteen cents. It was the least I could do for the country.

I could hardly pass through the neighbouring state of New Mexico without a visit to the Carlsbad Caverns. They were too near El Paso to miss and I made a detour to see them, doubling back 150 miles to the north-east of the city.

In arranging this trip I came up against the first and only deficiency in the Greyhound service, that was to create some problems later on. The vast mileage of roads covered by the company did not unfortunately include the side roads into the National Parks, which were the concession of the local bus companies and not open to the inter-state operators such as Greyhound. The nearest point that Greyhound could take me was a town called Whites City. For a $1.55 supplement to my ticket I could transfer to a local bus that would take me on to the Caverns.

On the road out of El Paso I enjoyed my first clear view of the Rockies, the beginnings of the continent's greatest upheaval. The ranges here were 5-8,000 feet, which made an impressive spectacle even when viewed from the high plateau land. The desert that I had seen as a kind of moonlit fantasy in the early hours of the previous morning was now an actuality, a burned-on yellow-brownness sprinkled with stones and scrub. The vegetation was very sparse and I was able to pick out, with a thrill of recognition, species of cactus and desert plants which before now I had only seen in English hothouses. Among the cacti, the staghorn and prickly pear were the most prolific, among the plants and shrubs the spear-leaved yuccas and fuzzy-flowered catclaw acacia. A desert wilderness which provided a captivating introduction to the wonders of Carlsbad.

Desert eventually gave way to mountain and we entered the foothills of the Guadalupe range, in which the Caverns were located. Rounding a bend we were confronted, after one or two earlier glimpses, with a massive citadel-shaped peak. This the driver identified as El Capitan, a hideout in the bad old days of none other than Geronimo and his Apache band. Obligingly he slowed down to let us focus our cameras. But we were too close, and without the smoke signals it wasn't much of a picture.

Getting into conversation with a Mexican couple sitting behind me I learned that they were on their way to visit friends in New Orleans and were very concerned about the effects of a hurricane that had hit southern Louisiana the previous evening. Remembering the reports I had seen in the paper that morning of the progress of 'Betsy' (some name for a 150mph terror) from Florida to the Gulf Coast, I could only share their concern, and wonder what had happened to my friends the Schroeders, who hopefully were now in Costa Rica. The stories of flooding, devastation and chaos were pretty hair-raising, and I was more than grateful that I had missed it and was heading in the other direction.

Transferring to the tourist coach at Whites City we went on to the Caverns, a series of vast limestone vaults 7-900 feet underground that had been explored for the first time in 1901 and later, as the world came to learn of their wonders, established as a National Park. The limestone formations that were their principal attraction were the result of an incredible million-year process; the caves themselves the work of earth movements, back in the age that had built the Rockies.

The tour started at a natural entrance a short distance from the Visitor's Centre, a vast and forbidding gape in the earth. Through this aperture a procession of about 150 slightly apprehensive tourists – myself included – were led by a ranger of the National Park Service, following a steeply descending path into what appeared, to glare-conditioned eyes, to be a pit of eternal darkness.

After a descent of about a hundred feet we had lost the daylight and were dependent on the electric lamps spaced along the trail, a hesitant glimmer that was just sufficient to light our way without disturbing the surrounding darkness. The black space above us, though impenetrable to the eye, had a presence that became more tangible as we went on, an uncanny aliveness that shortly manifested itself in a great whirring sound. As one, the procession froze.

Reassuringly our guide flashed his lamp upwards, revealing a flurry of tiny winged creatures close to the roof of the chamber. 'Bats,' he said. 'We got quite a few of them up there – about eight million.'

He continued, with disturbing nonchalance, to describe the evening flight of the bats, when they left the caves in search of food. This flight, one of the park's greatest attractions, lasted four hours. 'It was the bats that first drew attention to the caves, back at the turn of the century. Then they got opened up, on account of what they found here.'

His beam travelled downwards, to play over the floor of the chamber and the dark midden that covered it. The bat guano, rich in nitrates, made a first-rate fertiliser, and it was one of the original team of miners who had taken time off to explore what lay beyond the dim light of the mining lamps. His experiences were to become ours as we followed the path his uncertain steps had taken, sixty-odd years ago.

At the auditorium leading into the main corridor of the caverns the guide gave us some history. The first lesson was to distinguish between 'stalactites', which stuck 'tight' to the cavern roof, and 'stalagmites', which 'might' make it to the roof. Having equipped us with this basic geological knowledge he then went on to the more mandatory lessons, which included not wandering from the trails, not touching any of the limestone formations and not picking up any loose material. These were reasonable instructions, but I had to crib at the photography rule, which forbade flash or time exposures. Such photography, it was stated, caused not only potential damage to the light-sensitive formations but unnecessary delays to the progress of the tour, which had to cover a distance of three miles in the same number of hours.

The outward leg of the tour, taking us to a depth of 829 feet, was the most strenuous. The increasingly steep descent took us through huge rock-strewn passages that presented us with the first artefacts of one of nature's most extraordinary processes. This was the final phase in the development of the caverns: the addition of 'furniture' to the 'rooms' already created by the action of earth movements and water solution. Hanging from the ceiling and thrusting up from the floor were the pinnacle shapes of the limestone deposits, formed by the gradual seepage into the chamber of rainwater and snowmelt. On evaporation each droplet of moisture had left its mineral content to add to a growing deposit that over the centuries had achieved unbelievable dimensions.

Fulfilling the natural desire of Americans to put a label on everything, the 'rooms' bore such names as the 'King's Palace', 'Queen's Chamber', 'Green Lake Room' and 'Papoose Room' – names that described some feature of the chamber or its formations. The representational aspect of these had, of course, been exploited to the full, and although in most cases the association was obvious ('Queen's Draperies', 'King's Bellcord') there was some confusion in my mind about the 'Bashful Elephant' and the 'Frustrated Lovers'. And were those funny little knob shapes really meant to be papooses?

After a fifty-foot climb up 'Appetite Hill' – the most appropriately named of all – we arrived at the lunchroom. This, believe it or not, was the most flattening experience of my American tour. To toil for one and three-quarter hours down tortuous slippery paths to a subterranean depth of more than 800 feet and then to be confronted by Formica, stainless steel and soda fountains was, to say the least of it, disenchanting. It seemed that all the amenities, excepting overnight accommodation, were there: the few weeks' work of a catering concession effectively counteracting the work of 200 million years. Where else but America would you get a cafeteria and restrooms 750 feet below ground?

The last hour of the tour was spent in the 'Big Room', a modest title for an immense chamber that we were told covered fourteen acres and measured 2,000 feet from end to end, with a top ceiling height of 285 feet. By statistics alone this chamber was a cathedral among grottoes, with its spires, pillars and statues. The shapes were breathtaking: some huge and dome-topped and telescoping upwards, others long and narrow and hanging like giant organ pipes. Where stalagmite met stalactite their union created a long slender column from floor to ceiling, a fantastic creation which showed what nature could achieve if left long enough to her own devices. These 'live' formations, glistening with moisture, had a superbly translucent quality, like polished white marble. The most impressive was the 'Crystal Spring Dome', which added an inch to its stature every 6,000 years. Resting on its laurels at sixty-two feet was the 'Giant Dome', the work of four and a half million years.

Many of the formations were still growing, a fact dramatically illustrated by the guide when at the throw of a switch he extinguished all the lights and asked us to pause and listen for two minutes. In the eerie, hushed darkness the regular drip-drip sound was unmistakable.

From the Caverns the tourist bus took me via Whites City to the town of Carlsbad, a one-horse place whose only redeeming feature was the bus depot. My new destination, passing from the state of New Mexico to the state of Arizona, was Tucson, and here I met an unexpected snag. The ticket clerk had some peculiar notion that instead of going by the most direct route to Tucson – via El Paso – I would have to go via Albuquerque, 300 miles to the north. The reason for this, he said, was that the 99-day ticket prohibited me from covering the same route twice, and I could not go back to El Paso. I protested that I knew nothing of this restriction, and was sure he was mistaken. The El Paso bus, I pointed out, left in two hours, whereas the one for Albuquerque didn't leave until 7.15 in the morning. What did he expect me to do – spend the night in the bus depot?

His expression, or lack of it, implied that he didn't think this would be such a bad idea, which left me with only one option. Laying out my US map on the counter I asked his advice on the alternative routes to Tucson that were permitted by Greyhound, going by way of any city up to and including New York. He gazed blankly at the map, which covered the entire counter, and without saying anything began to trace a route westwards with his finger. After a moment or so he stopped, as though reaching traffic lights. Pulling a book of tickets from a drawer he wrote one out for El

Paso. 'Sooner they do away with these — ninety-nine-day tickets the better...'

Returning to a bench I sat down to wait for the bus. I was welcomed by an elderly lady who came to sit beside me, clucking sympathetically about the obtuseness of ticket clerks. To console me for my 'bit of trouble' she offered me an orange and a pack of sandwiches, which I accepted gratefully. Unwrapping them I was disconcerted to find a dollar bill tucked inside. Before I could say anything I was tapped on the shoulder and looked up to see the Mexican couple whom I had met on the bus to the Caverns. The man was thrusting a second dollar bill into my hand, taking advantage of my now total confusion to say how sorry he and his wife were that I had had the inconvenience and that this was the smallest thing they could do for me as I was such a long way from home.

I was touched, embarrassed and everything else – but knew better than to refuse the gifts. It was an act of spontaneous generosity that I would remember for a long time. For longer, I hoped, than the words (relayed to me by Michael) of the organiser of the English teachers' party on the voyage to New York. Laying down a code of ethics for the teachers during their stay in America he had suggested that 'although as Englishmen they were accustomed to a lower standard of living than the Americans they should try, if possible, to avoid accepting charity while they were in the States.'

Tucson to Flagstaff

A Waterhole in the Desert

I spent the two dollars on a steak and beer in El Paso waiting for the Tucson bus. The blow-out induced the right state of drowsiness for the night run, and I slept through until dawn reclaimed me on the outskirts of the city. It could not have been a better moment. My first glimpse of Arizona included a stand of saguaro cactus, a winking radio beacon and the pink pre-sunrise light on the Santa Catalina Mountains.

Arizona was surely the most wondrous of all the states, unequalled in the variety and splendour of its landscapes. It would be easy here to slip into the language of the scenic guide, the tourist hand-out. To spare the superlatives I will list just a few of its attractions, to give an idea of the range.

Arizona has the Colorado River, the Hoover Dam and Lake Mead. It has the Petrified Forest, the Painted Desert and Monument Valley. The prehistoric ruins of the Canyon de Chelly, Navajo National Monument and Montezuma Castle. The National Monuments of Tuzigoot, Wupatki, Tonto and Casa Grande. The

Tucson Mountain Park and the Saguaro National Monument. The Chiricahua National Monument, Meteor Crater and Sunset Crater. The San Francisco Peaks, Superstition Mountain and the Santa Catalinas. It also has the Grand Canyon.

On history it has less of a claim, if you are solely considering the story of the USA, which only entered these parts with the Gadsden Purchase of 1854. This was the acquisition of another huge chunk of real estate by the government (this time from Mexico), which added large areas of Southern Arizona and New Mexico to US territory. Before that, the tenancy of the American Indian tribes extended into prehistoric times, from the Cochise through the Basketmakers to the still surviving Pueblo culture. The tenancy of the Spaniards was less enduring – not quite 300 years – and that of the Mexicans a mere thirty. After them had come the trappers, the Mormons and the copper miners, the latter creating the boom towns that had given rise to another, more notorious trade. Less productive but more dramatic than mining were the activities of such gentlemen as Marshall Wyatt Earp, Doc Holliday and the Clanton brothers, in the streets and corrals of a town called Tombstone.

If you were looking for a real battle, i.e. one involving more than a few trigger-happy folk heroes, then Arizona provided the Battle of Picacho Pass (1862), the only military contest fought on her soil. This occurred in the Civil War and involved no fewer than sixteen Confederates and twelve Union soldiers, three of whom were killed in the encounter. Despite the military advantage that this would seem to have given the Confederacy, Arizona became a territory of the United States the following year.

Without any dates or events or National Historical Sites to preoccupy me I could devote my attention to my natural surroundings, delights for the eye that owed little to anything written in books. The saguaro, whose majesty had so impressed me in that early dawn glimpse, was the first object of my curiosity. After checking into the Tucson 'Y' I made immediate plans to travel out to the Tucson Mountain Park, which edged the Saguaro National Monument. My objective was the Arizona-Sonora Living Desert Museum, a unique exhibition of the animals, plants and geology of the region common to the states of Arizona and Sonora, Mexico. As with other attractions, I had learned about the Museum in my wildlife magazine, *Animals*. Located in the heart of cactus country, about twelve miles west of Tucson, it was unfortunately not very accessible. Public transport had not yet put it on the map and all I could do was to call the museum for advice.

My call was answered by Lewis Wayne Walker, the Associate Director and another *Animals* contributor who had corresponded with me. He was very keen to meet me and show me the museum, and suggested that if I waited outside the 'Y' someone would be along in about half an hour to collect me.

The 'someone' turned out to be a student who was doing weekend work at the museum. In a bouncy Ford utility we drove out of the city, following the West Speedway Boulevard for a straight five miles and then heading into the Tucson Mountain Park. This area, first flat and then undulating, covered by a green and brown forest of cactus and desert shrubs, contained one of the most unusual plant habitats in the world. In this unique community the saguaro was the sentinel, standing tall and motionless with its spiny arms braced against the sky. Amongst them grew the familiar desert trees, the paloverde and mesquite, and at their feet an undergrowth of smaller cacti and plants, the most quickly recognisable the spidery ocotillo, the organ pipe cactus, the pancake-shaped pears and the spiny, silver-whiskered cholla.

At an isolated junction we drove past an extraordinary sight that made me wonder for a moment which century we were in. A crumbling adobe wall surrounded a collection of weather-beaten frame buildings, straight out of the Old West. The signboard said 'Old Tucson', and I learnt from my companion that it was a Columbia movie set, built in 1940, that was now used as an amusement park.

A further three miles brought us the spectacle of a shallow, horseshoe-shaped valley, the open side of the horseshoe providing a view across a wide, far-reaching plain. Tucked into a corner of the valley was a group of adobe buildings, barely perceptible in the scorched wilderness of its surroundings. As we drove down into the valley I could not help wondering how it had come about that such a remote and unobtrusive place could command such interest and attention in the zoological world.

I soon found out. Pulling into the car park in front of the museum we were greeted by the tall figure of a man whose shirt, slacks and hair were matching shades of iron grey. This was Lewis Wayne Walker, Associate Director of the Living Desert Museum. A sage of the desert, who for many years had dedicated himself to a study of the region denoted by the two flags at the entrance: those of Arizona and Sonora. Through writing and photography he had conveyed the wonders of the region to a world-wide audience, and in the small enclosures and buildings was the essence of his experience – a living microcosm of the desert.

As he led me through to the exhibit area my host told me that 'living' was a word they used quite a lot at the museum. 'We have to, on account of this word "museum",' he said. 'Before they come here a lot of people think our animals are stuffed and our plants are in glass cases.'

In a moment I saw what he meant. Behind the offices of the museum was the garden that contained the zoological and botanical exhibits, concentrating a vast natural habitat into an area of little more than ten acres. Walking along a row of barless concrete enclosures I saw, among the larger animals, a black bear, a mountain lion and a jaguar. Further on were coyotes, raccoons, peccaries and porcupines, and in a delightful separate exhibit a prairie dog village. This took the form of a deep square trough about fifteen feet wide which had been filled with earth and turned over to a family of prairie dogs.

These ferocious burrowers had quickly converted the enclosure into a home of their own, riddling the earth with tunnels. 'Villages' such as this, I learned, had once been ubiquitous in Arizona, extending for hundreds of miles across the plains. Despoilers of grassland, the prairie dogs had represented a serious threat to farmers and stockbreeders, and had been all but exterminated in a concerted poisoning campaign. The survivors led a constrained existence in isolated areas and wildlife refuges, reduced to a sad fraction of their former numbers. Studying the amusing antics of these little creatures – one moment squatting, the next disappearing into their holes – I wondered how they could merit such persecution.

At the southern boundary of the garden Lewis traced with

an outstretched arm the broad sweep of the plain, hazed on the horizon to blend with grey-blue mountain ranges. Those distant ranges, sixty miles to the south, were in Mexico, marking the border between Arizona and Sonora. Stretching towards this infinity were the scattered markers of the saguaro, scratching vertical lines on the landscape as far as the eye could see. It would have been difficult to imagine a more perfect location for the museum.

Left by my host to explore on my own I followed a sign saying 'Tunnel Exhibit'. The path took me along one of the botanical walks of the museum, a pleasant ramble that introduced me to many unusual cactus and plant species. With the assiduous labelling on either side of the trail it was easy to become an expert, and more so when the names – like those given to coral reef fishes and other natural curiosities – were so apposite. Hedgehog, beavertail, barrel, flapjack, pincushion and organ pipe were all names that made future identification simple. But there were other, more lyrical ones. The Joshua Tree, for example, had been so called by the Mormons as a reference to its uplifted branches, related in their eyes to the supplicating arms of their prophet.

King of the cacti was the saguaro (*carnegiea gigantea*). To this succulent colossus the museum had devoted a complete *ramada*, or shelter, containing an information exhibit. The saguaro, I learnt, could attain a height of fifty feet, a weight of several tons and a life span of 200 years. Its remarkable water-storage system enabled it to survive up to two years of drought, a survival that was essential to the maintenance of many forms of animal life in the desert. Here was the essential role of the saguaro, as a formidable part of the desert ecology.

Its benefits to the desert creatures were numerous. In temperatures of 110° or more its shade was at a high premium. Additionally it offered nesting sites to such birds as the Gila woodpecker, which was able to bore a sizeable hole in the cactus stem, and to the tiny elf owl, which invariably came along to occupy it later. Food and moisture could also be obtained from the saguaro, in the form of its fruit, and its roots, chewed by such creatures as the peccary to restore the water content of its body.

The other necessity for desert survival was effectively illustrated by the Tunnel Exhibit, an answer perhaps to those frustrated naturalists whose daylight hours were consumed in scouring the desert in search of its wildlife. During the daytime that wildlife was, of course, right under their feet.

On either side of the tunnel, located twelve feet underground, artificial dens had been created to simulate the burrows of the desert animals that dwelt below the surface in the daytime. Each of these subterranean dens was connected with an outdoor enclosure, but during the daytime the animals followed their natural inclination and retreated below, so it was possible during normal visiting hours to see most of the dens inhabited. The open side of the dens was glazed for viewing, with illuminated push-buttons to light their interiors. Cautiously I groped my way along the tunnel, and jumped as the inadvertent touch of a button revealed a rattlesnake, coiled a few inches from my hand. Tapping the glass to make sure that it was there, I passed on to another button. This time I was reassured by the sight of a family of prairie dogs, snuggled cosily together in their burrow.

Among the other animals that I discovered in this remarkable construction were a skunk, ring-tailed rat, porcupine, ferret, kit fox and coati – all primarily night hunters that went to earth in the daytime. Less endearing, but quite fascinating, was a colony of fruit-eating bats, hanging from artificial stalactites in a realistic 'bat cave'. As the light flickered on them they blinked confusedly, as if uncertain whether it was night or day.

After a captivating ten minutes with a nest of long-legged black ants (the nest convincingly their own creation) I ascended the slope to the tunnel exit. Emerging again into the burning sunlight I could appreciate the wisdom of the desert creatures.

On the way back to the museum I met Lewis, who invited me to the staff restaurant for lunch. The interior of the restaurant, cooled by its thick adobe walls, was a pleasant respite from the furnace outside. During the meal other members of the staff joined us, including the Curator of Exhibits, Mervyn Larson. Mervyn had worked with Lewis on the Tunnel Exhibit, and was now talking enthusiastically about the next project.

'We're calling it the "Vampire Bat Display",' he said, 'Nobody's ever done anything like it. We've got real blood-drinkers, in a blackened cave. You want to see them at feeding time, it's a honey.'

Happily this was not an invitation. Instead I went to the Museum office, where the two men showed me a selection of their colour slides of Arizona wildlife. This was no ordinary collection. Sheet after sheet of 35 and 120mm transparencies were laid before my astonished gaze, a pictorial encyclopedia of desert species. Although some showed Museum animals, most appeared to have been taken in the wild. How else could one capture a bobcat padding through the scrub or a mule deer drinking at a waterhole?

The waterhole was a recurrent feature of the photographs, the flash pictures of its night visitors the most remarkable in the collection. The diversity of these creatures, drawn to the same spot by a common need, was fascinating. The peccaries were in herds and the deer in small groups, drinking tentatively. Other animals, pictured individually, were a skunk, bobcat, coyote, badger, ring-tailed cat and grey fox. I asked Lewis, who had taken most of the shots, how he had managed to get them without frightening the animals away. And where had he found the waterhole?

His answer was to lead me outside. 'Let's take a walk, and I'll show you.'

I followed him to a small group of buildings, about fifty yards from the entrance to the Museum. One of these was Walker's house. Taking me round to the back he showed me a small cement construction, partially concealed by scrub.

'This is our Wildlife Photographic Blind,' he said. 'We used it for all those waterhole shots.'

The building was about twelve feet long by six wide and included four windows with shelves for cameras. A battery of lights was fixed to the front, with four flash reflectors. A few feet away from it, shielded by a creosote bush and a large saguaro cactus, was a waterhole.

Bewilderedly, I said: 'But I thought all those photos were taken miles out in the desert.'

Lewis smiled. 'What d'you mean? They *were* taken miles out in the desert!'

I pointed at the flash reflectors. 'Doesn't the flash startle the animals?'

Lewis shook his head. 'They don't even see it. We use

stroboscopic light. It's pretty intense, and pretty fast – 1/2,000th of a second.'

The flash could either be synchronised with the camera shutters at the press of a button, or used in an open exposure. The latter technique was less often employed, Lewis told me, now that the whole area was illuminated with electric lighting. 'We have the lights on all the time at night,' he said. 'The animals have got pretty used to them – won't come near the place if they're not switched on.'

The whole idea of wild animals being photographed in this way seemed slightly improper: making *them* come to the camera rather than taking the camera into the wild. And sublimely easy; like switching on a TV nature programme. Perhaps I should admit to a degree of envy, that anyone could have such a wealth of wildlife wandering into his backyard every night.

Looking at the waterhole, a small rock-girt pool no more than two or three feet wide, I thought of a problem that so far Lewis hadn't mentioned. 'What happens in the dry season – doesn't the water dry up?'

He smiled. 'Not this one. Started as a leak in a water-pipe some time ago. The animals found it and used it as a drinking pool, so instead of patching it up we made it permanent. We keep a supply of water running into it, all year round, so that even when the other waterholes dry up – the natural ones – the animals have still got somewhere to drink.'

This artificial oasis, I learnt, was at times the only water supply in an area of twenty square miles. That helped to put the blind, and the waterhole, in their right perspective. Exposure to flash bulbs was, after all, a small inconvenience for a thirsty animal whose life might be saved by a drink of water.

One other potential hazard occurred to me. 'Some of the animals are a natural prey to others,' I said. 'What happens when they arrive together at the waterhole?'

Lewis nodded knowingly, suggesting he'd come upon an unknown secret of the desert. 'That's a new law of nature we discovered here. The carnivores such as the bobcat and fox give way to the deer, which always get the first drink.'

Back in his office Lewis gave me notes about the museum

for my article. Its key purpose, he told me, was public education. This did not merely involve the correct labelling of exhibits, but knowing how to talk natural history to a growing public. A constant flow of visitors, letters, telephone calls and TV programmes had underscored the Museum's standing as a leading natural history resource: supplying the right answers was the daily routine of a dedicated staff.

To illustrate the point the telephone rang, the caller a worried lady in Tucson. For a few minutes Lewis listened to her agitated voice, his expression growing increasingly quizzical. 'A rattlesnake – in your swimming pool? A *dead* rattlesnake? No, lady, I assure you. You don't have to change the water.'

Smiling, he put the phone down. 'Yet another example of the Museum's contribution to public education,' he said.

Mervyn Larson lived in Tucson, where he kept a very unusual pet. I first learnt about Frances on the way back to town in Mervyn's car, sitting on the front seat between Mervyn and his wife. Mrs Larson had come to collect her husband, and most of the way they were discussing Frances, who appeared from the conversation to be an elderly female relative, rather fastidious in her tastes and habits. It was only when I got to the Larsons' and went with them into the back yard, that I discovered Frances' real identity.

'*Frances! Frances!*'

My host, leaning over the gate of a small earthen compound, called the name softly. The sun had almost set and I tried unsuccessfully to discern a movement in the gloom. All I could see were the dark openings of one or two holes, burrowed in the earth, which considerably increased my curiosity.

A sudden scurrying noise alerted me and I beheld a thickset, cumbersome creature advancing out of the darkness. Dark-furred, flat-headed and barred from nose to tail with a broad white stripe. An unusual-looking beast, last seen in an underground tunnel in the desert. Frances was an American badger.

With a final scurry she flung herself against the gate, which Mervyn promptly opened. She waddled out, for all her squatness a rather imperial figure, proffering her chin for a courtesy tickle. We followed her at a respectful distance into the house. Once indoors she immediately assumed control of the household, scampering from room to room and inspecting each item of furniture to make sure it was in its proper place. Ten minutes of this slithering, scurrying activity were necessary before she could reach a pact with her surroundings and settle, with regal condescension, on a window-seat. She was then able to receive her admirers, responding rapturously to our stroking and tickling.

During dinner that evening the Larsons told me that Frances had been captured in the wild, and that her adoption as a family pet had been very much an experiment. Her transition to her new living quarters had been greatly assisted by the pen at the back of the house, in which she'd been able to burrow to her heart's content. The rest had been a question of her acceptance of the Larsons – as a friendly and accommodating pair of humans – and her adjustment to the life of suburban Tucson. After the rigours of the Arizona-Sonora desert it had been an unsettling change of scene. But Frances had made it. Like her fellow Americans, the good life had won her over.

One hunded and twenty miles to the north of Tucson, in the state capital of Phoenix, I was the victim of a holocaust. No other word can describe the effect of that naked Arizona sun, beating off the sidewalks in the downtown area. As I walked from the bus depot to the 'Y' I felt like a lizard emerging from beneath a stone.

Fortunately the 'Y' was only a short distance and I stumbled gratefully into the air-conditioned lobby. When I asked about the temperature, the desk clerk sighed. 'Same as yesterday, I guess. Hundred and five.'

The only refuge was the swimming pool. Swimming, I discovered, was just one of the recreations offered by the Phoenix YMCA, which for the sports fanatic must have been the nearest place to Paradise. Judo, wrestling, weight-lifting, basketball, karate and athletics were all on the programme, administered by a regiment of Mr Universes with 'Physical Staff' emblazoned on their vests. These trotting, chest-expanding figures were a natural hazard of the place, appearing unexpectedly at every turn of the corridors like human steamrollers. Rather than be (a) flattened or (b) recruited for karate I kept out of their way, either submerged in the swimming pool or stretched out on the sundeck. During my stay at the Phoenix 'Y' the only serious activity I pursued was the study of a map, detailing the location of Arizona's scenic attractions.

The problem was, as before, to discover which places were accessible by Greyhound, and which – of those not on the Greyhound routes – were a prospect either by local transport or hitchhiking. For all its tantalising spectacle Monument Valley, in the north-east corner of the state (featured in all those famous John Ford movies) had to be omitted as too lengthy a detour, and with it a number of Pueblo ruins that could be reached only by car. The great asteroid impact site, the Meteor Crater, was similarly unattainable.

I decided to devote my energies to the Grand Canyon – served by tourist buses from Flagstaff – and the area to the south-east of it, which included the Petrified Forest and the Painted Desert. Both of these were crossed by the famous US Highway 66, a major Greyhound bus route.

About eighty miles to the north of Phoenix, on the road to Flagstaff, I had marked one site with an affirmative cross – the Montezuma Castle National Monument. This was an indigenous cliff dwelling built about 700 years ago that was one of the few survivors of the Pueblo culture and a perfect example of their unique architecture. On the map it appeared to be just to the right of the highway, which made it convenient for hopping off the bus. But distances on the map were deceptive, as I discovered at the Greyhound Information Centre in Phoenix. Montezuma Castle was in fact five miles from the small town of Camp Verde, itself a couple of miles from the road. Greyhound did not offer services to either destination, but if I went across the street to Trailways they would fit me in on a bus to Camp Verde.

Transferring to Continental Trailways was rather like going over to the other side. But it appeared that the two major bus companies – whose routes did not entirely coincide – had an agreement to transfer passengers who wished to travel on any route that was covered by only one of the companies. Apart from their slightly differing routes, there was a similarity between the services, both of which offered the conveniences of air-conditioning, restroom, reclining seats and panoramic vision. And, need it be said, a regular and reliable schedule. An indication of the range of the rival Trailways system was the sign that I spotted in the bus which read 'Smoking on this Bus Prohibited by Law while in the State of New Jersey'.

The route north from Phoenix, the Black Canyon Highway, was a fast run through desert country that became, by a gradual processing of the landscape, the prospect of mountain and high mesa. The difference in elevation between Phoenix and Flagstaff was almost 6,000 feet, but the transition was made over a distance of 140 miles, the foothills looming larger with each turn of the road. In such a setting human beings seemed strangely diminished, ant-like creatures at the mercy of the forces that had thrown up the great ranges millions of years ago.

I watched a rickety wagon approaching, drawn by three burros and driven by a couple of hillbillies, that clung precariously to the side of the road. As we passed them, the Trailways driver raised his hand in salute.

'They was bus drivers, once.'

At midday we reached the Camp Verde turn-off and left the highway to drive along the winding, two-mile road that led us to the town, a one-horse place that before the advent of Trailways must have run the poor creature into the ground. As I got off the bus I was discouraged to learn from the driver that buses called there only once a day, and if I wanted to continue to Flagstaff that night I needed to hitch a lift back to the highway and flag down the next Trailways bus on the Glen Canyon route, which passed the turn-off at approximately 11.30pm.

So much for 'hopping on a bus'. Squatting on my rucksack at the side of the road, and watching the vehicle turn for its run back to the highway, I gave myself time for reflection. Touring America, it seemed, was not just a question of working out bus schedules. It was the first time, since starting out, that I had to think seriously about walking.

Leaving my rucksack at the Montezuma Inn, a bar-restaurant that doubled as the Camp Verde bus depot, I commenced my hike to the Verde Valley. In such a backwoods area I was reassured to find myself on a broad, paved road. If this was an indication of the popularity of the site, then I could hope for a procession of cars, driven by friendly natives, shortly to arrive. As it was the first time I had attempted to walk anywhere in the American wild, I needed that kind of hope to sustain me.

The road was peculiarly quiet and I must have gone three miles before I was offered a ride in a Chevrolet pickup. Unfortunately this ride was good for a mile only, and I was left to walk the last mile to the Montezuma Castle Visitor Center. So much effort deserved its reward and before I bought my ticket to view the ruin I had no less than three glorious, burpy Coca-Colas.

After this sublime self-indulgence any ruin would be an anti-climax and so it was with Montezuma Castle, a part-stone, part-adobe cliff dwelling built in the cavity of a hundred-foot wall of limestone. The shelf that supported it was about fifty feet up, and to my dismay I could find no way of reaching it. At one time, apparently, ladders had been in position, which could be withdrawn for defensive purposes. Nowadays these had been removed to preserve the ancient building from the ravages of scrambling tourists (and to preserve the tourists as well, I assumed). Two hundred thousand visitors a year was, after all, a slightly different proposition to the forty or fifty people who had originally inhabited it.

Montezuma Castle – so named by early Spanish settlers who believed it had been built by Aztecs fleeing from Mexico – drastically changed my picture of the legendary American Indian. No more the whooping brave, knee-hugging his palamino, but a quiet, sedentary artisan-farmer whose time was divided between agriculture, crafts and building. These Indians, the pre-Columbian Sinagua people, were of the Pueblo culture, which meant that they lived in stable communities with permanent dwellings, themselves known as 'pueblos'. They were confined to distinct regions of the south-west, notably the northern river valleys of what was now Arizona and New Mexico. But the differences between them and the much later nomadic tribes in neighbouring regions – particularly the warrior Apaches and Navajo – were considerable.

These differences stemmed from the inclination of the Pueblo builders' ancestors towards agriculture, an activity that over the years had become increasingly sophisticated. By efficient irrigation systems and the introduction of refined varieties of maize they were able to produce crops that were surplus to their needs: an important advance that allowed them to turn their energies away from farming towards other pursuits. For the Sinagua, when the battle for survival had been won, the work of perpetuation could begin.

In the Visitor Center I had seen the native beadwork, weaving and jewellery that were the artistic achievements of more leisured times. The practical achievements, on the other hand, had been in architecture, the gradual development of the Pueblo dwellings from simple stone-walled pit houses to the elaborate stone and adobe structures of four or five storeys of which this ruin was an example. The materials were the conventional sun-dried brick, made from clay mixed with straw, local limestone and timber – in this case the sycamore that abounded in the Verde Valley. The wooden joists, poking out from the clay-daubed walls, supported ceilings of branches and reeds bound with mud, the roofs of the lower rooms serving as the floors for the upper. If they'd been around at the time, the apartment builders of Manhattan would have looked no further for inspiration.

I wondered what had become of the Sinagua civilisation, which had reached its peak during Europe's Dark Age and then, quite unaccountably, disappeared. One could not, for once, blame the white man. One hundred and fifty years before the arrival of the Spanish the last of the ancient Pueblo villages had been abandoned, the inhabitants departing for reasons that remained a mystery. Drought, over-population, plundering by enemy tribes – any or all of these might have led to the exodus. In different parts of the south-west the Pueblo tradition had been maintained, but without the dynamic that had created the monuments of its golden age.

With a couple of hours' daylight in hand I started the walk back to Camp Verde. As bad luck would have it there were no cars going my way and it was dusk before I reached town, swaying into the main street like an unhorsed cowboy. My aching legs took me back to the Montezuma Inn, where I pitched into a stall with a groan of relief. I was hungry as well as tired and I ordered a halibut steak, bread rolls and coffee from a waitress who gave me the attention that I commanded as her solitary customer.

After despatching my meal in a little under five minutes, I looked at my watch and realised that I would need to take a little longer over the coffee. The Trailways bus was not due at the highway junction for another four hours. Allowing an hour for getting to the highway it would still need to be a pretty large cup.

The waitress, who must have been a mind-reader, came over and assured me that it was in fact a bottomless cup, and I could top it up as I pleased for no extra charge. The absence of other customers might have been a motive for encouraging me to stay, but I didn't question her generosity. It wasn't until I'd consumed my fifth cup that she began to cool off a bit.

Eventually one or two people came into the restaurant and her attention was happily diverted. In turn I was granted the diversion of an old-timer in buckskin who sat beside me with a drink and went straight into the story of his life. As most of it had been spent in Camp Verde the details were not very enthralling, the key facts being that he owned a pickup and drove around the neighbourhood doing odd jobs. When I told him I was about to set out for the highway to meet a bus, he acted the part I had written for him.

'Guess I c'd run y'up to the junction...'

With spirits soaring I picked up my rucksack from the girl at the counter and followed him outside. The car was a weather-beaten Ford that had been used, as far as I could judge, for carrying cattle. We got in and I listened while the old man tried the ignition a few times. All he got was a grudging cough.

In a flat voice he told me that the battery was gone, and there wasn't anything he could do. 'Don't look like I'm going to take you anywhere, son.' Those weren't my lines at all.

It was now completely dark, without the ghost of a moon, and once off the main street of the town I had to feel my way to the road that ran up to the highway. There was no road lighting and it was like walking into a black void, with the sensation that until each foot touched the ground there was nothing there. My only guide was the occasional pale glimmer from the porch or curtained window of a house, revealing itself unexpectedly after a tree-shrouded bend. To add to my discomfort, I was carrying the rucksack, the first time I'd attempted to go any real distance with it. Walking with the delicacy of an elephant under the forty-five-pound weight was a new exercise in self-torture and I was compelled at frequent intervals to rest, loosening the thing from my shoulders. The knowledge that it was only two miles to the highway did nothing to lighten the weight, nor the creepiness of walking on a strange road at night.

By the time the car arrived I'd given up all hope of getting a lift and was almost indifferent to the screech of brakes and the high school voice that called out to me.

'Wanna ride, pop?'

The headlights winked at me and I was tempted to ignore them. Being called 'son' and 'pop' in the same half-hour was not good for the morale. Fatigue conquered dudgeon however and I climbed in beside the tousle-haired sixteen-year-old.

At full throttle we sped up the road, my driver punishing the gears like a teenage Fangio. Above the roar of the engine I learnt that the car had begun life as a Chevrolet automatic before being converted to a four-speed gear-box. 'It's a hot rod – put it in myself.'

Such technical refinements were lost on me. I only knew that we were at the highway before my driver had reached overdrive. He seemed surprised that I should ask to be dropped at that point and I assured him that it wasn't anything to do with his driving or his car.

The half-hour that followed, while I waited for the Trailways bus, was a nervous ordeal. The turn-off was not a scheduled stop and at the right moment I would have to step out and flag the bus. In the darkness this wouldn't be easy, but to make it more difficult the spot at which I was standing and where the bus could pull in, lay just after a bend. The traffic was moving at about 50mph and I had only a second or two to decide which of the succession of headlights beaming into view belonged to Trailways. Those seconds were vital, if I wasn't going to spend the night sleeping under a hedge.

When it finally arrived the bus was unmistakeable, with its multiple roof-lights and glaring double headlamps. But it was also fifteen minutes late – time for me to have lost my last vestige of composure. As the bus approached I leapt out in front of it, waving my arms.

The driver, riding his air brakes, must have thought I was a madman. Attempting either to cause or prevent a major accident. When I climbed on board and asked if it was the Flagstaff bus he looked a little rancorous. Trying hard, no doubt, to remember his passenger courtesy rules.

The Grand Canyon

'Seven Hours Down and
Eight Hours Up'

A late arrival in Flagstaff, around 1am, meant a night at the depot, something I hadn't experienced since those twilight hours in the New York Bus Terminal. Sleep, to my dismay, was out of the question, the accommodation in the waiting room being confined to a row of tubular steel chairs designed to accommodate anything but the human frame. In an attempt to adapt their limitations to those of my anatomy I jammed two of them together and threaded my legs between them. Lying thus, with a third chair supporting my upper body and the rucksack a bolster for my back, I threw my open sleeping bag like a quilt over the top and pretended to be comfortable. After five excruciating minutes, however, I found myself helplessly trapped and obliged to seek the aid of a fellow 'dosser' in extricating me. This fellow, a student, had opted for the simplicity of the floor. It seemed that he had the right idea, but any inclination I might have had to join him was discouraged by the sub-zero draught that blew in from the street every time the waiting room door was opened.

At daylight I eased myself out of whichever chair was

supporting me and hobbled unsteadily to the restroom, there to gaze at the apparition in the mirror. Confronting me was a fugitive from society: a grey-faced, baggy-eyed, unshaven image that could have launched a thousand analgesics. Stroking the bristle on my neck and chin, I wondered if it was worth shaving, or whether I should come to terms with the fact that for the next few days I would be roughing it. In the midst of these deliberations my companion of the night entered, vigorously running his hands over his shaggy cheeks and through the mane of hair that hung about his shoulders. Turning a cold tap on full blast he stripped to the waist, revealing a bony chest covered in wire wool. In such company I was loth to undo the top button of my shirt, let alone produce a battery shaver.

In the Post House Cafeteria, chewing on the carbonised strips that masqueraded as bacon, I looked around at my assorted breakfast companions. A twilight gathering of well-wrapped and booted explorers who like me were on their way to view the greatest spectacle on earth.

Most of them were of the student-tourist fraternity, and I was soon approached by a couple of youths – a Scot and a Geordie – canvassing for passengers for a car they'd hired. They already had two girls lined up and the addition of a fifth person would reduce the cost to $4 a head for the ninety-mile trip. Calculating that this was little more than I would pay for the return fare on the tourist bus (there was no Greyhound or Trailways service) I agreed. By seven o'clock we were on our way in a smart new Ford Mustang, heading northwards for the South Rim of the Grand Canyon.

Entering the Colorado Plateau the road ran flat and straight and we maintained a steady 75mph, wavering only slightly when a high wind caught us or the Scots lad misjudged the steering. In addition to the cooler atmosphere we were able to enjoy sporadic glimpses of the tallest peaks of the San Francisco range, 12,000 feet or more.

Sagebrush-covered flats gave way to forested areas, a pleasingly varied landscape. But before I could compose any letters of approval to the Department of the Interior we drove past notices offering lots for '$5 down, $10 a month' rental. The 'scenic location' of the sites could not be disputed, but I wondered how the developers were describing their other virtues. What could one say, after all, about a bare strip of earth on a deserted roadside, without any visible amenities? 'Magnificent View of Through Route to Grand Canyon'?

At the south gateway we drove into the Grand Canyon National Park. In two miles, peering through the pine trees that fringed the rim, we had our first view of the mighty void. Stopping at a lookout point we jumped out and hurried to the edge of the canyon.

Camera at the ready, I tried not to be overwhelmed by the hazy vastness of the space before me, the work of seven million years, or by the knowledge that I was as immaterial as one of those tiny creatures from prehistory, recorded in the rock layers a mile beneath us. The job was to focus my lens, but that was near to impossible with the blurry rim of the north side nine miles away and the agglomeration of intermediate ranges rising from the canyon floor. With the picture taken, my vision cleared and I asked myself why I found it necessary to record an image that went beyond any visual bounds to enter the realm of the spiritual.

I saw the terraced layers of rock that made up the mountains and the walls of the canyon, immense shelving masses shaped by a river that through the millennia had scoured its way to invisible depths. In the bared stratification limestone, sandstone and shale combined in bands of red and buff and purple, colours that merged in the distance under the shimmering veil of the heat haze. It was a picture I had seen a hundred times, in photographs and films, and countless times in my imagination, during the long westward journey. But the experience I had not been able to anticipate was the silence. A magnificent, bombed-cathedral silence that reduced voices to whispers, thoughts to abstractions. How welcome at this moment to be spared the lecture, the breathless commentary telling us how wide, deep, timeless and majestic it was!

Words may have seemed an irrelevance, but further along the rim we found the Yavapai Museum and a park ranger who was doing his best to prove otherwise. Standing in front of an observation window, he recounted the story of the Grand Canyon.

'Seven million years ago that was just a flat plain out there, with the Colorado running through it. Now look at what that river's done – cut a great gash in the earth, 217 miles long, nine miles wide and a mile deep. How did it happen? Truth is, it wasn't just the river that did it. There were other natural forces, like earth movements. The land rose, all the time the river was cutting down, and the sides of the canyon were formed. Then landslides took the sides away, and the rocks that fell in the river acted like millstones on the bottom, gouging it deeper. If you go down into the heart of the canyon, you'll see the different rock layers that were exposed as the river cut through them – geological strata dating back to the Precambrian.

'There's something else you'll see if you go down into the canyon, and that's life zones. A life zone, as you most probably know, is an area in which you find an association of plants and animals peculiar to a particular climate. In the New World there are seven major life zones, ranging from the dry-tropical at the equator to the Arctic-alpine in the polar region. The zones occur mostly according to latitude, but some places you get different zones in a single latitude when the elevation changes from low to high. The bottom of the Grand Canyon lies at around 2,000 feet: the North Rim goes up to nine. At the bottom you'll find cactus, agave and yucca; on the rim spruce, fir and pine. On the bottom you'll find chuckawallas, rattlesnakes and other desert creatures; on the rim squirrels and mountain chickadees. Between the bottom and the rim lie five different life zones, all with their own indigenous animals and plant life.'

He went on to describe the characteristics of each zone, using a cross-section map of the canyon to show where they occurred. My explorer's instincts were aroused.

Later on we drove into the Grand Canyon Tourist Village. While the others shopped for a picnic lunch I slipped into the Park Headquarters. At the information desk I asked, rather tentatively, how long it would take to hike down into the canyon.

The man at the desk, who was probably paid to discourage such enterprises, nailed me with a penetrating stare. 'Coming up again?'

Uncertain whether it was a serious question, I nodded.

'Round trip fifteen hours,' he said. 'Seven hours down and eight hours up.' Handing me a leaflet headed 'Grand Canyon

National Park – Information for Hikers' he added, 'You better have a read of that, 'fore you think any more about it.'

Outside I examined the leaflet, which offered advice to anyone attempting a journey on foot into the canyon. My attention focused on the opening paragraphs, which emphasised that the experience was the reverse of mountain climbing, all the effort involved at the end of the trip rather than the earlier stages. The other points were not exactly encouraging:

'Canyon temperatures during the summer months frequently rise above 110°, sometimes as high as 120°, and cases of heat stroke or heat exhaustion are not uncommon.'

'Water supplies in the canyon are not dependable on any of the trails...'

'During high summer heat it is recommended that each hiker carry no less than one half-gallon of water per day while descending into the canyon and one gallon per day while ascending.'

'Emergency mule service is expensive...'

At the picnic table the others were discussing the question, but in a rather off-hand way that implied they had little intention of going the course. When I showed them the National Park guidelines they seemed glad to have confirmation of their doubts.

'An eight-mile trail to the Colorado River? That's sixteen miles, there and back.'

'And eight miles of it climbing up.'

'What would happen if you sprained your ankle?'

'They'd send a mule down, for twenty-five dollars.'

'How long would it take to get down there and back?'

'If we started now, we wouldn't be back 'til three o'clock in the morning.'

'And we only have the car for a day...'

Such down-to-earth realism was too much for me. In silence I ate a couple of sandwiches and downed a Coke, working on a plan to go it alone. I figured that if I set out immediately, and kept up a smart pace, I could reach the bottom by nightfall. Then, if I took my sleeping bag, I could spend the night by the Colorado and start the return climb at dawn.

With gathering resolution I went in search of a water canteen at the National Park's general stores. There was a rack full of them and I picked out a plastic one with '1.5 gallons' marked on the front. Turning it over I saw the price label: $6. This prompted some screwball calculations. Six dollars was more than a whole day's budget – a budget that I had already broken several times. On the other hand I would be spending a day down in the canyon, and could probably survive quite well on a gallon and a half of water. It seemed that I was going beyond the world of speculation into one of fantasy.

When I rejoined the others they were clearly waiting for some indication of my plans. I did, after all, have a stake in the car, and if I was going to disappear into the limbo they would want to know about it. To set their minds at rest I suggested a short excursion down the Bright Angel Trail, one of the two trails leading from the South Rim into the canyon. Measured against the 'through trip' to the river this could hardly rate as a compromise, but it did offer the essential experience of the canyon's interior, lost to those who merely viewed it from the rim. The faint-hearted Brits seemed happy with the deal.

Inside the canyon everything was stillness. The effect of this was difficult to define, but it seemed that once below the rim we were cut off from the world we knew and were entering another that was under the sovereignty of a supernatural power. An earthly Elysium where neither sound nor time had any place. By this token humans too would seem excluded, and effectively were. The physical features of the canyon presented a daunting obstacle to their incursions, and the trails to the bottom of the canyon – two on the south side and one on the north – though used for centuries by the native Americans, were clearly the last frontier.

The further we descended, the more the silence enclosed and enthralled us. It was like being inside a huge natural vacuum chamber, without a breath of wind to stir the branches of the juniper or the dusty leaves of the pinyon pine growing from the slopes. Then, as our ears sharpened, the other sounds began to intrude. The incessant vibration of the cicadas in the undergrowth, and the rustle of lizards as they skittered through pine needles at the side of the trail.

The birds, too, made their presence known, most conspicuously the elusive swallows and black, narrow-winged swifts, their darting shapes almost lost against the vastness of the canyon wall, their wing-beats swallowed by space. Elsewhere the distant chatter of a nuthatch or the whirring motor of a hummingbird's wings would have been a phenomenon, but here such sounds, natural to their environment, went almost unnoticed.

Others, man-made, came as intrusions. The toppling of a rock, dislodged from the side of the trail, alerted us to the emergence behind us of half-a-dozen muleback riders, led by a wrangler in a turned-down Stetson. These were, perhaps, some ordinary citizens who, experiencing a reawakening of the pioneer spirit, had leapt out of their armchairs and telephoned a reservation for a mule trip into the Grand Canyon. Looking down at the great abyss that lay below them, I wondered how many of them would satisfy their urge.

Far, far below I spotted another column of riders, moving like a line of ants across a projecting plateau. This was the Tonto Plateau, from which it was possible to obtain – at Plateau Point – the first good view of the Colorado River. Access to this point, about 3,200 feet below the South Rim, was from the Tonto Trail, which followed the south side of the canyon and involved from start to finish a strenuous seven hours on muleback.

What it would be like to get there on foot I couldn't imagine, but an illustration was shortly forthcoming. After the mule trekkers had passed, a lone figure appeared around a corner of the trail ahead of us, climbing with a ragged but unfaltering determination. Haggard, hollow-eyed and unshaven, with dust-covered hair and clothes and a water bottle hanging from his neck. A fugitive from justice? The ghost of a '49-er who'd taken the wrong turn on his way to the gold fields? When we stopped him we learned he was one of the intrepid few. A hiker who claimed he'd gone all the way, not only to Plateau Point but to the bottom of the canyon. Tapping his water bottle, which couldn't have held more than a quart, he said, 'I had to get down to the river, to get me a refill.'

As he trudged on up the trail we paused, glancing at one another with uncertainty. We'd gone about a mile already, and paused to ease our aching feet. When the Scots boy muttered something about the uphill climb being the hardest part, and how we shouldn't make ourselves too tired before we tackled it, there were no dissenting voices. In the wake of the true professional, we started back for the rim.

At Hopi House, on the way to the car park, we were attracted by a rhythmic drumming and jingling sound to an enclosed space where half a dozen American Indians were performing a dance in front of a small audience. The Hopi Feather Dance, among others, was a popular feature of a visit to the canyon, but whatever curiosity it aroused was quickly satisfied by the somewhat repetitive movements of the dancers.

The two central figures were an old chief, attired in a war bonnet, bear-claw necklace and ceremonial shirt, and a younger Hopi in a splendid headdress of red- and yellow-dyed feathers. This man also wore a feathered cape and arm bustles, and held bouquets of feathers in his hands. Bells stitched to his leggings jingled as he danced, a slow ponderous step that kept time with a tom-tom beat. The old chief, for his part, seemed happy to tap his foot occasionally and proffer a bowl to the audience.

The Hopi were a Pueblo people, descended from the native Americans who had inhabited the region in such ancestral sites as Montezuma Castle. Unlike the warring Apache and Navajo tribes of yesteryear their peaceful character ('Hopi' meaning 'peaceable' or 'civilised') facilitated their acceptance of reservation life in the area allocated to them in north-eastern Arizona.

After the performance we had a cool drink at a nearby refreshment kiosk. On our way back to the car we saw the Hopis again. This time the two men were in suits, shirts and ties, and smoking cheroots. Though the impact of American civilisation on these parts was not unknown to me I had to stop and stare as they split up and climbed into separate convertibles.

In our own car we drove out to Hopi Point, on the West Rim Drive. From here we obtained our first view of the Colorado River, a brilliant snake of whiteness trapped in the deep cleft of the Inner Gorge. The late afternoon sunlight, rapidly failing, picked out the twists and turns of its course below the dusky red fortresses of rock that cradled it. These too, deprived of shape and colour during the day, were now sharply defined, their outlines accentuated by deepening shadows. In the softening light the quality of the canyon's various colours had also emerged: reds and golds, browns and purples, greys and blues. As we watched, the colours slowly fused together, so that finally there were only the two ends of the spectrum juxtaposed. The deep red of the canyon walls, inflamed by the dipping sun, and the dark violet of the indented shadows. And matched against them the pearl-grey of the sky, so intensely luminous it hurt my eyes. The contrasts were enthralling, the limitless beauty of the scene impossible to behold as anything but the most superb natural revelation. The Grand Canyon in daylight was the summit of sights. At sunset it was the pinnacle beyond.

Route 66

Getting My Kicks

In the waning light we drove back to Flagstaff. The return journey
was even faster than the outgoing one and I detected a sense of
urgency in my companions. It turned out that they were 'seeing' the
States in two weeks – a two-way, coast-to-cast marathon that even
I, with my appetite for mileage, would never have contemplated.
One night out of every two, and fifty per cent of their journey, was
being spent on board the Greyhound, leaving just enough time for
side trips like the Grand Canyon. For British students working in
the States during their summer vacation this punishing schedule
was, I learned, obligatory. The work-study courses in which they
were engaged were invariably of ten weeks' duration, which
left them two weeks of their three months' vacation to do their
sightseeing. In comparison with this my ninety-nine days seemed
a lifetime.

At the bus depot I left them queuing doggedly for a bus to
Albuquerque, the next stage of their trip to New York. As to my

own plans I was down for a good night's sleep, and was here ready and willing for the next negotiation. With students milling everywhere with propositions (most of them legitimate) I could not fail in my endeavour. A couple of Scandinavians who'd found a room in a hotel near the depot came up with the best deal, at $3.50 split three ways. To make it really attractive they offered me, for an additional fifty cents, the use of the bed.

Ten hours on a mattress was a good preparation for the day ahead, or more precisely the forty hours that would pass before I lay on one again. My plan for the day was a visit to the Painted Desert and the Petrified Forest, heading east again on Route 66. The two sights were near one another, and I was ready to believe the travel guide that said they could be viewed 'virtually in the same breath-taking glance'.

Another convenient feature of the two areas was their location near the highway. By arrangement with the driver of the Albuquerque bus I was dropped off at the access road to the Painted Desert Visitor Center. As I approached it I fully expected to see a huge spectator window inside the building, offering an immediate wide-ranging panorama.

Inside the Center a park ranger put me straight. There was no single comprehensive view of the Painted Desert, which covered a vast irregular area, stretching from here to the Grand Canyon National Park 120 miles to the north-west. At its southern end it adjoined the Petrified Forest National Park.

The ranger went on to inform me that in 1896 a law had been passed prohibiting the removal of petrified wood from the park. This 'wood' was Federal property, and people caught with it in their possession were liable to prosecution. As he gave me the warning the ranger looked me up and down, as though working out what quantity of the stuff I was capable of carrying out of the park. With my rucksack deposited at the Visitor Center, and no more than my trouser pockets to fill, I assumed that I passed his inspection. But the ranger's attention was already drawn elsewhere. Behind me a large station wagon had pulled up, plastered with souvenir stickers and loaded with countless children.

The road wound upwards to a ridge and in a short time I had reached the top and was getting the first miraculous view of the

Painted Desert, the most evocatively named natural spectacle after the Grand Canyon.

The artist, of course, was nature. The canvas volcanic ash, the pigment iron oxide. The medium, water.

The effect was stupefying. Over a landscape of badland formations – humped, striated deposits rolling like waves from the horizon – were washed a variety of soft yet vibrant colours. Rust-red was the base, banded by thin brush strokes of blue, brown and greeny-white: a combination of hues so delicately blended that no artist, however gifted, could have matched. I saw a rainbow, descending to earth.

The miracle remained, for all such notions, a natural one. About 160 million years ago, during the geologic period known as the Triassic, this region had been close to sea level, an enormous marshland that had been slowly covered with the layers of silt, sand and volcanic ash deposited by rivers and floods. In these deposits were minute quantities of iron oxide and other minerals which had created the colours. In a later period the reverse process of erosion had commenced, with driving rains and shifting streams gradually stripping away the sediments and creating the shapes of the badlands. What I could see now was that most paradoxical of natural phenomena, a desert created by water.

As I gazed out on the desert it seemed for a moment that the bands of colour were moving towards me, a kinetoscopic effect that had me spellbound until I realised I was looking at the shadows of clouds, passing like wraiths over the landscape. These shadows, overlaying gentle tints, served to enhance them, creating for the spectator an ever-changing panorama of colour.

After a three-mile walk, taking pictures from the rim overlooking the desert, I turned back to the Visitor Center. At the admission gate I told the ranger that he didn't have to search me for petrified wood, as so far I hadn't seen any. He nodded, in a way that implied he could have told me that before I started.

'How far did you go? Three miles? Too bad. If you wanna see the giant logs, you gotta go another thirty-three.'

Examining the scale on my map of the park I saw that he was right. So much for 'the same breath-taking glance'.

Collecting my rucksack I positioned myself at the exit to

the parking area. Exactly in the centre of the driveway, so that anyone pulling out would have to run me over to get to the road. Fortunately the first driver lacked homicidal tendencies and I was offered a lift in a small Volkswagen.

My companions were Jewish – the man who was driving, his wife and mother-in-law. They were from Israel and had only arrived recently as immigrants in the United States. Squeezed in the back between the mother-in-law and my rucksack I realised I would get to see little of the trail but would learn a great deal about how the family were adapting to their new life in California.

At the point where I had abandoned my first excursion the road looped and headed south over the highway to the Rainbow Forest, the lower area of the park where most of the petrified trees were located. In the bare, eroded terrain we saw a scattering of the logs, but these were nothing in comparison with the concentration we found at the end of the road, at the southernmost entrance to the park.

After taking my leave of the three new Americans I went into the museum and Visitor Center and helped myself to a trail leaflet, which directed me to a circular walking tour of the Long Logs Trail.

The logs, I learned, were the remnants of trees that had flourished during the Triassic period. By natural processes the trees had died and fallen into the mud of flooding streams. Their rapid burial had prevented their decay, and the sediments, laden with mineral silica, had commenced their work. Gradually water had filtered through the logs, depositing silica within the cell tissues of the wood. This had formed tiny quartz crystals which ultimately replaced the wood and created petrified replicas of the original trees. As time passed the log-bearing layers were buried deeper and deeper, and it was not until later upheavals that they were uncovered, the earth movements producing deserts that had subsequently been worn away by erosion to reveal the incredible forest of stone that lay beneath.

At the start of the trail I picked up a piece of petrified wood (an act that was not prohibited by Federal law, as long as you put it back) and studied the subtle range of its colours. These were the effect of the minerals that had seeped into the wood all those millions of years ago: red, yellow and brown from oxidising iron;

black, purple and blue from manganese and carbon. An hour earlier I had seen nature's spectrum spread before me in a huge, sweeping panorama. Now I was holding it in the palm of my hand.

The Long Logs Trail led me through the largest accumulation of petrified wood in the park. Like the debris of a mighty tornado, the giant logs lay everywhere. Although broken into fragments of various sizes they retained perfectly the form of the original trunks, and with diameters of up to seven feet, one could imagine the immense height of the living trees. Perhaps the most extraordinary sight on the trail was a log jam formation where dozens of trunks, more or less intact, were piled together. These were the trees which, instead of being buried where they fell, had been carried away by the streams and thrown together on sandbars or in shallows. Millions of years later they had lain under 3,000 feet of mud and marine sediment: millions of years further on, erosion had exhumed them. To see them now, lying in the same chaotic heap in which they had originally accumulated, was to experience a dramatic telescoping of time. Here was a scene from the age of the dinosaurs, frozen for the perpetual wonder of humankind.

Back in the museum I discovered a variety of exhibits that increased my wonder: beautiful polished segments of petrified wood and minerals that had been extracted from the wood and finished as gemstones such as agate or jasper. The value of the petrified wood, and its recognition as part of the nation's heritage, was best illustrated by a letter prominently displayed in a glass case. It came from a woman visitor to the park, who'd had a serious transgression to clear from her conscience.

To the Superintendent,
Petrified Forest National Park

Dear Sir,
Nearly two years ago, as we were driving thru Arizona, we visited the Petrified Forest National Monument. While my husband was taking pictures of the logs etc. I looked down at my feet and saw some slivers of bright coloured rocks. I picked them up and put them in my pocket. (Being a 'rock-hound' is one of my hobbies.) My husband didn't know I had them, and as we were leaving the

Park, he answered 'no' to the question 'have you any Petrified Wood?' That was my sin, sitting there quietly and not telling my husband and the man at the gate the truth. It's bothered me ever since. I knew I should send them back to you, but somehow never got up the courage to do so.

This Easter season, when I was going to Communion in my church, I knew I couldn't live with myself if I didn't 'straighten out' even a little sin like this one. So I promised God, I'd forget my fear of what would happen to me, when you found out, and I'd send back the 3 slivers of Petrified Wood I'd picked up that day. Would you please do me a favour? Some day, when you are driving near the north gate of the Forest, and see a small chunk of Petrified Wood by the roadside, will you please drop these pieces near it in the sand. That's where I found them.

Every once in a while I start to deplore the lack of integrity in people in this day and age, and then with a shrinking heart I realise that I'm not any better. Perhaps, now, I can feel 'clean' again.

Sincerely,

P.S. I am mailing the wood in a separate small package with this letter today. I am still frightened, though. When my husband hears about this, it may break up our 31 year marriage. I can't see whatever possessed me to pick up those pieces.

Beside the letter there were the three slivers of petrified wood, no more than two or three inches long. Disturbed, chastened and abashed, I slipped out of the museum and when no-one was looking quietly dropped my small piece on the ground. Then, returning to the souvenir shop, I bought an identical piece for fifty cents.

Rainbow Forest was crossed by Route 180 and just before sunset I left the park and headed west on foot, with the firm expectation of being picked up before dusk and taken to Holbrook, where the road met the US66. But I had reckoned without the Arizona sunset. After half an hour, at about 6.30pm, the sun had gone completely and darkness fell like a curtain on the desert road.

Holbrook was nineteen miles away, and it took two of them to realise that I wasn't going to get there that night. The road was totally deserted, and there wasn't even the whisper of a car engine to give me hope. The rucksack lay like a petrified log on my shoulders, and my legs were aching. As the moon rolled out from behind a bank of cloud, shaking a ghostly hand with the desert, I came to an enthralling conclusion. I would spend the night in the desert.

With this idea firmly in my mind, and resisting the thought that a car might suddenly materialise, I started to look for a nesting site. A cool wind was blowing in from the mountains and I cast about for cover. Here I was subject to the limitations of the terrain, which was disappointingly thin on hedges and mossy banks and offered only an indifferent covering of sagebrush, snakeweed and cactus. I'd never slept al fresco – and tentless – before, and now was my chance – but how did I shelter behind a prickly pear?

Eventually, by dint of perseverance, I found my windbreak. Looming up out of the darkness ahead of me was a large square shape which turned out to be a signboard for the park, marking its westward boundary. Thankfully I dumped my rucksack on its leeward side and laid out my sleeping bag. The ground was hard, but zipping myself tightly into the bag, and with the rucksack as a pillow, I hardly noticed it. How could I concern myself with such a minor discomfort, when the star-speckled sky was up there above me, the breathy desert air in my nostrils? How could I feel anything but the glorious sense of exhilaration that came from being totally isolated, abandoned to the rawness of nature?

After lying there for a few minutes, watching the feathery movements of the snakeweed and other desert plants that grew nearby, an unnerving thought occurred to me. I remembered from my visit to the Arizona-Sonora Desert Museum the descriptions that Lewis had given me of some of the deadly species of the region. Creatures like the prairie rattlesnake, the poisonous lizard known as the Gila monster, the rock or bark scorpion, the black widow spider. He'd given me an information sheet about them, so that I'd know them when I saw them. The rock or bark scorpion, I remembered, could be distinguished from the harmless giant hairy scorpion by its slender 'tail', and the black widow spider by the reddish colouring of its underparts. But how could one observe the underparts of a spider in the darkness?

The knowledge that neither the sting of the scorpion nor the bite of the spider was necessarily fatal did little to ease my mind. Ploughing to the depths of the sleeping bag I pulled the zip up from the inside and for five breathless minutes lay rigid in its hot, cotton-wadded interior. An airhole being necessary, I reopened the zip an inch or two, using the slit to breathe through and to keep a wary eye on my surroundings.

I was almost ready to relax when I felt a tickle on my calf, inside the trouser leg. With a single frenzied movement I unzipped the bag and struggled out, beating my leg like a delirious Hopi. When I could pause for breath I rolled up my trouser leg, gently feeling the skin, but there was no swelling and my panic subsided. Wearily I climbed back into the bag, wondering if this was how I was going to spend the night. To cut a long story short, it was.

Merciful dawn came at 5.30am and I eased myself from the bag, stretching my near-rigid limbs. Fortified by a cat-nap that may have lasted all of thirty minutes, I rolled up the bag, hoisted the rucksack and started out on the seventeen miles to Holbrook. At first I felt quite light-headed, the effect of sleep deprivation, and the rucksack was a featherweight on my shoulders. Then, with the sun warming through and the road steadily climbing, I adopted the more familiar pack-horse mode, plodding under the forty-five-pound weight with a gnawing hollowness in the pit of my stomach which reminded me of my other deprivation: a hot, strong coffee.

The distant drone of a car switched me into hitch-hiker mode and I flagged down a genial Hopi in a large and battered Buick. As I sank gratefully into the front passenger seat he told me that he did the run twice a day, to deliver and collect his Navajo girlfriend who worked at the Visitor Center. At Holbrook, twenty minutes later, he dropped me at a snack counter. With a seventeen-hour fast to eliminate I did energetic justice to a plate of fried eggs and waffles, and after a freshen-up under a cold tap outside I was ready for the next stage of my journey, which would take me across the breadth of Arizona to the state of Nevada.

I was dismayed to have to wait until midday for a Greyhound, one of only three a day that stopped at Holbrook. The distance to my destination, Las Vegas, was 350 miles and the late start meant that I would arrive there at night, which was possibly the best time for a city constructed almost exclusively of neon.

At Flagstaff the sky greyed over and in a short time we were driving through heavy rain that drew itself like a net across the landscape, erasing perspective. The forest colours merged into the same neutral shades and after the brilliance of the previous day I felt strangely cheated. The rain persisted until dusk – or at least as I recall, having succumbed by this time to a deep sleep.

Sometime later my reviving senses became aware of two things. The sound of canned music and car horns, and a winking kaleidoscope of lights making spatters of colour on the wet glass of the windscreen. As bags were pulled down and people jostled to get off the bus I asked someone if this was Las Vegas. The question was received in amazement, followed by a concessionary nod when the person realised I was from another planet.

Only half-awake I descended from the bus and started towards the downtown area of the city. The walk was an extension of my waking dream, with the sound of music, voices and fruit machines erupting from an endless avenue of casinos, and the wet pavements splintering the light from their dazzling exteriors. In night-time Las Vegas, the gamblers' capital, nothing was real. Only the hope, perhaps, that cemented the neon and the noise, the driving force of the people who inhabited the place, bound to it by one of man's strangest compulsions.

I saw them briefly through the glass of the casino doors, groups of punters huddled round the gaming tables or standing at the fruit machines, working the levers like robots. The click of a coin in a slot, the cascade of a jackpot, reminded me of the one tangible commodity in this tinsel city.

Before my dream became a nightmare I turned off the strip and headed into the comparative obscurity of the neighbouring blocks, where the gaps in the neon made it possible to separate the hotels from the casinos. Las Vegas was a popular place and I must have checked a dozen desk clerks before I found one who could give me a room.

'Last one in the house,' I was told, with the added qualification: ''Fore you take it, you better know something. It's inclined to be a little noisy.'

I shrugged, wondering how he could imagine that a sleep-walking zombie could give a fig about noise when there was a bed in reach. But caution prevailed. 'May I see the room?'

He led me up a poky flight of stairs to a dark stuffy mummy-chamber barely lit by three flickering light bulbs. Once I had located the bed however, I had no further questions. Least of all about the music, drumming dully through the floorboards. When the man had disappeared I fell out of my rucksack and clothes and into the bed.

After listening to the music for an hour or so I could identify some of the tunes. *Waiting for the Robert E. Lee* was the favourite, followed by *Swanee*, *Get Out and Get Under* and other evergreens. Through the distortion of the loudspeaker systems in the room below they hardly came over as individual numbers but more as a monotonous lethargic drone. Normally such melodic mush would have carried me straight to the land of nod, but every five or ten minutes a voice came over the system to interrupt it and jar me back into consciousness.

'Jackpot, five-two-one, paying eight dollars, jackpot...'

The voice, flat and mechanical, might have belonged to a talking computer, with just enough variation in its announcements to keep me hanging on.

'Jackpot, three-nine-zero, paying five dollars, jackpot...'

Las Vegas was called the sleepless city, and by seven o'clock the next morning I knew why.

Las Vegas

The Music of Falling Coins

In the unreal silence that followed the last piped chords of music, the last clatter of a roulette wheel, the last tinkle of an expectant dime, I re-donned my clothes and rucksack and went down to the lobby. The clerk, propped on an elbow, did not meet my eyes but with his free hand took my four dollars. Sleep? A game of chance.

In the combined light of dawn and guttering neon I found my way back to the bus depot and boarded a bus heading north on the interstate highway. My precipitate flight from Las Vegas was partly due to fear of my own human frailty (didn't I still have 250 dollars in my possession?) and a desire to see a nearby scenic attraction.

A special feature of the neighbouring region – the canyon country of south-western Utah – was its unique erosional forms. As in the Grand Canyon, water and earth movements had done their work, but here the principal agent was wind. With a vigorous deftness it had carved a mass of elaborate architectural shapes from the rocky plateau: walls, spires, pinnacles and ramparts that together created vast natural citadels and fortresses. The three outstanding examples of these formations were at the Zion and

Bryce Canyon National Parks and the Cedar Breaks National Monument, all of which lay in the same corner of the state of Utah in the right angle of its borders with Arizona and Nevada. Determined not to be misled this time by the scale on my map I sought the advice of the driver on how I should reach them.

He started off by shaking his head. 'You'd've done better a couple of weeks ago,' he said. 'They got tourist buses going out to all of 'em, from Cedar City – but they finished early September. Only way now is by car, from Cedar City. How come you missed the season?'

The only answer to that, of course, was that I hadn't known about any season, or any suspension of tourist services. If I had, I wouldn't have attempted the trip. But now I was on the bus I might as well enjoy the scenery.

Stony desert thinly skimmed with Joshua trees reminded me that I was now in Mormon country and entering the state that these singular people had made their own. Zion, or 'Heavenly City of God' had been their name for the canyon they had discovered in 1860, whose temples of vari-coloured stone had roused their spiritual wonder. My own view of the Zion National Park was limited to its backdrop, visible after a long climb into forested mountain country. To the west lay a massive barrier of cedar-clad slopes, their heights enhanced by an unexpected dressing of snow. After staring at the desert for so long, the sight of that celestial powdering made me momentarily lose my bearings.

Further north the snow lay more thickly, and by the time we reached Cedar City, a featureless and weather-beaten mining town, we might have been in the middle of a Tyrolean winter. Once off the bus I felt strangely abandoned, and daunted by the distance (twenty-four miles) to the Cedar Breaks National Monument. A sign put me on the right road and I started out, setting my teeth against the fine drizzle of snow. To my astonishment and relief a friendly Dodge soon rescued me and I was driven all the way to the Cedar Breaks turn-off, three miles from the Monument.

Before I had covered ten yards I was delighted to be rounded up by another car, this one a Volkswagen with three college boys on board. Somehow I squeezed into the back among an arsenal of sporting rifles and they drove me up to Cedar Breaks, firing questions at me all the way. Like where was I from and what did I think of America? And what was I doing with a parachute in the middle of a forest?

Arriving at the Cedar Breaks Lodge, close to the most spectacular chasm, one of the boys suggested that he accompany me to the edge, to watch me jump. Laughing him off, I accepted his invitation to leave my rucksack in the car, as they were going back to Cedar City later and could stand me a ride. Taking my camera I trudged off through a belt of snow-girt trees to the rim of the chasm.

After the Grand Canyon and the Painted Desert I didn't think I'd have much breath left to catch, much awe left to inspire. But here I stood, at the edge of the Cedar Breaks, gasping and gaping all over again. The reason was simple. With the grander spectacles, I'd known beforehand what to expect, and the degree to which they would impress me. The secret of Cedar Breaks was its surprise.

A break in the trees, and suddenly, stupendously, a drop into infinity and the revelation of a great mauve and russet amphitheatre, tiered by crenellations of wind-scoured rock. The snow had stopped but had left its mark, a white trim on the cliff-tops that perfectly set off the colour of the rock. At 10,700 feet the clarity of the light lent further brilliance to the tints of red, brown, mauve and lavender, the snow-burdened clouds a contrasting background wash of pearl-grey. I shivered, discovering that in the few moments of standing there, in the gallery of this miraculous theatre, I had become oblivious of the abrasive wind that even now was doing its work, sculpting the craggy walls.

I turned back, my boots wet inside from the snow. It seemed unlikely now that I would make the distance to Bryce Canyon, or see more of Zion, but with Cedar Breaks I had got close enough to the Promised Land.

The college boys took me back to Cedar City by a devious route, heading off on a twisting narrow road that was little more than a snow-covered trail through the woods. I clung nervously to my seat as we slewed around hairpin bends on the pine- and aspen-clad slopes, wondering if this would be my final experience of America's natural wonders. To my dismay my companions seemed to be enjoying themselves, hooting with glee as the car slid from side to side of the track or spun into snowdrifts.

Every so often one of the youths who wasn't driving would shout 'hold it!' This would force the car to career giddily for a few yards and then jerk to a standstill, its nose jammed into another drift.

The cause of the distraction would be a fleeting shape, moving through the trees. 'Look at that beauty...'

To my alarm the boy beside me in the back seat reached for one of the rifles and thrust himself through the open roof of the car. From the way he swung the rifle without sighting it I guessed he was only play-acting. I did not, however, doubt his sincerity. The next time we stopped I saw what they were looking for. In a gap between the trees, a few yards from the car, stood a white-tail deer with a fine head of antlers, immobilised by surprise at our slithering arrival. On the spur of the moment I followed suit and poked my head and shoulders through the sun-roof, flipping open my camera case. I managed to get a quick, blurry shot before the animal scampered off.

Back in my seat I expected some kind of ribald response to my action. Instead I found a mutual despondency. 'Just think of it,' my back-seat companion was muttering. 'A great, mossy, son-of-a-bitch twelve-pointer, right there sittin' by the road, and we ain't even near the season...'

We drove on. I wasn't sure whether to be disappointed that it was not through my act alone that the creature's life had been saved, or pleased that the game season was not yet under way. Come November, or whenever it was, I guessed it wouldn't make any difference.

When the three young hunters were through wetting their lips we'd covered thirty miles of the most hair-raising but wildly beautiful scenery I'd ever driven through. In that wonderland of snow-powdered ponderosa, shaking aspen and unfathomable slopes I could overlook the purpose of the excursion and turn a deaf ear to the hunting stories of my companions. The most remarkable thing I learnt was that one of them did his hunting with a bow and arrow, presumably to give himself a greater feeling of integrity. As an innovation to the hunting scene this weapon had been highly popularised, and in some states it was possible to obtain a licence to hunt with it in advance of the normal hunting season. Then, if you missed your target with an arrow, you could always get another license and bag it with a gun.

At a place called Panguitch we got onto a paved road and headed south. Forty miles of highway, cut through massive lava beds, took us to Cedar City, passing on the way the beautiful Lake Navajo. By the time we reached the town it was six o'clock and under a cold grey sky the light was going fast. The boys dropped me at the bus depot and I set about fixing my night's accommodation, the 12.51am bus to Las Vegas.

In Cedar City I met my first native American. He was standing on a street corner near the depot, slapping his arms against his sides. It was the coldest night so far and I was in such a hurry to find a warm interior that I at first ignored him.

He was signalling that he needed a light. I looked at his cold, lined face, shielded from the street light by the limp brim of a Stetson, and the patched, paper-thin coat and trousers. It was more than a light he needed.

I nodded towards a café, but at my suggestion of buying him some soup he looked a little hesitant. I went ahead, holding the door open for him, and with a quickening step he followed me into the café. We sat down at the counter, and in the brighter light I saw he was quite a young man, and that the lines on his pale, leathery face were not from age but from some long-endured privation. His name was Charlie Sunrise.

The soup helped him talk and he told me he was from Oklahoma, where he ran a small farm. Unfortunately he'd suffered a crop failure in the past year and he'd been forced to travel west in search of work, leaving his wife and three children behind. They were dependent on the money that he sent them week by week, working as a farm labourer. He was constantly moving on, either because the work was temporary or the money poor. His present employer, a Mormon, had outsize scruples about a fair day's pay for a fair day's work, which at a dollar an hour cut little ice with Charlie.

'He won't pay me no more, 'cause I'm Indian,' he said. He made it sound like an accepted fact of life that could not be disputed. I could find no trace of bitterness in his voice. He was a Comanche, descendant of the Southern Plains tribe subdued by the US military and government in the 1870s. His wife was an Apache, whose grandfather had 'run around with Geronimo'. As a sign of the changing times, he had fought with the US army in Korea, but his acceptance by the military had not extended later on into acceptance into white society. He had always been an outsider, fighting to get away from reservation life and compete on equal terms with other Americans.

Becoming a land-holder had seemed like a move towards this ideal, but his subsequent misfortunes had returned him to a position of dependence on white employers, whose attitudes towards migrant labour did not seem to have improved much since the days when the first 'Okies', deprived of their farm plots by the Great Depression and the Dust Bowl, had moved west.

To be a member of a deprived minority in the richest country in the world was something that had to be borne, like having one leg longer than the other or a tooth with a hole in it. This, at least, was how it seemed to Charlie. 'We're contented, I guess. We have to be.'

I thought of his once proud and formidable nation, a human barrier to the tide of an alternative civilisation, that was now a picturesque embarrassment tucked away in the reservations of the south-west. Then my memory flashed back to that hotel lobby in downtown Washington and I thought of another minority in their big-city ghettoes, that right now were painting protest banners and making petrol bombs. Like Charlie Sunrise, they wanted status, but for them that meant more than a dollar-fifty an hour.

After we'd had some more soup and a cup of coffee we went out into the cold night again, to discover a town that save for a few street lights and slowly moving headlights had been extinguished. The snow had returned, ghosting the sidewalks, and the Comanche looked uncertainly up and down the street, drawing his collar round his throat. When I asked where he was going he said 'to the church', because it was warmer there.

If anyone had ever suggested that I might be intrigued by a Penstock Rivet, I would have had to ask what it was before I shook my head. But after my next local excursion I might have taken that person seriously.

To get a close-up of this remarkable object the tourist is invited to travel to the Hoover Dam, a well-known pre-war construction in the Black Canyon area of the Colorado River, between the states of Arizona and Nevada. Here you will find all the information you need, on anything from a Penstock Rivet to the amount of concrete in cubic yards used to build a dam 1,244 feet wide, 726 feet deep and 650 feet thick at the base.

At the end of the thirty-mile run from Las Vegas I was able see the impact of the dam on the local landscape. Its most impressive creation was Lake Mead, a vast reservoir held in a rugged embrace of volcanic rock. Dotting the surface of the lake, like white chips in a blue glaze, were the tiny sailing boats that reminded me of Lake Mead's other function as a National Recreation Area.

At the foot of the lake the giant rose, a massive wedge of concrete between the canyon walls. The bus dropped the tourist group at the east end of the dam and with Lilliputian trepidation we walked on to it, making our way across the road bridge which ran along the top. From my notes I saw that this road, forty feet wide, represented little more than a sixteenth of the width of the dam at its base, which gave a good idea of the overall scale. Looking down from the parapet on the south side of the road I saw the Colorado River, its progress restrained to a gentle flow by the filter feed of the dam. Here the dam sloped outwards in a curving cascade of white concrete: on the other side there was a sheer drop to the waters of the lake.

A Department of the Interior guide called us together at the service entrance to the dam and gave us a brief history of its origins. 'You all know why dams are built,' he started hopefully, 'because we couldn't, quite simply, live without them. Before the Hoover Dam there was no control for the Colorado, which can be a pretty powerful river, as anyone who's seen the Grand Canyon will appreciate. In the spring and early summer the river used to flood, drowning the crops, and in late summer and fall it used to dry up, so there was no irrigation during the drought period. Something had to be done, and that was how Reclamation began.

'The Hoover Dam, named after the pre-war Democratic President Herbert Hoover (and known as the "Boulder Dam" to the Republicans) was the pioneer project, and since its completion in 1935 there's been no flood or drought on the Lower Colorado. The reservoir, Lake Mead, stores more than two years of average river flow, used for irrigating one and a quarter million acres of land and supplying the municipal and industrial water for a population of ten million, including Los Angeles. Additionally, it generates about four and a half billion kilowatts of hydroelectric energy annually. Shall we go inside?'

With the other members of the tourist group I was ushered into an elevator, which plunged us into the heart of the dam. At the bottom our guide told us we had descended 560 feet and were now going to inspect the power plant. I followed the group into a tunnel, trying not to calculate how many cubic yards of concrete lay on top of us.

We emerged into a towering oblong chamber that comprised one arm of the power plant complex. From a lofty gallery we had a vision of the space age: eight generators standing in coldly-illuminated splendour on a shining floor without a human being in sight. Half of the Hoover power plant's generating capacity came from this chamber, but it was impossible to imagine the power output that this represented. I could only share the blind faith of the busy Los Angeles housewife, 300 miles away, plugging in her hair dryer.

From the power plant we passed through another tunnel into a small chamber which allowed a view of some of the huge steel pipes that carried the water through the dam. These, the guide informed us, were the 'Penstocks'.

The climactic moment had come. With some ceremony he unlocked a small safe and took out a large metal object, about a foot in length, which he needed both hands to hold aloft. Then, to his enthralled audience, he announced:

'This is a Penstock Rivet. It weighs thirteen pounds. In each band securing a section of this water pipe there are 277 of these rivets. Each section of the pipe is twenty-two feet long, and weighs an average of 150 tons. The pipe is thirty feet in diameter and 4,000 feet long.' He paused, allowing his audience a moment of tension before adding: 'It's the largest in the world.'

At this there was a gentle sigh of relief from the group. A flow of questions followed, technical and otherwise, about the construction and operation of the dam, all effectively handled by the guide. The most awesome piece of information was, of course, the amount of concrete that had been used to build the dam. Three and a quarter million cubic yards... Once again I couldn't absorb the figure. Much easier to think of it as a highway, sixteen feet wide and four inches deep, stretching from New York to San Francisco. Or a continuous flow of concrete going on for two years, twenty-four hours a day...

Drunk with statistics we found ourselves back in the elevator. But even that didn't spare us, taking us to a height, we were told, of a forty-four storey block in just over a minute. Emerging gratefully into daylight I crossed the bridge to the reservoir side to gaze at the pleasant blue expanse of Lake Mead. In the setting of excavated rock, transformers and power cables, asphalt and concrete, it was difficult to overlook the fact that this too was man-made.

It was strange to recall that after my visit to that 'Eighth Wonder of the World' – the Astrodome in Houston, Texas – I thought that I had seen everything. But Hoover went one better. A bronze plaque mounted on the parapet of the bridge stated that – in civil engineering terms at least – this was one of the Seven.

The night the English did Las Vegas commenced on a note of trauma. It must have been four days since I'd looked at myself in a mirror, and in the hotel room that evening I was confronted by a spectre. My travelling clothes, the buff windcheater and jeans, were unrecognisable as those I'd worn at the start of the journey. Layered with dirt and grease, torn or frayed in a dozen places, they would have roused the compassion of a hobo. My uncut hair was like matted kapok, curling round my ears. My beard – if a sparse six days' growth could be so described – belonged to a baddie in a 'B' Western. I clearly wasn't ready for the 'Entertainment Capital of the World', and knew that if I entered the Strip looking like this I'd collect more dimes than the fruit machines.

The battery shaver had its limitations and I nervously committed myself to the hazards of a razor blade, scraping my chin and throat until I looked like a schoolboy's first experiment. A hot shower removed the six-day grime from my body, a shampoo the last evidence of the Painted Desert. This left me with the problem of my clothes.

From my rucksack I resurrected a shirt, fresh socks, blue lightweight jacket and crease-resistant terylene trousers. Although the latter had lived up to their description I was mortified by the shirt and jacket, which had to be opened like road maps, fold by fold. Fortunately the shirt had a stiffened collar which could be pulled into shape with a tie, and I was able to concentrate my efforts on the jacket, vigorously dabbing a sponge over it until the creases had smoothed out.

With a freshly laundered tuxedo and a pocket full of dimes I was ready for Las Vegas. Setting off along the downtown Strip, the music of falling coins was already in my ears.

In the city of Las Vegas there were, I'd been told, 22,000 fruit machines. My problem was to find the right one. The gambling joints of the Casino Center that lay behind the welter of neon were world famous: The Mint, The Golden Nugget, Diamond Jim's, The Nevada Club, The Golden Gate. Inside they were indistinguishable, full of the same obliterating noise. Clanking slot machines, gargle-voiced callers, cascading coins and background music. There was no escape from it, or from the glitter and glare of the brightly-coloured machines, gaudy carpets and chairs, spotlights and glass-panelled ceilings. One had either to submit or run. Inside the glass doors of The Mint I hovered on the edge of running.

A girl in fishnet stockings and little else approached with a tray of cigars and chewing gum. With a six-inch Havana and wad of Wrigley's in my jaws I felt more the part and sauntered up to an unmanned fruit machine. Looking at my fellow gamblers I was mortified to see that they were less formally dressed than me, the men in cowboy shirts, jeans and riding boots and the women in sweaters, slacks and slingbacks. Their uniformity of dress was matched by a uniformity of stance and movement as they stood in line along the endless ranks of machines, inserting the coins and jerking the handles with a hypnotic rhythm. They appeared hypnotised, gazing fixedly at the little windows with their revolving fruits.

For two five-cent pieces I got an orange with a pear and a plum and a bunch of cherries with a plum and an orange. Disgruntled, I transferred my attention to the gaming tables, where the stakes were a little higher. With hands in pockets, guarding my traveller's cheques, I mingled with the more serious punters. Blackjack, roulette and craps were the main attractions, but the tables were so crowded that I could see little of the play. Dealers in white shirts and felt aprons jostled with tight-waisted women and broad-shouldered men for elbow-room on the baize, and I caught only the occasional flash of dice or the spin of a roulette wheel. Any further involvement was deterred by my natural aversion to taking risks of any kind – particularly with money.

From the Casino Center I continued to the more exclusive Las Vegas Boulevard. Known simply as The Strip, this avenue of naked vulgarity ran through the heart of the city: as far as the freeway to the south and to the point in the north where it disappeared in the desert. The Strip was too exclusive for public transport and I was soon wearied by the walk, with the cars swishing past and the sidewalks empty. On either side stood the hotels, casinos and entertainment venues that had created Las Vegas' most enduring image: architectural aberrations that were little more than glorified advertisement hoardings. Their exotic names flashed and glowed against the night sky in a furious discharge of kilowatts, challenging the primeval environment on which they were projected.

The tropics exerted a strong influence, but it was uncertain whether The Sahara outdid The Sands or The Dunes in anything but size. Similarly The Thunderbird was no more than a match for The Flamingo, and The Stardust outshone The Satellite only in the variety of its constellations. With little desire to approach the exclusive frontages, which muted even the ring of the fruit machines and the rustle of dollar bills, I decided to return to the downtown Strip – by comparison the poor man's Las Vegas.

On the way I had a closer look at a different aspect of the sinful city, promoted with some zeal by the local Chamber of Commerce. In a publicity handout it had declared that 'Las Vegas has more churches per capita than any city in the nation, with more than eighty-two churches representing all major denominations'. This had seemed a reasonable atonement for Gomorrah – but that was before I saw the churches.

First there was The Wee Kirk o' the Heather. Could this be the home of good old-fashioned Nevada Presbyterianism? I wondered if it mattered, when there was an illuminated sign outside, advertising a wedding chapel 'open day and night'. And a steeple outlined in neon, topped by a flickering cross that beckoned the faithful divorcees.

Then The Little Church of the West, built of timber, whose traditional twee-ness had no doubt secured its popularity as 'The Wedding Place of the Stars'. And nearby The Cupid Wedding Chapel, offering a 24-hour service and a five dollar ceremony, with a free tape-recording thrown in. Aliens landing in Las Vegas who would have been unaware of the peculiarities of Nevada State Law, which permitted instant marriage as well as instant wealth or poverty, might have been a little bemused.

I finished my evening in The Mint, donating $1.75 to its good causes. The seventy-five cents were a gift to the one-armed bandits and the dollar the price of a beer – and a show – in the showroom. I hardly tasted the beer, spreading it in slow sips over the two-hour length of the show.

Returning to my hotel I saw something that underlined the status of gambling, in the only state in the Union where it was legal. Marching up and down in front of a casino was a lone croupier, carrying a placard that read:

'On Strike. This House Fires Non-Winning Dealers'.

Southern California

'This is Muffin, and I'm Bernie'

There was a lot to see in California, so I had to start early. Leaving Las Vegas to sputter and yawn its welcome to the day, I took the Greyhound on the desert route west. This was the beginning of the Mojave, a 200-mile stretch of emptiness and desolation reclaimed only by the orange groves and urban sprawl of Los Angeles. It was the nearest thing to total desert that I'd seen so far: a flat, sandy waste relieved by little more than a sprinkling of juniper and sagebrush and the gesticulating arms of an occasional Joshua tree.

Just before the Nevada-California border a huge sign reared up ahead of us, reminding us that we were still on the sacred soil of the Gambling State. Standing in front of a dilapidated neon-wired building it made the dramatic announcement:

'State Line Bar. Last Chance – This Is It.'

Needless to say we didn't stop, and if we had it was unlikely that any of the passengers on the bus – still nursing their slot machine elbows – would have been able to drum up a solitary nickel. Most of them, anyway, were asleep, catching up on their lost night.

Somewhere in the middle of the desert I discovered I was in California. A uniformed figure waved us down and I saw that we were passing through the California Inspection Station, where all westbound vehicles were examined to make sure they were abiding by State Law and not bringing any fruit across the border. As the biggest fruit-growing state in the Union, California was touchy on this point, and in the interest of pest control every orange, apple or grape – even if it originated from California – had to be surrendered. As the inspector came aboard I kept a poker face, thinking of the beautiful ripe Jonathan apple in my rucksack. Nothing in the world would induce me to part from that.

Over on the horizon, as we continued westwards, I saw the peaks of the Sierra Nevada, the last mountain range before the sea. Among those peaks was the mighty Mount Whitney, at 14,485 feet the highest in America outside Alaska. This last huge land barrier, shutting off the moisture-laden winds of the Pacific, had created in the great basin that lay in its eastern shadow the notorious Death Valley.

Named in memory of a party of '49ers who'd tried it as a short cut to the gold fields – with dire consequences – Death Valley was the lowest, hottest and driest part of the United States. The fact that it was now a National Monument under the administration of the Department of the Interior did not make it any less of a hazard for anyone undertaking a trip across its 150 waterless miles, even on the paved highways that cut through it. For once, passing the turn-off at Baker, I could resist the challenge.

Three or four hours later we were through the mountains and entering the more fertile country east of Los Angeles. On either side of the road lay the orange groves and vineyards that were the most famous features of the Golden State: further on we ran into her most notorious. A long, sinuous arm, eight lanes wide, reached out to us – the first tentacle of Greater Los Angeles. This freeway, the San Bernardino, was the beginning of the complex network of motorways that dominated the city.

Spraying out like the branches of a tree were the interchanges for the satellite towns which lay about fifty miles to the east of the main conurbation. Passing over them on the elevated highways I thought about the population boom that had transformed

California from a little-known extremity of Mexico, inhabited by American Indians and a handful of missionary settlers, to a state more wealthy and populous than any in the Union. Eighteen million people were there to prove it, and it wasn't all because of Sam Brannan.

A stream in the Sacramento Valley and a shallow pan had brought Sam's fortune, and the most spontaneous mass migration in American history. In 1849 upwards of 100,000 fortune seekers had joined the Gold Rush, the first citizens of the new California. Conveniently, America had annexed the territory the year before, after her victory in the war against Mexico, and within another year California had become a state. Gold had made her an immediate magnet, but even a century after Sam's discovery, when the '49ers were a legend and gold was something they kept in Fort Knox, the migrants were still coming. The present rate was 1,200 a day, which over the year was more than four times that first hot-footed influx. Could it be that something shone more brightly than gold in the modern migrant's eye?

In a typical year the southern part of California, centred on Los Angeles, could claim an enviable 292 days of sunshine. An average temperature of 70°, sandy beaches and rolling surf were the other attractions that drew the migrants from the rest of America. With such attributes, 'LA' needed no promotion. Rather, a deterrent, which it was conspicuously in the process of creating. When the beaches of Malibu became a lengthy commute from the centre then perhaps it was time for the flow to subside.

In the meantime, what did California's eighteen million do with all that sunshine? Were there enough beaches for them all to sunbathe in comfort? In a state that, taken as a separate nation, would be the fifth most prosperous in the world, the question was academic. Apart from those heliocentric coast-huggers of Santa Monica, Long Beach and other popular stretches, the majority of southern Californians probably saw a beach only once or twice a year. For the rest of the time they had the job of maintaining the dynamic of growth that was the essential generator – and support – of their life style.

In a state in which the average yearly rainfall was less than half that of the rest of America, water supply and irrigation schemes were the first priority. Mention of the two 300-mile aqueducts bringing water from the Colorado River and the Owens River east of the Sierra Nevada to the farmers and housewives of the Los Angeles area was enough to give an idea of the scale of the problem in the south. In the Central Valley, the potential of millions of acres of fertile soil had been realised by the harnessing of two rivers (the Sacramento and San Joaquin) running into the San Francisco Bay. This vast alluvial tract – the biggest kitchen garden in the world – gave birth to every imaginable fruit and vegetable, providing unlimited employment for those economic migrants who had forged much of the state's prosperity.

Gold, sunshine, grapes and oranges. And like any other progressive 'nation' California had its share of industry: iron and steel works, motor assembly plants, ship-building and missiles. The latter was the most significant development, an extension of the aircraft production of the war years that had given manufacturing its greatest boost and brought a new level of prosperity. But even that was not the whole story. One had to remember the achievements of a small Los Angeles suburb called Hollywood.

Any expectation of stepping from the bus into a throng of movie moguls, cool starlets and tanned swashbucklers was dispelled by my arrival in downtown LA. This area could only be described as a place where buses stopped, cars kept moving and traffic cops waited to be relieved. Its apparent nonentity overlooked the fact that just south of here lay the district of Watts, scene of the recent riots that sprang from the high level of deprivation and racism that existed in the city.

I wasted little time in calling Bernie Crampton. She was my principal contact in southern California, an animal lover who in the few weeks before my departure had become a pen-friend. It had all started with a letter to *Animals* magazine, asking permission to use a little drawing I had done for the Christmas issue in a book of animal cartoons she was compiling. Coming at that moment, her request had met a ready response.

The lady, I noted, lived in the town of Hemet near the city of Los Angeles. Writing back, I had enclosed the original of the cartoon, saying that she was welcome to use it and suggesting – with a finely-honed opportunism – that as I was shortly coming to

America I could perhaps call on her and collect the ten-dollar fee she was offering.

To my surprise this somewhat unsubtle approach had been received with great enthusiasm, in a letter that had bounded back across the Atlantic with an open invitation for me not only to call but to stay for as long as I liked at 475, North San Jacinto. By what might have seemed design rather than luck it turned out that Mrs Crampton ran a motel.

When I called her she was expecting me and I took the first Greyhound to Riverside, a tentacle town from which I took a local bus to Hemet. The journey, to my dismay, took four and a half hours, which showed how misleading the reference 'near the city of Los Angeles' could be.

On the way to Hemet I re-read a couple of Mrs Crampton's letters, deciding in advance that she must be a bit of an oddball.

'I have two loves in my life, and that is animals and photography. We've got a pair of chuckawallas that I'm trying to tame, so my daughter and I can take them out on location. One of my favourite places in southern California is the San Diego Zoo. May I take you there and introduce you to all our wonderful animals? I'm frequently asking our guests if they need a guide, so maybe I should ask you. Wouldn't know where I was going, but would get there...

P.S I mentioned you to a friend of mine who keeps three lions and a cheetah. You might like to meet him. The lions are from 3 years to 10 years of age. Aug 19 will be the 4 yr old's birthday party. He got the idea from our Pekingese's birthday parties...'

Nervously, I alighted from the bus at North San Jacinto and walked a few blocks towards a sign that said 'Hemet Motel'. Bernie Crampton was there waiting for me, right under the sign. She presented the kind of figure that I had anticipated. Flamboyant, sun-burned, smiling. Red hat and red hair, with earrings and lipstick to match. Pekingese under left arm.

'Well, hi there...' To my bewilderment I was offered not a hand but an inert paw, which I shook with a certain diffidence. 'This is Muffin, and I'm Bernie...' From the start, I was given the right sense of priorities.

Bernie was a photographer and spent her time doing studies of small creatures in various untypical situations for children's picture books. Her own menagerie consisted of various mice, hamsters and goldfish and two desert lizards called Chuck and Walla. These two received any affection left over from Muffin, who was, of course, the star turn.

'Isn't he my own flesh and blood baby?'

Such qualities, it seemed, made Muffin a very special kind of dog. If not of a higher order of mammals, then at least a bit up on the social scale. Wasn't his birthday formally celebrated, with a champagne party, to which all his canine friends were cordially invited?

Before I forget I should mention that Bernie also had a husband and two children. The children were high-school teenagers and the husband a mechanic with a full-time job in Riverside, which left Bernie with the running of the motel. This was hardly, it seemed, a full-time occupation, as Bernie was willing to seize any opportunity to 'take off' in her TR3 and do something 'different'. From the warmth of her reception I guessed I was the best opportunity for a long time.

For me, too, it was an opportunity. My first hot shower for several days, a spotless motel room, and spare ribs with the family. Spare ribs are the roast beef of America, a traditional meal rivalled only by steak in its popularity. Afterwards, it was Bernie's evening, with an enthusiastic presentation of her photographic work that showed the full range of her own peculiar talent. Kittens in beer mugs, dogs in funny hats, mice playing miniature pianos, frogs on a checkerboard. Animals straight and comic, wild and domestic, clothed and unclothed. Animals in national parks and zoos. Animals on location, in strange situations that only humans could devise.

When I asked Bernie if she had ever considered submitting her photographs for publication she showed me with some pride a book she had prepared for this purpose, made up of text and pictures. The story was of a frog in search of a lily pad, which in the middle of the Californian desert was nothing if not original.

The next day we went to San Diego. From the start it was a memorable day, with Bernie knocking at my door at 9am armed with Muffin and a glass of fruit juice. 'I called the Director,' she announced, 'but he's away at some zoo conference. The Curator of Mammals is going to take you round instead.'

I nodded, drinking the fruit juice and shielding my gaze from the bright sun blazing through the motel doorway and the vision of Bernie Crampton in a crimson sun hat. Her shoulders were bare, revealing her rich California sun tan, and she looked more as if she were on her way to the beach. She'd been up two hours already and swum 150 lengths of the motel pool, a daily ritual that represented 500 miles swimming each year – or half the California coastline – before breakfast. This kind of fantasy fulfilment was hard to beat, but in a few moments I saw the supreme example. Bernie Crampton with Muffin under her arm and a Hasselblad hanging from her neck, climbing into the TR3.

Just before we started she remembered dogs weren't allowed in zoos, and Muffin was handed protestingly to Cynthia, Bernie's daughter. 'Now don't you fret at all, 'cause your mommy's going to be back real soon...'

With Bernie at the wheel it was a pious hope. As we swept along the Palos Verdes Drive, with its captivating first views of the Pacific, I was reminded of a hair-raising passage in one of her letters.

'Two weeks ago I was driving down to the San Diego Zoo in my English Triumph sports car and had a blow-out on a rear tyre, so after whiplashing across the freeway, spinning two circles on the road, it landed over an embankment 20 feet down. I never drempt of coming out of that alive, but all it did to the car was ruin the tire, which was ruined at the first bang. That was about the weirdest experience I've ever been in. I've always loved fast cars and fast driving, but after all this mess I've turned into a rather slow, pokey driver, almost scared to death. Hope I've not frightened you to the point that you'll not drive with me.'

That all happened at 80mph, and if I hadn't known about the accident I would have been quite relaxed, as Bernie maintained a cruising speed of fifty all the way. As it was, I didn't see too much of the scenery and got to San Diego, at the farthest southwest corner of the United States, with only the memory of Bernie's speedo reading and the traffic overtaking us on the inside lane.

San Diego Zoo lay in what must have been one of the most luxuriant parks in the northern hemisphere. The vegetation of Balboa Park reminded me that I was once more in a sub-tropical region of the States, with a profusion of trees, ferns and flowers more typical of the rainforest regions of South America. This variety of natural foliage, coupled with a superb climate, ensured the welfare of animals whose chances of survival outside their natural habitat would otherwise be non-existent. The climate had been the most important factor in the growth of the zoo, which was now one of the largest and best-planned in the world, with an unequalled variety of species.

This much I had known before my visit. Now, with the Curator of Mammals as my guide, I could appreciate for myself the advanced design of the zoo. A natural outdoor environment for the animals had been created by an informal layout of mesas, grottoes and islands, screened from each other by plantations of trees and shrubs. In the congenial local temperature (never going much below 55° in the winter) such outdoor enclosures were acceptable to most of the animals throughout the year. In the Great Ape Grottoes it was possible for once to see gorillas, chimps and orangs disporting themselves in the open air, without the fear of them succumbing at any moment to a bronchial infection. Other animals more customarily in the open were a natural feature of superbly realistic landscapes, without a bar or brick wall in sight. The elephants had an extensive area surrounded by a moat, the giraffes a similarly moated exhibit with a 'butte' in the background concealing an interior giraffe house.

From the enclosures, my admiration was diverted to the animals. The rarities were, as usual, the most interesting. Indian rhinos I had never seen in captivity, nor the legendary okapi. The proboscis monkey was one of a pair that were the only specimens outside Indonesia. And how about that moon-faced, rather diffident little creature, hiding in the branches of a eucalyptus? Was that really a koala?

'We've got eleven of them here,' the Curator announced proudly. 'The only koalas outside the continent of Australia. Nine live births, all successfully reared. We're able to grow the right species of eucalyptus in San Diego, which is an advantage, as they won't eat anything else.'

Bernie trained her camera. 'Aren't they the cutest little darlings?'

My own photography was assisted by the zoo photographer, who did most of my work for me by driving us around in a truck and stopping at the vantage points. To help out on the angles I was allowed to climb on the roof of the truck, which gave me some excellent views of the larger enclosures. The experience of being on the same level, eye-to-eye, as a giraffe is one that I recommend to anyone with the smallest inferiority complex.

For the rest of my tour of the zoo I was accompanied solely by Bernie, who proved – in her unique way – as good a guide as any. She'd been here regularly once a month, and was an authority on all the new arrivals, from the baby apes in the Children's Zoo Nursery (who spent their first few weeks in diapers) to a 'wee, wee baby hippo' which Bernie had been trying to persuade the Zoo Director to allow her to photograph from inside the moat. The closer Bernie could get, the better – even at the risk of being trampled by two tons of irate motherhood. Herein lay the difference between Bernie and myself. Like me she believed that animals were a superior kind of human being, but unlike me she was ready to prove it, by embracing every available llama, tree lizard or giant tortoise. I began to wonder if we shouldn't all just change places.

Once upon a time someone had told me that Knott's Berry Farm was the most authentic reconstruction of a 19th-century frontier town in America. When Bernie offered to take me there I was prepared to put my life-long credulity to the test.

To get there we had to retrace our route along Palos Verdes Drive, the coastal highway that had brought me my first views of the Pacific the day before. The crisp breakers, white sandy beaches and flower-filled verges were the spectacle I'd relished since leaving New York. Behind me lay the width of a continent: before me the limitless ocean.

To make the pilgrimage more meaningful Bernie paused at the Wayfarer's Chapel, built on a height overlooking the sea by none other than the great Frank Lloyd Wright. This chapel – which even for the arch-innovator had been something of a departure – was one of the showplaces of the West Coast. When Bernie called it 'cute' I expected to see something slightly blasphemous, like a Las Vegas wedding chapel. I was in no way prepared for the plate glass structure that confronted us, its gable jutting sharply from a shrouding mass of creepers. The building was completely transparent, allowing the visitor to view the altar from outside and the sky and natural world from within. According to Bernie the idea behind it was that the weary traveller, while seeking spiritual renewal, was still surrounded by the familiarity of trees and flowers, sky and ocean. At home, not only in the House of God but in the lap of Creation.

Entering the chapel we were greeted by the sound of piped organ music, wafting out from a hidden source. In a hushed voice Bernie said: 'This is where Jayne Mansfield got married.'

I nodded with the proper reverence and we walked together up the aisle towards an altar flanked by a trickling waterfall. Although there was no-one else in the chapel I was aware of an uncanny presence, of something living and growing around us that was in no way supernatural but just there. On either side of the chapel I saw what I could feel: potted ferns and creepers embracing the glass walls, vying with the luxuriant foliage outside. It was warm inside the chapel, so warm that the comparison with a greenhouse could no longer be avoided. I wondered if the air conditioning had failed, or if the plants preferred it that way. Maybe the Great Architect (not F.L.W.) had something to say on the matter.

Continuing along Palos Verdes Drive we passed America's last frontier, the sleek villas that clung like an elastic girdle to the Californian coast. These houses represented the climax of the American Dream, the ultimate horizon of the countless immigrants who had followed the lodestar of the Golden State. The balconied sun-palaces with the ocean view were the mark of their achievement, shrines of a status cult second only to that of Beverly Hills.

Having found it all, I wondered what was left for those latter-day frontier seekers. The estates they had created spread inland like an urban growth, banking the hills. Their drives sported Oldsmobiles, their yards a swimming pool, their sun porches a potted palm. The sea lay in front of them, the past behind them, and there was no point in moving sideways. Where did they go from here?

Bernie unwittingly answered the question when we drove past a high-walled enclosure with glimpses of fir trees, cypress and white stone. 'Forest Lawn Memorial Park,' she said. 'Everybody wants to get in there, but they only take the people who apply way in advance. To get a vault you have to pay a premium.'

I remembered a poster I'd seen in the downtown area, that had taken the point a little further. Two men, soberly dressed, sitting at a table in a restaurant. One of them raising a cup of coffee to his lips and looking at the other with an expression of cordiality and gratitude. The caption: *'I'm glad you recommended Pierce Brothers Mortuary'*.

On to Knott's Berry Farm and the most elaborate piece of hokum on the tourist beat. A reconstruction of a 19th-century pioneer town, complete with a gift shop, steak house and ice-cream parlour.

It had all started with Walter Knott's berries, which had been the local rage before the war. Jams, jellies and cakes, Mother's Home-Baked Pies and endless preserves had been the products of his fertile soil. The farm and berry market, an increasing attraction for visitors, had been extended to include a Chicken Dinner Restaurant, run by Mrs Knott, with the famous pies as an inviting extra. Casting about for a further development of his golden acreage Mr Knott had spotted a ghost town from the mining days and dreamed up the idea of creating his own detailed replica. By a remarkable feat of transplantation he had done it: dismantling derelict buildings at a number of similar sites and re-erecting them at Knott's Berry Farm. The reconstruction featured all the components of an authentic pioneer town: gun shop, livery stable, school house, saloon and general store. Additionally, to complete the illusion, a gold mine with a sluice box and an 'iron cayuse' engine and passenger cars, genuine rolling stock of the period. The latter were still in working order, and the visitor could choose between a train ride along a mile of railroad or a trip in an old-time stage coach.

The children, of course, loved it. Especially the elderly bald ones, in their knee-length socks and Bermuda shorts. As we wandered through the ghost town we saw these enthusiasts, hustling their wives and barking at their trailing offspring. 'Keep up or you'll miss the train ride.' 'Let's leave the candy, kids, 'til we've taken the auto ride.'

Here, it seemed, were Mr Knott's ideal customers. This didn't mean the history buffs had been overlooked, rather that they had not been taken too seriously. If they cared to look for a Southern Pacific Railroad Camp Stove, an 1880 Waffle Iron or a Hand-turned Chord Music-Box of the Civil War Period these scholars would probably find it; but not until they had picked their way through a barricade of Hand-Made Articles, Personalised Gift Items and Speciality Souvenirs. Gazing blankly at the hand-loomed nylon placemats, engraved plastic handbags and flower-decorated candles (scented or plain) they would recognise a disturbing truth about their country. That however hard it tried to revive the past, it could never escape the present.

Bernie, thank God, had seen it all before and we didn't spend too long being disillusioned. By the time we were on the highway again, however, it was past five. There was no time to do anything else, and we realised it was the parting of the ways. At Anaheim I unloaded my rucksack from the car to transfer to the Los Angeles bus. Demurely I returned Bernie's hug with an English kiss, and told her it had been the fastest two days of my trip. From the top of her red sun hat to the heels of her red shoes she glowed.

'Well... I've been mighty glad to take you round, Paul. Next time you come over, we'll maybe arrange a little more time.'

I nodded and said that perhaps when I came to America again she would be able to take me to that friend of hers, the one who kept three pet lions and a cheetah.

Los Angeles

Fruit of the Stars

Number 11734 Wilshire Boulevard was not an address you could take lightly. In England, it had seemed like the other end of the world: in downtown Los Angeles it was a few blocks further. The fact that I was standing in Wilshire Boulevard at the start of the journey gave me little encouragement. An inch-to-the-mile street map of Los Angeles opened out to four feet and I had to go across four folds from downtown westwards to reach 11734, on the junction of Wilshire Boulevard and Barrington Avenue.

There were no buses in sight, so I started walking. I didn't seriously consider going the whole distance on foot, but I'd learned a bit about the Los Angeles public transport system. In a city where there were half as many cars as people such public services were extraneous – except of course to those who really needed them. I remembered a newspaper article which had pointed out one of the anomalies of Los Angeles: a city with the most advanced freeway system in the world and yet with a high proportion of its population on public assistance and unable to afford a car.

Spurring me on was the thought that at the end of the journey I would find someone I knew. In a totally anonymous city like Los Angeles this was no small incentive, particularly when that person was a fetching redhead who used to share an editorial office with me in London. This girl, whose name was Sarah, had travelled to the States a month after me and was staying with her sister's in-laws in their luxury apartment. She was a girl who liked doing things in style and I remembered her excitement at the prospect. The location, after all, could not be bettered. To the north of the apartment lay the movie-star hideouts of Bel Air and Beverly Hills; to the west the beaches of Santa Monica.

I counted six blocks and then paused hopefully at a bus stop, watching the traffic. After a twenty-minute wait two buses came along, but they both terminated short of my destination and I carelessly let them go. I went on a few blocks, glancing wistfully at the sleek cars that swept past me. Another story about Los Angeles that I'd treated as a joke came back to me with an unnerving clarity: that in some parts of the city walking was illegal. Of all the LA myths, this was the most believable and was borne out by a police officer in a passing patrol car, who asked, not very politely, where I was going. He shook his head disbelievingly when I told him.

A few minutes later a car wove unexpectedly into the kerb and a Latino with half-closed eyes leaned out of the window. His voice was slurred, and what came out was only what I thought he said.

'You wanna ride, buddy?'

I nodded and pointed up the road, to infinity. 'Santa Monica?'

'*No es problema.*' He opened the passenger door and I climbed in beside him, the rucksack still on my back. As we pulled away from the kerb I realised my mistake.

Instead of continuing along the nearside lane he pulled immediately into the next one, without looking in his mirror. Luckily the traffic was thin, but it was soon piling up behind us as we drove unerringly along the white line between the lanes.

'Y' know the way to Hill Street, buddy?'

Straining my ears, I asked him to repeat the question. He didn't seem to hear me, and I anxiously noted the sagging angle of his head as he concentrated his gaze on the white line. Tough break, I'd been picked up by a wino.

As we maintained our course in the middle of the road the horns started, rising rapidly to a crescendo. To avoid further embarrassment we went through the red light at the next intersection, leaving our pursuers at a standstill. Fortunately there was no cross traffic at that point and no need for me to grab the steering wheel.

'Y' know the way to Hill Street?'

That was what I thought he said. And what he'd probably said first of all, when he pulled up at the kerb. He wasn't going anywhere near Santa Monica, but to Hill Street. Wasn't that in the downtown area?

'Missed a coupla' turnings, back there...'

Well, that's what happens, when you've been drinking cheap wine all night. All he wanted was to get home and sleep it off.

At the next intersection we stopped. The lights were green, but I didn't think to mention it. My companion leaned across to me, his potent breath heavy on my cheek. 'Hey, buddy – you drive a car?'

When I'd got out and was about halfway along the block I looked back and saw the car still at the lights, a line of other cars strung out behind it. Looking at the number on the nearest building I saw that I'd made some progress. Another hundred blocks and I'd be there.

A bus that by some miracle was going to Santa Monica took me all the way: ten miles that confirmed my expectations of Los Angeles. The cross-section of the city sliced by this endless boulevard was as representative as any of the more affluent neighbourhoods that I had travelled through so far. The architectural sources of America's most eclectic city were a conundrum: Spanish-American, mock-Georgian, Renaissance palazzo, 20th Century Fox. And plain bizarre: how could I forget Wilshire Boulevard's greatest feat of eccentricity, a restaurant in the shape of a bowler hat? (You've got it, The Brown Derby).

I could never imagine what it would be like to live in Los Angeles, but at 11734 Wilshire Boulevard I came uncomfortably close to finding out. Here, behind a resplendent exterior, lay the essence of the 'Dream'.

The block consisted of apartment buildings and shops, surrounding a central plaza. Walking down a slope I mistook for the entrance passage I found myself in a huge underground car park. A pillared hall, that at this hour of the day was like an empty bowel, its contents spread around a city of freeways, parking lots and multi-storey car parks. I doubt if I'd seen anything more suggestive of the omnipotence of the motor car.

A door on the far side led me into a laundry. Once more I beheld the triumph of the machine, with humans its willing accomplice. Between the humming rows of washers and spin driers walked the (largely female) occupants of the apartments, keeping a watchful eye on the suds and pausing intermittently to touch a button. Dressed in exquisite trouser suits, their hair dyed and lacquered, they might have been taking a break between cocktails.

Through another door I found my way to a foyer, which from all appearances was the official entrance. Standing in the carpeted hallway in my hobo's outfit and rucksack I felt extremely furtive, like a down-and-out after an illicit night in the broom cupboard. To my relief there were no janitors around and I slipped quickly into an opening elevator. Taking the third digit of the address number as the floor I pressed the button marked '7'.

My hunch proved correct and on the seventh floor I found the magic number: 11734. There was an eyehole in the door and as I pushed the buzzer I stood discreetly to one side. In a few minutes a middle-aged man in glasses opened the door and peered out. Seeing me, he started and withdrew.

Before he could shut the door I managed to announce myself and in some bewilderment he paused. 'Not Sarah's friend?'

I nodded, and with some uncertainty he ushered me inside. He was Sarah's sister's father-in-law, and inside the apartment, rising from a divan to greet me, was Sarah's sister's mother-in-law. Her reaction to the sight of Sarah's friend, whatever it may have been, was superbly masked by a smile of welcome. 'I guess you'd like to see Sarah.'

She picked up a telephone and in a minute or two Sarah – who was in another apartment – joined us. By the time she arrived I had eased the rucksack off my shoulders, hoping this made me more acceptable to Wilshire Boulevard society. To my surprise, Sarah greeted me in the same way as the others – as a bit of a curiosity. That was what two weeks on Wilshire Boulevard did for you.

We went for drinks on the balcony, from where I could look down from a height of seven storeys on the central plaza. In the middle of the plaza there was a swimming pool and sun court; on two sides a shopping area built specially for the apartments. I saw a sign that said 'Supermarket' and another 'Pet's Parlor'.

After travelling across a continent it was hard to imagine that this was, for some, the limit of their world. For all the pleasures of her new existence, I discovered that Sarah had declared against going native. She was a country girl and her 'heath and heather' instincts had rebelled against the tyranny of the car, imposed on her whenever she wanted to go anywhere. It had been hard to identify any need – from buying a newspaper to having her hair done – that might take her further than the plaza; but when she did she was driven all the way. Such was the rarity of existence on Wilshire Boulevard.

The two days of my stay with Sarah did little to recall reality. On the first day following my arrival we went to Disneyland, the pleasure park that every fun-loving American wants to visit sometime (if only he can persuade his children to take him). The park, laid out on a 160-acre former orange grove near Anaheim, south of Los Angeles, had been the inspiration of Walt Disney, a man long dedicated to entertainment in another form.

The invention of Disneyland had come from Walt's awareness that even the cinema had its limitations, and that to get people really involved in the business of enjoying themselves you had to make them do extraordinary things that they would normally never think of doing. Like riding on a monorail, blasting off in a moon rocket, exploring the ocean depths in a submarine...

For five dollars we were allowed fifteen of these 'adventures'. This might seem a lot of money, but no-one who goes to Disneyland will begrudge it. Where else, and for what kind of money, could you recreate the fantasies of childhood?

The first adventures were in 'Tomorrowland', an area devoted to the space age and high-speed thrills. Here we climbed a replica of the Matterhorn, 140 feet high, built of steel, concrete and plaster, and took a bobsleigh ride down its slopes, plunging into a watersplash at the bottom. We rode over the first monorail system in the west at 40mph, took a Swiss cable-car over Alpine peaks, and whizzed dizzily around in a flying saucer. We took a journey to the moon by spaceship and a voyage to Atlantis in a submarine.

The latter experience was the most (synthetically) thrilling of them all. Here was a 'genuine submarine' that actually travelled under the water. With no hint of irony its creators acknowledged the fact that 'Tomorrowland''s submarine fleet was 'the world's eighth largest'. It was also the only one in the world that ran around on rails and offered its passengers consecutive views of sunken galleons and submerged cities, coral reefs and polar ice, giant squid and sharks.

In a landscape that had been cleverly adapted to suit the location of the 'adventures', Walt's imagination took us everywhere. As well as 'Tomorrowland' there was 'Fantasyland', 'Frontierland' and 'Adventureland'. Within the same 160 acres we could take a jungle river cruise, a steamboat up the Mississippi and a pack mule ride through the desert. By the end of the day we felt like a couple of worn-out globe-trotters, our impressions as varied as they were unreal. All of which brought me to the conclusion that if I had only one destination left in the world that I could go, it would have to be Disneyland.

Our plans for the second day needed little discussion. We knew exactly what we wanted to do, and the only problem was how to do it. How, for example, did we get to see Doris Day in Makeup, or Tony Curtis off set, downing a highball? How to get inside one of those fabulous movie lots, whose streets were camera tracks? The magnificent studios, the mansions of the stars?

We'd heard about a Hollywood tour bus that departed from a downtown hotel at a certain time, but the Wilshire Boulevard buses – predictably unreliable – ensured that we missed the connection. With only the vaguest sense of direction we started walking up one of the long avenues that ran north from Wilshire, with the tenuous hope that it would eventually join the mythical Hollywood Boulevard.

On our way we discovered the Farmers' Market, a rambling emporium beloved of the movie stars. The open-air stalls exhibited a rich variety of produce, most of it from the farms of the San Fernando Valley to the north. The display of fruit and vegetables was breathtaking; no less than one would expect in a state so blessed by its rich soil and sunshine. The most compelling quality of the produce was its freshness – something that Sarah and I would appreciate at the lunch counter. To palates adjusted to the flavours of canned, cartonned, foil-packed, deep frozen and hygienically sealed foods, the freshly-cooked helpings of roast farm-bred turkey and autumn vegetables were irresistible. The meal gave us the energy to explore the luxuriant avenues of produce that stretched for what seemed miles around us.

'What on earth is that?'

Sarah was pointing at a plump, star-shaped fruit. She picked it up to examine it more closely. Just then, as though responding to a cue, a man in a blazer and gold tie-pin popped up from behind the marrows.

'Allow me to introduce myself. Andrew Hosack, 20th Century Fox...'

With some uncertainty we shook hands. Gold teeth mirrored the tie-pin as he gave Sarah an expansive grin. 'You know, lady, I couldn't resist the way you wrinkled up your nose just then, when you were lookin' at the fruit...'

My heart sank. At any moment, it seemed, Sarah would be whisked away for a screen test. But happily it transpired that Mr Hosack was not a producer, director or even talent scout. He was a driver for the 20th Century Fox Transportation Department.

'You know, it really is a great thrill to meet a couple of young English people out here in Hollywood. We get a lot of visitors all year, but I always keep a special eye open for our friends across the pond.' He paused, his grin spreading further, and we eyed him with increasing suspense. 'Most visitors like to get a look inside the studios, but unless you got some kind of intro, it's pretty difficult...'

Catching our expectant gaze, he looked at his watch. 'Right now they oughta be shootin' *Daniel Boone*...' A moment's deliberation was followed by a wink, and a discreet softening of his voice. 'What would you say if I smuggled you in?'

We fell at his feet. He didn't really have the authority, he told us, but thought that he could get us through the gate without too much difficulty. He led us to his car, which had '20th Century Fox' emblazoned on the side. It was like being given an entry pass to heaven.

As we drove to the studios we learnt that 'Andy' had been with Fox for forty years and had been involved with most of their productions. His job was to ferry the stars and directors around, but frequently during his career he had been asked to drive on the set as well as off it. His most recent role, in *Those Magnificent Men in their Flying Machines*, was the one that he recalled most proudly. Remember that scene at the aerodrome when the fire engine went berserk and drove through a hangar? Well, that was Andy Hosack at the wheel.

In a dream sequence that was pure cinema we went through the gates at 20th Century, the guard waving us on as though he recognised us from our last visit with Daniel F. Zanuck. Thereafter the fantasy abated as we drove around a complex of anonymous office and studio buildings, without so much as a glimpse of Tombstone or the Forum Romanum. As Andy explained, 20th Century Fox – like most of the big studios – had seen days of greater glory. Once upon a time it had boasted the largest film lot in Hollywood, but since the advent of TV and the rising cost of making films for the big screen, it had undergone the inevitable transformation. The lot had been sold for $43 million, and seventy-five acres rented back to provide studio space for making television series. The only compensation for this sorry capitulation to the 'box' was the knowledge, however unpalatable, that this was what the public wanted.

The two series currently in the pipeline were *Daniel Boone* and *Twelve O'Clock High*. With the furtive briskness of a security guard in a nuclear missile plant our guide led us through a side door and along a narrow corridor to the studio where '*Boone*' was in production. Taking elaborate care not to trip over cables, lights and other bits of apparatus we crept into a corner behind the scenery and were there treated to a close-up of the ghost of the old Hollywood.

A forest of fibreglass cottonwoods stood against a painted backcloth of sky and mountains. Grouped beneath a tree in the foreground was a posse of half a dozen men, armed with rifles. Their leader was gripping a rope, slung over a branch of the tree, looped around the neck of an 'Indian' who stood impassively awaiting his fate, his hands tied behind his back. To the left of the 'Indian' stood another man, armed with a shotgun. Tall, bronzed and buckskinned, he was immediately recognisable. In unison we whispered 'Fess Parker' and Andy raised his finger to his lips, either to prevent us mobbing the star or to warn us of the imminent 'action'.

In the next half-hour I discovered the truth about film-making. Far from being glamorous and exciting it was in fact a somewhat tedious business, with the director and crew in eternal confab between takes, and the takes themselves winding up in successive retakes. The action looked straightforward enough (Daniel Boone, backwoods hero, intervening to save innocent 'Indian' from lynching party) but nothing seemed to go right. Either Fess would miss his cue, the microphone get tangled in the cottonwood, or the 'Indian' grimace too unstoically when they jerked the rope. I could think of easier ways of earning a living.

During a break in the filming Andy signalled to Fess Parker, and to our tremulous delight the star of the show came over to greet us. I remember little of the encounter, save a towering six-and-a-half-foot frame, a smile like the split bark of an oak and a backwoods grip that left my hand half-paralysed. And a touch of gallantry that belonged just as surely to the pioneering days. Seeing that Sarah had nowhere to sit, Fess found her a stool. 'Out on the frontier,' he declared, 'we like our womenfolk to be comfortable.'

Sarah was, of course, thrilled, and it was clear that Fess welcomed the diversion. Even for a hardy frontiersman, standing under a dummy cottonwood all day could become a little tiresome. In a moment the 'Indian', who had somehow slipped his noose, came to join us. Under the sweat and greasepaint he looked a little haggard, as anyone might after hanging at the end of a rope all day.

After a brief visit to the *Twelve O'Clock High* set (the TV series, not the Gregory Peck film) Andy obligingly took us on to Hollywood Boulevard. Dropping us at the famous Walk of Fame, he suggested we look around and 'find a good movie'. We thanked him for giving us a perfect day, and he responded by saying how glad he was that he had spotted us earlier at the Farmers' Market.

He had a farewell shot for Sarah. 'Remember that fruit you were wrinkling your nose at? It's called "star fruit"...'

The Sequoias

Living Monuments

Unless your heart lies in San Diego, the Golden State has only one alternative destination to LA. Perched on a peninsula 400 miles to the north is the other major settlement, the urbane and historic city that disclaims any relationship to its sprawling rival. Los Angeles might be a suburb in search of a city, but San Francisco – to its increasing detriment – was the reverse.

The stretch of California that separated the cities provided some interesting contrasts. The coastal strip that one day – if the real estate people had anything to do with it – would be their unifying thread, was backed by the coastal ranges of the Central Valley, which in turn was backed by the higher mountains of the Sierra Nevada range. These mountains were famous not only for their scale (Mount Whitney was one) but for their beauty, the work of earth movements and glaciation and the defter application of wind and water.

Scale and beauty also applied to those great natural phenomena, the sequoias. A trip to see the giant trees, and the country around them, presented a natural breathing space between the cities. When a single tree was marked on a 1:21 map then I could have no other objective. The tree was the 'General Sherman', believed to be the world's largest living organism. It stood in a grove on the western slopes of the Sierra Nevada, in the Sequoia National Park.

To get there I had to take a bus north, through the San Joaquin Valley, with a town called Visalia as my jumping-off point. The 200 miles of US99 that took me to the Greyhound stage at Tulare covered a great variety of scenery, with live oak forest and scrub-mantled hills running into semi-desert and then the more fertile stretches of the valley. A low-flying aircraft spraying pesticide, droning like a giant winged insect overhead, was a marker for the crop that flourished here almost as prolifically as in the South: cotton.

For miles the fields reached out to the horizon, giving way eventually to the orange groves. Tulare was at the centre of orange country and from here I took a local bus to Visalia. As far as I could see there was no public transport beyond this point and I was left with the problem of how to cover the extra fifty miles to the park.

The most direct route was on State 198 and for the first time I found myself on foot on a major freeway. Knowing that there were laws against hitch-hiking on these roads I did not make my intentions too obvious. I kept my eyes to the front without a single glance at the passing traffic. This did not mean, of course, that I expected to go unnoticed.

No one stopped and after a while I realised that the drivers too had the state laws in mind when they sailed by at the permitted maximum of 70mph. Fatalistically I awaited the scream of sirens and the arrival of a police car to escort me from the carriageway.

The Sheriff of Tulare County did not show however and I was obliged to throw down the gauntlet. Taking off my rucksack I dug out a piece of card and wrote 'SEQUOIA' on it in large letters with a piece of charcoal. Cellotaping the card to the rucksack I resumed my journey. Within two minutes I was picked up by a farmer in a truck.

He was not going into the park but offered to give me a boost. This turned out to be a distance of twenty-nine miles, as far as the park gates. To get there my driver, who was 'always pleased to help

THE SEQUOIAS

a Limey', willingly extended his journey beyond the plantation where he worked. When I told him how much I had longed to see a ripe Californian orange growing on a tree he smiled. 'There's plenty of them, up my place.'

A few miles short of the gates he turned off the road and drove me to the plantation, a forest of orange and lemon trees that he'd nurtured for most of his working life. A walk around the perimeter of the grove gave me a glimpse of one of the many problems involved in their cultivation. Between each row of trees stood a line of smudge-pots, the oil burners that were lit at night to protect the trees from frost in the winter months. At the end of our tour the farmer showed me another product of his devotion of which he was justifiably proud: an avocado pear tree heavy with green, globular fruit.

Deposited at the park gates I hailed the ranger on duty and asked him how far I was from the General Sherman Tree. The ranger, a crop-haired veteran, looked at me with a degree of caution. 'Seventeen miles, or thereabouts.' His eyes ranged over me, fixing on my rucksack. 'You plannin' on hitch-hikin'?'

I nodded, but as it was 4.30pm said I wouldn't be starting out until the following morning. He shook his head, slowly and decisively. 'There's no hitch-hikin' allowed in the National Park area.'

Did he just hit me between the eyes? The same rules had applied on the freeway, but surely this was different? I had to ride the blow. Temporarily acknowledging the authority of the Baden Powell hat and well-ironed uniform, I retreated to a motel on the park boundary.

It proved a good strategy. The following morning when I returned to the gates there was another ranger on duty, a young man of about twenty. His attitude was more accommodating than his colleague's and he offered to arrange a lift for me into the park – the simplest way of getting round the rules. In half an hour the first vehicle arrived, and the ranger flagged it down.

I could not have wished for a more convenient, or appropriate conveyance. A Dormobile van with a Union Jack sticker on the windscreen and a GB plate on the back. The first British-registered vehicle I'd seen in America.

203

On board was an Australian family, four intrepid round-the-worlders who'd bought the van in England and shipped it out to America. By shifting some luggage they made space for me in the back and we drove up to the Giant Forest, a seventeen-mile haul that took us from 1,700 to 6,000 feet. On the way up we had tremendous views of the country that made this area one of the most sought-after for the addicts of mountain landscape: the forested uplands of the Sierra. Between them, the Sequoia and the King's Canyon National Park to the north covered 1,300 square miles of picture-calendar beauty, reaching its climax in the majestic High Sierra to the east.

And in those tree-Titans whose seed, one could imagine, had wafted on the wind from Mount Olympus.

When a living thing was three or four thousand years old one could only describe it in the language of mythology. More so when it was the survivor of a species that flourished millions of years ago. The 250-mile stretch of the Sierra extending west from Sequoia to Yosemite National Park was one of the few natural habitats of the *Sequoia gigantea*, the world's greatest living monument.

Driving through the forest we became aware of the tremendous size of the trees. With their lowest branches as much as a hundred feet from the ground, they resembled colossal fluted pillars, up to thirty feet in diameter. Only when I arched my neck backwards could I see the foliage of the lower branches, a canopy of green that obscured any further view of the trees. Parking off the road, we went to inspect the 'General'.

How do you find a single tree in a forest of giants? Simple, you check the grid reference and then follow the road signs. Walking along the trail to the famous tree I wondered what the indomitable general would have thought about having the world's largest (living) block of wood named after him.

At the end of the trail there was a large grassy clearing, filled with straining photographers who had not cricked their necks like this since their visit to a famous building on 34th Street, New York City. The limitations of my own equipment were only overcome by going back the furthest distance I could and then lying on my back, with the camera pointing upwards. At this angle I was able to get most of the tree in the picture, with a bit of sky to spare.

But this alone could not convey the scale of the giant. I had to find some human beings, to provide a contrast. After a fruitless search for thirty large men who would kindly volunteer to link their arms around the trunk I settled for the Australian family. They thought it was a 'bonza' idea, and handed me their own cameras for the shot. Under my direction they stood against the tree, looking rather like insects that had just emerged from a crack in the bark.

The General Sherman tree was 272 feet high and 101 feet around the base. Its nearest rival, the General Grant, was 267 feet high and 107 feet around the base. Even standing in front of them such dimensions were hard to comprehend.

Leaving the Australians to a picnic I returned to the road and headed south towards the Visitor Center. The two-mile walk through the forest was a daunting experience. It was not only the height of the trees but the thought of their age that impressed me; the idea that any form of plant life could endure the hazards of nature for so long.

Among the towers that loomed over me were some that had been saplings when Columbus discovered America, or had first sprouted from the earth before the birth of Christ. Such historical comparisons, though putting the age of the trees in perspective, offered no explanation for their existence. For this I had to take a closer look at the trees themselves.

The forensics lay in the bark, a fibrous reddish-brown cladding with a thickness – revealed by the fissures in the wood – of several inches. This was the armour that had preserved the trees for centuries from the scourges of insect pests, disease and fire. Their resistance to the latter was strikingly illustrated by the black fire scars on many of the trunks, evidence of past conflagrations. These were gradually being covered by an envelope of new bark, leaving the scar an inverted 'V' on the side of the tree.

Why the trees were confined to such a small area of the country was a mystery, though it was thought that these were the places that had escaped glaciation in the last ice age. There could certainly be no other explanation for the survival of the species, whose antiquity had been established by the fossil remains uncovered elsewhere. But apart from this accident of nature, and the cast-iron constitution of the trees themselves, they had another point in their favour. Old age brought little diminution of their powers. After 3,500 years General Sherman was still procreating.

At the Visitor Center huge sections of trunk were on display, laid on their sides to reveal in cross section the record of their incredible age. One or two people were counting rings, which was the sort of activity I preferred to keep for a rainy day. Leaving the dendrochronologists to their pleasures I departed along the trail to Moro Rock.

The summit of this odd, sugar-loaf rock afforded a grand view of the High Sierra, a panorama of mountain wilderness. From here I returned to the trail and thumbed a lift back to the Visitor Center from an elderly couple in a station wagon. Obligingly they took me on a detour to the Tunnel Log, featured on many postcards of the park. This was a fallen redwood through which a road – leading nowhere in particular – had been cleverly routed. The tunnel that had been carved out of the log allowed a headroom of about ten feet. According to my much-travelled companions, this was nothing. In the Yosemite National Park, to the north, they'd carved a road tunnel through the trunk of a *live* redwood...

The sequoias, of course, were conifers, but any hope I might have had of tripping over a football-sized cone was disappointed. The cones that I saw were a standard two or three inches in length, which hardly made them unique specimens. More remarkable was the potential of the tiny seeds they carried. I slipped one into my pocket for luck, wondering what the chances were of starting a colony on Hampstead Heath.

Anxious to leave the park before dusk I took up my now familiar stance outside the Visitor Center on a gently sloping hill. That day the Fates, bless them, were lined up beside me. Within a few minutes my transport had arrived, though not in quite the form I had imagined.

The vehicle that hissed and clanked to a halt was unlike anything on wheels I'd ever seen. A huge, mechanised dinosaur, painted bright yellow. From the elevated driver's cabin a distant voice hailed me, inviting me to join him.

With the rucksack dragging on my shoulders it was like an attempt on the Eiger. The wheel of the juggernaut was taller than me and I had to reach up for the mudguard to pull myself onto the hub cap. From here I transferred to a footplate below the passenger door, and on the driver's instructions off-loaded the rucksack into the centre of a spare wheel mounted on the back of the truck. By a superb gymnastic feat I opened the passenger door and tumbled into the cab.

My shouted thanks were drowned by the roar of the diesel engine as the monster got under way. My voice froze and my attention was magnetically focused on two things: the road, barely visible below us, and the robotic action of the driver as he propelled the vehicle into the descent.

Despite his skilled handling I was convinced that the thing had a will of its own, and only by a grudging act of submission would allow the person at the wheel to control it. The dashboard in front of me bristled with a bewildering array of knobs, levers and dials: progressive shifts for snow clearance, fuel and air pressure gauges, main and auxiliary transmission levers. A choice of twenty-four transmission shifts, to cope with unimaginable feats of hauling, lifting, ploughing and clearing.

With a juggernaut momentum we plunged into the bends – each one poised on the brink of the nothingness below. For a few moments on each bend, my life was in the gyrating arms of the driver. Only when he'd pulled us out of it could I think again about the rest of my life. For him, of course, it was just routine.

Until we'd reached the fourteenth hairpin there was little communication between us. Then the driver caught a glimpse of my face in his mirror. 'You never bin in an Osh-Kosh?'

I shook my head, unable to think of any other occasion. I'd never even heard of an Osh-Kosh. Clearly it was a name I would remember.

By a combination of Providence and the driver's brute genius we made a safe landing on the valley floor, after a descent of 5,000 feet, and executed a cautious turn into the Park Headquarters. This was about a mile from the park gates, but my stars were still favourable. No sooner had I descended from the Osh-Kosh than a car pulled up beside me and a door was thrust open. It was the young ranger who'd helped me with the lift into the Giant Forest.

'Where you going?'

When I said the park gates, he looked astonished. 'Is that all? Didn't you say you were going to San Francisco or someplace?'

For the second time I lost my voice. As I climbed in beside him he said: 'I can drop you at Modesto, if that's any good.'

Modesto was 150 miles away to the north on US99 – about eighty miles from San Francisco. The ranger – a student who had been working in the park for his vacation – was on the way back to his home in Sacramento. In the gathering darkness we drove out of the park towards Visalia, the starting point of my hike the previous day. Another five miles took us onto the US99, and from here it was either divided highway or controlled access freeway all the way to Modesto, a run of two and a half hours.

Modesto was a Greyhound stage, and after a steak and coleslaw in an 'all-nite' diner at the depot we parted company. Having no idea of the times of the buses to San Francisco I was encouraged to find that I had only an hour to wait. Time to reflect on the tally of a day's hitch-hiking that measured, by any standards, as a freakish success. A Dormobile, a station-wagon, an Osh-Kosh and a fast car. A fantastic view of the mountains and valleys of the Sierra, and the Titans of the Great Forest. How many tourists could combine that variety of transport with that amount of spectacle?

The San Francisco Greyhound was almost empty and I took a seat at the front behind the driver, for the benefit of a widescreen view of our arrival in the city. The front seat on the other side of the bus was taken by an irrepressible character in Greyhound overalls, who was making the most of an opportunity to chat with the driver. In defiance of the regulations (which as an employee he should have known about, regardless of the notice) he maintained an endless banter, firing anecdotes at the driver and any passenger who was in range. Presenting himself as a professional 'bum', he recalled some highly-coloured experiences, drawn from a lifetime of apparently aimless roaming. The stories, though implausible, were impossibly funny, and in the midst of my own laughter I wondered how the driver, with his quaking shoulders, was able to hold a straight course.

In response to my applause the yarn-spinner fixed me with a beady eye. 'You ever bin to Wyoming?'

I shook my head, and he added: 'Then you won't have seen a jackalope.'

The driver's shoulders were still quivering, suggesting that he'd heard this one before.

'In Wyoming they cross the jack-rabbits with the antelopes. That's how they get jackalopes. If you wanna know how to spot 'em they've got long ears and long legs – run faster than a racehorse. They use 'em for herdin' sheep.'

'That's nothin',' the driver said. 'What about the turquitoes?'

His friend nodded, his face as straight as a board. 'That's in Texas. Mosquitoes are so large down there they cross 'em with turkeys...'

With entertainment like this the journey evaporated – a comic interlude with changing scenery. In a short time, staring through the windscreen at the lights ahead, I had a renewal of the sensation I had experienced on that misty morning two months ago, when the *Queen Elizabeth* had sailed under the Verrazano Bridge and into the Narrows to afford the first magical glimpse of New York City. Now the lights ahead of us belonged unmistakably to the other great city, separated by the width of a continent, that stood as dramatically on its own peninsula. As we drove, via a complex structure of feedways, on to the massive approach road of the bridge, the driver beckoned me down into the well of the bus beside him. From here I had a Cineramic view of the night-time San Francisco with its steeply-banked streets and tiered skyscrapers forming a curtain wall of light behind the shimmering waters of San Francisco Bay.

As we sped towards the city, the great curving span of the San Francisco-Oakland Bay Bridge lifted us in its embrace. At the central anchorage of Yerba Buena Island we passed momentarily through a tunnel, about 500 feet long, and then came out on the West Crossing of the bridge, from where it was possible to glimpse simultaneously the illuminated spans of the two other bridges that completed the girdle of the bay. To the north, the Richmond-San Rafael. To the west, the fabulous Golden Gate Bridge, a slender sparkling thread across the opening to the Pacific.

San Francisco

Diagonals and Verticals

At four-thirty in the morning Market Street was a wind tunnel. Violent gusts, driving in from San Francisco Bay, scourged me as I battled my way southwards from Golden Gate Avenue to Hayes Street. On the tenth day of my California experience, after a restless night before that icy dawn, I feared I might be leaving more than my heart in San Francisco.

The only light in Hayes Street led me to the San Francisco Casual Labor Office. For a dimeless itinerant, whose six-dollar-a-day budget had begun to falter, this was a place of destiny.

In the murky inner office, fogged with the fumes of tobacco smoke and unwashed bodies, I discovered a Ben Shahn photograph. A dozen or so day-haulers, reincarnations of the Okies of yesteryear, were slumped on three or four rows of benches, waiting for what the day would bring. They all looked as if they could use a shave, a shower and a hot breakfast. Some were asleep, some muttered incoherently to one another and some stared wanly at the late arrivals as we joined the line to have our employment cards stamped. Duly registered, I found a space at the end of a bench and sat beside a gnarled, sullen-looking individual in patched overalls.

My muted 'good morning' did me no favours. His look of bleary incredulity told me that he'd seen nothing like me, in his whole tomato-picking life.

'First haul?'

Diffidently I nodded. He sighed, but I wasn't sure whether it was in contempt or sympathy. With soil-ingrained hands he gently rubbed his patched-up knees and thighs to get the blood flowing. 'You name it, I've picked it,' he said.

I regarded him with interest. 'What are tomatoes like?'

For a moment he pondered. 'Small round things that grow on the ground in rows about a mile long. They're OK, if you like bustin' your back.'

A steady flow of people was coming into the office, the one-day hopefuls for whom the ungodly hour was bearable, if it meant a day's work. As tomato-pickers they were improbable.

Some looked as if bending down would be their last act. One couple – he with beads around his neck, she with hair to her waist – were clearly in the wrong place at the wrong time. They all shuffled, sheep-like, to the counter, ready to play their vital role in the nation's economy.

Grudgingly the seasoned workers who'd arrived on time made room for the newcomers on the benches. Soon the place was full, and everyone settled down to await the day-haul bus. This was due in about half an hour at 5.30am. With everyone asleep or half-way the time was passed in silence, broken only by desultory murmurs.

'Where we goin' – San Jose?'

'Pickin''s pretty tough, right now.'

'How much they payin'?'

The long-haired girl sat in front of me and through half-closed eyes I studied her bottom. More correctly, the seat of her jeans, which iconographically was of more than passing interest. Inscribed thereon, in ball-point pen, was an assortment of graffiti that included a heart shape, surmounting the words 'Pot is Hope' and a tomato incorporating a nuclear disarmament symbol.

The bus was an hour late. By the time it arrived, at 6.30am, you could have cut the atmosphere with a knife. When the driver put his head around the door and shouted 'San Jose!' it was as if he'd announced the discovery of gold. A concerted, almost involuntary surge carried me to the door.

Outside, the struggle continued as fifty people tried simultaneously to board the bus. It wasn't all good-natured, particularly when the hippy – he with the beads – pushed in front of my companion with the patched overalls. Finding his breath again after being dug a few times in the ribs the veteran exploded in scorn.

'How much pickin' *you* ever done?'

The youth, pulling his girlfriend after him, hardly turned his head. 'Plenty, man.'

'Pickin' a frickin' guitar, that's all!'

Though recognising that saying 'after you' was not an option, I was the last person on the bus. My timidity had cost me a seat and I was one of a dozen people left standing. The driver climbed aboard, with no more than a single pained glance at his payload, and pulled a piece of typewritten paper from his pocket. This, it turned out, was a list of the farms where seasonal work was in progress.

San Jose was a fifty-mile run, straight down the Bayshore Freeway. As we drove south, through the dark empty streets of the city, my senses swiftly blurred, lulled by the movement of the bus. If sleep had been possible, standing shakily on one foot in the midst of a crowd of fifty whiffy tomato-pickers, I would have succumbed. Instead, my thoughts wandered back a few days to my arrival in San Francisco.

Getting off the Greyhound at the Market Street depot I had said to myself: 'This is it, Young Man, You've Gone West'.

Time to check the greenies.

Truly I had gone west, with less than a quarter of my funds remaining. Two months ago I had started out with a conviction that I would see the States for six dollars a day. The alien registration card that made me eligible for employment was an insurance to tuck into my wallet. But here I was, two-thirds of the way through the trip, with less than a third of my money left. Even I, with my limited logistical skills, could do the calculation. The budget that I had considered adequate for my needs was a theory scribbled on the back of an envelope.

The pre-dawn hours passed on a tide of letter-writing. It was the only occupation left to me after renouncing, during that traumatic night in Flagstaff, any further attempt at sleeping in a Greyhound bus depot. At 5.30am, with the last letter to my loved ones sealed, stamped and surrendered to US Mail, I wandered out into Market Street.

Following a routine recommended to all travellers arriving in an unknown American city in the small hours, I found the nearest all-night garage and asked the attendant for a street and vicinity map (you know, one of the free ones courtesy of Chevron?). A sleepy wave directed me to a rack, and with a practised hand I helped myself to San Francisco, the Peninsula, the East Bay Cities and Marin County. I would like to have asked for a battery check as well, or even some gasoline, just to show my appreciation.

With the help of the Downtown map I soon located the 'Y' on Golden Gate Avenue and checked in for the night. The night in question was, of course, the following night – but the desk clerk was a humanitarian and gave me immediate possession of a vacant room. This, hopefully, would serve as two nights for the price of one. The first 'night' lasted five hours, a deep sleep on a made-up bed that took me round to eleven o'clock and put me in good shape for my first sortie into San Francisco.

A good way of exploring a city of this size and complexity, I discovered, was to find the State Employment Bureau. Having found that, to then locate the office of the Department of Employment that could hopefully provide me with a job. The Department was pretty diversified, and I tried three different offices before I got the right one. According to the Bureau, all these offices were 'just off Market' which sounded pretty parochial until you looked at a map and saw that Market was the street that ran in a diagonal line from the docks north-east of the city to a point in the southern residential area five miles away.

The street was not only the longest in the city but also the widest. Being originally a wharf it had an unusual feature: the streets to the east of it, where the Bay had been filled in, ran at a different angle to the streets to the west of it. To add to this peculiarity, the angle was vertical as well as horizontal. To the west of Market the streets started to climb to the heights of the city, those impossibly steep hills that were San Francisco's most celebrated idiosyncrasy.

Fancying my chances with the Professional and Commercial Department I walked twelve blocks to the office on California Street, 'off Market'. Needless to say there was nothing doing in the professional and sales line and I had to go back fourteen blocks to Industrial and Service, on Mission Street. Here I queued diligently with the other applicants for Industrial Work, Laundry and Garment, and Hotel, Restaurant and Domestic, only to find that my qualifications were not exactly what they were looking for. Moving back another three blocks I found myself at the Casual Labor Office on Hayes Street. Stuff this for a game of Snakes and Ladders.

Inside I gazed blankly at the vacancy notices, which offered me four alternatives. I could either join twenty-five roustabouts in setting up a carnival (about six hours' work), distribute samples in Oakland for $1.20 an hour, go fruit-picking on a day haul, or sell blood to the San Francisco General Hospital. At $10 a pint the last proposition was the most attractive, but I couldn't see myself tackling many hills thereafter. Being neither a sixteen-stone roustabout nor a seven-stone sample distributor, I was left, like the Okies, with but a single choice.

The choice was tomatoes, and the place San Jose. On the card that the clerk gave me, my occupational title was entered as 'Elem. F.W.' When I reported for work (Farm Labor), I had to bring the card with me. The day haul started at 5.30am every day, reporting time 4.30. To my relief I could report any day I chose, which meant that for a day or two I could bookmark my fate.

The vexed question of employment being settled, I could turn my thoughts to pleasanter things. From a phone booth I put through a call to Elizabeth Mendell, now returned to Stanford University after her vacation. The call, which had been pre-arranged during my stay in Houston, did not come as a surprise and was another successful piece of timing. Elizabeth was driving to San Francisco the next day with Marsden and three children from his family they were taking out for the day. They were going to the Fleischhacker

Zoo, on the west side of the city, and could pick me up afterwards at the YMCA. 'After that, you must come down to Stanford,' she said. 'We've got everything fixed.'

Those magical words were instant balm to a lone Englishman in America. At a gentle pace I commenced my long anticipated exploration of the city.

At the farthest reach of my tour, the City of the Bay could be described (even in the context of America) as a transcendent urban experience. This definition could also be applied to New York, which was its opposite, not only in its location but its character.

I considered the differences. Where New York was awe-inspiring, San Francisco was sedate, where the 'Big Apple' was frenetic its West Coast sister was, undeniably, laid back. The hard-edged capital of commerce had something of the nature of its doughty and competitive colonisers – the Dutch and the British – in its make-up, whereas the capital of hedonism on the other side owed its beating heart to the Spanish who arrived here in 1776 and made it their northernmost port in New Spain. And, to no less an extent, to the new Americans who came here in the middle of the following century, lured westwards by a vision of El Dorado. For these pioneers San Francisco meant little more than a harbour where they could anchor their boats after the long journey up the west coast from Panama or Cape Horn, before they headed east for the gold diggings of the Sierras: but it would also mean a bolt-hole where they could raise hell if they struck lucky. I would soon discover that the raffish spirit of the makeshift city of shanties, saloons and opium dens had survived into the 1960s.

As chance would have it my first 'point of interest' was the legacy of the people who had given their toil, tears and sweat not only to the gold workings but the construction of the rail lines which had brought the pioneers westwards. On the Grant Avenue tangent of Market Street I found the area of the city unique for its pagoda-style roofs, dragon-entwined street lamps and shop fronts emblazoned with Chinese characters.

Of all the enclaves of the Orient that had grown up in the last century in foreign lands, San Francisco's Chinatown was probably the most prolific. Eight blocks deep and three across, it was the home of the descendants of the first immigrants who had sailed across the

Pacific to the 'golden hills' in the early 1850s, and the thousands more of their kind who had later been imported as cheap labour for the construction of the Union and Central Pacific Railroads. They now comprised the largest Chinese community in the West.

Sadly, although the Americans greatly benefited from the 'coolie trade' – the export of labourers under contract from China – their appreciation was not shown in the rates of pay for the construction gangs ($1 a day for the Chinese, $3-5 for the whites). This exhibition of prejudice against the new Californians was further demonstrated when the railroad was completed and the labour market was flooded with 15,000 unwanted Chinese workers. Anti-immigration laws such as the 1882 Exclusion Act were passed: the resulting outbreak of mob violence, including lynching, cast an indelible stain on the land of the free. Until the repeal of the Act during World War Two (when a different enemy was perceived), the Chinese population of the city showed a steady decline and had only recently recovered the numbers of the boom years of the 1870s.

Wartime solidarity against a common foe – Japan – provided only a brief reconciliation. Apart from the inevitable freezing of relations between the two countries, the Communist takeover in China in 1949 had a bizarre consequence: the banning of all imports of art goods from the Chinese mainland. As a result the Chinese Americans, who had worked so hard to promote their culture, were deprived of the essential commodities. I had been alerted to this by reading – in a current and one-hundred-per-cent serious piece of travel literature – the following bland assurance: 'Most of the things you will see', it read, 'although Chinese in design, are imported from Japan, but the discerning visitor should no longer pass them by. The quality of Japanese workmanship is quite different today from that of several years ago'.

Along the parade of restaurants, bars and shops on Grant Avenue I was reassured to see signs such as 'Sun Tao Yuan – Genuine Chinese Food' and 'Canton Bazaar – Chinese Art Goods'. Tempted, just momentarily, to test the authenticity of 'The Concubine Room' I settled for a chop suey at the next- door diner.

That should have done it, for Day One. But the map was still a temptation. Noticing that I was only a couple of blocks from

Broadway I thought that I should educate myself further in the cultural life of San Francisco.

In tiny Adler Street, which made a quadrilateral with Grant Avenue, Columbus Avenue and Broadway, I found myself at the City Lights Bookstore. Though I knew this to be a sacred precinct of the Beat Generation I had not, as yet, studied the form. Jack Kerouac's *On the Road*, William Burroughs' *Naked Lunch* and Allen Ginsberg's *Howl* were unread bibles. Browsing diffidently among the book stacks, jammed with the literature of the West Coast avant garde, I didn't fully appreciate that with all these noble characters still around, the place was not just a shrine but a living organism.

It was given its vitals by the man who'd set it up in '53, a poet by the name of Lawrence Ferlinghetti. The motive force for a lot of what subsequently went on came with the publishing business that he added on upstairs, which enabled him to promote the work of the Beat poets and novelists whose overriding thesis was the damnation of current society with its emphasis on materialism and social conformity. Ginsburg's *Howl*, a poem banned for obscenity on its publication in 1956, was their *Sanctus*.

For the opposite point of view I needed to look no further than my guide book, which described the bookstore as 'representative of the serious literary and artistic aspects of the local Bohemia, rather than the exhibitionist, self-pitying current that is also here, as in other cosmopolitan cities'. It continued: 'Though some of the "beats" of the late 1950s were part of the literary group, important members of it such as Kenneth Rexroth and Alan Watts were quite independent of and even antagonistic to the defiantly disengaged.'

It was inevitable that a guide book that put the word 'beat' in quotes would not be too finely tuned to another famous San Franciscan community. The word 'gay' meaning 'homosexual' was not generally recognised and I had to do some work with the index. In their respectable publication the editors at Random House made no mention of gay people or of the Castro (the district of San Francisco where most of the community was concentrated). The 'risqué factor' of the Broadway Strip and the city's other pleasure zones was attributed to jazz, hard drinking and that catch-all vice, Bohemianism. Where homosexuality was concerned denial was, it seemed, a comfortable alternative to outright prejudice. I was fully aware, however, that San Francisco's Police Department had compiled a blacklist of its gay citizens and made a regular habit of raiding gay bars and arresting people. It was an attitude that must have seemed, even in such moralistic days, to be contrary to the whole ethos of the city.

Stepping from the cerebral enclave of Adler Street into the fleshpots of Broadway was, even in that city of disparities, a culture shock. For all their roistering inclinations, the old-timers would have found it even more so. The 'Forty-Niner' décor of many of Broadway's bars was a gratuitous nod to the city's pioneering days, but it was a pretty sure thing that those red-blooded gold-diggers, longshoremen and roustabouts of yesteryear would have had little affinity with the street's modern entertainments.

They might have fired a few shots into the ceiling of the Chi Chi Bar to get Miss Keiko to go a stage further with her 'Dance of the Serpent', or chucked their gold nuggets at the ladies of 'Leila's Topless Revue' at the Moulin Rouge to persuade them to go all the way, but they would have drawn a blank at Finocchio's. Here they would have been confronted with the outlandish spectacle of Messrs. Francis and Blair, the 'Two Old Bags from Oakland' who were, the entrance sign declared, 'The World's Greatest Female Impersonators' with 'Lavish Revues Nightly', running from 9pm to 2am.

I looked at my watch. Suddenly it seemed like a long day. Heading south down Golden Gate Avenue I was ready for its most compelling attraction, the 'Y'. The desire to capitalise on a legitimate, paid-for night's accommodation was overwhelming.

The real 'Frisco Frisson' awaited me next day at the junction of Market and Powell. This was where the diagonal met the vertical and everyone went for a ride.

Like the hills that had created their need, San Francisco's cable cars were a part of its legend, outdated and uneconomic but totally sacred. A national monument on wheels that was, it turned out, more than just tourist bait. The locals liked them too, and a history of controversy surrounded attempts in recent years to replace them with more up-to-date forms of transport. This was, paradoxically, the motivation of their inventor, Andrew Smith Hallidie, who on seeing a team of straining horses trying to get one of the old horsecars up a hill had set out to devise, in the early 1870s, a method of hauling tramcars by a continuously revolving cable. The invention, which had won the immediate support of San Francisco's business community, had been of no small benefit to Hallidie, a local wire rope manufacturer.

As the idea caught on, cable car lines had been introduced in other American cities. Sadly their working life had been threatened by the arrival of the electric trolley, and by the 1890s San Francisco had been the only city to retain the system. Motor buses too had made their incursion, and of the eight original lines only three now survived. This was about as near to extinction as a species could get, and put the cable car, for American conservationists, somewhere between a bald eagle and an eighteenth-century building.

At the foot of Powell Street I witnessed an unusual spectacle. A picturesque vehicle, not unlike a Disneyland street car, was being rotated on its axis by a number of men and women of various ages thrusting their weight against it. Other people were less helpfully climbing onto the car as it revolved, others getting off. This was one of the famous turntables, the terminal point for the two lines that ran from here to the waterfront. If I'd been looking for an example of the San Franciscans' dedication to their oldest form of transport it would have been the picture of a middle-aged woman gripping the handrail of the car and giving an extra tug before she got on.

The car marked 'Hyde and Beach' was the best one for Fisherman's Wharf and I climbed into the front section, as near to the controls as I could get. The flat fare was fifteen cents – cheaper than anything Disneyland could offer.

The operation of the car was simple, depending on a clamp that extended beneath the vehicle into a slot in the street where it engaged with a moving cable. The driver – or 'gripman' – controlled the car by means of a grasp which either connected the clamp to the cable to make the car move or released it to make it stop. In addition he had a braking mechanism to prevent the car either running backwards or forwards on a slope when it was stationary.

As we wound our way up the first hill I noticed how the traffic lights changed to green at our approach, stopping the cross traffic at the intersections. Between the foot and summit of the hill there were about eight of these intersections, where the street levelled out. Towards the top of the hill the street became much steeper between the intersections, so that any traffic on the next horizontal was invisible. It was like going up a giant staircase.

Nob Hill, the San Franciscans called it. The name came from its occupation by the wealthy 'nabobs' of the city who had built their homes here after the construction of the California Street cable-car line in 1874. The four biggest fish at this time – Leland Stanford, Collis P. Huntingdon, Charles Crocker and Mark Hopkins – had all lived here, commuting daily by cable car to their offices on Market Street. Between them, these four had built the western railroad, the Central Pacific, which had joined with the Union Pacific in 1869 to create the United States' first transcontinental railway line. Control of all the rail shipments had ensured the Big Four's financial domination of the West right up to the early 1900s when the rival Western Pacific Railroad had been opened. Until then the great board palaces on their summit had represented a kind of Palatine Hill, viewed with a mixture of awe and ridicule by the natives.

At the top of the hill I had a closer look at the two buildings that now dominated it. Both were hotels, the best known in the city. One, The Fairmount, had been built as a memorial to 'Bonanza Jim' Fair, who'd made his fortune in the Comstock Lode Strike in the Nevada silver mines. The other was The Mark Hopkins, built on the site of his mansion on California Street. The main attraction of this hotel was its high-level bar, the 'Top o' the Mark', which at 537 feet provided the best central views of the city and bay.

On the other side of the hill we took a sharp turn left – a bonus thrill as the slot curved and the car lurched round giddily on the cable. One or two children, hanging from the handrail of the open section at the back, made it an even bigger thrill. On Hyde Street we turned downhill again and I balanced precariously on my seat to get a shot from one of the city's most celebrated viewpoints: Hyde Street Hill, dipping like a camel's hump to the Wharf. Beyond it, the fishing boats and motor launches on the grey-blue waters of the bay, with Alcatraz Island in the middle distance and Angel Island and the backdrop of Marin County beyond.

The popularity of Fisherman's Wharf had its origins in the activities of the fishermen who once sold their catch on the sheltered quay. Since then it had become a magnet for seafood gourmets and curio hunters and exploited beyond any semblance of the original. Now the restaurants were doing the selling, serving up the fruits of the sea in many guises. For the length of several blocks they hemmed in the waterfront, interspersed with the souvenir shops that were the automatic appendage, and despoiler, of the 'picturesque'. In defence of the place, I should admit that my reaction was purely visual, and that I did not try for the real flavour by sampling a 'Crab Louis' at Tarantino's. In defence of myself, I should admit that my tastes were pure and simple, and that if I could have found any, I would have settled for a bag of prawns.

Having reached the northern end of the peninsula, my sights were fixed elsewhere. From Pier 43½ Fisherman's Wharf I would embark on one of the most unpredictable of all San Francisco's excursions.

Standing at the bow of the Harbor Cruise boat, my camera poised to snap the views of the bay, I had little inkling of the vagaries of the San Franciscan climate. October was a warm month in the bay region and the sun was shining brilliantly on the choppy harbour waters as we moved away from the pier. The cruise followed a lariat loop westwards, snaking under the Golden Gate Bridge, and then curved backwards round Alcatraz Island and as far east as the San Francisco-Oakland Bay Bridge, whence it completed the loop to Fisherman's Wharf. On the way out to the Golden Gate Bridge I noticed a layer of haze, lying across the mouth of the bay. Expecting to discern the shape of the bridge emerging from it I was disappointed. The closer we got, the thicker the haze.

It was only when we were in the midst of it that I realised that we had run into a sea fog. Visibility was little more than twenty yards and the giant span of the Golden Gate Bridge, just ahead of us, was a spectacle available only to my imagination. And to the unfaltering commentary, relayed by the loudspeaker: 'Ahead you can see one of the world's most beautiful man-made constructions...'

For an unrecorded description I had to turn to a man in a peaked cap, standing by the rail. The fog, he told me, was a common event on this part of the coast in the summer and autumn, when the cold water rising from the ocean depths met the warmer surface air. The resulting fog bank, stretching up to six miles along the coastline, found an opening at the Golden Gate, from where it penetrated inland. 'Bad time of the year for seein' the bridge,' he said.

Turning back, we soon re-entered the sunlight. Passing the island fortress of Alcatraz I could read the warning signs on the jetty, identifying the notorious Federal prison. 'Keep Off – U.S. Property' and 'Only U.S. Government Boats Allowed Within 200 Yards' were hardly invitations to view. The prison had closed two years previously and at that distance I had to be satisfied with the legend. Al Capone, Morton Sobell, the Birdman of Alcatraz. The names, echoing from the loudspeaker, were a roll-call of the Hall of Infamy.

To add to the drama, we heard about the escape attempts. There had been fourteen such attempts, all but two of them foiled. The remaining two were inconclusive, in that the five convicts involved had disappeared, never to be seen again. Given the location of the island, a mile and a half offshore and encircled by sharks and icy currents, such disappearances were hardly a guarantee of success.

From the grim isolation of Alcatraz we continued around the head of the peninsula to the magnificent continuity of the San Francisco-Oakland Bay Bridge. The thrill of crossing the bridge on the night of my arrival was fresh in my mind: greater still was the sensation of passing under it and gazing up at the giant steel trusses that spanned the towering concrete piers. In two days, I'd enjoyed more simulated experiences than even the studios of Walt Disney might conceive: a trip to Canton, a ride on a roller-coaster, a ghost ship voyage. Surely the 'Forty-Niners' never had this kind of fun.

Stanford

Phi Alpha Male

'Hi! You must be dog-tired, after riding all those Greyhounds!'
Climbing into the car I laughed at Marsden's joke, feeling a pleasant surge of reunion as I joined him and his fellow passengers, Elizabeth and three candy-sucking Blois grandchildren. Following their trip to Fleishhacker Zoo they were picking me up on their way south to Palo Alto, home of Stanford University.

I told them about my adventures in Arizona, Southern Utah and Sequoia. They were impressed but clearly mystified, wondering why I should want to go to all those parks. And *hitch-hiking!* Could you still do things like that?

A journey that had taken me twenty-five days had taken them little more than three, travelling most of the way on Route 66. But having stretched their vacation to the limit, they had to admit to a greater sense of urgency. 'This is our senior year at Stanford,' said Marsden, 'and as seniors we have to act responsibly about things like turning up for the start of semester.' I caught his wink at Elizabeth.

From the end of Market Street we drove to Twin Peaks, the grass-covered heights that even in a city of hills were a conspicuous feature. From Christmas Tree Point we were treated to a stunning view of the entire northern tip of the peninsula.

It was possible for the eye to travel, slowly and pleasurably, from the Golden Gate Bridge at the entrance to the bay on the west to the great natural barrier of the San Bruno Mountain to the south, taking in the whole of northern San Francisco, the Bay Bridge and the shores on the far side of the bay. The details of the latter were erased by a soft blue mist, hanging over the bay. On a clear day, Elizabeth told me, it was possible to see the campanile of the University of California at Berkeley, twelve miles to the north-east.

Using the broad passage of the distant Market Street as a guide, I was able to delineate the area destroyed by the San Francisco earthquake. This was, of course, the Great Earthquake of 1906, a calamity that senior San Franciscans recalled not as 'The 'Quake' but as 'The Fire'. It was the ensuing fire and not the initial convulsions that had caused the main damage, destroying almost the entire area that now comprised downtown San Francisco. Many of the old buildings had gone up in smoke, most notably the board palaces on Nob Hill. A total of 450 people had been killed – the worst disaster to strike an American city.

Driving down from the Peaks towards the Bayshore Freeway on the east side of the peninsula we passed through a district that characterised the city's rapid recovery from devastation. The Mission District – named after the Spanish mission founded here in 1776 – was another area that had been ravaged by fire. But evidence of its immediate resuscitation was in the uniform, early twentieth-century style of these houses, with their bay windows and wood-framed gables. The sight of such quaintly-mannered buildings – last of their kind before the onslaught of modernism – was pleasing.

Not so charming was the development to the south of the city, which became more pronounced as we headed for Stanford. Viewed from the freeway the tiered hills were cut like a grocer's cheese in huge, bare slabs. Spaced along them were uniform pastel-coloured cubes, row upon row, that I recognised as the 'cracker-box' architecture that was devouring the scenic hinterland of San Francisco. A tunnel through the San Bruno Mountain had taken the Southern Pacific Railroad southward in 1907, establishing a commuter link with the city for the growing residential areas in the lower part of the peninsula. The result, sixty years later, was a dense and continuous urban development along fifty miles of the bay shoreline.

A forty-five-minute run brought us to Atherton, a small town north of Stanford where Marsden's family lived. Depositing the children there we continued to Palo Alto, a town that geographically – and historically – was an extension of the university. At No 318, High Street, I discovered just how well Elizabeth had organised everything.

'Remember Brad?'

In response to Elizabeth's toot on the horn a figure in jeans, roll-neck and sandals appeared at the front door. Even without the beard he'd worn in Sicily it was unmistakably Brad Friedland, one of the other students whom I'd met, with Elizabeth, on that railway platform in Taormina a year ago. Seeing me, and no doubt recalling the frenetic figure of the English archaeology buff clambering over the ruins of the ancient theatre of Syracuse, he gave a whoop of greeting.

'Hi, Paul – still got your guide book?'

Four more figures appeared, wearing the student uniform of sweater and jeans. In quick succession I was introduced to Oz, Randy, Brad II and Jay. They all lived off-campus, at No 318. After we'd shaken hands Brad said: 'Thought you'd like to meet the guys you're rooming with.'

I looked blankly at Elizabeth, who was smiling at me. 'Didn't you always say you wondered what it would be like to be an American student?'

My first lesson at Stanford was geography. I commenced my studies at the woman's residence, Lagunita Court, where Elizabeth was on hand with an itinerary. Before I could ask her how long it would take for me to see every faculty, she produced a campus map covering an area of 9,000 acres and pointed to a small square in the middle. 'Make a start with the Quadrangle,' she said. 'Then, if you're still feeling energetic, go over to the Museum. You want to borrow a cycle?'

Picturing the phalanx of cyclists we'd passed on the way into the campus, riding four or five abreast, I declined. 'Thanks, but I might get caught in the traffic.'

As it turned out, not such a good call. A walking tour of a campus the size of Stanford was challenging. Back in 1884 Governor Leland Stanford's gift of his 8,800-acre Palo Alto stock farm for the site of a university had been more than generous. Now, even with a complex of academic schools, laboratories, libraries, staff and student residences and electronics research firms (the 'think factories') filling out the acreage, there was still room to spare for future enlargement.

Standing as the centrepiece of one of the most advanced universities in the States, Stanford's Quadrangle struck a strangely incongruous note. The buildings mixed the styles of Spanish Colonial and Florentine Renaissance, with rough-hewn sandstone walls, Romanesque arcades and palm-shaded courtyards. The Memorial Church, in the middle of the Quadrangle, was adorned with a mosaic on the upper part of its façade – a further touch of the Romanesque. Although these were the original buildings of the university they looked strangely unrelated to the complex, with its contemporary urban layout.

More in context, but no less incongruous, was the adjacent Hoover Tower, Stanford's 'phallic symbol'. Built in the 1940s to house a collection of the former President's political documents, the 280-foot tower looked like a Saturn rocket that had failed lift-off. The one advantage of such a construction should have been the view from the top, but this – by order of the university authorities – was denied me. When I questioned a passing student about access to the tower he looked cryptic and muttered: 'Last year, not everyone went up there for the view.'

I registered a blank. Did this mean that the students of Phi Delta Theta, bored with their endless tutorials, had formed a Two-Hundred-and-Eighty-Foot-High Club? Or had they, less entertainingly, simply jumped?

A visit to the Leland Stanford Junior Museum was worthwhile, if only for one item. Amid a welter of mementos of the Stanford family – the Governor, his wife and the son after whom the university had been named – I saw the object that truly celebrated a golden age. The Golden Spike, driven by a silver hammer, with which the Governor himself had united the two lines of the Union Pacific and Central Pacific at Promontory Point, Utah, creating the first transcontinental rail link. A tap of the hammer that in 1869 had opened up the West – and the bank deposits of four gentlemen named Stanford, Crocker, Huntingdon and Hopkins. I wondered if the 14,000 Chinese labourers who had hacked out the formidable route through mountain and desert, laying track at the rate of ten miles a day, had been there to applaud the ceremonial tap.

Without a car, the Seventeen Mile Drive was hardly a proposition. But the copywriters egged me on. 'The Most Famous Scenic Drive in California'; 'Monterey Peninsula – Internationally Known for its Beauty'. Such songs of praise were guaranteed to exploit my greatest weakness.

The ninety-mile run to the peninsula made it a natural objective for a day out from Stanford, and on the second morning of my campus sojourn – before my 'fellow-students' were awake – I was on my way south on the Greyhound's central highway route. At San Jose – where I had a momentary vision of ripening tomatoes – I switched to another bus destined for Monterey. From Highway 101 we turned west to reach the part of the coastline forming Monterey Bay.

The peninsula was shaped like a hook, enclosing the southern end of the bay. From what I had learned, the views around its coastline were stunning: rocky headlands, groves of pine and cypress, pocket-sized coves, sweeping pebble beaches. Of all this, I realised, I could expect to see only a fragment.

The first problem was the starting point. Should I approach the much-lauded route from Monterey, to the north, or the 'village' of Carmel, to the south? In the bus depot at Monterey the question was answered by a tourist poster with a colour photograph of the Mission of San Carlos Borromeo de Carmelo, near Carmel. This was the most celebrated of the chain of missions established on the Californian coast by the Spanish during the eighteenth century. A peep at the past that drew me irresistibly to Carmel.

A local bus took me across the peninsula to Carmel. Getting off the bus before it turned into the village I continued on foot along the highway. In a short while I reached the Mission, a small group of orange-coloured sandstone buildings just off the road by the Carmel River. The simplicity of the buildings had an immediate appeal.

The Mission, founded in 1770 by the Franciscan Junipero Serra, had originally been sited in Monterey, an early Spanish settlement. The purpose of this and the other missions had been the pacification and conversion of the local Indian tribes, a task that the friars had undertaken with an unholy zeal and energy. Their difficulties had been enormous: not only the physical ones of establishing themselves in a completely unknown and unmapped territory, among primitive and hostile people, but the political ones of dealing with recalcitrant governors and soldiery. The favourite recreation of the soldiers – lassoing Indian girls from horseback, and shooting any members of the tribe who intervened – had not greatly improved relations between settler and native, and a year after its foundation the Mission had moved to the quieter pastures of Carmel.

Here the church had been built, using the forced labour of the (newly baptised) native Americans of the Ohlone and Esselen tribes. The result was a rugged little homespun building with a suggestion of the Baroque but none of its elaboration. A squat bell-tower, topped by an onion-shaped dome and barnacled with the mud globes of swallows' nests, was its most charming feature. Around the flower-filled courtyard of the church were grouped the other buildings of the Mission, formerly the storehouses, workshops and living quarters of the friars and their dependents. Apart from its ecclesiastical function the Mission had served as an efficient working community, the friars supervising their native work force in farming and stock-raising and in various crafts. After four or five decades the work of the Californian missionaries added up to a considerable achievement, their influence extending along a chain of twenty-one missions from San Francisco to San Diego.

But for all their success, the missions were destined to extinction. In the 1830s the Mexicans arrived and, taking exception to the continuing loyalty of the missions to the Spanish church, forced the removal of all religious supervision from the missions. Deprived of their spiritual direction the natives had returned to their tribal life – and paganism. Like so many historic buildings in the States the missions fell into decay, only to be rediscovered and restored later as cherished monuments. And after a long journey of missionary endeavour that had started in 1869 with the founding of the Mission San Diego de Alcala in Southern California, a tireless and indomitable Franciscan friar had reached his ultimate destination. When the state of California had been asked to nominate two of its founders for memorial statues in the nation's Capitol in Washington, Padre Junipero Serra was one of them.

Returning to the highway with my own mission as yet unaccomplished, I flagged down a passing car.

'Seventeen Mile Drive?'

The driver, a middle-aged woman, shook her head. 'Sorry, I'm going the other way. But I'll take you to Point Lobos, if that's any good.'

It sounded like a good option. Instead of heading north to the Monterey peninsula I would be going south to a miniature and less touristy replica. I jumped into the car and in four miles was dropped at the entrance gate of the Point Lobos Reserve State Park.

Through a fairy-tale forest of pines trailing whiskers of Spanish moss I followed the mile-long road leading to the point. There were no cars on the road, no sign of life, and I had the glorious feeling of having the place to myself. Drawn by the sharpening scent of the Pacific I ran the last stretch into the open, emerging breathlessly onto a rocky wind-pummelled headland.

If an effective cure could be found for stressed-out businessmen, seeking respite from smoke-filled rooms, ulcer-provoking sales graphs and high-calorie lunches, it was Point Lobos. A walk to that tip of rock was a purgative with a tonic chaser: clean and vitalising. And more than just a walk. With the exuberant mix of shrubs and trees that abounded on the headland, the tidal pools that floated in the rocks, the vistas of sea and sky that changed at every step, it was an exploration. The tang of kelp was heavy on the breeze and I clambered down among the rocks, looking for molluscs. The surf had thrown a lot of seaweed onto the rocks and I was intrigued by the amount of kelp, the strange brown seaweed that was a feature of this coast. A few yards from the shore I saw a great heaving bed of it, the tight bladders at the end of the stalks like tiny heads bobbing out of the water.

I searched among them for the profile of that rarely-seen creature that was especially associated with this coastline: the Californian sea otter. I should have known better. In the 1920s, after 150 years of human predation (particularly by the Russians, whose trade in furs took them halfway down the west coast) the otter had been pronounced extinct. Spotted again a decade later, it had immediately received the strictest protection, and its declining numbers had rallied. But it was still very rare.

A faint barking sound diverted my attention to the wildlife that was, at a distance, visible. On a surf-buffeted island of rock I saw the glistening bodies of a colony of sea lions, the *Lobos marinos*. These animals, secure on their outpost, were the big attraction of the reserve, whose modest 350 acres had more to offer per square yard, it seemed, than many of America's major parks.

A hiking trail led me across the headland to what was identified as one of the last natural groves of the Monterey cypress, which the reserve had been created to protect. Confined to a stretch of coast only two miles long, the cypress clung to the shoreline as though seeking a last line of defence. Its tenacity was remarkable – several specimens perching on the longest spearhead of rock within a few feet of the frothing ocean. Lobos faced north and I was entranced by the red lichen that furred the trees overlooking the sea. It lent a fiery halo to their outline, providing a vivid contrast to the icy blueness framed by their branches. The shape of those branches intrigued me. Like crooked arms, begging the elements – and humankind – for mercy.

Rather than return by the road I decided to make my way along the shoreline to Carmel, and satisfy an aspiration I had carried with me from the east coast. After skin-diving in the Atlantic, I was determined to put at least one foot in the Pacific.

With the spirit of adventure soaring high I clambered through the perimeter fence of the reserve and raced across a stretch of open land, the spectacle of Carmel Bay before me. Another fence – this one of barbed wire – slowed me down a little, but once through it there was nothing more than a downward scramble over rocks to separate me from the beach.

As far as the word can be applied to the west coast of America, the beach was a virgin. A natural stretch of pure white sand, screened by cypress trees, and completely desolate. Apart from a distant view of Carmel the only habitation in sight was well in the background, half-hidden by trees. I later discovered that this was a Carmelite convent, which – together with the barbed wire – might have had some bearing on the purity of the view.

The water looked cold and I took my time about getting into a costume. When I finally made the plunge it was a baptism by ice and it took all my willpower to go deeper than knee-level. Even then, when I was totally immersed, it was impossible to swim. The beach shelved steeply and there was an aggressive swell that had me floundering like a fly in a bubble-bath. Within a few minutes I'd had enough and scrambled out, gasping for breath. So much, I thought, for '*Surfin' USA*'.

A quick work-out with the towel and I was jogging back to Carmel along the beach, tingling all the way. I doubt if I had ever felt so good.

In addition to its industrial park, research laboratories and eight Nobel Prize winners, Stanford was also well known for its Eating Clubs. The mainstay of the student body, the idea behind these clubs was extremely simple. Eating Clubs were a community thing, with more than a hint of the kibbutz. The students of a particular fraternity or sorority contributed equally to the food and to the effort, sharing the duties of serving and washing up. The only hired help was the cook, who officiated at the midday and evening meals. (The preparation of breakfast, which involved little more than flipping a hamburger, was open to all comers.)

My return to student life that evening was marked by a barbecue. This event, thrown by the Eating Club, was in honour of a new intake of female freshers who conveniently outnumbered the males of the Club. In their company I suffered an acute conflict of identity, not sure whether I should pass myself off as a mature student on a travelling scholarship or a very junior Visiting Professor.

'Hi, you Phi Alpha?'

I found myself gazing into the dark lustrous eyes of Natalie Wood. The *very* image, tucked tightly into her roll-necked sweater, plastic belt and pleated skirt. My mind raced. 'Not exactly,' I said.

Intrigued, she looked at me quizzically. Though I had little resemblance to James Dean's character in *Rebel Without a Cause*, I might at least be a bad boy from a good family. Another girl, in a Stanford Indians vest, came to my rescue. Interposing herself between me and Natalie Wood she gave me a hug. 'Hey, you must be that friend of Elizabeth's, the guy from Oxford?' Nodding at the first part of the question, I tacitly acknowledged the second. I could see, after all, that the freshers were not only young but impressionable.

From that point it was a home run. Although I'd never been to university my seminar on English academic life was a sell-out. Anecdotes about punting, leaping off bridges into the Cherwell and climbing college drainpipes after late-night binges had Natalie and Co. hanging on my words. When the party moved on to Brad's place I maintained my role, working diligently for my PhD, debating at the Union and cavorting at the May Ball. My American students were entranced and my friends, Marsden and Elizabeth, were my loyal accessories.

My powers of invention saw me comfortably through the evening. But even if they hadn't, my success was guaranteed. A California state law forbidding the sale of alcohol to persons under twenty-one made me the most sought-after person at the party. Any time I wasn't discussing my sociology course I was two blocks down the street in an 'all-nite' bar, purchasing large quantities of Dutch lager for my under-age friends.

The party ended with me crashing out on Brad's sofa, where I remained for several hours in a state of suspended animation. It was a poor preparation for the following day.

A major event on the Stanford sporting calendar – and for college students the nearest thing to religion – was football. My trip had spanned the sporting seasons, and from the refined technicalities of baseball I was transported to the gore, grit – and technicalities – of American football. The big game that Saturday, a celebration for all but a pagan minority, was the Stanford 'Indians' versus the Oregon 'Ducks' – a contest that promised to give the faithful their ritual orgasm.

The sacred precinct was about a hundred yards long and fifty wide, an oblong of green turf marked off in ten-yard sections and surrounded by a tiered oval of seating, eighty rows deep. This was the mighty Stanford Stadium, capable of holding 100,000 spectators. When Marsden and I arrived the stands were already half-full, with half an hour to go before the start of the game. Passing through the Student Gate and presenting my 'Student Only' ticket I followed Marsden to the Stanford student section, which covered most of one side of the stadium. The benches here were filling up quickly, but on the other side – allocated to Oregon – they were more thinly spread. In the west corner of the stadium I noticed that there were no spectators at all, for no apparent reason.

The spectacle of American football was lampooned in Britain as much as it was revered in the States. The pageant was always more than the performance, and unless you were one of the converted, i.e. a citizen of the United States, it could promise a seriously dull experience.

To ensure that the right level of frenzy would welcome the players, the whipping-up process was shortly under way, with the bands of the rival colleges – Stanford and Oregon State – striking up simultaneously and the cheerleaders springing into action. No ball game, it seemed, could get off the ground without the preliminary chant of support, led by half a dozen crew-cut cheerleaders bouncing up and down in front of a row of microphones on a raised platform. Their red sweaters and white Bermudas – Stanford colours – were repeated in the outfits of the 'Indian maids' – a team of college girls who pranced about on the edge of the field in North American Indian costume.

At the right moment, just before the crowd got tired of shouting for them, the players arrived. It was an invasion, a stream of helmeted, padded giants pouring onto the field and lining up in their opposing teams on either side. Each team had upwards of fifty players and I tentatively asked Marsden if all one hundred were on the field at the same time.

He laughed. 'You want someone killed?' Only eleven men a side were played, he told me, the remainder acting as substitutes. The teams were divided into two separate sets of players: offensive and defensive. An offensive team was reckoned to be on the attack if it had advanced ten yards in four 'plays'. If it failed, the other side took possession of the ball and the team that had originally been on the offensive would be replaced by a brand new defensive team. No one had much of a chance to get tired, and with a reserve of fresh unbroken bodies to draw from, injuries were of little account. I couldn't help comparing the game with our English equivalent, Rugby Union, where barring substitutions for injuries or fouls the same fifteen men finished that had started, and no one wore much more than a shirt, shorts and a pair of boots. When I pointed this out to Marsden, and asked why the American players wore so much padding, he looked at me in frank astonishment. 'You really *do* want someone killed!'

In the opening minutes of the game I saw what he meant. A dozen heavily-armoured eighteen-stoners crashing together in a welter of flying limbs and heaving shoulders, one side trying to clear the ball, the other trying to stop them. That the attempt to clear the scrimmage (American equivalent of the English rugby 'scrum') invariably failed was hardly surprising, with each player being blocked by his opposite number and the man in possession of the ball disappearing under several hundredweight of bone, muscle and armour. Unlike the English game, tackling was not bound by any rules, the methods varying from a bear-hug to a neck-grapple or a bulldozer shove.

Despite a stonewall defence by both sides there were moments of real excitement later in the game when the ball carriers began to break through and get the ball downfield either by fast running or dexterous passing. When the game was moving, the cheerleaders went wild, baying into the microphones and leaping in the air. But the crowd was usually ahead of them. It only needed the Ducks to be pinned down on their goal line and the Stanford student section was calling for their blood in an incoherent tribalistic chant – ending with the frenzied exhortation '*In–di–ans!*'

Nothing, of course, compared to the delirium that followed when the Stanford quarterback broke the line and scored. The first touchdown, worth six points to the Indians. For the next couple of minutes, I wondered if the world had gone mad. The college band was marching past the student section, blowing its lungs out, but I couldn't hear a peep above the noise that engulfed us. Bursting popcorn bags, drumming feet, the united roar of ten thousand

Stanford students. And then I nearly leapt out of my skin. A cannon standing in the south-eastern corner of the field, which until then I had thought was an ornament, suddenly billowed smoke and flame. For a moment, my ears vibrating with the explosion, I feared the worst. California had declared war on Oregon.

What I had witnessed, of course, was a dramatic variant of the Astrodome scoreboard, with its computerised firework display. The home team had scored, and the cannon had roared. When the smoke had cleared and I could see across to the far side of the stadium I understood why there were no people sitting there.

As they ran out the Stanford players echoed the chant, and in my battered ear Marsden shouted: 'Next game's against U.S.C. – University of Southern California. That'll be a walk-over –'

With substitutions stopping the clock every few minutes the game seemed to last forever. In the end a late touchdown took Stanford to 17-14, a lead they held until the final ball. In the moment of triumph, hell again broke loose, with the conquering team charging off the field to shouts of 'U.S.C.! U.S.C.!'

Getting to our feet to leave the stadium, I caught a glimpse of the last group of players to leave the field, a dejected-looking handful in green shirts and yellow leggings. The poor old Ducks couldn't even raise a quack.

Sunday was the last day of my 'semester' and to make it properly memorable Elizabeth and Marsden presented me with a ticket for another event that perfectly rounded off my week at Stanford. It also fulfilled a lifelong ambition. That afternoon, sitting in the open-air Frost Amphitheatre, I was privileged to hear the gravelly voice and lilting trumpet of that great jazz legend, Louis Armstrong.

With his veteran All Stars, Louis had come to take part in the Stanford Jazz Year, a festival of concerts and other activities compiled to celebrate the achievements of fifty years of America's greatest art form. If ever there was a living embodiment of jazz it was 'Satchmo'. To hear his breath vibrating that horn was good enough – but here was the maestro himself...

Rolling his eyes and swabbing his face with his famous table-cloth handkerchief. Cracking his eternal joke about not wiping off the Man Tan. Wooing his already conquered audience with a few simple notes that captured an evergreen melody. As a jazz experience it couldn't compare with the intimacy of New Orleans' Dixieland Hall, but that didn't matter. Louis wasn't going to deliver a concert-hall performance any more and didn't need to. His larger-than-life personality had taken over where the horn had left off, defying the disadvantages of an open-air auditorium with loudspeakers and an 8,000-seat audience.

Sadly the concert, and the whole Stanford experience came to an end and I was left with only a few goodbyes to celebrate my departure from academe. Toasted in Coke at an Eating Club send-off I responded by offering all present, including Brad and his room-mates, a return match in an English pub. I should have realised, of course, that with either military service or a stint in the Peace Corps in prospect, England was the last place they'd be going for a while.

From the club I was driven by Elizabeth and Marsden to the Palo Alto bus depot, collecting my rucksack from Brad's place on the way.

The final goodbyes were hard and we kept them short. I was at a loss to know how to say 'thank you' for everything they'd done for me.

'Send us a postcard,' said Elizabeth. 'And make sure it's Big Ben.' She looked at me curiously. 'Where are you going next?'

I kept a straight face. 'San Jose,' I said. 'To pick some tomatoes.'

San Jose

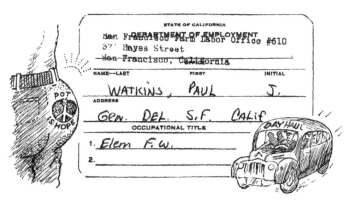

STATE OF CALIFORNIA
DEPARTMENT OF EMPLOYMENT
San Francisco Farm Labor Office #610
37 Hayes Street
San Francisco, California

NAME—LAST   FIRST   INITIAL

WATKINS, PAUL J.

ADDRESS

Gen. DEL. S.F. CALIF

OCCUPATIONAL TITLE

1. Elem F.W.

2.

The Tomatoes of Wrath

The sharp jolt of the bus stopping brought me back to earth. Looking out of the window I saw a huge unfenced field, covered by straggly knee-high plants. A scattering of figures, barely visible in the early light, were bending down and filling boxes.

Emotions on seeing my first tomato field were mixed. I can only describe them as somewhere between awe and dismay. As the overseer climbed on the bus, I hid behind the man standing next to me.

'I want six. Experienced.'

With a proper deference I made way for the professionals. Surprisingly, after the initial assault on the bus at the Labor Office, there was no great rush but some animated discussion, focused on the information that it was a second picking. Everyone wanted to know whether piece rates were being offered, or if payment was by the hour. With a grudging acceptance of thirty cents a box the six eventually came forward.

As we drove off to the next field there were mutterings of discontent.

'Thirty cents a box on a second pickin'? What kinda deal is that?'

The tomato pickers had their representative. He of the patched overalls was the voice of dissent, a weathered protagonist of pickers' rights. The second picking, it seemed, was an area of controversy. The extra work incurred in gathering the sparser fruit left over from the first picking made an hourly rate preferable to a rate per box, but that wasn't always the way the farmers saw it. For them, piece rates were more economic when it took longer to pick a box. The logic could not be denied, any more than the thirty cents. Despite their agitation over the years, the fruit pickers had not yet been able to form a union.

I had no information on how many tomato fields there were in the Santa Clara Valley, but in the next hour we did the grand tour. Employment was not as plentiful as we'd been led to believe and we were turned away from several ranches in succession. Working through the list of names on his sheet the bus driver got increasingly frustrated, calling the heavens down on the people at the Farm Labor Office who had compiled it. From the start, his dearest wish had been apparent: to get shot of his disgruntled load and head back on the Bayshore Freeway.

The next ranch to offer work was even less attractive than the first. Here the weeds were higher than the plants, and – as the overseer pointed out – the tomatoes were 'kinda small'. His offer of twenty-five cents a box met with an almost united derision. The eight or nine spirits that did succumb were all 'greenhorns' – weakened by the prolonged bus ride and an oppressive desire to get down to some picking. Their feeling was in no way shared by the rest of the bus, who seemed prepared, despite the protestations of the driver, to sit tight until the right job turned up.

For another hour the fruitless search continued with the driver intermittently pulling up and plunging into telephone kiosks at the side of the road. His purpose was plain: to get through to the office and find out what the hell he was supposed to do with a bus-load of redundant and bloody-minded tomato pickers. The last time he climbed back on the bus he slammed the door with sufficient fury to wake even the half-dozen or so diehard sleepers in the back seats, who had not stirred since San Francisco.

'Boy, I wish them goddam tomatoes would dry up!'

Eventually, as I was about to write off the State of California

Department of Employment as a lost cause, we struck gold. At the entrance gate of one ranch a station wagon came out to meet us and we were hailed by the driver, who turned out to be the rancher himself. He offered to take all of us, for thirty cents a box or $1.40 an hour.

Nobody could crib at that, but I was astonished by the continuing reluctance of one or two people to get off the bus. Their motives for going out on a day haul were difficult to fathom. Perhaps they were enjoying the ride, or the chance of a chat and a smoke with their friends. After counting heads the rancher sorted the sheep from the goats, calling on the novices to stand in one group and the pickers with three or more days' experience in another. Fifty per cent seasoned and fifty per cent green, we were marched off to the nearest field and given two rows each to pick.

A wiry man in a check shirt, working in the next row, showed me how it was done. 'Turn the plant over, and scoop 'em in your hand,' he said. It looked simple. I started on the first row, and was amazed when I had filled my first box after only ten minutes. Working steadily for an hour I achieved the giddy total of five complete boxes, which compared favourably with the efforts of my more experienced neighbour. From this result I could see the advantages of the piece rate system. Five boxes at thirty cents each equalled $1.50 – or ten cents more than the hourly scale. The incentive was clear, but to make anything out of it you had to know how to pick tomatoes. To my profound dismay I learned that I was not one of the gifted people.

In the second hour I picked four boxes, in the third only three. The energy with which I had started perished gradually among the weeds, the stinging undergrowth that grew thicker and thicker as I progressed along the row. The heat, too, slowed me down, and the painful declaration of untried muscles somewhere in the small of my back. As the tomatoes took longer to find, and the box longer to fill, I began to see the merit of the hourly scale.

A blessed diversion was the arrival at midday of a catering truck, replete with cold drinks, hot dogs and sandwiches. For ten minutes tomatoes were forgotten as the pickers jostled for refreshments. This time I was up at the front – and recoiling at the extortionate prices. For a 'Poor Boy' roll, Pepsi-Cola and packet of chips I was obliged to pay a whole dollar. A price that could afford to be inflated when the nearest competition was nowhere in sight. And how much of the dollar went into the rancher's pocket, for providing the business?

With renewed determination I returned to the tomatoes. Setting an example was my energetic neighbour, who had by-passed the lunch break and – with fifteen boxes to his credit – was still picking like a robot. In a few minutes, as I was stacking up my twelfth, the checker came along and punched my card – a neat hole in the figure '12'. He was a young hustler, the son of the overseer. His job was to keep a tally of the boxes picked, and make sure all the boxes were full. Eyeing my haul he told me about the remarkable Mexican *braceros*, who could pick up to 150 boxes of tomatoes a day on a first picking. To obtain a higher output the Mexicans competed with one another, to see who could pick the most.

'In Mexico they would earn only forty cents an hour. Here, working on the piece rate, they can make up to forty dollars in one day.'

The contrast with my own achievement was fairly pointed. In fact, with people like the Mexicans around, I wondered why they troubled with rabbits like me. Later on, talking to my neighbour in the next row, I learned the unhappy truth.

'You won't see no *braceros* on these fields,' he said. 'They stopped 'em coming over here last year, by Federal Law. Sounds crazy, but they were doin' too many people out of a job. Weren't nothin' to do with the farmers, of course. They'd only hire *braceros*, if they could. They work for less money, and they're twice as fast. Now there's trouble comin' up. The pickers want to form a union, so they can get a fixed rate. The farmers are gonna fight them, all the way down the line.'

And meanwhile there were several thousand *braceros* sitting on the border, waiting for a change in Federal Law. I suddenly realised how lucky I was, not having to depend on this work for my existence. A thought to cheer me as I pressed on into the jungle.

The weeds grew thick and fast, stinging my arms as I turned them over to uncover the plants. The pain in my back was increasing, and I realised what they meant by 'stoop labour'. An occupation for which I had little natural bent.

By mid-afternoon the work began to tail off, with many of the pickers packing up after their fifth or sixth hour and having a recuperative smoke. At 4pm the catering truck reappeared, but this time did not do such good business. Backing out of the lane between the fields it ran into a stack of boxes filled with tomatoes. This would not have been so bad, if the man who had picked them had not been resting against them. A big man with a red shirt and a bushy black beard. His work for the day completed, he was dozing gently as the ripe red avalanche fell on him.

'You — Simple Simon!'

The driver, who didn't like being called that, climbed down from his cab. He was a small man, but there was no mistaking the belligerence of his stride as he advanced on the fallen boxes and the heaving pile of tomatoes.

'What – did – you – call – me?'

Tomatoes sprayed everywhere as the Beard got to his feet, dwarfing the truck driver. Undeterred, the driver grabbed the Beard by the front of his shirt. 'Repeat – what – you – said – !'

The Beard obliged, shouting in the other man's ear while he lifted him skywards. For about ten seconds the threat display continued, the Beard swaying from side to side as he held the driver aloft, repeatedly shaking him so that the money jumped out of the changers on his belt. Returned to the ground, the driver was too furious to pick up the money and leapt back into the truck, yelling abuse. Before the tomato pickers, in a gesture of solidarity, could turn the vehicle over, he had driven off.

After we'd collected the tomatoes and shared out the dimes we called it a day. Someone had said something about the pay-out being at 4.30pm, so it seemed a good time to break off. My final tally was seventeen boxes, which in my eyes if no-one else's was a spectacular achievement. On checking with my fellow-pickers, I found there weren't too many who'd done better. Most of them, being realistic, had opted like me for working by the hour. When the overseer arrived for the pay-out there couldn't have been one individual who didn't know, to the last cent, what he was owed.

Surprise, then, when the overseer told us. As we lined up by the truck for our money we learned that an hour had been deducted for lunch; a startling revelation that no one – not even the experienced hands – had anticipated. When he heard the news, one man went almost berserk. This was my industrious neighbour, who had worked solidly from 10am to 2.30pm, without lunch, in the full expectation of being paid for four and a half hours. The money that they offered him, for three and a half hours, was less than five dollars.

He wouldn't accept it. 'Nobody told me about no lunch-hour,' he protested. 'I didn't stop for no lunch, for Chris' sake. Worked straight through, from ten to two-thirty. Ask him –' He pointed at me, and I nodded, almost by reflex.

The overseer, looking fatigued, pointed to a car parked beside the truck. 'Go talk to the manager,' he suggested.

Sensing that my support was required, I followed the angry man to the car. The manager, darkly scowling, was sitting behind the wheel, smoking a cheroot. When my companion launched into his protest, it was apparent that his words were falling on deaf ears. With some determination I asserted the justice of his complaint.

Hearing my English voice the manager regarded me with curiosity, and I weighed in with all the eloquence at my command. Like a seasoned tomato field lawyer I put my neighbour's case: that he had worked exactly the number of hours he claimed and that there had been no mention of a lunch-hour when we arrived at the ranch. If he'd worked four and a half hours then surely he was entitled to four and a half times the hourly rate?

The manager closed his eyes, as though the effort of speech was too much for him. 'Hour for lunch is the rule. You askin' me to go roun' checkin' every darn picker, to see if they're workin' that hour?'

Relentlessly the car window wound up. The glazing-over of a fraud, with no other reason than the exploitation of the worker. No wonder the pickers were rebelling.

My own lunch-hour-deducted money came to the grand total of $7.70. Pre-empting any objection, there was an entry on the payslip to show that if I had been paid on a piece rate basis I would have earned only $5.10. Rather than accuse my employers of any meanness, I should be grateful.

As we drove back through the valley into a green and gold sunset I recalled the moment in John Steinbeck's great epic novel of pre-war migration, *The Grapes of Wrath,* when Al Joad had stopped the truck bearing his expectant family westwards and cried: 'Jesus Christ, look!' and Pa Joad had responded 'God Almighty!' and 'Ma, come look, we're there!' and little Ruthie had exclaimed: 'It's California!'

And most telling of all, little Winfield had cried: *'There's fruit!'*

How the hopes of those yearning, impoverished Okies had been dashed, in the desperate days to come, by the struggle to earn enough money between the whole family, picking fruit at five cents a box, to buy a side of bacon for the evening meal; by the mendacity of the owners forever forcing the pickers' wages downwards; by the brutality of their hired heavies whose pick handles vanquished all dissent. The fruit of the Joads' promised land had tasted more bitter than mine.

The tomato pickers of California were, as already depicted, an assorted bunch. Returning on the bus to San Francisco I discovered just how assorted. Sitting next to me was an individual I recognised as one of the 'greenhorns', a sandy-haired youth who had given up after ten boxes.

'What time you reckon we'll get back to 'Frisco?'

It was the third time he'd asked me, and I was getting tired of shrugging my shoulders. I couldn't see that it made much difference what I said, as he had made up his mind that we should be back in the city by 7.30pm, in time for this very special date.

'Going to see P.C. Jones,' he said. 'You know, the fabulous P.C.?'

I nodded, as though I instantly recognised the name and envied him his good fortune. Eventually, of course, I had to ask him who P.C. Jones was, so that he could look at me with the right degree of surprise and wonder.

'You never heard of P.C. Jones? Where've you been all this time? Hec, man – he's just about the greatest female impersonator in San Francisco –'

I was ready to believe him, until the two men in the seat in front of us intervened. They were none other than the Beard and the Patched Overalls, who up to that moment had been engaged in a hostile review of the iniquities of California's ranchers.

---

* John Steinbeck 1939, published by Penguin Books 2001.

The Beard said: 'You're talkin' through your ass. There ain't no drag queens come close to Francis and Blair.'

The Greenhorn would not be swayed. 'You're sayin' that 'cause you ain't seen P.C. Jones.'

'P.C. Jones? Wouldn't cross the road for her.'

Beginning to feel out of the conversation, I tried to reassert myself. P.C. Jones sounded great, I ventured, but was it the kind of show you'd take a girl on a date?

For the Greenhorn, bafflement now topped wonder and surprise.

'Who said anythin' about takin' a girl?'

At that point I changed the subject. The only relevant topic being tomatoes, I asked how much he had made.

He shrugged. 'Not too much. Enough to buy some makeup, I guess.'

Yosemite

Raccoon in the Headlights

I was taking a bit of chance that Michael would be at home. Without a phone number I'd been unable to warn him that I would be turning up on his doorstep late at night with a request for a bed. If he was at all embarrassed by the sight of a dishevelled compatriot on his doorstep he didn't show it. As he opened the door in his dressing gown we simultaneously apologised.

The best I could do was: 'God, I hope you weren't asleep...'

He let me in, shaking his head. 'Forgive the night attire. It's crazy, but I have to go to bed by ten. Up at six, first class seven-thirty. That's how they work you over here.'

He was teaching at the local Junior High School, trading places with an American teacher who had taken over his class at his own school in Dorset. He wasn't sure which of them was getting the best out of the deal, but one thing he did know. The Americans were not getting the best out of him.

The timing of my arrival made my situation clear and my unwitting host obligingly laid a mattress on the floor of his room. I collapsed on it gratefully, using my rucksack as a pillow. Michael in turn lost little time in nipping back into his bed and switching out the light. For about an hour we talked away in the darkness – two displaced Englishmen exchanging experiences of a country that was, by mutual consent, bigger than both of us.

Michael's problems centred on the transmission of ideas to the fifteen year-olds in his class, an even mix of Mexicans and white, black, Hispanic and Oriental Americans. Having such a mixture in the class made communication very difficult, particularly when the youngsters came from poor homes where there was little encouragement to learn. He described himself succinctly as 'a lion-tamer in the Blackboard Jungle'.

On the credit side, however, Michael was being feted by his hosts – his fellow teachers and a large number of the locals who were persistently wining and dining him. To the Americans he was something of a curiosity, and was being constantly plied with questions about himself and his life in England.

The 6am rising was grim, but we made it. Michael was being collected at seven by a colleague, and we had time for a quick breakfast before he arrived. I felt a bit apologetic about using Michael as a rest stop, but he was OK about it. After talking non-stop with the natives for a couple of months it had been a relief, he said, to 'chew the rag' with a fellow countryman.

I got a lift from Michael to the bus depot and there embarked on a Greyhound heading eastwards. My next destination, not far from the Nevada border, was clearly marked:

'Yosemite: from the Sierra Indian name for grizzly bear, "U-zu-ma-ti". Mountainous region of unusual beauty; inspiring gorges with sheer granite cliffs; waterfalls; groves of giant sequoias'. By all accounts, the most spectacular part of the Sierra Nevada.

For a car-less traveller of limited means, the way to Yosemite was not easy. With exasperating deference to the local bus services, the Greyhound went no further than Merced, a town eighty-four miles west of the park. A tour bus was waiting at the depot, but my enquiries went no further than the $8.75 fare. Resigned to my fate I took a piece of card from my rucksack and wrote 'YOSEMITE' on it in large letters.

Clearly labelled, I sought a means of delivery. Eighty-four miles was a fair distance and I wasted no time in setting out, heading for the east-west highway that by-passed the town. Once on the highway I kept to the central division, a stretch of flattened earth between the carriageways. It was like walking a tightrope, with the traffic streaming past on either side.

Sixty-mph convoys are rarely conducive to happy hitch-hiking. I'd learned that on the road to Sequoia, and now the lesson was repeated. Conspicuous as I was, nobody was going to stop for me. They weren't going to risk a multiple pile-up for the pleasure of my company. After five miles I decided to rest awhile and wait for a break in the traffic.

My chance came with a lone Ford that had a reasonable gap behind it. My cheerful acceptance of the lift was deflated, however, by the driver saying that he was only going as far as the next turn-off, a mile ahead. As a consolation he suggested that if I waited at a nearby gas station I should be able to get another lift fairly quickly.

Deposited at the gas station I went over to one of the pumps, where a bony bespectacled man in cap and windcheater was fuelling a station wagon. As I approached he gave me a quick once-over and nodded at the car.

'If you wanna ride, climb in.'

'Thanks!' I was too surprised – and relieved – to say anything else. Easing off the rucksack I put it in the back of the car, lodging it amongst a stack of newspapers. Going round to the front I opened the passenger door, where I had to stem an avalanche of more newspapers, these tightly rolled and piled high on the seat. Clearing an adequate space I eased myself in.

Making a space for himself where the newspapers had tumbled over on his side, my host climbed in beside me. He had a large pipe in his mouth, which he proceeded to take out and fill with tobacco. At that point I thought I had better ask him where he was going, and whether it was anywhere near the Yosemite National Park. With a disconcerting vagueness he nodded, and jabbed his pipe at the pile of newspapers. 'That's the way I'm headin' with this lot,' he said. 'Gotta take a few back roads, but you'll get there quicker'n walkin'.'

When the pipe was going well enough we set off. I was dismayed when in three miles we turned up a narrow unmade road, leading through orchards. In about half a mile I saw the first house, lying off the road to the right, and was mystified when my driver asked me to wind down the nearside window. A second later I ducked as his right arm jerked out and a rolled newspaper flew out of the window and over a wall to land in the front yard of a house. Another spun almost immediately out of the window on his side, to land in the drive of the opposite house. The bombardment continued all the way along the road, the car swerving from side to side with unnerving dexterity as the missiles hurtled to their targets.

I'd often wondered, when watching American films, if those newspaper boys on their bicycles, lobbing accurately from a range of about twenty yards, were fact or fiction. Now I had the answer.

The 'few back roads' turned out to be a tour of the local county that took in everything but the Yosemite National Park. My driver's antics, which at first had seemed remarkable (have you ever tried simultaneously to steer a car, smoke a pipe and score a bull's eye on a front porch?) eventually palled, and with them the novelty of ducking my head every few seconds to avoid a serious contusion. We fetched up finally in Mariposa, a small town on a crossroads which according to my map was thirty miles from Yosemite.

With his last missile dispatched, it was the end of the road for the newspaper man. Tapping out his pipe on the steering wheel he gave a prolonged yawn and suggested that as he lived nearby I might like to accompany him to his home for a bite of food and a quiet half-hour or so watching TV. 'You won't get into the park tonight,' he said. 'Maybe I could run you up there in the morning.'

Looking at my watch I politely said 'no'. It was, to my dismay, almost 4pm. After starting on my journey that morning at 6am, nothing could now deflect me from my purpose – to reach Yosemite that evening. The newspaper man was clearly disappointed by my rejection of I Love Lucy and a TV snack.

Walking up Mariposa's main street I was aware of a sharp drop in temperature, which reminded me that I was now on the flank of the Sierras. Positioning myself at the junction of the two state highways on the outskirts of the town I prayed for a prompt and reliable deliverance. I stood there, as far as I can recall, for two and a half hours, getting colder and more dispirited as time wore on. The traffic was very light and it was obvious that no one would be driving into the park at that hour of the day. The only person who stopped was a highway patrolman, who was less than helpful. 'You're wastin' your time, goin' up there. Park shuts at dusk – won't be no one goin' on that road tonight. If you want my advice, you'll stick aroun' Mariposa.'

From the tone of his voice I knew this was more than advice. After his tail lights had faded into the gathering gloom I started walking, knowing that if he came back and found me in the same place I would be provided with alternative overnight accommodation.

The road was steep and tree-lined and in half an hour completely dark and soundless, without the glimmer of a house light or the murmur of a car. I remembered the last time it had been like this, on the road from Camp Verde. With one difference, of course, that could not be ignored. On that walk, there had been the knowledge that within two miles I would reach a highway and pick up a bus: now there was no such certainty. I was faced by thirty miles of chilling darkness.

After an hour the jitters overcame me and I sank down at the roadside, wondering what on earth I was going to do. My strength had withered, and with it my resolution. I was cold and hungry, not having eaten since my early breakfast with Michael. The only thing I was sure about was that I could go no further. Shedding my rucksack I stood it in the road with the 'YOSEMITE' sign facing the traffic.

The US Cavalry were nowhere in sight and I became resigned to another night under the stars. The difference here was that the temperature was several degrees lower than in the Arizona desert. Picking up my rucksack I turned towards the undergrowth.

By some miracle a pair of headlights flooded the road just then and a battered Volkswagen pulled up short of me. I leapt out from the verge, waving, without thinking how much I might be scaring the driver.

As it happened, Alex E. Kolaski wasn't short of courage. As an employee of the Yosemite National Park, daily exposed to the menaces of black bears, cougars and other wild beasts of the Sierra, he wasn't going to be frightened by the sight of wild-looking hitch-hiker with a placard. On the contrary, he was glad to have the company.

Gratefully I sank into the car. 'You're going to Yosemite?'

'Sure, I work there. I'll take you right into the Valley.'

We drove off into the night on the desolate, slowly climbing road. Alex – or 'Al' – as he preferred – was full of talk, telling me about his life in the park. As a member of the work force servicing the various facilities of Yosemite Village his work was fairly menial, but this was more than compensated by his surroundings, the most scenic in California. His only regret was that the work was seasonal, and that he had to look elsewhere for a job in winter. 'Every year, I come back here,' he said. 'Ain't no place like it nowhere in the world.'

In a while the road joined the Merced River, which ran down from the High Sierra through the Yosemite Valley. Through narrow gorges and valleys we followed the twists and turns of the river, driving within the arc of our headlights. The bends were deceptive, exaggerated by the phantom shapes of rocks and trees that leapt into the panning beam. Al drove pretty fast, and although he knew where he was going it was scarier than anything those three boys had done, up by the Cedar Breaks. Did he know for certain that nothing would be coming the other way? Ahead, at the end of the road, lay the camp grounds and Park HQ: he was probably assuming no one could be leaving the valley at that time of night. And not thinking about what might be crossing the road ahead, round one of those blind corners.

Clunk.

A pair of startled eyes, gazing out of a black mask, were all we saw before it happened. Al groaned and punched the steering wheel with his fist. 'Raccoon. So help me, I got a raccoon.'

For the next half-mile he cursed fluently, and chided himself for not going back to see whether he had killed the little creature. Following the incident he drove with extreme caution, particularly round the bends. It was fortunate that he did. In a mile or so we came upon a mule deer, standing in the middle of the road with her fawn. Caught in the glare of our headlights, the two animals gazed at us inquiringly and did not move until our brakes were screeching and they were forced to jump out of the way. If it hadn't been for the earlier incident with the raccoon, these two unwary creatures might well have contributed to a statistical monstrosity.

Was it a fact that in a single year 70,000 deer were slaughtered on American roads?

A seemingly impenetrable forest of conifers shrouded the entrance to the park. It was a relief when we finally reached Yosemite Valley, and were welcomed by the wink of lights through the trees. On either side of the road lay the tents of the campgrounds, and here and there a timber lodge or cabin. The thrill of being in the park at long last was enormous. Only question: where would I spend the night?

Al, bless him, had already considered the question. 'What'd you say to shackin' up in my tent? There's only one other guy 'sides me; we can fit you on the floor, someplace.'

It was the gesture of a kindred spirit, and what one might expect from someone who could pick up a stranger on a dark mountain road. Parking by the employees' campground, Al led me to his tent, where he showed me my space by the stove. Then we went to the club room, where I made quick work of three hot dogs and a coffee. During the meal I was introduced to some of Al's fellow employees, a boisterous crowd who made me more than welcome.

On the way out of the club room I glimpsed a small scampering form, disappearing into the shadow of the porch. It shortly danced back into the light and I recognised, with a start, the creature that had been trapped momentarily in our beam, before its final oblivion. I cautioned Al and we stood there silently, watching the raccoon as it picked up a crust of bread with delicate fingers and nibbled it furiously, pausing every few seconds to dart anxious glances at us out of its strange harlequin mask. Allowing for its reputation as a camp-follower, I was still astonished by its boldness. When it had finished the crust it looked at us appealingly, its tiny forepaws raised in the air. It was more than Al could bear. Telling me to wait he went back for another hot dog.

A stiff back and muzzy head were the legacy of a night on the floor of Al's tent, stretched out beside the oil stove. The best remedy for both was a climb to Glacier Point.

Glaciation and erosion were the architects of the valley, their work creating a nave for the great cathedral of the surrounding mountains. The Merced River had laid the foundations, cutting through the granite of the last uplift: then the glaciers had flowed down from the mountains, transforming the 'V' into a 'U'. The debris from one of the last glaciers had caused a partial damming of the lower end of the valley, creating a lake and slowing the progress of the river. Over the millennia the river had deposited sediments that gradually filled in the lake, creating a flat valley floor a mile wide.

Hiking across the tree-covered floor to the start of the Glacier Point trail I remembered the ranger at the Grand Canyon talking about life zones. The elevation here in the valley was 4,000 feet, the transition zone where the conifers began to displace the oaks and other broad-leaved trees. Most prolific were the white fir and incense cedar, tall shapely trees growing out of a carpet of yellow fern. Autumn colours had by now asserted themselves, the tawny leaves of oak and maple providing a contrast to the dark evergreens. Crossing the placid Merced, I was offered one of the most brilliantly composed scenes in the tapestry of the wilderness: a montage of river, firs, mountains and sky with a centrepiece so perfect that it might have been contrived for that single view. The Half Dome was Yosemite's crowning glory, an extraordinary formation of rock shaped during the glacial period. With tremendous force the ice flow had sliced away half the granite mass, leaving a gigantic sculpted headstone to dominate the upper end of the valley.

A strenuous two-and-a-half-hour climb brought me to Glacier Point, 3,000 feet above the floor of the valley. From here my roving gaze took in the whole spectacle, a generous reward for the climb. Raised to the same elevation, I could view the Half Dome in profile: an extraordinary sight with its rounded, hump-like back and sheer, knife-cut face. Directly in front of me I saw further evidence of glacial carvings in the sheer north wall of the valley, grained and indented where the layers of rock had been stripped away. Out of a crevice in this wall sprang the Yosemite Falls, the most famous feature of the park. From what I had read about the falls, I was able to identify the long spear-shaped stain on the face of the rock which traced the flow of water. The falls were now dry and I could only wish that I'd been there in the springtime, when the snows melted on the high ground and the water spilled into the valley in a white cascade.

The noise of a truck engine was the last thing I expected to hear at that moment and I pirouetted in surprise as a tip-up appeared from nowhere, reversing towards the edge of the rock. I stood frozen, watching the rear wheels of the vehicle approach the brink. Was I about to witness a new kind of tourist attraction, to rival the Yosemite Falls?

To my relief the truck stopped a few yards short of the edge and deposited a load of redwood bark, adding to the pile already there. I had no idea what it was for, and was more interested to know where the truck had come from. As it drove off I followed on foot in the same direction and was astonished to discover a paved road, running down the other side of Glacier Point. At the sight of this, and the chalet-type lodge that lay back from the road, I suddenly felt rather cheated. Two and a half hours' climb, and I'd made it to the Glacier Point Hotel.

In front of the hotel I found a couple of women tourists, feeding nuts to a bevy of ground squirrels and chipmunks. The little creatures were very friendly and without too much enticement were taking the nuts from their feeders' hands. Offering my services as a photographer I borrowed each of their cameras and took the appropriate snaps. The women, who were from Long Beach, were delighted.

Pursuing my success I inquired as to whether they had come up to Glacier Point by car. They nodded, looking rather surprised by the question. When I asked if they could give me a lift back into the valley they looked even more surprised, until I explained that I was travelling without a car and had hiked into the park from Merced. At this piece of information the older of the two women gawped. 'Oh my – you ain't the feller we passed on the road yesterday, carryin' that Yosemite sign?'

I nodded, and they were immediately propelling me towards their car, saying how terrible they'd felt about not picking me up, but it was on a freeway and there *were* police regulations...

We drove down into the valley, a circuitous route that took us past the charming and softly-flowing Bridal Veil Fall and the huge glacier-planed rock of El Capitan. Throughout the drive I was flattered by the women's attention. They asked me to let them know whenever I wanted to stop for the view or take a photograph. It was an act of contrition that became almost embarrassing. When we reached their village hotel – the splendid and historic Ahwahnee – they insisted on inviting me to dinner, a gesture which in the circumstances I could do little to resist. Sitting in the vast baronial dining hall and presented with a fresh, crisply-grilled mountain trout, served with asparagus and French fries, I was totally in their thrall.

As much as I enjoyed the trout, my companions appeared to enjoy my company. Their questions were unwavering and my answers, though brief, seemed only to encourage them further. What did it feel like, carrying that heavy bag all day? Didn't I get a sore back, not to mention sore feet? And how about the buses? Were the seats comfortable, and did I have to travel overnight? What did I think of America? Did I like it here more than in England? And where, might they ask, was I staying the night?

Before they could book me into a room at the Ahwahnee I told them.

'Private accommodation?' Their eyebrows lifted. 'Gee, you must know somebody –'

When I got back to the tent Al was resting. He'd been shifting furniture around most of the day in the Yosemite Lodge, for 'one o' them durn conventions'. He had been unsure as to whether I would be staying in the park for a second night, but was glad to see me back. 'Why don't you stop around for a few days? This is your home, for as long as you like.'

I made one of those hopeless, indecisive gestures, which were becoming habitual. 'Thanks,' I said. 'I'll probably leave tomorrow.'

To help me make up my mind – about staying – Al drove me out to see the Firefall. This was a short-lived but sensational event, first created in 1872, that brought the tourists out every night, to gather below the dark tower of Glacier Point and then watch the fiery cascade spilling onto the valley floor 3,000 feet below. Parking in a convenient spot we were able to glimpse the preliminary moment – a tiny fire glimmering on the point above us. This, Al told me, was a bonfire, lit every night during the summer season at about the same time. I remembered then the pile of bark that I had seen unloaded at the point the previous day.

'There she goes!'

The flicker of light became a brilliant blossom, spreading its fiery red petals over the edge of the rock. I watched as the fire plunged downwards, a glowing cascade trailing into the darkness. For a minute or so, before the last embers were scattered into space, the Firefall continued, a 900-foot cataract that burnt itself out on a rocky ledge high above the valley floor. It was a wonderful sight that would ignite my memory for years to come.

I just hoped that Smokey Bear wasn't looking.

With the sad realisation that even Yosemite couldn't hold me I started out again the next day, loaded with my rucksack, sleeping bag and a toothpick inscribed 'Ahwahnee Hotel'. This was a parting gift from Al, one of those simple tokens of goodwill that become strangely enduring mementos. I might not have stayed at the hotel, but I had the toothpick.

Walking through the village I was warmed by a great sense of satisfaction. I had seen the Yosemite Valley in comfort and style for practically nothing. With that kind of fortune there seemed no limit to what I could achieve. With reinforced bravura I flagged down the first car that came in sight.

That car was guided by my stars. It was a Morris Minor and the occupants were English, a man of about thirty and his father. More than that, they were leaving Yosemite by way of the Tioga Pass. This was the only eastern exit from the park, on a road that joined the US395 at Lee Vining – the Greyhound connection for points east. It was not, by all accounts, a good road, but it would save me from the alternative trek back to Merced and the roundabout journey out of California via Sacramento.

The younger man, who was driving the car, was a naturalised American. His home was in Santa Clara, Cal., his father's in Sheffield, Yorks. The six weeks that the two were spending together were being devoted to trips into the back country, camping and hiking, and leading the sort of life that wasn't possible for them either in Santa Clara or Sheffield. Amidst an eccentric tangle of gasoline cans, fishing gear, tin kettles and packs of canned beer I settled down in the back to what I anticipated would be a relaxing and scenic drive.

So it was, as far as the Tioga Pass. Sixty miles of raw creation, at altitudes of 8-10,000 feet. The road, which traversed the entire width of the park, was only open in the summer and autumn months, when the snow had cleared. Just as the rock debris in the creek and river beds spoke of the glaciers of the past, so the granite cliffs betokened the avalanches to come. In the middle of October, with the autumn colours well advanced and a tang of winter in the air, the landscape seemed in a state of suspension, waiting for the soft cloak of the first snow to be laid on its shoulders.

On the way to the pass we drove through a stretch of countryside that at this level was totally unexpected. At 8,600 feet, in their nest of high peaks and fir, the Tuolumne Meadows – in the eastern part of the Yosemite National Park – were like a glade in the thick of a forest, a restful expanse of open grassland speckled with alpine flowers. The Meadows were the site of a ranger station and the main High Sierra campground, a major centre of camping and hiking activity.

My first intimation that the journey might not turn out as expected was the sign that confronted us on our arrival at the pass, saying 'Road Closed'. For a minute or two we sat there, nonplussed. Then a ranger came out of a hut and strolled towards us. Poking his head into the car he explained that construction was in progress on the road ahead, and that it would be closed until two o'clock that afternoon.

My companions, who did not seem too concerned by the news, had a short conference. As it was only ten o'clock they decided to go for a hike, to explore the Tuolumne Meadows, and continue their journey later when the road was open. It would have been an obvious choice for me to accompany them, but when they suggested it I shook my head and with heroic resolution donned my rucksack and bade them farewell.

Somewhere at the back of my mind a small voice reminded me that it was fourteen miles to Lee Vining from that point. That I was carrying a forty-five-pound pack, and that according to the National Park Service the road was still under construction and closed to traffic. Another voice, not quite so loud, told it to shut up and put a little more faith in those currently favourable stars.

From the pass, at 9,940 feet, the road took a gentle descent which made the first two or three miles easy going. The surface was in good repair and once I got past the road works I imagined it would be the same right through to Lee Vining. Then, even if there weren't any trucks to help me on the way, I could walk the distance comfortably and reach my destination before the road was reopened to traffic at the Tioga Pass.

On that descent my heels were winged like Mercury. It seemed that nothing could stop me. But as the descent levelled out and I came within sight of Lee Vining Canyon my feet turned to lead.

The canyon, seen from a distance, was an awesome sight. Banked by huge granite cliffs, it stretched into the blue infinity of the Sierra. Along its north side I could pick out the course of the road, a needle line scratched into the rugged contour of the granite. It seemed to go on forever. I paused, resting the rucksack on a boulder. There was no one in sight, and not even a cricket in earshot. I couldn't have felt more numbingly helpless and alone.

In the stillness of my surroundings I was hardly prepared for the muffled *crump* of an explosion, somewhere around the next bend. Fearfully I approached the corner, expecting to see either a massive fall of rock or a crater gaping in the middle of the road.

What I found was a sign, painted in bold red letters. 'WARNING', it read. 'NO RADIO TRANSMISSION. BLASTING AHEAD'.

Rounding the bend I witnessed one of the most energetic rapings of Mother Earth that one could expect to see in an area of such isolation. Two 'cats', two bulldozers, a mechanical excavator and a fleet of trucks were pummelling away at a gouged-out embankment of earth, widening a right-angled cut in the mountainside. As far as I could determine from the map, I was somewhere on State Highway 120.

Cautiously I advanced on a man in a helmet and orange waistcoat who was directing the operations. When I asked him if there was any danger on the road ahead he looked at me blankly, tipping back his helmet.

'Safest stretch in Mono County,' he assured me.

Taking strength from his words I pressed on, climbing over the rubble of earth and rocks. In a moment I was cowering against the embankment as a huge diesel-engined juggernaut bore down on me, swinging round at the last moment to bury itself in a wall of earth. The next three miles were like walking a gauntlet between a minefield and a tank training ground, exposing me to the dual threat of being detonated into the heavens or bulldozed into the earth. The most systematic intimidation was imposed by the giant excavators, the width of the road, which suddenly appeared from nowhere and swept past me like a mechanical avalanche, wafting me bodily against the rock face. Following them the water carriers, spraying the churned-up dust and turning the legs of my jeans into damp sticking plasters.

The seventh or eighth mile brought me down by a hairpin bend to the floor of the canyon where I rested a while, bathing my feet in Lee Vining Creek and listening to the arguments. Voice One, the strongest, was saying how incredibly fit I must be, to go eight miles with a rucksack that a few weeks ago would have disabled me in half the distance. For someone in my condition another six miles would be no problem at all. Voice Two, in a quiet undertone, suggested that I wouldn't last another yard.

The argument was resolved finally by a procession of cars, wending their way down into the canyon. Looking at my watch I discovered that I'd completely lost track of time. The road had been opened at Tioga Pass an hour ago, and these vehicles were the first off the start line. Pulling on my shoes and other trappings I climbed stiffly back to the road.

My thoughts were unrepeatable as the first car, and then a dozen more, sailed past me, without so much as a friendly 'V' sign to cheer me on my way. What kind of people were they, who could ignore a poor footsore hiker who'd been walking eight miles? Motorised zombies!

Toot toot. Half-expectantly I turned as the car pulled up beside me. My heart gave a leap. It was a Morris Minor, with two Englishmen on board.

'Going our way?'

At my thankful nod they both grinned and the father asked if I'd enjoyed my hike. But I didn't mind. For the privilege of being able to collapse again into their back seat I could take any amount of Yorkshire humour.

They took me the last six miles to Lee Vining, a town whose only claim to fame was its main street, the US395. Left alone in that spot I felt rather like a used-up car tyre, deflated and worn, abandoned at the side of the road. My jaded spirits lifted a little when I saw the bus depot further up the street, and when I got there they lifted higher. Over the entrance was the familiar sign of that leaping quadruped, symbol of merciful relief to one whose hiking days – hopefully – were over.

The Greyhound for Reno, Nevada, left at 6.19pm. I doubt if I had ever been so pleased to see a vehicle as that great aluminium-clad Scenicruiser, coasting into the depot with lights blazing and engine pulsing, or to climb once more into its cool interior and drop into my favourite seat, behind the driver.

Leaving California was a bit of a wrench. I'd been there three weeks, longer than in any other state. A period in which I'd seen much of the condition of American life – and an abundance of her landscape. Nevada, which had the misfortune to be on the dry side of the Sierra range, was the canvas reversed. Arid and empty, with its life grafted on. How else could one describe those repetitive miniature Las Vegases, spreading their jackpot growth into the desert?

At Reno, 'The Biggest Little City in the World' (modelled on its big sister to the south with its casinos and wedding chapels) I changed buses for Salt Lake City, Utah. This was a run of 530 miles, across countryside that like much of the return trip would be lost in darkness – a necessary sacrifice in the cause of saving time and hotel bills. My experience of northern Nevada was accordingly confined to the rest stop at Elko, where I broke my slumbers for a pancake stack at the Post House.

Though darkness made a mystery of the next 400 miles, daylight came at a good moment. With the first tinge of grey on the horizon I became aware of a flat, limitless expanse that looked as if it had been laid using a spirit level, blemished only by the tenuous shadows of scrub. This was the Great Salt Lake Desert, the dry basin of a great lake that had existed in glacial times. The name of the lake – Bonneville – had a modern association as well, as the site of successive world land speed records.

The lake had formerly occupied most of the western half of what was now Utah, and unlike its remnant, the Great Salt Lake, had been a freshwater lake fed by rains and meltwater from the glaciers. The salt deposited by the rivers flowing from the nearby salt mountains had not been sufficient to predominate, but as the glaciers disappeared and the climate became drier the freshwater supply diminished and the lake sank down below the level of its outlets. Deprived of its drainage system the salt had gradually accumulated as the lake contracted, and now, in an average depth of only twelve feet, the salt content was twenty-three per cent – six times more than that of the Pacific.

By the time we came in sight of the Great Salt Lake the sun was up and I had to shield my eyes from the glaring white surface of the water, the brilliance of the salt deposits spreading from its shoreline. The bareness of the view was awe-inspiring: a bleached-out print on which the charcoal sticks of the telegraph poles and the occasional squatting hulk of an abandoned car were the only distinct images. The desolation had a stark purity that one could see, in a visionary moment, with the eyes of Brigham Young and his followers, driven more than a thousand miles westwards in search of a spiritual sanctuary.

Salt Lake City to Yellowstone

Divine Revelations

'Here will be the temple of our God.'

So decreed Brigham Young, standing with his Mormon followers on a spot of ground in the Salt Lake Valley at the end of their epic westward journey. On the same spot – now Temple Square, Salt Lake City – I gazed up at the legacy of his words. A towering granite temple, reproducing in its spires and crenellations a bizarre mixture of Gothic and Oriental. But for all its oddity the Temple of the Church of Jesus Christ of Latter-Day Saints was a prodigious monument to the faith of its builders.

In 1853, when construction had commenced, the only method available to transport the granite was by ox-cart, a round trip of forty miles to the nearest quarry. Three to four yoke of oxen would be necessary to haul a single block, and the journey might take three or four days. The advent of the railroad had speeded up the work, but it was forty years before the temple had been ready for dedication. To one outside the Church, it was hard to see the point of all this zeal and devotion. But it invited my curiosity.

Who were the Mormons? And what was this strange faith of theirs, that in a country whose foundation stone was religious tolerance had provoked so much wrath and persecution?

Mormonism – the only home-grown American religion – derived from the teachings of Joseph Smith, a young man from Palmyra, New York. In 1820, when he was only fourteen, Joseph had received the first of a series of divine revelations, culminating in the visit of a holy messenger who had instructed him to go to a hillside near his home and there uncover a stone box containing a set of gold plates. These plates had been engraved with an ancient script which the young man had immediately set about translating. The result of his efforts, the Book of Mormon, was an account of an ancient Hebraic people who lived in America, centuries before its discovery by Europeans. This evidence of the existence of the chosen people on the continent of North America, thousands of years ago, was a foundation for the belief that in time to come the Land of Israel – Zion – would rise again here, and that the resurrected Christ would reign here on earth. A myth, certainly, but no greater than any of the others.

Nothing too provocative in any of this, but the inevitable persecution of an ordinary being who claimed divine revelation followed its historical precedents. Joseph Smith's new interpretation of the Gospel, prescribing certain doctrines and principles of conduct that ran against the standard concepts of the time, inevitably goaded the opposition.

One could not ignore the fact that one of those doctrines embraced polygamy, a practice that could not have been popular at a time when frontiers were being forged and women were a rare commodity. In 1844, after he had tried unsuccessfully to establish his church in four different states, Joseph Smith had paid the price of his beliefs at the hands of a lynch mob in Carthage, Illinois. For the movement, of course, this had done nothing but good. The cause that had suffered from the martyrdom of its leader had yet to be recorded. The Church of Jesus Christ of Latter-Day Saints, founded in 1830, had ultimately achieved a membership of one and a half million.

Not being one of this number I was prohibited from going into the temple and turned my attention to the other bizarre – and universally celebrated – building on Temple Square. If I had been asked to conceive of a suitable vehicle for the Mormon Tabernacle Choir, my imagination could not have done better than a huge silver dirigible, freshly descended from the heavens. For the more technically minded, the Mormon Tabernacle is an achievement of sheer ingenuity, considering the period of its construction. In the 1860s, in a pioneer community, steel was not available, and the only materials the Mormons had to work with were wood and stone. The great ovoidal roof of the Tabernacle was built entirely of wood, a bridgework of timbers supported by arches spanning the complete width of the building. The roof, originally covered by shingles but now by aluminium, rested on sandstone pillars with doors opening into the Tabernacle.

Through one of these doors I followed a file of people who were being conducted into the auditorium by a guide. I was disappointed to hear that I had just missed an organ recital, a half-hour performance given every day to demonstrate the remarkable acoustics of the interior. Sitting down at the back of the auditorium, I could only imagine the effect of the colossal instrument that towered above us, in combination with a 375-voice choir. After hearing so many broadcast recitals of the Mormon Tabernacle Choir it was a pity to miss the real thing.

In the context of the twentieth century it was difficult to imagine the awe with which the pilgrims from the east must have beheld the Tabernacle, after trekking across 1,000 miles of wilderness from the Missouri frontier.

Later on, having travelled here on the Union-Pacific railroad, they would have been equally enthralled by the completed temple, which took forty years in the making. The hardship and sacrifice endured by the Mormons shaping their new life was amply illustrated by the exhibits in the Temple Museum, to which we were next conducted.

The first plough used by the pioneers was a favourite with the guide, who devoted equal attention to a battered old piano that had been hauled across the plains by ox-cart. For the Mormons, playing music and tilling the soil were the same thing: an act of dedication.

On the matter of dedication, we could not have found a better exemplar than our guide, a young man who in addition to being a local attorney was a priest of the Mormon Church. He was, he told us, one of 350,000 similarly ordained, the offices of the Church being open to every male member over the age of twelve in good standing. Such participation was inevitable in a foundation that was held to be the resurrection of the original Church of Christ, a concept that required a degree of faith – and committal – far beyond that of other Christian denominations. 'Latter-day Saints' was a description used to distinguish the Church's elders from the original saints, a necessary distinction when the President of the Church (also known as the 'Prophet') was supported by a Council of the Twelve Apostles.

Other theological concepts had more personal connotations. Our bodies, the guide informed us, were regarded as the tabernacle of the human spirit: there could accordingly be no contamination of them by unclean substances, such as alcohol, tobacco, tea or coffee. 'Or narcotics,' he added as an afterthought. Also, for the advancement of God's kingdom, it was considered a duty of Mormons to contribute a tenth of their income to their Church, a further act of devotion that made offertory-box Anglicans such as myself feel a bit mean.

Old Faithful Geyser. Fountain Paint Pot. Grand Prismatic Spring. Grand Canyon of the Yellowstone.

Anyone in search of the essence of the Great American Outdoors should visit the Yellowstone National Park. An area sixty miles square containing the greatest variety of scenery and natural phenomena in the United States.

Tucked into the northwest corner of Wyoming – the northernmost point of my journey – Yellowstone had until now remained a remote objective, a climactic experience that had been stored and treasured like the few remaining rolls of unexposed film in the pocket of my rucksack. My arrival at Salt Lake City, however, had put me in striking distance.

Armed with the certain knowledge that Yellowstone was the only National Park served by Greyhound, I turned up next morning at the depot, only to learn from the ticket clerk that the service had been discontinued five weeks ago. That was in early

September, the end of the American tourist season. The nearest place that Greyhound could take me was the town of Idaho Falls – 104 miles from the park.

Forlornly I examined the soles of my shoes, to determine whether the holes in them were also in the soles of my feet. Before I could dispel this troublesome notion I was approached by a young couple in camel-hair coats who had been in front of me at the ticket counter. They, too, were anxious to go to the Yellowstone and had been asking the same questions as me. Why didn't we team up and hire a car at Idaho Falls?

I couldn't think of a better idea. They were German and newly married, on a five-week tour of the States. The methodical type who had earmarked all the sights and were not going to miss anything. While Jutta got the bus tickets Hellmut telephoned Budget Rent-a-Car.

An 8.15am start gave us a good springboard for our run to Idaho Falls, a distance of 220 miles. Crossing the border north of the Salt Lake from Utah into Idaho I tried immediately to pick out some outstanding feature of the scenery, that would implant the state of Idaho in my memory. But America didn't work like that. Not every state could be a California or a Texas, and the ones that weren't deserved respect for their integrity. Idaho was such a state: virtuous and unmemorable. In 1805 the explorers Lewis and Clark had trekked across its terrain in search of a river passage to the Pacific: sadly they never found it. In 1861 a more successful trail blazer, Captain John Mullan, would construct the first wagon route across the Rockies, leaving his carved initials on a tree stump now on display in the state museum. History apart, one cannot mention this state without reference to that sturdy product of the Idaho soil, currently playing to packed restaurants alongside Tad's Dollar Steak. The real beauty of the Baked Idaho Potato, as opposed to other national monuments, was that you didn't have to go all the way to Idaho to enjoy it.

Renting a car is never as easy as it says in the advertisements. When we reached Idaho Falls, at around 1.30pm, our first task was to find the agency we had contacted, which was like trying to find a brand of crackers in a supermarket.

The bus depot was surrounded by car rental firms, a sure

indicator of the scenic countryside now within motoring range. But despite the number of rival firms the spirit of competition was strangely lacking. After its telephone offer of five dollars a day Budget Rent-a-Car went into reverse by saying that it could no longer guarantee this and now could only offer a car at seven dollars a day. In addition to this there was a one-dollar insurance charge and a mileage charge of eight cents. For a day and a half, and an estimated mileage of 350 miles, the total cost would be about forty dollars. That such an amount was beyond our collective reach was emphasised by our collective response. The traditional Dutch auction ensued.

'One way you could have a reduction is to put your own gas in the car. The mileage charge would be reduced to five cents a mile.'

'What about the hire charge? Seven dollars a day is more than our budget. Can you reduce the charge for the second day?'

'Any time over the hour is reckoned by the hour at a dollar rate. If you're planning on a day and a half then you need to be back here by the evening, before we close. That allows you another four hours on top of the day.'

'At a dollar an hour?'

'Look – I'll cut you a deal. Be back here by five-thirty tomorrow, and I'll only charge you for the day.'

A deal it was. In a stylish Ford Galaxie, checked for dents, we swept out of Idaho Falls on the road to Yellowstone, Hellmut handling the big American car as if he'd never driven any other. With a bit of luck we hoped to get to the park while it was still light.

As we headed north the sky got grey and heavy-looking, and it looked as if we were running into a storm. Jutta said that at the altitude of the park – around 7,000 feet – there was a good chance of snow. It seemed strange to be in mountain country again, so soon after my trip to Yosemite, and I had to look at a map to convince myself that I was no longer in the Sierra Nevada but the Rocky Mountains. Over to the east we had tantalising glimpses, through pine forests, of the Grand Tetons, a range of massive flint-edged peaks created by mighty glaciers. These peaks were the outstanding features of another, eponymous, National Park lying ten miles to the south of Yellowstone.

'Welcome to Montana – the Big Sky Country'. I did a double-take on the sign as we flashed past. Montana? Looking at my map I saw that we were just crossing the Continental Divide, which formed the Idaho-Montana border, and entering the tiny thumb of Montana that poked between the adjacent states of Idaho and Wyoming. With the promise of the 'Cowboy State' ahead, the 'Big Sky' country was a bonus.

The park was mainly in Wyoming, overlapping stretches of Montana on its northern and western edges. As we entered it at West Yellowstone the first wisps of snow appeared, blown into sinuous shapes by the wind gusting along the tree-girt road. Although it had only just gone four, the trees – the closely-growing lodgepole pine – combined with the pall of the sky to create a premature gloom that forced us to slow down and concentrate on the road.

In a mile or so we were relieved when the forest gave way on one side of the road to a river bank and a view across an open stretch of meadowland where a large herd of American elk were browsing. The first sight of Yellowstone's wildlife filled me with excitement. Next to its fame as a huge thermal amphitheatre, the park was best known as a wildlife sanctuary, in which the animals could roam freely with little fear of man. The late afternoon, when they emerged into the open areas to feed, was one of the best times to see them.

At Madison Junction we turned right onto the Grand Loop Road, a scenic route providing a 147-mile circular tour of the park. The river bank steepened and we were soon driving on an overhang looking down at the swiftly-running waters of the Firehole River. The river, fed by rushing mountain streams, was a rousing prelude to the drama of Yellowstone, a series of frothing white cascades breaking over silver rocks and throwing their sparkling spray into the gathering dusk. The snow was falling thickly now, suspending the car in a kind of vacuum.

'Look!'

In the moment Jutta caught her breath I saw the first geyser, an uprush of white vapour just visible through the curtain of snow. Straining my eyes, I could make out other wraith-like shapes beyond it, caught in the eddies of snow. Eager to have a closer look we pulled into a parking area and left the car to explore. A sign reading 'Fountain Paint Pot Nature Trail' led us into a landscape that belonged to another planet. A bleached, sulphurous waste that stretched into an unreachable nothingness. In our frozen awe we could find no words for it. The aftermath of a seismic holocaust? The debris of Armageddon?

Strangely, in the face of such desolation, there was no sense of extinction: rather of a tremendous pulsating life force that made the very ground tremble under our feet. The earth was breathing!

A snow-covered boardwalk led us to the miraculous events. Treading gingerly in each other's footprints we aimed for the nearest billow of steam, glancing warily at the pie-crust of earth beneath us. With my limited knowledge of geology, I tried to picture the infernal processes at work beneath us: the underground plumbing system that created the spectacle. At the Silex Spring I encountered my first clue – a pool of bubbling, steaming water about fifteen feet in diameter. This was the surface opening of a fissure in the rock descending many hundreds of feet, an escape route for the superheated water rising from below. The water in this pool was at boiling point and barely visible through the wreaths of steam: further on there were other pools whose water was cooler and more placid. The colours in these pools were as beautiful as they were unexpected, vitreous blue on the surface and underneath a variety of hues that formed a colour ripple from the centre – yellow edging into green edging into reddish brown. These colours belonged to different species of algae that flourished at certain temperatures: the yellowish forms on the lip of the fissure where the water was hottest and the brown species on the outer rim of the pool where it was cooler.

The level of the ground water supplying the springs varied with the level of the earth. On the higher ground it was not so near the surface, and the springs appeared as 'paint pots' of heaving mud. A rise in the ground brought us to the most extraordinary of these, the Fountain Paint Pot. A cauldron of varied colours that gasped and steamed and trembled, on that hesitant edge of boiling that made watching it a gentle agony of suspense. The steam bubbles, breaking through the surface, were a fascinating sight. Globules of mud that grew larger and larger and then burst with a delicious *plop*. This was a part of the mixing process that created the different hues, a blending of clay and silica with iron oxides. The finished effect was a pinky-grey, with the odd streak of citron yellow. On the outside, where the mud had caked and dried, the mixture needed a stir, the tiny mounds and craters making a lunar landscape in miniature.

Agape and agog, and oblivious of the cape of snow that hung on our shoulders, we continued our exploration of the geyser basin. The variety of thermal activity was astonishing. Apart from the hot springs and paint pots there were such oddities as the fumaroles, shafts in the rock that provided gas escapes for the liquid furnaces of the magma. In most cases this was a direct release of volcanic heat, without any interference of ground water. Occasionally, though, during a seasonal change in the water table, a fumarole might take on the activity of a spring. An example of this was the Red Spouter, a bright red jet of water that took us by surprise, spurting out of the ground a yard or two from the boardwalk.

After the experience of walking for about a quarter of a mile on the lid of a pressure cooker it was a relief when the lid blew off. At the furthest loop of the trail we were surrounded by the star performers of Yellowstone, the geysers. All around us the jets of water built their rival columns, their scalding spray hissing in the wind-chilled air. As the surging jets intermittently wavered and died others sprang up in their place, like synchronised fountains. Gazing at their spectral shapes through the snow-laced twilight I felt that I had been touched by a wand and conveyed to a mystic world, where Nature, in her most beautiful guise, was the only inhabitant. What could make purer poetry or deeper mystery than the play of steam and white water in the dusk, veiled by the magical rhythms of the falling snow?

For a while we had been enchanted out of any awareness of time, or of the snow melting in our hair. But now it was getting dark and we started back to the car, walking as quickly as we dared on the slippery boardwalk. The half-light, combined with the descending veil of snow, played some strange tricks on our eyes. A series of black upright spikes, jutting out of the ground, were like the spars of a sunken vessel: only on closer examination could they be identified as dead trees, stripped of their branches, like a grotesque vision of the Western Front. How they had met their death was hardly a cause for conjecture in this bleak, tempestuous wilderness: one could only wonder if they had ever had the gift of life.

Our end of season arrival, though granting us free access and saving us from the summer hordes, presented us with a minor problem. The only available accommodation was at the Old Faithful Lodge, whose elaborate backwoods architecture and roaring log fire in the reception suggested top-of-the-range. This was of course a personal response – but one that I was obliged to communicate to my companions. After they had booked their room I asked Hellmut if he could let me have the key to the car, so that I could arrange my own accommodation. The two of them looked at me with curiosity. 'Where will you go?' asked Jutta. 'This is the only place that's open.' With some diffidence I told them that my destination was the back seat of the car and a sleeping bag. They were nonplussed. 'You'll freeze to death,' Jutta said.

Ten minutes later I was in their room, stretched out in my sleeping bag at the foot of their bed. As Hellmut put the light out and wished me goodnight I had a troublesome thought. For these young newly-weds a trip to America must signify a very special kind of holiday. Although I was warm I had to confess to misgivings, about how far one could stretch the bonds of international friendship...

Travel cynics might suggest that 'natural wonder' was a uniquely American expression, applied to everything from a mountain peak to a blade of grass. And the Great Outdoors, with its National Parks and National Monuments, not as the creation of nature but of a group of commercial interests, ready at the drop of a waterfall or a pine cone to move in with the catering concessions. They would paint a picture of crowds of US tourists with cameras, light meters and guide books, gathered round a hole in the ground.

It was a crisp, sparkling morning at Old Faithful and we stood expectantly at the sacred spot, accompanied by other watchers in parked cars. In front of us a sign identified the 'Old Faithful Geyser', and further away a smoking mound that marked the opening to the underground steam funnel. A technical description of the workings of a geyser being beyond me, I must resort to images.

A vertical pipe filled with water. At intervals, poking into it, the spouts of several kettles, steaming away merrily. The water in the pipe acting as a pressure valve against the steam pressure from the kettles, until forced by that pressure to overflow a little from the top of the pipe. The steam building up in the kettles, and the waterload in the pipe getting lighter and lighter with the increasing overflow. At a certain point the water in the pipe losing its stability and suddenly flashing in a steam-driven jet from the mouth of the pipe. Substituting an underground vent with connecting chambers for the pipe and kettles, you have the anatomy of a geyser.

The big question was: how long did it take the water to boil? This varied greatly from geyser to geyser, depending on the extent and capacity of its underground system. Some were less reliable than others, but this one wasn't called 'Old Faithful' for nothing.

The eruptions came at intervals of sixty-five minutes, and we were fortunate in not having to wait too long. We'd only been there a few minutes, in fact, when half-a-dozen car doors opened simultaneously and the camera-wielders advanced. As they joined us the geyser began to spout, right on time. We watched entranced as the white froth of the overflow gathered to a head and then shot upwards in mounting tiers of hissing foam, to reach a pinnacle more than a hundred feet high. For several minutes the great fountain gushed into the air, a massive volume of steam and superheated water. When the supply of water, rushing up through that underground pipe, was finally exhausted, the pillar of foam gently subsided. It was as if a tap in some deep cavern of the earth had slowly been turned off.

Though unmatched for size and splendour the Old Faithful was just one of 200 geysers in the park, one of 10,000 thermal features that made Yellowstone one of the most varied and extensive areas of its kind in the world. The existence of volcanic activity so near to the surface was a freak of nature, found only in such scattered parts of the world as Iceland, Japan and New Zealand. Its repertoire, we discovered, was inexhaustible. After last night's thermal adventures we thought we had seen everything. A walk along the Firehole River, flanking the road into Old Faithful, proved us wrong.

Following the self-guiding nature trails on either side of the river we came across a number of springs and geysers that had their own unique features: the peculiar formations created by the deposit of minerals from the springwater. The Punch Bowl Spring, with its brew bubbling in a self-built cauldron of white and bronze silica, was the best example; others were the Grotto Geyser, the Scalloped Spring and the Castle Geyser, whose names forestalled one's own powers of invention.

No wonder the first explorers, bringing back stories of their discoveries, had been so sceptically received. It wasn't until 1870,when a proper expedition had been organised to follow in the tracks of the fur traders and God seekers, that the stories – or most of them – had been confirmed. After that the wheels of official recognition had begun to turn, and in 1872 an Act of Congress had created the United States' first National Park. Like Yosemite its name came from a Hidatsa Indian word, in this case a translation of their name for 'Yellow Rock River'. A mark of respect for the people who had, after all, been the first to appreciate its wonder.

It was to the Yellowstone River that we now headed, continuing our journey round the Grand Loop. Though the snow had fallen heavily overnight the road was drivable and we could go at an easy 35mph without any hazard. The mysteries and miracles still surrounded us, and we kept our eyes fixed on every break in the trees.

On a thickly forested stretch of the road we saw a couple of parked cars ahead of us and slowed down, expecting to see something extraordinary. We were not disappointed.

Leaning against one of the cars was the huge dark shape of a bear, with its forepaws resting on the driver's door and its nose pressed against the window. *Ursus Americanus*, the American Black Bear. We slid to a quiet stop, a few yards behind the second car, and reached for our cameras.

To our delight we saw that the bear had a cub in tow, dancing around its mother's legs. A bag of popcorn, thrust through the top of the car window, fell at the mother's feet and was immediately seized by the cub, who tried to shake it open. They started young in the Yellowstone.

Hunted elsewhere, the Black Bear was well protected in the parks, to the extent that it spent almost as much time at the side of the road and in the campgrounds as in the forest. Its forwardness was, of course, inspired by the easy pickings offered by either careless or foolhardy tourists: the ones who left boxes of ham lying around in campsites or proffered goodies from car windows. The latter – expressly forbidden by park regulations – was an act of bravado that many of the park's visitors could not resist, regardless of the obvious dangers. What matter if Junior got hugged, swiped or chewed, as long as he could tell the other kids he'd fed a real live Smokey Bear?

Another car pulled in and we drove on, not wishing to contribute to a 'bear jam'. Further on we saw a second, sedentary bear and this time pulled up some distance from it. Slowly the bear got to its feet and started towards us, lumbering ponderously down the middle of the road. In defiance of another regulation Hellmut and I got out of the car and focused our cameras. A word of warning here: never photograph an advancing bear with a twin-lens reflex. Everything is less distinct in a ground-glass screen, and when you're peering downwards you can't check distances with the other eye. As the bear got closer I waited for the right moment to shoot, unaware of the real speed of that leisurely, flat-footed creature. When I'd taken the shot and saw the bear a few yards away and looking hungry I followed Hellmut back into the car with a Nijinsky-like leap.

From the forest area we drove on to the shoreline of the Yellowstone Lake, which lay at an altitude of nearly 8,000 feet. The road rose above the lake and most views of it were over the snow-covered tops of pine trees. Those glimpses were like sips from a spring, refreshing expanses of ice-blue water stroked by the lowering clouds of a pearl grey sky. At the outlet of the lake, by Fishing Bridge, we turned north along the Yellowstone River, heading towards the celebrated canyon and falls.

On the way we allowed ourselves a diversion on foot along a trail marked enticingly: 'The Black Dragon's Cauldron'. The trail wound steeply up a hillside through an area of mud geysers and pools, yet another variation of the thermal landscape. Over bridges, duckboards and slippery paths we made the climb, continually astonished by the spectacle of thick snow on one side of us and simmering, translucent pools on the other. At the end of the trail we were confronted by a weird and wonderful scene, straight from that underworld where our imaginations had been dwelling since our arrival in Yellowstone. A lake of fire and brimstone, a dark forest, a river of hell. This was the Black Dragon's Cauldron, a throbbing bed of mud created by an earthquake in 1948. The steam from its craters mingled with the steam from a vast pool of overflow water, stretching beyond it to the retreating tree line. In the midst of this pool stood the same frozen spikes that we had seen the night before, and now appeared clearly as the relics of drowned trees. Their bleached bases showed the effect of their long immersion in the mineral-laden water. Slowly, the wood was turning into stone.

It was on this trail, making the descent to the road, that we saw our first bison. A dark, humped shape silhouetted sharply by the snow, browsing among the trees. Leaving the trail we cautiously approached it, moving from the cover of one tree to the next so as not to disturb it. Stalking it like that I felt strangely guilty, as though it wasn't a camera in my hands but a rifle. I couldn't help remembering the terrible beating that these creatures had taken in the last century, when the campaign of slaughter carried out by the settlers and railroadmen had reduced their number from tens of millions to less than one hundred. The equivalent, on Bill Cody's reckoning, to a box of cartridges.

Following the valley of the Yellowstone to the north we came at last to the Upper Falls, the first of the two great cascades that carried the Yellowstone River into its canyon. An outcrop of rock, a short walk from the road, gave us a stunning close-up view of the falls as they plunged over the ledge only twenty feet below us. The drop here was something like a hundred feet: half a mile further on at the Lower Falls the river fell again from a height of 300 feet to the floor of the canyon.

At different points along the rim we were treated to splendid views of the canyon and falls, the pinnacle sights of Yellowstone. The Grand Canyon of the Yellowstone was aptly named, though for different reasons, I supposed, than its Arizona rival. As a 'young' river valley it could not boast the depth of the other Grand Canyon – 1,200 feet against a mile – but could offer other aspects of grandeur that to the less hungry, more discerning eye were equally sublime. First and foremost were its colours, peculiar to the rock that had given the river its name. The mineral rhyolite, a decomposed lava, varied in shade from rust red to peach yellow – a radiance of colour that defied the grey sky and gifted the canyon with a ready-made sunset. To bring out the hues, the canyon did not lack for contrasts. The pine trees that grew from its sides – with what seemed little more than a toehold on the rock – had their fine dusting of snow. The river, rushing at breakneck speed below, was jade green scalloped with white. And at the head of the canyon, adding a finishing touch to the scenic masterpiece, was the long white streamer of the Lower Falls. Gazing from the precipice at that lovely sight I realised I'd found the thing every traveller was looking for, but often didn't see until they looked at the photos. Perfection.

Wyoming and Colorado

Frontier Days

The Grand Loop Road was shaped like an '8'. Obliged by shortage of time to cut across the centre of the park we drove west and rejoined the US191, heading back to Idaho Falls by the same route as our outward journey. Coasting into Budget Rent-a-Car with an empty tank and five minutes to spare on our time limit we were thankful to be charged only thirty-six dollars, which for a run of 340 miles was a gift. My third share of twelve dollars could be favourably measured against the hassle of 'going it alone'.

At 12.15am we were back in Salt Lake City, delivered by a dutiful Greyhound. We were all exhausted. With a Teutonically straight face Hellmut asked me where I was planning to spend the night.

'On the 3.30am bus to Cheyenne.'

Shaking their heads in sympathy, Hellmut and Jutta wished me *'Gute Reise'*. Before we parted I made a note of their address in Germany. Unlike many of the people I'd travelled with, I thought of them more as friends than as chance travelling companions who'd helped me with the mileage.

My exhaustion was not so great that I missed the dawn in southern Wyoming. I had often heard of the uniqueness of the Wyoming landscape, but was hardly prepared, after the pine-clad mountains of the Yellowstone region, for the windswept prairie-land that lapped like a brown sea against the highway. This was the high grazing country that belonged, inextricably, to the Wild West. In the tall grass stood the dark shapes of browsing cattle, and to complete the picture the occasional lone rider, herding a string of horses. But perhaps the most emotive sight, to one who had only seen it on celluloid or in the picture books of childhood, was a covered wagon, driven by a sheepman behind his jostling herd. In such 'prairie schooners' the pioneer migrants had journeyed a hundred years ago, forging the early trails and expanding the western frontier.

Noting the crossed sabres on my map I could see that they hadn't had it all their own way. These symbols marked the clashes of a 25-year war, the battlegrounds that were either monuments to the courage of the US Cavalry or to the heroic actions of the American Indian tribes (Crow, Arapaho, Lakota and Cheyenne) – depending on your point of view.

A return to the high country heralded our approach to Cheyenne, the state capital. Essentially a railroad city, born of the Union Pacific, Cheyenne was also famous as the home of the 'Cheyenne Frontier Days', the biggest annual event in the rodeo calendar. Any hope that my visit might coincide with this bronco-busting, steer-roping jamboree was dashed on arrival. The next event was not until the following July. In the meantime, what could Cheyenne offer me?

Essentially, a bed. One of the last uncontacted addresses in my pocket-book was of a cousin of my uncle's, an ex-railroad man called Charlie Standen. A bachelor in his late sixties, Charlie was only too pleased to have my company for a couple of days. And to entertain me by the best means at his disposal: a spacious six-seater Ford.

Ten minutes after my call from the bus depot the car arrived, with a smiling Charlie at the wheel. In the next forty-eight hours I got to know that car pretty well.

The bed was a sofa in Charlie's apartment, the convertible kind that allowed for a six-footer. After a week of tents, bedroom floors and buses it was a blissful experience, and one which I could only wish had been longer lasting. Charlie, it turned out, was one of those inveterate early risers whose day began with the first glimmer of light. At 7am I was wakened and presented with grapefruit, orange juice, bacon and eggs – between yawns the best breakfast I'd had in America. As I worked my way through it, my host made the point that he wanted me to eat well as we had 'a pretty heavy schedule'.

The local sights commenced with the city centre, but the intermittent rain and snow forced us to concentrate on the Wyoming State Museum, where I took the opportunity to crystallize my hazy knowledge of frontier history. Charlie must have been there a hundred times, but he walked me round the cases with a scholarly enthusiasm. Cheyenne had started out, he told me, as a Union Pacific townsite at Crow Creek Crossing in 1867. Initially inhabited by a handful of railroad employees, it was thought that the place would suffer the same fate as many other railheads and disappear into the prairie as the tracklayers moved on. But the construction of a fort consolidated the location and the 'end-of-tracks' encampment became a thriving town, supplying goods to other pioneer settlements. Named in honour of the Great Plains Indian tribe, Cheyenne eventually became the state capital of Wyoming.

Later in the day we drove out to Laramie, the next townsite on the Union Pacific Railroad, and met up with a friend of Charlie's – another railroad veteran. For the two old-timers it was a good opportunity for a day out and a spot of reminiscence; for me a chance to enjoy the effect of a fresh fall of snow on the same landscape I had seen the day before, the white-powdered prairie relieved only by the dark clusters of sturdy black Angus cattle. Seeing the barriers that had been raised at the roadside to catch the snowdrifts I wondered what it would be like in three months' time, when the actual winter set in.

The trip to Laramie was just a run-up to the real adventure, which Charlie had arranged for the next day. This was a drive into the Rocky Mountains via the town of Boulder, Colorado,

Wyoming's neighbouring state to the south. Accompanying us on this trip was a special friend of Charlie's, who we picked up in town. Not a railroader this time but a wispy-haired lady in her seventies, who answered to the name of Clare. She was very thrilled about the outing and from the moment she joined us she continually thanked Charlie for his kindness and me for putting up with her. Although I could never be sure about these matters I suspected that she was an old flame of Charlie's, and that they were secretly engaged.

At 5,000 feet, Boulder was a gateway to one of the highest regions in the United States. Within a forty-mile radius towered some of the greatest peaks in the Rockies, many of them over 14,000 feet. Fortunately the road did not attempt these heights and for the most part followed the network of creeks that furrowed the lower ranges. The weather was in a happier mood than the day before and we were spared the distraction of falling snow, which would have made some of the bends a little hairy.

The popularity of the area was evident from the number of wayside inns. Most of these had been built on the lines of a Swiss chalet, and the one that we chose for lunch – the Black Forest Inn – advertised 'Authentic German Food', 'German Outdoor Beer Garden' and 'Ratskeller', a degree of ethnic obsessiveness that one could not expect to find anywhere, it seemed, but a mountain-top in Colorado. Inside it was all Teutonic shields, ornamental steins, glockenspiels and Johann Strauss. The 'authentic' German dishes were accompanied, naturally enough, by black bread and Bavarian wine.

On a circular route to Denver we passed through Central City, a relic of the boom years of the mid-nineteenth century when men had gone into the mountains with their pick-axes and shovels in search of the 'mother lode'. Walking up the main street, it was apparent that the small settlement, which retained some of its picturesque shanty dwellings, was still sitting on a gold mine – this time from the profitable vein of tourism. Endless racks of picture postcards of the old-time workings, and displays of souvenirs, including imitation gold nuggets, paid tribute to the rip-roaring early days.

From Denver, state capital of Colorado, I would be continuing my journey to the east, and had arranged for Charlie to drop me off. After a surprisingly gentle descent we were soon on the highway to the city, and I was gazing with some degree of awe at a splendid landmark: the Coors Brewery. Through much of the western United States I had seen the signs advertising the beer 'brewed from pure Rocky Mountain spring water'. Now I had to believe it.

When we reached Denver I calculated with some concern that Charlie had driven 200 fairly arduous miles, and that by the time he got back to Cheyenne he would have driven a further hundred. The equivalent of travelling in a day from London to Sheffield and back.

But to Charlie, descendant of the iron men of the Union Pacific who'd spanned a continent, it was just 'a day out'. He thought nothing, he told me, of driving Clare down to Denver for an evening's theatre – 'if they had a decent show on.' At this point Clare reminded him about the tickets he needed to order for the symphony concert that Saturday.

There was only one word I could find to describe Charlie. Indefatigable. And the same went for Clare.

For my Wild West farewell I could have settled for a night on the town in Denver. 'The Mile-High City', 'Queen City of the Plains', 'Home of the Pioneers'. But such was the perversity of the region – with one scenic miracle tucked away behind another – that the parting could not be so abrupt. Thus it was that the following morning – after a night in the Denver 'Y' – I was wilfully heading south, to Colorado Springs and Pikes Peak.

Here lay the essence of the Rocky Mountain 'Spectacular'. The special virtue of this area was its accessibility, the mountain roads (created originally for the stage lines and mining camps) snaking out from Colorado Springs. To obtain the view from the 14,000-foot Pikes Peak you had to choose between the Pikes Peak Toll Road and the Manitou and Pikes Peak Cog Railway, both of which took you close to the summit. My inclination being towards novelty, I started out on foot for Manitou Springs, the terminus of the cog railway.

On the way I was intrigued to see a signpost inscribed 'Ghost

Town'. After the fakery I had encountered elsewhere my response was perhaps a little unguarded. But wasn't it true that most of these old towns, the relics of the mining boom, were located in Colorado?

Turning up a side road I followed the signs to a large building, rather like an aircraft hangar, with a fence masking the exterior. Painted on the front in large emphatic letters were the words 'GHOST TOWN'. Assuming this to be either a museum or administrative building for the historic site I approached the entrance. To my dismay the door was locked, and to my annoyance there was no notice saying when – or whether – the place was open to the public.

Determined to view the sombre relics I slipped through a hole in the fence and walked round to the back of the building. Expecting to come upon a scene of derelict shanties, caved-in plankwalks and petrified tumbleweed, I was disconcerted to find that there was nothing to see behind the structure. After completing a circuit of the building I peered through one of its grimy windows, looking for a clue. A chink in the backcloth draped inside the window revealed all I needed to see. The Ghost Town was inside the building.

With the knowledge that there were, supposedly, no fewer than seven hundred ghost towns in Colorado, I had to assume that most of the others were not protected and hidden from view. My feeling of disillusionment was hardly dispelled by my arrival an hour later at Manitou Springs. The activities of the cog railway, I learned, had been suspended until the following spring, and my only consolation was the opportunity to inspect a rather magnificent railway engine, mounted on a block, with 'Manitou and Pikes Peak Railway' painted on its side.

Deprived of my climactic view of the Rockies I had to settle for the best available alternative: a walk through the Garden of the Gods. By some quirky error of omission this was not identified as a National Monument but merely a Famous Natural Feature, under permanent contract to the picture-postcard industry. It was, quite simply, a glorious geological freak, a relic of the chain reaction to the enormous earth movements that had created the Rockies. The strange rock formations that I saw on my walk were the result of the uplift of Pikes Peak: a forcing up of the buried layers of sandstone. The vertical slabs of strata thus formed created an interesting optical illusion. The elevation view gave an impression of mass, like giant buttes viewed from afar. In profile, however, they were barely visible.

Further curiosity was added to the shapes by the work of erosion, giving the scenic labellers a field day. The 'Siamese Twins', the 'Pulpit Rock', the 'Sleeping Indian' and the 'Tower of Babel' were an artful interpretation; so contrived that one could picture those imaginative people from the National Park Service, sizing up each peculiarly-shaped rock. 'Hey, Elmer, look at this – I got the "Kissing Camels"!'

With the 'Balanced Rock', of course, I could dispose of such imagery. Wind and rain had undercut it to such an extent that there was nothing left but a gigantic poised boulder, looking as if it might topple with the next puff of wind. So precarious that there had to be some human agency supporting it. Keeping a cautious distance I examined the rock more carefully – and was confounded. No steel braces, no cement, no underpinning. Not even an ad for Wrigley's Chewing Gum.

My last view of the Rockies was joyful: an MGM fade-out. Pikes Peak viewed through the rock gateway of the Garden of the Gods. Sunset imminent, and a pair of sore feet to remind me of the fifteen miles that marked the zenith – and finale? – of my US hiking career.

For a truly personal service I could not have done better than the Greyhound van that took me from Colorado Springs to the town of Limon, Colorado. Limon was the first stop on the Denver-Kansas City run, and although the short cut from Colorado Springs did not merit a full-sized coach, I felt more significant as the only passenger in the van, bounding along in the darkness with the driver yelling jokes at me all the way. At Limon, connecting with the Scenicruiser, I settled down for the twelve-hour run to Kansas City.

To pass the time I tried reading the Denver daily that I'd bought on a news-stand. But previous experience of American newspapers should have deterred me. Hard news and editorial pieces were drops of water in a desert of society news, obituaries and supermarket ads. The only light relief was in a report headed 'Seven Hunters Die in One Week in Colorado'. This gave an account of hunting incidents in the past week in which no fewer than seven men had died in pursuit of game, either from heart attacks or accidental shooting. One of the men who had been shot, I read, was dressed in bright yellow.

The daylight stretch of the journey took us through the state of Kansas, in the heart of the Great Plains. Despite the enormous mileage (the state was something like 400 miles across) my memory of the landscape was unvaried, an endless sea of grassland, corn and wheat fields. Surprisingly, the predominant colour was green – the green of winter wheat and the new grass breaking through the combed earth. The driver, in the inimitable style of his calling, summed up the feeling of monotony in one of his periodic announcements:

'Our next rest stop will be at Manhattan, Kansas, in three hours' time. In the meantime I'd appreciate it if you folks were a little quiet so the driver can get some sleep.'

Why was I heading east by way of Kansas? Why not take to the hills – the Black Hills of Dakota? And the Badlands – 'that part of hell with the fires burned out'? The answer was simple – to save time that could not be given to other diversions. But between buses at Kansas City I could find a moment for William Rockhill Nelson.

Co-founder of the *Kansas City Star*, Nelson was best known for the fine art collection he had gifted the city for the creation of one of the nation's premier art museums. In a bustling cow-town, built around a railhead on the Missouri River, it was quite a revelation to discover a Caravaggio *St John*. Not to mention the cloister of a medieval monastery and the restored alcove of an eighteenth-century Venetian palazzo. The latter exhibit, complete with Louis Quinze clock and Bombe commode, was a reminder of America's European roots.

Art endowments apart, Kansas City had little of historical interest other than its identification with Independence, Missouri, now a separate satellite of the city to the south-east of the Missouri River. Known as the 'Queen City of the Trails', Independence had been the starting point in the 1850s for the journey to the goldfields of California and Oregon and for the Santa Fe trail which had opened up the south-western states.

The modern Kansas City, spanning the Missouri River, was now large enough to have its name shown twice on the map, as a city in two states. It was from Kansas City, Missouri, that the Greyhound departed for Chicago.

That wasn't until 5pm. In the meantime I had to find something to eat. The search, unfortunately, was not appeased by the expensive calorific creations of the Post House Restaurant:

Barbecued Beef Sandwich: Choice Beef, with a Spicy Sauce Served on a Sesame Seed Bun with Crunchy Cole Slaw. 90c.

Post House Italian Spaghetti: Covered with Zesty Meat Sauce and Grated Parmesan Cheese Garnish, Served with Crispy Green Salad. $1.20.

My needs being for simple *pan* rather than panegyric I looked elsewhere. The 'Supermarket' sign led me through automatic doors into a huge humming concourse lined with shelves of food and drink. In this consumer's mecca the simple quest of choosing a snack was almost impossible, the showcards extravagantly outbidding one another in the promotion of their products.

With gnawing entrails I stared at the Special Fed Plump Young Frying Chickens, Whole Body 29c lb; the Chubs of Fresh Lean Ground Beef, 33c lb; and the Canned Chunk Tuna, 4c-off deal. Longingly I beheld the 'Pictsweet' Assorted Vegetables in Poly Bags and the Grade AA Fresh Eggs in the X-large Cartons. Controlled freshness and packaged preparedness, fully realised in the tinfoil triumph of the TV dinner:

'NOW! With Tangy Cranberry Sauce! Roast Farmbred Turkey, with Brown Gravy, Whipped Potatoes, Peas in Butter Sauce!'

For ten cents I bought a Washington Apple, a big glossy thing that weighed at least a pound. At the checkout, in the procession of baskets and trolleys piled high with cans, packs and cartons, I couldn't help feeling inadequate.

That was, until I reached the till. Presenting my five-dollar bill and polite apology to the girl at the counter I was treated to a mesmeric gaze and sigh of wonder. 'Heck, you English have the cutest accent! Please say somethin' else!'

For a moment I paused, seeking inspiration in her melting gaze. 'May I have my change, please?'

Chicago to Dearborn

From Windy City to Tin Lizzie

At 7.15am on a wet and windy morning Chicago offered a chill reception. Behind me lay a ten-hour run through Missouri and Illinois (via St Louis), a journey passed in darkness and deep sleep. Emerging from the swing doors of the bus depot I wondered where I was. No more the cornfields and cattle ranches that had been my last view of the Plains, but black granite buildings and a whirl of traffic that I'd not seen since New York.

This was Chicago, America's third most populous city, national rail hub and capital of the Midwest. Located on the west shore of Lake Michigan, its port had access to the Atlantic Ocean from two outlets each 1,000 miles distant, linked to the city by a network of rivers and canals: the St Lawrence Seaway to the north-east and the Mississippi to the south. Inconceivable, but so was every other aspect of Chicago – until it was conceived. Think of the first skyscraper, the first vacuum cleaner, the first electric dishwasher. The Ferris wheel, the zipper, the chocolate brownie. Frostbite and hypothermia.

The nickname 'Windy City' was no joke and before I'd covered the first block en route to the 'Y' I was shrinking against the side of the buildings, lashed by a powerful Force Eight. The name on the corner of the block, 'Lake Street', was the clue to its source: the great expanse of water that lay to the east. Lake Michigan, one of the five Great Lakes, was only a few blocks away, a vast conductor for the icy winds blowing down from Canada. In a helter-skelter of beer cans, cigarette cartons and newspapers I hurried south along Wabash Avenue to the shelter of the 'Y'.

It was like running the proverbial gauntlet, the assailants not only wind and rain but the clamour of the waking city. At that time of the morning the level of traffic was stupefying, and I was baffled by the number of blue and white police patrol cars, prowling across the intersections like wolves in search of prey. Overhead an elevated railway – part of the city's rapid transit system – rattled and thundered. By the time I reached the 'Y' my ears were as numb as my fingers and I was ready for the security and comfort of 2,000 rooms, communal shower and toilets.

After breakfast in the cafeteria I had to decide what to do with the day. With the weather so bad I could hardly contemplate sightseeing. Instead I followed up a transatlantic friendship by telephoning my cabin mate on the *Queen Elizabeth* (way back in another age), with whom I'd shared some of the joys of New York. Leslie Morris lived at Oak Lawn, a suburb ten miles south of Chicago. Ten weeks had passed since our arrival in America, but the voice of welcome didn't fail me. The remarkable thing about Americans was that whenever you called them, they sounded as if they'd been hanging on the phone.

With Chicago's public transport system – surely the best in America – I had no difficulty in reaching Leslie. From State Street I took a rapid transit car (my first rail journey in the States) and then a suburban bus at a place called Englewood. The ticket issued at State Street was good for the bus and saw me through to 103rd Street and South Pulaski, where Leslie was waiting in his car.

'Good job you called on a Sunday,' he said. 'The rest of the week I'm at school.'

The carefree Leslie who I remembered from the voyage, breathing in with deep relish the salty breezes of the Atlantic, was no more. In the four-minute drive I learned how things had changed since his return to America.

Leslie's experience had been no more fulfilling than Michael's. Like Michael his return had been less than joyful. Problem Number One was a new Principal, installed during Leslie's absence. The new man was pretty demanding, and expected Leslie – the Assistant Principal – to be an extension of his dynamic self. Problem Two was a legal difficulty over the purchase of his new apartment, and Problem Three a dent in the back wing of a parked car, incurred when Leslie was backing out of his drive to come and fetch me. Despite that welcoming voice I had the feeling that I might have picked a better time.

In the suburb of Oak Lawn I learned a new word: 'Condominium'. This American-sounding bit of Latin (or Latin-sounding bit of American) was used to describe a building containing separately-owned apartments. Leslie's 'condo' was tailor-made for the bachelor life, with the kind of stream-lined, push-button kitchen that looked as if it only needed a gentle smacking of the lips to produce a four-course meal. Almost apologetically, he took me out to a steak-house for lunch.

Ten weeks after his return from a year's teaching in England, Leslie still nursed a nostalgia for High Barnet. But every time he thought about working for a longer period in England his bank account twitched. As a teacher in America he earned roughly three times as much as his counterpart in England – which for him resolved the problem.

'How about you? You fixed on where you're going to settle?'

I was jolted back to the Sports Deck on the *Queen Elizabeth*, and conversations with Leslie about my future in America. Could I be really honest, and say that if there was one thing I hadn't given half a second's thought to in the last ten weeks, it was the future?

Leslie was disconcerted by my response. 'You want to work in Chicago. As a journalist you'd earn three times the money.'

Possibly, but would I not be writing about the Bergers being united to the Elafsons at the All Saints Episcopal Church, and the regrettable number of jay-walkers being arrested each day on Michigan Avenue?

Chicago was an architect's city, which even non-architects, if they selected the right vantage point, would appreciate. In 1871 the city centre had been destroyed by a fire (the Great Fire of Chicago) and to the amazement of Chicagoans it was not only the old wooden buildings that perished but also the new 'fire-proof' structures, built on a framework of cast iron. New methods and new materials had been the order of the day, and to meet the demand, a ready influx of architects and engineers from the east.

Their major achievement had been the replacement of cast-iron with steel and the construction of the first conventional skyscraper: a prototype that was to undergo many refinements that would maintain the basic principle of the weight-bearing steel frame enclosed by light freely-fixed walls. It was a method that called for, but did not always receive, simplicity of treatment. For many years the challenge of producing a building that was larger and more splendid than the last proved too great, particularly for the merchant princes to whom a skyscraper stood in for an outsize advertisement hoarding. The worst excesses, perhaps, were in Manhattan – though Chicago had its share.

It was some time before function reasserted itself, and architects like Louis Sullivan, who at the end of the nineteenth century was advocating an end to ornament on buildings, were able to show the way. It was to his credit and that of his followers that the European architectural revolution of the 1920s would find its ultimate home in Chicago.

My own vantage point was the bridge that carried Michigan Avenue over the Chicago River. From here I could admire two early-1920s buildings, perhaps the best known in the city, that stood to the north of the river, forming a gateway to the 'Magnificent Mile' of North Michigan Avenue. To the left the Renaissance-style Wrigley Building (monument to America's favourite habit) and to the right the neo-Gothic *Chicago Tribune* building, an artistic concoction greater than anything they'd ever set in type. Both buildings were a tribute to the age of grandeur that preceded the post-Sullivan modernists.

The view west along the river was a jolt into the present. At the first bend rose the twin towers of Marina City, a piece of pure science fiction that was, incredibly, the home of some 1,500 people. For the non-technical there was only one image that could describe it. A gigantic double-stack of long-playing records, with the spike of the turntable sticking through the middle.

In reality what I was looking at were two circular sixty-storey buildings, each topped by an enormous television mast. Completed in 1963, Marina City had achieved worldwide celebrity as America's highest apartment building. It contained no less than 895 two-room apartments and all attendant amenities, including parking space for cars on the first nineteen floors and boats in the basement.

For those determined to elevate themselves above their fellow-citizens, Marina City was obviously the latest thing. And yet it was hard to believe that the two great cylinders actually contained people, living and breathing in their quarter-quadrant of air-conditioned space, gazing out from their celestial balconies at Lake Michigan and three states. Were they real people, or the two-dimensional type that were used to illustrate scale? And what was this panorama of treeless embankments, concrete piers, single-span bridges, curtain walls and hull-core towers if not a perfect architect's model, blown full-size?

To reduce it all to more manageable proportions I returned to Michigan Avenue and ascended the heights of the new Prudential Building, opened in 1955. The fortieth-floor observatory was reckoned to offer the best overall view of the business district, and as much of the city as weather conditions would allow. The only problem for a penurious tourist was the price of admission: fifty cents.

On the assumption that the view from the thirty-ninth floor would be as good as the fortieth, I retreated one flight down the Emergency Stairs.

Confronted by a swing door I marched brazenly through, with the innocent enquiry 'Is this the observatory?' already forming on my lips. Fortunately there was no one on the other side of the door and I made my way between two rows of lockers towards the nearest window space. It was on the north side of the building and gave me an unbeatable panorama with Lake Michigan to the east and the central business district to the west. Lining up my camera on the long straight furrow of Michigan Avenue I prepared to take my shot.

'Yes, sir?'

The voice of authority belonged to a shirt-sleeved, broad-shouldered man in a peaked cap. In the male employees' locker room of the Prudential Assurance Company the words I'd rehearsed had a slightly empty ring.

'No, buddy, this isn't the observatory. That's next floor up. Where you got out of the elevator.'

With as much grace as I could muster I thanked the man and rejoined the non-erring, non-straying flock on the floor above. Paying my fifty cents I went through the barrier and found a space at one of the observation windows. It was not a good moment for the film winder to get stuck.

Chicago, in sum, was less than my hopes. A city that had gone through the birth pangs of the frontier and the cattle barons, the adolescence of boom, the maturity of civic pride and achievement. The stockyards still existed, but without the stink or the stigma of that period when Chicago, on the backs of thousands of hard-pressed immigrants, had built itself into the meat and grain capital of the west. The Lithuanians, Poles, Slovaks and other exploited 'foreigners' were now the professional classes, and Upton Sinclair's excoriating masterpiece *The Jungle* was an indictment of another age. Almost as remote was the Prohibition era of the twenties, when the bootleggers had taken over whole suburbs of the city and turned them into liquor markets. It seemed incredible that one arch-racketeer – Al Capone – could have been big enough to dominate a city the size of Chicago, running it like a personal fiefdom in which the opposition was eliminated without any questions asked.

It wasn't that I'd hoped for, or even anticipated, an exchange of bullets on Wabash Avenue, or a St Valentine's Day Massacre on the steps of the Pru. It was just that the contemporary Chicago, with its architectural wizardry and systematized living was too ordered (the traffic excluded) and too self-aware. This didn't mean that violence had died with Capone, or that Chicago had never tried to beat the world. But now the stockyards and the Police Department were open to tourists, and the violence was mainly dictated by protest.

In this respect Chicago's problems were shared by Detroit. Both were large industrial cities, with dense black populations that had inherited the role of the underprivileged from the immigrants of fifty years ago. The only difference was the industries they served.

In Chicago it had been meat-packing and construction: in Detroit, my next destination, it was the motor car. The Ford plant at Dearborn was alone responsible for something like forty per cent of America's total car production, which in an average year ran up to seven million: an astonishing figure until you remembered the ninety million cars and trucks on American roads.

For automotive enthusiasts a visit to Detroit was inevitably a visit to Ford, to count the vehicles off the assembly line at the Rouge plant and to explore the twentieth-century legend of Henry Ford at Greenfield Village. The overnight drive, eastwards across the state of Michigan, took seven and a half hours, spanning the broad peninsula between Lake Michigan, Lake Huron and Lake Erie. Detroit itself stood on the river that was part of the link between the two last-named lakes: hence its name '*Detroit*', or 'strait'. The Frenchman who'd founded the fort and fur trading post here in 1701 had bequeathed another famous name: Antoine Laumet de la Mothe, Sieur de Cadillac.

On the subject of names, whence Michigan? Had I been a student of Algonquin, I might have got a clue from the Michigan licence plates, all of which bore the motto 'Water Winter Wonderland'. But of course, '*Michi Gama*': 'Land of the Great Water'.

Another clue was the steady drizzle that greeted our arrival at the city's downtown bus depot. The aspect of rain and grey buildings, reminiscent of my arrival in Chicago, was appropriate to my mood. A pre-dawn check of my finances had revealed that I was down to my last fifty dollars, allowing me an average of less than four dollars a day for the remainder of my trip. The six dollars a day was dying a brave death: to help it on its way I settled down to a Post House breakfast of Grilled Ham, Hash Browns and Coffee. Total one dollar.

'Mind if I join you?'

If I'd been searching for a soul mate, then this was he. A walking hangover in a dented hat, who tested the chair before he sat down. With the help of a black coffee and his current prescription he gave me the story of his life. Or was it the story of last night? Whatever it was, he needed to get over it, and the best treatment was a stranger with a sympathetic ear. Though the slurred voice was incoherent I could gather quite a lot from the visual aids. Iron pills, headache pills and tranquillisers, tipped into his palm. Cascading from his billfold, a mixture of credit cards, tokens and pay-checks. To capture the essence of the American way of life you don't have to travel 12,000 miles.

Paradoxically, the fellow seemed to want to help *me*. He was concerned that a stranger should come so far and not have anyone to meet him and show him Detroit. Before he could offer his personal services I enquired if he knew the way to the YMCA.

'YMCA?' He looked at me quizzically. 'Why would you go there?'

'I'm a member.'

He sniffed. 'Three dollars seventy-five a night! You don' wanna pay that kinda money. Follow me. I'll show you a place for three dollars.'

We hurried through a web of cold streets, lashed by wind and rain. Our destination was a sullen dingy alleyway that in better days might have passed for Detroit's Skid Row. There my guide abandoned me, pointing erratically at a weathered sign with the inscription 'Hotel'.

Inside, in the lobby, it was very dark. I had some difficulty in picking out the desk clerk, who was in deep shadow and revealed himself only by his upturned eyes. When I asked for a room they stared at me balefully.

'Number Seven.' He handed me the key and I felt my way along an unlit passage. The doors on either side had no visible numbers and I tried the key in each until I found the right one. Entering the room, I stiffened at the tangy whiff of B.O. Like the room in that other budget hotel in New Orleans – which as I recalled was fifty cents cheaper – it had no ventilation. The semi-darkness suggested the absence of a window, but I was disinclined to switch on the light for confirmation. Shrugging my rucksack on to the bed I locked the door on the room and went off to Dearborn.

Henry Ford's village of Dearborn, some fifteen miles from Detroit, had grown into a town of 115,000 inhabitants. In the 1870s, when

Henry was working on his father's farm, this was the population of Detroit. Almost a century later, that population was roughly four million: in the 1770s there were about as many people in the whole of the United States. From such figures one could gain an idea of the extraordinary growth of the country, and of the unusual power of a man like Henry Ford, who could unite town and village in one colossal industrial enterprise.

At the Ford Central Office Building, an isolated block overlooking an expressway, I switched from the suburban bus that had brought me from Detroit to a motor-coach marked 'Rouge Plant'. Tours of the plant left every half-hour, between the hours of nine and three; a schedule that was essential to cope with the regular flow of visitors.

They came, good car-owning Americans, to study their origins: the bits and pieces of mechanical wizardry that went to make up the sleek saloon or convertible of their choice. And at the Rouge Plant they could see the very genesis, in the blast furnaces of the iron foundry. Herein lay the miracle of the Rouge: a production plant in which every single process in the manufacture of the motor car was accounted for. As well as the iron foundry there were steel mills, an engine plant, a tool and die plant, a glass foundry, frame and radiator plants and – at the end of it all – the assembly plant. The Rouge generated its own electricity, ran its own fleet of freighters (the Rouge River flowed through the plant) and boasted its own railroad system, with something like eighty-five miles of track and eighteen diesel locomotives. It was one of the few fully integrated industrial complexes in the world, dependent only on imports of iron ore and coal. If part of its 1,200 acres were to be made over to crops and the raising of beefstock, the Rouge could have flown its own flag.

Predictably, the tour concentrated on the engine and assembly plants. In the engine plant we viewed the different stages in the assembly of the Ford V-8 engine, a breakdown – or should one say build-up – of the components that was both fascinating and instructive.

Most impressive was the mountain of cylinder block castings, newly arrived from the foundry, that awaited transmission to the conveyors for machining and assembly into finished engines.

Under the guidance of a Ford technician we followed their progress along the assembly line, watching with mounting curiosity as the different parts of the engine were installed. Camshaft, crankshaft, flywheel, tappets. We watched as the cylinder bores were checked for the correct gauge and the pistons and connecting rod assemblies fitted. One tourist, curious about the coloured spots painted on the side of some of the cylinder blocks, received an interesting reply from the guide.

'That's a special earmarking for California,' he said. 'All those engines with the spots have to be fitted with a special exhaust system that changes the carbon monoxide to carbon dioxide. It's a state law, on account of all the smog they get over there.'

Once the exhaust manifold had been fitted we were treated to a 'hot test', in which the engines were run for twenty minutes. We were then transferred to the assembly plant, where the engines, travelling on overhead conveyers, were lowered into the car bodies. The tempo of production was electrifying, geared to the output of more than a car a minute. The biggest crowd-pullers were the men who, working to the customer's specifications, added the finishing touches. One man's sole occupation was the addition of a chrome strip to the fender, using a special adhesive strip. When the same questioner asked, as tentatively as possible, what these men would expect to earn, the guide shrugged.

'Maximum's around four hundred a week.'

Big money was a Ford tradition, going back to 1914 when Henry Ford had doubled the daily wage of his workers from $2.34 to $5. By anticipating their demands, he'd kept the unions – his bête noir – out in the cold. Apart from top wages his avowed cause had been the reprieve of his workers from drudgery and the advancement of their leisure and recreation. How far had these ideals been fulfilled? The guide, confronted by the open mouths of his audience, gave us the answer.

'That's for a sixty-hour week, of course.'

In shining procession the Mustangs followed the Falcons, two popular series (the Mustang only recently off the drawing board) that between them offered a range of thirteen models. Ford's production line that year carried no less than forty-nine models, and with trucks and other commercial vehicles the total output was something like 12,000 vehicles a day. For the statistically-minded, this represented slightly more than America's daily birth rate. More Fords than babies? It didn't seem natural. But then – as Henry Ford would point out – it was what the public wanted.

The Tin Lizzie! What pictures that name evoked, of an age that seemed as far away as the frontier! I remembered one I had seen in a magazine, taken in the 1920s in the main street of a town in the mid-west. All the cars parked on the street were Model Ts – the most popular car of all time. Between 1908 and 1927, Henry Ford had made fifteen million of them, working to a formula that remained a constant for all those years. The People's Car would be a straightforward, practical, four-cylinder vehicle, and it would be painted black. And because it was mass-produced, it would be very cheap.

To see one of those originals (how many had survived?) I needed to extend my tour with a visit to the Henry Ford Museum. Returning to the Ford Central Office Building on the tour bus I decided to walk the mile or so to the museum, following the expressway in what I judged to be the right direction. Unfortunately the orientation of the map was not very clear and I ended up on the Ford Road, at the gateway of the Henry Ford Community College. Opting for guidance while I was still warm I went over to a police car parked at the side of the road. Affixed to its body were the notices 'Be Nice to People' and '$100 Fine for Throwing Trash on Highway'. The mobile patrolman, who had a nicer way of saying it than most of his kind, asked me where I was going.

'Henry Ford Museum? You're outa your way, feller. But while you're down here, why not take a look at the Henry Ford Home?'

Offered the services of a police car, I couldn't refuse. As we drove off, however, I felt a little uneasy. Was this how the Detroit Police Department picked up their vagrants?

I was reassured in a few minutes when we turned up a wide gravel drive and drove towards a rambling, ivy-clad mansion. This was the Henry Ford Home, no longer occupied by the family (Ford died in 1947) but as yet preserved from the public gaze. As a special concession, I was allowed a 'look-see' while the policeman checked for prowlers.

Feeling something of a prowler myself I slipped round to the back of the house and regarded its bizarre architecture. Battlements and gables were not a happy combination and it seemed that the Ford image had never been clearly determined. Country house or castle? The garden was more conventional, sloping down to a stretch of water fed by artificial waterfalls. It was very peaceful here, a happy retreat for Henry Ford from the pressures of the production line. But although he promoted leisure for his employees, there couldn't have been too much of it for their hard-working president.

For all their goodwill – and the speed of their patrol cars – the Detroit Constabulary could not beat the clock. When we arrived at the museum, it had just closed. So too had Greenfield Village, created by Ford, which was a sort of superior Knott's Berry Farm, comprising a collection of colonial and nineteenth-century buildings transported from different parts of America and reconstructed on a 200-acre site. Henry Ford, as everyone knew, had his own opinions about history. Greenfield Village and the Henry Ford Museum were his way of expressing them. The history of a people came not so much from books, he claimed, but from the objects of their everyday life. Such objects could be an iron kettle or a 125-foot locomotive: it didn't matter as long as it had been created for practical use. 'A piece of machinery or anything that is made is like a book, if you can read it...'

And what could one read in the satin-smooth finish of the 7-litre Ford Galaxie, superbly stationed against the backdrop of green turf and colonial architecture? The biggest individual success story of all time.

Canada and Niagara

Roll Out the Barrel

'Get out!'

Surprisingly it was my own voice, issuing from somewhere inside my cramped, nerve-wracked body. It was one o-clock in the morning, and someone had just unlocked the door of my room for the second time that night. The first intrusion, half an hour ago, had provoked a polite 'Do you mind?'– but this time I was screaming. The ordeal of getting to sleep in an odorous, airless room was bad enough. To be twice roused from that sleep by some dumb hotel porter was more than ragged flesh could bear.

But that was not the end of it. At 2.30am, when I'd just managed – for the third time – to drift into a semblance of sleep, a terrific hammering noise dynamited my senses. Some disorientated drunk, who might have been staying at the hotel but more probably had wandered in from the street, was trying to force an entry. Aware of the dangers of counter-provocation I lay silently knotting the bedclothes, waiting for the hammering to stop. The door held and the fellow got tired, giving it a final hefty kick before staggering off. With a deep groan I sank back into the damp pit of the mattress.

On my way out of the place the next morning I accosted the desk clerk. Unfortunately this was not the one who'd checked me in the previous evening or even the one who'd been there last night. This one, whom I'd never seen before, had just come on duty. As I related the story of my tragic night his finger wandered down the register.

'What number room?'

'Seven.'

He frowned, turning back a page. 'What time you check in, boss?'

'About seven o'clock yesterday morning.'

He nodded to himself, tapping the register with a pencil. 'Looks like you got wrote down for the wrong night.'

By the time I'd bought some aspirin, back at the bus depot, the total saving over a night at the YMCA was twenty-five cents.

The 7am Greyhound for Buffalo, New York, was the start of another leg of the journey east. But with a difference. This time I was doing it in daylight, and travelling through a different country. Passing under the Detroit River by way of the Detroit-Windsor tunnel the bus crossed the border into Ontario, Canada.

I didn't know what to expect of Canada. 'Dominion Within the British Commonwealth' was a kind of abstraction, like an honorary club membership. My National Service in Cyprus had shown me what British influence in a former colonial protectorate was like (rule of law, red telephone boxes) but there the comparison ended. Cyprus had gone its own way politically, whereas Canada, though independent, maintained old loyalties and traditions (outside the areas of French influence of course). Ontario was an English-speaking province whose capital, Ottawa, was Canada's seat of government, supporting the Monarchy, the Commonwealth and Federal authority, a country that had no desire to become part of the United States.

Entry formalities were minimal. At the immigration office on the Canadian side we had to take our passports to an official for stamping, but baggage inspection was reserved for passengers stopping off in Canada. As we drove out of the bus station I had my first real look at the country. If my intention – other than taking an essential short cut along the US-Canada border – was to ascertain Canada's essential Britishness, I was quickly satisfied.

On the journey through Windsor my only uncertainty was to the location of the Castle. The Crown was a recurrent symbol, on post boxes, policemen's caps, road signs and buildings. I saw a Prince Edward Hotel (celebrating the Queen's latest arrival – or perhaps an earlier departure?), a church in the English Perpendicular style and a notice that said 'Vote Conservative'. The signposts bore names that read like a scrambled AA route guide: London via Chatham, Leamington via Maidstone and Essex. Beyond Windsor the countryside continued the theme, the cornfields interspersed with woodland rich in autumn colours, the apple and pear orchards with genteel farm dwellings and square, bay-windowed houses. The early morning frost – the first I had encountered in America – was a reminder of my last English winter, a powdered-glass landscape under a tarpaulin sky.

By midday the snow that had been threatening began to fall, blurring the view. Eventually we pulled into the forecourt of a large roadhouse, our scheduled rest stop. Filing into the restaurant with the other passengers I marvelled at the sight of the white tablecloths. After three months of swabbed formica they were a wonder to behold. And the bottles of sauce – not those funny packets or squeeze-me things. Starting towards the counter I was diverted by a trim figure in a lace cap who directed me with a reassuring smile towards a table. *Waitress* service?

Brown Windsor Soup. Roast Lamb and Mint Sauce, Boiled Potatoes and Carrots. Apple Pie and Custard. Had the sun ever set on that menu?

After lunch I examined the postcards in the rack by the counter. The choice seemed limited to the Niagara Falls in full spate and Her Majesty the Queen at her Coronation, 1953. The age of the card had not improved the four-colour process and the Queen looked equally aged, closer perhaps to her Silver Jubilee. Postcards, I decided, could wait until I reached the Spectacle.

The first signpost for the falls was near the Welland Ship Canal, a 28-mile passage from Lake Ontario to Lake Erie. The canal was part of the St Lawrence Seaway, serving as a by-pass for the falls. The difference in the level of the lakes – half of it represented by the falls – was 326 feet, a problem that had been overcome by a system of locks large enough to allow the big ships to pass through.

The Seaway, opened in 1959, had revolutionised North America's inland navigation. Starting at Montreal, on the hazardous southern stretch of the St Lawrence River, it had forged its way by a series of canals and locks to Lake Ontario. From here the Welland Canal carried it through to Lake Erie (which was at the same level as Lake Huron) and with a terminal 22-foot lock conquered its final obstacle, the drop between Lake Huron and Lake Superior. The combined achievement was a stretch of 2,000 miles of navigable water, from the mouth of the St Lawrence to the head of Lake Superior. The commercial effect of this opening to the Atlantic on such lakeside cities as Chicago, Detroit, Cleveland and Toronto was immeasurable.

The greatest commercial success, of course, belonged to a stretch of water that was entirely *un*navigable, except by loonies in barrels with a yen for eternity. The Niagara Falls, flushing into the river that served as the US-Canada border, served both countries as a leading scenic attraction. The people who flocked here year by year were drawn by a combination of spectacle and mystique: the gapers and the lovers jostling for an eye-hold on the wondrous cascade.

Before re-entering the United States by way of the International Bridge I got off the bus. The Canadian side offered a better view of the two Falls, the American and the Canadian. Stowing my rucksack in a locker I started off on the short walk along the parkway to the spectators' platform.

It was cold on the parkway and I caught my breath as the wind slashed me, cutting like a honed razor through my clothes. Buttoning my plastic mac around my neck I thought that I must be mad to be wearing the same clothes that I had worn in the deep south, two months ago. But it was not a new lesson. The first victim of rucksack travel is contingency planning.

A hundred yards or so from the bridge I found a path leading from the raised parkway to the foot of the gorge opposite the American Falls. From a rock promontory I could view the falls, separated by a stretch of the limestone overhang. The drop was about 170 feet, and I watched in shivering wonder as the water foamed over the edge and washed into the gorge. A mountain of debris, lying at the foot of the falls, illustrated the process that would eventually eliminate them. Beneath the overhang lay the soft shale that was slowly being eroded by the falls, causing the limestone on the top to break away. Gradually, Niagara was retreating, taking the head of the falls back to Lake Erie. What would happen when it got there was an interesting, if rather arcane speculation. The Lake Erie end of the Niagara River was 326 feet higher than the Lake Ontario end, prompting the speculation that one day there would be an even greater spectacle when the whole lot went *phut*.

Doubled against the wind I returned to the parkway and hurried on to the Canadian Falls. These were also known as the Horseshoe Falls and formed a curving link between the two countries. With thirty-four million gallons of water pouring over them every minute the link was purely visual: one could hardly imagine attempting a crossing. From the observation plaza, only a few feet above the falls, the noise of the crashing water was stupefying. Hands over ears I gazed spellbound at the brink of the falls, the point where the green turbulence plunged into the cataract. From the rocks below, the spray rose in a dense silvery mist, catching the fading sunlight in its threads.

It was a scene for lovers, but lovers there were none. Apart from myself the only people on the plaza were a few men in thick belted coats, hanging on to their hats in the wind. A sign over the Table Rock House, overlooking the falls, suggested where the rest of the crowd might be. 'Scenic Tunnel' was the clue and I pictured the multitude on their ledge a hundred feet below, clad from head to foot in oilskins and reaching out ecstatically to touch the great wall of water as it descended in front of them. Unfortunately Niagara was closing down for the night and it was too late for me to join the throng.

So much has been written about the beauty of the falls that there is little to add. One can only subtract, by contemplating what we humans have done to diminish nature. The splendour of the American Falls, viewed from the Niagara Scenic Parkway on the Canadian side, was marred by the skyscrapers that rose beyond it in the city of Niagara, USA. From the American side it was hard to escape the newly built Skylon Tower across the river in Canada.

Perhaps the best view was from the inside of a wooden barrel, launched into the falls in 1901 by 63-year-old Michigan schoolteacher, Annie Edson Taylor. On emerging unharmed from the barrel, she exclaimed: 'No one ought ever do that again.'

Boston

'The British are Coming!'

From Buffalo, NY I took a late bus on the final lap of my journey to the east coast. Most of the journey was passed in darkness, with first light at Albany, the capital of New York State. Breakfast at 5.30am in the Albany Post House was not my most cherished memory, but the coffee served to keep me awake for the run along the Massachusetts Turnpike to the city of Boston. My wish to catch the dying splendour of the New England Fall was sadly unfulfilled. From all appearances the peak of the spectacle had passed some weeks earlier, and I had to mentally garb the thickly-wooded landscape – now partially bereft of foliage – with those glorious shades of russet, gold and amber that were, for a month of the year, the pride of these parts.

After starting my tour (historically) with Philadelphia it seemed appropriate to make my penultimate destination Boston. The clarion call to the new nation that had rung out from the Assembly Room of the Old State House in Philadelphia was, after all, the echo of the first shots fired against a Boston mob by Redcoats in

1770; the resounding splash of 340 chests of tea thrown into Boston Harbour; the galloping hooves of Paul Revere's horse as he rode out to Lexington in advance of the British column. Boston, founded by the Massachusetts Bay company in 1682, had been one of the earliest Puritan settlements on the east coast, established only eight years after the historic landing of the Pilgrim Fathers at Plymouth, Massachusetts. With its proudly independent families, nurturing their patriot sons, Boston had become the cradle of the American Revolution a century later, a key point in history commemorated by the city's numerous monuments.

To pay homage to these memorials, sited along Boston's 'Freedom Trail', was the obligation of the patriots of today. The Mayor of Boston, inaugurating the trail, had signed a Declaration to this effect, calling on every true American to complete his or her education on the hallowed route. And not only Americans. Lest the footloose foreigners should imagine themselves exempt from this obligation, it was also declared that the trail 'continued as ever to be open to the peoples of the world' who were urged to walk along it and share in 'part of the world's heritage of freedom'.

Historic Boston awaited me, but at twelve noon, shortly after my arrival at the Huntingdon Avenue 'Y', I decided that it would have to wait a little longer. As I opened the rucksack my socks made their own declaration. Tucked into shoes and poly bags I found no less than six dirty pairs. In addition, a pile of soiled shirts and underwear that represented the slough of a fortnight or more. For an hour I did penance in the washroom, commandeering four basins and working them in rotation. Soak in one, scrub in the next, rinse in the other two. An excellent method of disposing of large quantities of washing simultaneously. Similar methods were applied to the drying, with every available cupboard door, chair back and bed rail serving as a clothes horse. By the time I'd finished my room looked like a Chinese laundry, with my entire wardrobe spread out to dry and me in the altogether. It seemed a good occasion for a celebration. The only problem was that I couldn't go dancing in the street at that precise moment, Boston being a singularly respectable city.

A good night's sleep brought me fresh to the door of No 280 The Fenway, Boston. A stately building, just off Huntington

Avenue, that had attracted my interest long before I had thought of going to Boston. Among all that city's curiosities, the Isabella Stewart Gardner Museum was undoubtedly the most quirky and fascinating.

Isabella Stewart, born in New York in 1840, had come to Boston after her marriage to a wealthy businessman, John Gardner. Her stars, waxing bright in the social firmament of that city, had led her in time to Europe, where she was to travel extensively. In Venice, wandering through the grand palazzi, she had fallen under the thrall of the Renaissance. It was the beginning of an act of dedication, realised in later years by an art collection that embraced not only the high point but many of the other periods of European art. But much as she enjoyed collecting, this could not in itself satisfy her aspirations. When her husband died in 1898, leaving her in command of his fortune, she had set about building a museum that would provide a proper setting for the varied items of her collection. Her plan to model the building on one of the palaces she had admired in Venice went a stage further with a laborious reconstruction.

The process of building, which took three years, was masked by great secrecy, enforced by the outer walls of the courtyard, that must have stretched the nerves of Boston society to breaking point. Then, to a fanfare of Bach, the doors of Fenway Court had been opened, and the chosen few who first entered its space could join in admiration of Isabella's creation.

Framed by cloisters and overlooked by the arched windows of the upper floors, the courtyard was a glimpse of the Venetian Cinquecento. On the far side of the court a fountain murmured beneath a pair of plunging stone dolphins; above it the balustrade of the stairway leading to the first-floor galleries was covered in flowers. The same flowers – chrysanthemums in a variety of glowing colours – were massed on the floor of the court, faithfully reviving one of Isabella's most subtle inspirations. Every three months or so the flowers were changed, bringing a new seasonal mood to the court.

In her voluminous correspondence with Bernard Berenson, the art historian (and former Harvard prodigy) who had helped her acquire many of her paintings, Isabella had not overlooked the smaller details. The cloisters were her 'bottom drawer', containing a collection of architectural elements from virtually every period of civilisation. Two of the marble columns flanking an archway carried Roman capitals: their bases were Venetian lions. A French Gothic gargoyle gurgled into an Italian holy water basin: on the opposite side of the cloister it met the blank stare of a Graeco-Roman Apollo. The incorporation of these assorted pieces in the fabric of the building, in such a way that they seemed a natural part of it, was a triumph of ingenuity. One could especially admire – without any feeling of fraudulence – the little fountain that Isabella had assembled herself, from a variety of 'odd pieces'.

It should be mentioned, of course, that those 'odd pieces' – plus much of the fabric of the palazzo – had been shipped stone by stone across the Atlantic.

The same diversity marked Isabella's art collection, which was displayed on the three floors of the museum. On the ground floor, in the small room off the North Cloister, I found Manet, Whistler, Turner and Degas. On the first floor the early Italian masters, the painters of the 'Golden Age' (Raphael, Botticelli, Bellini) and the Dutch and Flemish masters (Rembrandt, Vermeer, Rubens and van Dyck). On the second floor the Venetian giants (Titian and Veronese) and a variety of other works that I could not hope to categorise. As with all collections of this kind, which start selectively and then, gaining momentum, enlarge to take in a broad spectrum of period and style, it was difficult to make a general assessment. One could only recall the works which for one reason or another were the most significant, and offered the finest judgement on the person who chose them. What could one say of the superb *Rape of Europa*, painted by Titian in his 85th year, that was reckoned to be the most important painting in America? Or *The Concert* by Vermeer, purchased by Isabella for $6,000 and now worth a million? Or the Raphael *Inghirami*, a portrait on wood certified by Berenson as the original version of an 'inferior' painting in Florence?

And what could one say of the painting of Isabella Stewart Gardner herself, executed by the dexterous hand of an admiring John Singer Sargent? A lady of great elegance and perception, attentively portrayed. Wearing a gown, cut daringly at the throat, the latest creation from the House of Worth. A rope of pearls, hung with a ruby, to show off the neck: a double rope to show off the waist. And the strange tapestry – or was it wallpaper – that made a kind of rosette pattern behind her head, like the halo of a medieval saint.

A strong element of single-mindedness was apparent in the unsmiling face, the soul-searching eyes. It was also apparent in the arrangement of the museum, which under the terms of Isabella's will was maintained permanently in its original form. One would have to know this to understand why one painting, hanging in the dark space between two windows, was almost impossible to see; and another, hanging over a door, almost impossible to find. The stipulation included the positioning of furniture. In the Tapestry Room I spent some time trying to work out the significance of a series of orange spots marked on the floor. I consulted the attendant, who was standing by with an air of polite resignation to answer the question. The Tapestry Room, he explained, was still used – as in the late Mrs Gardner's day – for musical recitals and concerts. These performances required a repositioning of the furniture, and to ensure that everything was put back in the right place the location of each table and chair leg was marked on the floor. It was a special request of the owner that nothing should be changed: this, after all, was what gave the museum its special character...

Forty years after her death Fenway Court was still the home of Isabella Stewart Gardner, the pole star – and the enigma – of Boston society. Her presence was impressed on the arrangement of every curtain, the position of every chair, the hanging of every picture. To some it might have seemed an impossible imposition: to others a privileged insight into one woman's taste and devotion. Sceptical visitors should be directed to the Titian Room, to admire a painting of great delicacy, ascribed to Giorgione, of *Christ Bearing the Cross*. In front of the painting I was touched to see a silver vase, arranged with violets. The flowers, I learned, were changed every day.

The cloistered charm of Fenway Court and the bustle of the Boston subway was the difference between the old world and the new. The downtown train carried me in a few minutes to Park Street, on the eastern edge of Boston Common. This was the start of the Freedom Trail, scene of the final rift between the Old World and the New.

To give a detailed description of the monuments on this trail would be like reciting the Federal Constitution or Samuel Francis Smith's *America*. Between them, just three summed up the spirit of Old Boston.

In the Old State House 'the child of Independence was born'. This spirited eighteenth-century building – on whose cornices a lion and a unicorn were still, inexplicably, rampant – was the former seat of the colonial government, whose administrators had included some of the men who had later signed the Declaration of Independence in Philadelphia. From the balcony of the building, overlooking State Street, the Declaration had been read to an excited crowd, ready to confront the King of England. Fourteen years later, when the battle was over and the new Republic finally launched, the first President of the United States had stood on the same balcony, receiving the acclamation of the new Americans.

The first sacrifice of the Revolution was recorded a few yards further on, at the site of the 'Boston Massacre'. Here a guard of nine British Redcoats, driven to distraction by the missiles of a resentful mob of colonists, had committed the grave tactical error of opening fire. Their muskets, felling five doughty Bostonians, had ignited the tinder whose flames would be adroitly fanned by the patriots. At the ensuing trial of the soldiers two virtuous Boston lawyers, John Adams and Josiah Quincy Jr, had appeared for the defence, with the result that all but two of the soldiers had been acquitted. Convicted of manslaughter, the unhappy pair had suffered the penalty of being branded on the hand. Subsequently released, they had stood as Cain-like witnesses to the growing infamy of British rule, and as 'beneficiaries' of honest American justice.

Another memorial to the colonial (anti-colonial?) period was the Faneuil Hall, the Forum of the old town of Boston, where the outraged voices of the citizenry had been raised against the taxes imposed by the British Crown. Unfortunately the hall, which I'd been told housed an armoury of weapons from Revolutionary times, was closed, and I had to transfer my attention to the vast market building that lay behind it. The sight of the huge orange pumpkins piled high on the ground by the vegetable stalls reminded me of a forthcoming festival that meant more to the Celts of Boston than to the English: Hallowe'en.

Pumpkins aside, Old Boston seemed near to home. The streets here were irregular and narrow, like those of the City of London, with the same grey stone buildings and atmosphere of mercantile prosperity. At the end of the trail I found the most salient echo of all. A white steeple in the style of Wren, poised elegantly over a tree-lined mall. The Old North Church, built in 1723, was the oldest surviving church in Boston. In one of the oldest US cities, that made it something of a landmark. But the clue to its real fame lay in the equestrian statue at the opposite end of the mall. On the night of April 18th, 1775, a rider named Paul Revere had set out with a companion to beat the Redcoats to Lexington and Concord, two nearby towns where rebel activity had been reported. Two lanterns, hung in the steeple of the church, had signalled the departure of the British troops, whose orders were to capture stores of ammunition that had been hidden by the colonial militia. Riding through the night ahead of the Redcoats, Revere and his companion had given the warning to the Americans, who had gathered forces to intercept the British. The first military engagement between the two sides followed shortly at Lexington: 'the shot heard around the world'.

It was amusing to conjure up the possible sequence of events if in 1775 the British had managed to forestall the revolt for a couple of hundred years. In such unlikely circumstances, would the Paras have flown in from Wiltshire? And patriotic Bostonians, their eyes fixed on radar screens, reach for the telephone to alert the Pentagon? Would US-based missiles intercept the Phantom jets? Viewed in the light of the Old North Church, our modern age looked sadly unromantic.

New York Encore

The Night the Lights Went Out

How an Englishman spends Hallowe'en is hardly a matter for speculation. I would like, however, to record my experiences in the New York Bus Terminal Waiting Room, on the night of October 31st, 1965.

I started off feeling rather low. I was suffering that three-o'clock-in-the-morning, end-of-bus-ride feeling that I should have been used to by then. The most sobering thought was that I had now completed my tour of the United States. The landscape that had seemed without horizon or limit was gone, and there were no more 'scenic wonders' for my gaze. No more mountains, canyons, lakes, prairies. No more sunsets over desert, clouds over jagged peaks, winds over grassland. No more open road, with the thrill of a National Park or the glimpse of a distant sierra. Twelve thousand miles of asphalt had turned the dream into a memory.

It had also ended a very happy relationship, lasting from the time I'd first sat in this waiting room at the start of my journey. For three months, and for most of those 12,000 miles, my companion had been that lithe, streamlined beast that ranged freely and inexhaustibly across America: a creature with the added virtues

310

of punctuality, courtesy and a smooth ride. My appreciation of the beast could find no better expression than in a tatty little book of coupons, tucked into my hip pocket. Inside was one international 'See America' ticket, issued by the Greyhound Corporation. The last survivor, from two books of thirty-six tickets. The idea that I still had one more journey I could make... Would Miami ever seem so enticing?

A second empty book caused me more concern. In the Bank of Boston I had parted with my last traveller's cheque, to finance a bowl of Homemade Soup, price thirty cents, at the Boston Post House. This left me with a balance of nine dollars and seventy cents, plus the odd nickel tucked into a coat lining. With that figure in mind, I didn't care to check my sailing date. Two more days and I'd be on the Bowery.

In the meantime the New York Bus Terminal Waiting Room was the nearest thing to home. The second time around, I almost had a sense of belonging. I could have sworn that I'd seen a lot of the people before, veterans of the night of my arrival. One such was sitting opposite me, felt hat tipped forward over his unshaven face. I imagined that I had seen him in a dozen bus depot waiting rooms, right across America. His only claim to individuality was a lapel button inscribed: 'To Hell With Girls'.

Apart from the odd kit-bagged serviceman and long-distance traveller, most of the crowd were, I suspected, residents, waiting with a conditioned resignation for the next police raid. With every seat taken and some people (in the main, legitimate travellers) standing in protective groups around their baggage, there was a sense of security in numbers.

The limited dormitory facilities meant that even the contortionists, accustomed to lying across three raised slats without screaming, had been forced to accommodate themselves on a single seat. Such luxury had been spurned however by a befuddled black guy, who was lying on the floor. Signs of life came spasmodically as he groaned and flapped his arms like a walrus.

My heart sank as three Hallowe'en revellers arrived on the scene. I had met them earlier, on my way to the waiting room: three teenage girls in witches' hats whose encounter with the spirits, I guessed, was confined to the bottle of rum that they passed between them. A late-night 'Ghouls 'n' Ghosties' party had cost them the last bus home and now they had to spend the night in the terminal. Crazy, man.

Seeing me they advanced in formation. Three little nymphs in cotton dresses, their feet bare, walking unconcernedly between the benches of ogling men.

'Hey, you wanna come to a party?'

I looked at them blankly. 'Where?'

'Well, right here, of course.'

The invitation was extended, bench by bench, to the whole waiting room. The response was a mixture of whistles, groans and lustful glances. But the young things persisted, like sweet-voiced sirens beguiling a ship-load of tormented voyagers. The only one they failed to enchant was the prostrate wino, who like Ulysses was safe from their charms.

There was a blast of cold air suddenly as two policemen came in by the street entrance, smacking their nightsticks in the palms of their hands. Bad spirits, come to haunt the living.

Carrying out what was apparently a routine operation they went straight to the front bench and commenced jabbing their sticks at the sleeping occupants, cutting off their snores in mid-throttle and ejecting them from their seats. At first I thought the entire waiting room would be evacuated, but then I realised it was the residents they were after.

'Whadya fink this is – a hotel?'

Challenged to show their bus tickets, some of the accused were fumbling. Two elderly ladies, borne down by plastic bags, took evasive action and checked out. A bearded nomad, sitting on the bench marked 'Reserved for Women and Children' was not so vigilant.

'Cain't you read English?'

The man regarded the notice dumbly as one of the policeman pointed at it. He shook his head, and in a moment was hoisted to his feet and marched to the exit. The NYPD avengers were soon back and row by row the purge of the benches continued, a ritual flushing of the bums. Although I looked as bummy as the rest of them I was gratified that the policemen passed me by, their eyes fixed on other targets. A lesson to all transatlantic travellers passing through the New York Bus Terminal Waiting Room: hang on to your Cunard labels.

I looked anxiously at the black guy, still gyrating on the floor. It was obvious that the policemen had saved him till last, zeroing in like vultures swooping on an upended turtle. For a moment they stood over him with hands on hips in a classic threat posture. Then with precise co-ordination they delivered their demonstration of resuscitation techniques, as practised by the New York Police Department.

While one held the man's flailing arms the other thrust an ammonia capsule up his nose. An application to both nostrils producing little effect, they each grabbed his jacket and hauled him upright, or so that his bent knees were just clear of the floor, and walked him to the door. Where the ammonia had failed, only one treatment could succeed. The invigorating air of a New York street at four in the morning.

Their pogrom completed the policemen departed, thigh-whacking their nightsticks. Behind them they left the waiting room half empty, a scene of desolation. When my nerves had stopped jangling I realised I'd just witnessed an event unique to New York City life. A dawn raid on the Port Authority Bus Terminal.

The events that followed the policemen's departure cannot be recorded with certainty. In the small hours, after a long overnight journey from Boston, kept from sleep by sheer discomfort, I could be forgiven if my mind began to wander. Everything that happened then had a kind of abbreviated absurdity, like clips from a Mack Sennett movie.

First up was the wino, who had found his way back into the waiting room, this time in an agitated state. It appeared that he was now a victim of street theft, the second mugging of the evening. Paradoxically he was appealing to the same NYPD that had carried out the first one.

'*Polis! Polis!* They done taken my money!'

After several frenetic circuits of the waiting room he ran out into the main concourse, where his voice could still be heard, echoing into oblivion.

Next event was the reappearance of the girls, who had slipped out quietly on the arrival of the policemen. Once more they headed straight towards me, but this time, clearly, it wasn't to invite me to a party.

'Hey, whadya say we borrow your sleepin' bag?'

Before I could respond they had grabbed the bag, unzipped it and wrapped themselves up in it, tucking it under their bare feet and round their shivering bodies. Three white-faced pupae, sharing a cocoon. I wondered when they'd finally discovered that a draughty bus depot at four o'clock in the morning was not such a crazy scene after all.

Wasn't it, though? In a minute I was questioning my sanity as the street door swung open and a man in Highland costume marched in, complete with bagpipes under his arm. The spirit of Hallowe'en? Halting in the centre of the waiting room he gave us all a long, withering look. Any moment I expected a rendition of *Scotland The Brave*, followed by at least three reels and a lament. Such a thought might have occurred to the piper, but his disdainful expression suggested he was seeking a worthier audience. Without so much as a moistening of the lips he turned on his heel and marched out again.

After that the waiting room began to refill, mostly with the people who'd been evicted earlier. It seemed that this was where I'd come in. Not wishing to sit through another reel of the Keystone Cops I decided to try my luck with an early check-in at the Sloane House 'Y'. Shaking the three chrysalises from my sleeping bag I slipped out into the cold embrace of Ninth Avenue.

At the Cunard office the next day my worst fears were confirmed. The next *Queen*, they regretted, scheduled to sail in a day or two, was fully booked. I would have to wait a week for my return trip to England.

With six dollars in my pocket it was a hard punch to ride. I'd spent three dollars on the previous night at the 'Y': another day would see me clean. What then? The thought numbed me. I had one of three alternatives. A fast in Central Park, the British Consul, or the Department of Labor on 54th Street.

The first idea was ruled out not so much by my dislike of privation (since when could I afford that?) but by a natural fear of the jungle. I didn't know much about the muggers of Central Park, but was sure they didn't ask questions like 'Have you any money?' before they mugged you. The question of temporary financial assistance was equally unacceptable. It would be like a channel swimmer donning water wings in the last fifty yards.

By this process of elimination I found myself in a queue at the New York State Department of Labor, in what must have been one of the busiest offices in the city. It took me an hour to reach the counter, to be confronted by a poker-faced woman in glasses who looked blankly at my alien registration card. My hopes of being offered immediate employment at the Waldorf-Astoria evaporated in her draughty glance. 'Do you have a Social Security Card?'

Without one of those I couldn't work. Directed to Social Security Administration I joined another queue almost twice the length of the first to obtain a card with a magic number. Equipped with this cipher I returned to the Department of Labor where in due course I found myself face to face with the same frosty woman.

'What do you want to do, exactly?'

In the twin crystals of her spectacles I saw a seductive image of jewelled women sipping champagne at damask-covered tables, bathed in candlelight. And their companions, cigar-smoking, middle-aged playboys with dollar bills tucked under sideplates. 'Waiter?'

As though momentarily willing herself to be in another time and another place, the woman closed her eyes. 'Ninth floor. Service Industries Office.'

The end of the trail was a room reminiscent of the bus depot waiting room, its occupants sitting in quiet rows waiting their turn to be called. On an empty chair I found a form which I filled in and handed over the counter: my application for employment in the service industry. Sitting down I studied the figures around me, vaguely reminiscent of the tomato-pickers of San Jose. Bowery bums and winos, sad-looking Puerto Ricans, women (or men?) with false hair and tinted eyebrows. Some recovering lost sleep, others staring into space with a studied indifference to their neighbours and their surroundings. And probably to their fate.

In an hour or so I was called to the counter. A job had been allocated to me, in the CBS restaurant on Fifth Avenue. My joy was hard to contain. I looked at the introduction card, which I was instructed to take with me. Reporting time was 8pm and I was referred for the position of Dishwasher.

The only way of conquering a feeling of inferiority (and in New York even millionaires felt small) was to take a trip along 34th Street to Fifth Avenue, and then to the top floor of the large building on the corner. From here you could look down on the whole sinful world.

At the time of writing the Empire State was the world's tallest building, measuring 1,472 feet from ground level to the tip of the mast on its TV tower. Getting to the top was no problem, with a choice of seventy-four elevators. Before taking one, however, it was worth confirming that I'd come to the right place. Displayed in the lobby were dramatic presentations of the *Eight* Wonders of the World, done in illuminated stained glass. Starting with the Pyramids of Giza and ending with the Empire State, the only one built in the twentieth century. (What price the Astrodome, or the Hoover Dam?)

To reach the 102nd floor observatory at the top there was a climb of 1,860 stairs. This was one reason for using an elevator. The other could be appreciated by anyone familiar with a Cape Kennedy 'lift-off'. To experience the thrill of those first moments after firing it was not necessary to undergo the rigours of an astronaut's training. At eighteen feet per second, in the elevator of the world's tallest building, you got the full effect. And if someone was standing on your toes you didn't need to tell them to get off. Weightlessness occurred fairly rapidly, at some point after the fiftieth floor.

The trip to the eightieth took fifty seconds. A quick switch to another space capsule took me to the eighty-sixth, the lower of the two observatories. Leaving the elevator and groping for a life support system I made my way to the threshold of space. What I saw from that vertiginous height was not a view but a three-dimensional map, stretching away to infinity. The features were clearly marked, outlined by the sharp unclouded sunlight. I was looking south, at the prow of Manhattan island advancing into the Atlantic. The skyscrapers of the financial district, at the very tip, stood out like masts against a horizon, as outstanding here as when

I had first viewed them from the harbour. Defining the prow were the entrances to the two rivers that made Manhattan a peninsula. To the west, the broad opening of the Hudson River, separating New York from New Jersey. To the east the narrower entrance of the East River, spanned by the three bridges that connected the boroughs of Manhattan and Brooklyn. Through the thin mauve haze that hung over the Upper Bay I could just distinguish another of New York's five boroughs, Staten Island. And in the bay the tiny figure that had hailed my arrival at the golden door: the green goddess of Liberty, thrusting her beacon 300 feet in the air. But more exciting still were the twin verticals, like soft pencil marks on the horizon, that marked the opening to the Atlantic. The piers of that giant bridge under which I had sailed into the miracle of America, three months ago.

Walking around to the other side of the observatory I beheld the quite different view to the north. Here the buildings were the whole spectacle, a massive concentration of skyscrapers between 34th Street and Central Park. From this angle the sunlight threw the buildings into sharp relief. Each one stood out against its shadow, cast on the flat wall of its neighbour. The avenues, running north to south, were similarly defined like deep knife cuts. The guideline was Fifth Avenue, carving its unfaltering way through the heart of Manhattan and along the east side of Central Park. The park, three blocks wide and fifty-three deep, was a neat section cut out of the city, a green oblong that lay like a realtor's dream between the East and West Sides. From that height the apartment buildings of Fifth and Eighth Avenues, facing each other across the park, were like two rival armies, drawn up in close order and awaiting the command to advance.

Partly blocking the view of Central Park was the huge pile of the RCA building, the centrepiece of the 'city within a city' complex of the Rockefeller Center. Its tiered grandeur, which must have made it a landmark in the Thirties, now looked strangely out of place set against the more avant garde skyscrapers surrounding it.

Now that I was in outer space the superior view from the 102nd floor offered little more. But once again I had the sensation of being up there with the angels, in that tiny dark room with its reinforced windows. I would like to have planted a Union Jack there, just to show that we, too, were a nation of pioneers.

The man-made heights of Manhattan had other thrills to offer, beyond the expectations of a lone backpacker. An opportunity for high-altitude nightlife arose from my pre-trip correspondence with Dee Knapp, a journalist friend of my uncle's who had spent her working life in New York.

One telephone call on arrival and she'd risen to the occasion, offering to take me to dinner at the 'Top of the Sixes' (666 Fifth Avenue, only a few doors down from my dishwashing assignment at CBS). It was a splendid offer, and one I couldn't refuse, no matter what the social rules prescribed. I didn't tell Dee that I was down to my last four dollars, but she may have guessed.

A meal in a rooftop restaurant is always a different experience. In New York it was unforgettable. Surrounding us as we dined was a night-time panorama of the city: mighty towers of a thousand lights that shone in bright checkerboard patterns in the foreground and in tall shimmering beacons in the distance, where the lights coalesced. The view lent an edge to my already well-honed appetite.

Awaiting the starter, I tried not to disgrace myself with the breadsticks, but managed to consume not only my own but Dee's. The grilled shrimp that followed received similar summary justice; so too the rib-eye steak and chocolate sorbet. The conversation added extra relish. With that glimmering backcloth we could talk of only one thing: the phenomenon of New York City. The gigantic dynamo that seemed to be eternally self-generating: the supercharger of the world. Could it ever fail?

I told Dee about my earlier views of the city and how glad I was that I had a few extra days to take in some more. With the practicality and finesse that distinguishes all good journalists Dee told me exactly where I should go and how much time I should spend looking at so-and-so. The days from now until my sailing date were satisfactorily filled, with everything from the United Nations Building to the Metropolitan Museum of Art and the Solomon R. Guggenheim Museum. That left only the nights.

There came a moment in the evening when, with a brandy at

my lips, I glanced furtively at my watch. It was nearly eight o'clock, which meant I had to break another of the social courtesies. With some embarrassment I emptied my glass and asked Dee if she could possibly excuse me, as I had to go and do the washing up.

At first I thought it would be easy. The machine looked capable enough – a stainless steel giant that hummed and steamed at the touch of a switch. Clad in my official CBS kitchen staff overall I was ready to take command.

The steward had other ideas. 'You load the dishwasher,' he said tersely.

Like all back-stage Neros, he had his empire sewn up. A canvas chair, a cigar and a couple of submissive slaves. For a closer definition of my duties I needed to consult the other slave, who was called Joe.

Joe was an old hand who had worked in most of Manhattan's downtown restaurants. His ability to distinguish one end of a dish-washing machine from the other was demonstrated by the fact that he had positioned himself at the clean end, ready to receive and stack the plates as they came out of the rinse. My position, as the apprentice, was at the dirty end.

The routine was simple. As the trays came out of the hatch and along the conveyor belt I had to catch them and pile the crocks on the moving rack that fed them into the machine, checking for invasive items such as chop bones and melon rind.

For the first couple of hours my only thoughts concerned the dark habits of the diners in the restaurant upstairs. Anyone imagining the excesses of the affluent society were a myth should spend an evening with a dishwasher in New York's West Side. In two hours I must have scraped off enough food to avert a famine in darkest Africa.

Other depravities were in more personal rituals. Paper napkins used as cosmetic aids, twisted neatly through the handles of coffee cups. Toothpicks broken in half and wedged into liqueur glasses. And most loathsome of all, the cigars. Half-smoked and squashed to extinction in coffee cups, *hors d'oeuvre* dishes and finger bowls.

I purged my revulsion by watching the plates shuttle into the dishwasher, disappearing into the steaming jets of water. The steady hum, hiss and throb of the giant at work was compelling: I felt a strong urge to be not merely the agent of the machine but its master. A panel of switches on the side caught my eye, labelled with instructions ranging from 'Wash Water' through 'Rinse' to 'Final Rinsing Spray Water'. And then – most tantalising of all – 'Booster Steam Switch'.

A devilish scheme formed in my mind, to throw this switch and recreate the climactic scene from Fritz Lang's *Metropolis*, the moment when the machine-dominated future-world was finally transformed into chaos. But my plan was foiled by the kitchen steward, who chose, whenever I got too close to the switches, to make his own move, inspecting the steam pressure gauge and adjusting a valve. Had he suspected my intentions? I couldn't be sure, but the great director had asserted his authority and the revolt of the proletariat was crushed.

By 11pm the flow of crocks had abated and I guessed that the restaurant had closed. A pleasant illusion that my duties for the evening were discharged was, unhappily, short-lived. In a few minutes the first pans began to arrive.

I beheld them in wonder. Giant oval cauldrons a foot deep, their insides cakes of culinary sewage. Frying pans the size of dustbin lids filled with ice rinks of fat. Baking trays of every shape and size, blackened by burned-on grease. And then the utensils: kitchen knives like relics of the Bronze Age, giant ladles and spatulas, roasting forks and tongs – all encrusted with the thick residue of cooking.

All these, of course, had to be cleaned by hand. From the world of automation it was back to sweated industry, working in a sink with a brush and scourer. For two hours I did battle, scraping, scouring and scrubbing until my hands were raw. There were lessons to be learned and I learned them quickly.

Lesson One: Vegetable strainers have perforated bottoms and should not be scoured too vigorously. *Lesson Two:* Frying pans have naturally black bottoms, which need not be scoured at all. *Lesson Three:* The burnt-on grease in most saucepans has been there a long time and should be left alone.

By 1am the procession of ironmongery had ceased, and I groped warily in the sink – now a dark, noisome morass – for the last submerged pan. The crisp rustle of dollar bills and the scent of freshly laundered YMCA pillows were now dominating my senses and I could hardly believe it when the steward presented me with a floor mop and said: 'See what you can do with this.' Dishwashing, it seemed, had a pretty wide interpretation.

By 3am I'd mopped the floor, cleaned the sinks, scrubbed the draining boards and emptied the garbage bins. If Joe helped, I didn't notice. All I noticed, eventually, was the money in the calloused palm of my hand. Eleven dollars and seventy-five cents.

In the next couple of days I did two other jobs. Neither, mercifully, as bad as the first. But both instructing me in the less endearing aspects of human nature.

Al's Italian Villa got off to a bad start by being somewhere out in the farthest reaches of Queens, the largest and most featureless borough of New York City. The subway (Flushing Line from Times Square) was a new experience, but one that rapidly palled, indistinguishable from a trip to Leytonstone or Watford Junction on the London Underground. My appointment was for 3pm and when I finally got there I was very hungry, having forsaken lunch in Manhattan. I hoped, naturally enough, that a sympathetic Al would help me out.

As I paused in the front of the restaurant he came out from behind the counter. A squat, hairy, garlic-smelling man with an engraved scowl. When I announced myself as the dishwasher he looked surprised, as though he'd been expecting some completely different kind of person. But when I asked if I could have some lunch first, before I started work, the surprise turned to suspicion.

'You wash dishes. Then you eat.' He paused a moment, before adding: 'If you're good, for nothin'.'

In a small kitchen I was confronted by a pile of plates, submerged in a sinkful of water. From the contents of the water, and of the saucepans stacked on the draining board, I gathered that the speciality of the house was meatballs. From the modest quantity of the dishes I also guessed that they were not the most famous meatballs in the borough of Queens. The work, accordingly, was easy, a fact impressed on me at intervals by Al as he brought in the plates.

'Nice job you got here.'

On average he must have said that once every half-hour while I was working, and two or three times as I sat chewing my way through six meatballs and a pile of spaghetti. I felt like making a humorous reply, like it would be even nicer if he had a dishwashing machine, but I didn't think he'd get the joke. A warning voice told me to play it straight until I'd finished.

The golden moment never seemed to come. The hours before the restaurant closed stretched like the endless skeins of spaghetti in the chef's pan, eased only by the latter's wisecracks about the contents of his *stracciatella*. At 11pm, when the last customer had departed, I was called into the restaurant by Al. Anticipating the heady *ching* of his cash register I was mortified once again to receive a mop. One of those awkward things that had to be wrung out in a specially adapted bucket. My technique being all wrong I was obliged in a few minutes to return the mop to the proprietor, who applied it with aggressive skill to the area behind the counter. Quickly tiring he passed it back to me, suggesting that I do the rest of the floor the same way.

The cleaning-up process lasted until midday. Enough time for me to make a finite calculation of my earnings. At $1.25 an hour and allowing for social security tax, I couldn't expect less than $11.25. The only thing that I hadn't allowed for was that Al might not be so good at mathematics. Bemusedly, I watched him count out ten one-dollar bills.

At my protest, his scowl deepened. If I thought I was getting more than ten dollars I was mistaken. 'That's what I agreed with the employment office,' he said. 'And anyhow, didn't I do part of your job for you?'

In the face of such low cunning it was all I could do to maintain calm and dignity. But Al wasn't worried about that. 'Don't come back tomorrow,' he said. 'Friday's a busy night, you know?'

Something he added about giving me a recommendation, if I needed one, was lost in the fresh night air as I marched outside. Heading for the subway I made a stern vow. Never to wash another dish, for anything but love.

By some miracle I was able to keep the vow the next day, when I graduated from dishwasher to 'bus-boy' in the restaurant of the Coliseum Building in Columbus Circle, Central Park. The art of 'bussing' dishes was unknown to me, but proved infinitely preferable to washing them. All I had to do was go round the tables with a trolley, clearing the crocks and whisking away the crumbs without spilling too much of the customers' lunch in their laps. To convey the right impression of cleanliness and efficiency I was given a white cotton suit and paper cap to wear, which made me look like Dr Kildare on his ward rounds.

The only snag – and there had to be one – was my co-worker, a woman with cow-catcher teeth who drove her trolley like a steam locomotive between the tables, whipping up the crocks and wiping the tables with a daunting precision. A lifetime of 'bussing' had given her the veteran's antipathy for the novice – a category in which she unerringly placed me. Although we were responsible for separate sections of the restaurant she was forever coming over into my half, with criticism or advice. How she found time to attend to my duties as well as her own was beyond me.

'I do a good job here. They don't complain about *my* work.'

This comment and similar were delivered at regular intervals throughout the morning, establishing not only my colleague's superiority but my own inadequacy. As her chariot bore down on me I cast nervous glances at my salt and pepper pots, to ensure they were properly aligned, and that the ketchup cap was properly screwed on. Her scathing glance was enough to tell me, every time, that I had failed.

Relief from surveillance came only during the lunch hour, when the Coliseum staff poured in for their self-service snacks and there was too much for the cow-catcher to do to worry about me. As it happened I was well able to look after myself, and to impress countless awestruck diners with my efficiency. One old lady, admiring the deftness of my movements, asked if I was, by any chance, an out-of-work ballet dancer.

If I had a flair for the job, the last person to tell me would have been my fellow 'busser'. The nearest I got to encouragement (apart from the certain promise of $1.50 an hour) were her assurances that 'It's always a little harder the first day' and 'They pay a bonus here at Christmas'.

My last few days in New York passed pleasantly on the tide of my earnings, which by some miracle carried me through to the sailing date. In those few days I was able to see the best things in a city that had become in a few decades one of the cultural capitals of the world.

A culture not inherited, but earned – and no less spectacular for that. European visitors to the Metropolitan Museum of Art on Fifth Avenue, seeing the massive appropriation of their nations' artefacts, might well feel deprived. But before their protests became too vociferous they needed to consider their own record. What would Madrid's Prado have been without Isabella of Castile, the French Louvre without Napoleon? And the 'Met', with its 234 galleries and collections spanning five millennia, could be ranked beside them.

Three hours in the Metropolitan could be compared to three months in America: a diverse and demanding experience that left me, in the end, asking for more. The pattern of my journey, from state to state, from city to city, was replicated in my tour of the museum's galleries, devoted to classical and ancient Egyptian art, the Renaissance and modern European movements, plus everything you needed to see in nineteenth- and twentieth-century American art. It seemed that there was always another painting to admire, a staircase to be mounted, a gallery to explore. And then, when you thought you'd covered the ground, there was another museum to visit. Back in the entrance hall of the museum I discovered that there was a medieval section up in northern Manhattan, called the Cloisters. (I would visit that splendid institution the following day, walking all the way uptown through Harlem.)

A few blocks south of Central Park, the Museum of Modern Art – by nature of its exhibits – was potentially even more demanding. My view of art beyond Cezanne being of a dark corridor, I needed all the help I could get to lighten the way. The collection, from Arp to Zorach, was immense, but to my relief it was carefully phased to show the evolution of each of the movements and their influence on one another. There were arrows to guide me from room to room, and a fold-out plan of the floors to show the location of the different schools and the individual masterpieces, such as the Monet *Water Lilies* and the Picasso *Guernica*. Despite these aids I had ultimately to admit defeat, the impact of the endless rooms becoming both physical and cerebral. My only relief was to pause, at intervals, to study the progress of the more enlightened and aware, the sandal-footed aficionados who gazed earnestly at the cubes, circles and blots, occasionally making notes.

Easier on the cerebrum – and the feet – was the Solomon R. Guggenheim Museum. I like to think that when he designed this building Frank Lloyd Wright had people like me in mind. An elevator to the top, and then a walk down a spiral ramp at a gentle three-per-cent grade. Looking at the pictures arranged in orderly succession around the circular walls was little effort (even the sombre Edvard Munch was approachable under these conditions) and before I knew it I had descended to ground level.

When it opened in 1959 the museum had taken the worlds of art and architecture by storm. From a French Impressionist base the collection had expanded to the outer reaches of contemporary art, and the architecture owed its inspiration to natural forms. A snail was certainly the progenitor of that extraordinary coiled exterior, which reflected the inner spiral of the ramp. One in the eye for the 'Met"'s great Renaissance palace further down the road.

In the rapid surge of innovative cultural architecture that was transforming the life – and the face – of New York, the performing arts had their place. Up on Columbus Avenue at 62nd Street I found the new Lincoln Center for the Performing Arts nearly finished, with the Philharmonic Hall, Metropolitan Opera House, New York State Theatre and Vivian Beaumont Theatre complete and the Juilliard School of Music in the last phase of construction. The crisp white buildings, uniformly faced with travertine, made an interesting complex that offered a diversity of architectural facets. Most harmonious was the view of the Vivian Beaumont Theatre from the central plaza, with the little square pool in the foreground dominated by the majestic two-part bronze *Reclining Figure* by Henry Moore.

From the moment of setting foot in New York I had resolved to cross to the other side of the city to the East River, to gaze upon the building that was on every visitor's check-list to view, whether from a skyscraper, bridge or harbour cruise. No essay on the city's architectural innovations would be complete without a mention of the United Nations Building.

A crosstown bus, out of the rush hour, proved the quickest method of getting there. From the stop on 42nd Street and First Avenue I had only to cross the road to the six-block stretch of international territory that gave New York the proud, though diplomatically unmentionable title of 'World Capital'. Standing in classical isolation on their waterfront site were the principal buildings of the headquarters – the Secretariat and General Assembly. The one a slim, curtain-walled tablet, rising sheer against the clear sky, the other a low, gliding wedge of white limestone. I entered the building through the north side to join the gathering of visitors in the public lobby awaiting the guided tour.

We were not kept for long. With a precision and expertise that recalled my visit to the White House and Capitol, we were ushered through the General Assembly auditorium and various chambers in the Conference Building by a photogenic guide in United Nations blue. In a tape-recorder voice, adjusted to the acoustics of each chamber, she gave us an explanation of their different functions, and a description of the organisation of the UN and the work of its various agencies. With neither Assembly nor Councils currently in session, I had to conjure up my own gathering of delegates in exotic head-gear, filling the semi-circle of desks in the hall of the General Assembly.

But that wasn't all. Apart from the delegates I had to imagine the President of the General Assembly and the Secretary-General, sitting on the raised podium which dominated the hall under the UN emblem: the speaker at the rostrum, the advisers and official guests on either side and the interpreters, press, radio and TV people in the two tiers of glass-walled booths above the auditorium. It was like trying to recreate a gathering of the Roman Senate in the modern-day ghost of the Forum.

But even those who had missed out on the *shoe-banging had plenty to enjoy in the building itself. First credit belonged to the team of architects, led by the great visionaries Oscar Niemeyer and Le Corbusier. In addition, the work of Scandinavian schools was to be seen in the design and décor of the Council chambers, with meticulously chosen materials and colours, from the different woods used in the panelling and furniture to the fabrics of the curtains and tapestries.

---

* Refers to Nikita Krushchev's protest at the General Assembly, 12 October 1960.

The only piece of interior design that I found slightly baffling was in Sven Markelius' Economic and Social Council Chamber. In the delegates' area the lighting had been subtly concealed above a suspended ceiling. In the public gallery, however, the pipes and ducts of the heating and ventilation systems running across the ceiling had been left exposed, and painted with rectangles of black, grey and white. One could only guess at the designer's motives. To prove that the United Nations was not, as so many claimed, an abstraction, but a practical, functioning organism?

On the day before I sailed I remembered that I had to go and see Montezuma.

Montezuma was my last contact in America, engineered through the offices of *Animals* magazine. A distinguished contributor, whose story had featured in the magazine and whose photograph had appeared on the front cover.

Montezuma lived down in the Village, in an apartment on Horatio Street. He'd come all the way from Ecuador and was one of the Village celebrities. His exotic name, proclaiming his pre-Columbian roots, was a workable alternative to his scientific nomenclature: *Felis wiedii*. Montezuma, as zoologists will already be aware, was a margay. Related to the jaguar and ocelot, but smaller. Nocturnal natives of the tropical rainforests of South America, margays were lithe and long-limbed, with spots and stripes and coal-black eyes.

Like any wild creature domesticated at an early age, Montezuma was innocent of his birthright. Sensations of prowling in dark forests, alert to dangers and opportunities, were unknown to him. Even the pleasurable experience of mauling a farmyard chicken had been denied him. Instead he was obliged to follow the natural instincts of his two Persian housemates, Sinbad and Shah, and go on welfare.

This could, in his case, extend to the luxury of a chuck steak, which was beyond the dreams of his companions. As congenital domestics, they had to settle for Nine Lives or Fish 'n' Chix. They might however draw the line at some of the other specialities, such as bananas, which were on hand to satisfy their equatorial cousin's more exotic tastes.

Despite his seeming innocence Montezuma could show atavistic behaviour. All it took was a ball of wool, converted with a feral flick of the paw into a helpless rabbit that could be tormented at will. Such primeval playfulness was not without its cost. In the process of unravelling the wool the Merrills' apartment became Monty's jungle. The carpet was the forest floor, burred with skid marks. The sofas and drapes were the tree roots and trailing vines, anchor-points for tooth and claw. The ornaments were the tropical fruit, falling from the canopy.

My contact, who shared the apartment with Montezuma, was a Mrs Si Merrill. Mrs Merrill, who had written the aforementioned article about her pet entitled 'Cat With a Difference', was delighted that I should want to do a piece of my own about 'Monty', and take a few pictures. In her letter to me she had suggested that I give her a call during my stay in New York and fix an appointment. Warning me that she was often out during the day and that if I didn't reach her first time to try again. Beyond this I had no idea whether Montezuma himself was willing to talk to the Press.

With no reply to my first call I decided to leave it until later in the day. The morning was young and I took the subway down to the South Ferry stop on Battery Park, at the southernmost tip of Manhattan. From here I took the obligatory ferry trip to Staten Island, which must be about the cheapest sightseeing trip in New York. For five cents I travelled the eight miles across the harbour to the island, and for another nickel made the return trip to Manhattan. As an experience it could hardly match my first voyage into the harbour on the day of my arrival. But it was a refreshing escape – particularly for deck braves like myself – from the concrete canyons and traffic fumes of the city. Landing back at the Battery I felt pleasantly invigorated, both by the sea breezes and the sense of joy that came from seeing Manhattan once more on the horizon.

At this point, on the tip of Manhattan, I was within quarter of a mile of the Financial District, that great mountain range of buildings that had been my first view of the city. From the root of Broadway, at Bowling Green, I wandered up to Wall Street, the innermost canyon that ran in a straight line from Broadway to the East River. The walls of this narrow passage were lined by America's major banks, brokerage houses and investment companies, and its bedrock contained a significant amount of the nation's gold reserves and currency. But the money wasn't just lurking in the basement vaults. You could see it in action too, from the Visitor's Gallery of the New York Stock Exchange.

Here was a scene that made the floor of the London Stock Exchange look like a bingo parlour. From corner to corner of the vast hall a sea of humanity eddied and whirled, hundreds of terylene-suited men scurrying around with bits of paper and tickertape in their hands. Shouting instructions at one another and pausing spasmodically to check the magnified tape that wound continuously along two sides of the hall. This tape recorded every transaction – and the faces and gestures of the brokers the reaction.

The one mopping his neck with a handkerchief was no doubt assured that General Dynamics were holding their price: the one knuckling his brow wondering why some mutt dealer in Pittsburgh was selling off his Consolidated Electronics. It was pure theatre, with entertaining elements of comedy and tragedy.

It was interesting to recall that Wall Street owed its name to the wall that had been built by the Dutch colonists three centuries ago, to mark the *northern* boundary of their settlement. Whatever happened to Nieuw Amsterdam?

From Wall Street I continued north to City Hall, passing on my journey the aptly named 'Cathedral of Commerce', otherwise known as the Woolworth Building. Completed in 1913, this monument to the retail pioneer Frank W. Woolworth was in the fastidious style known as 'American Gothic', which on closer examination revealed spires, gargoyles and flying buttresses. Until 1930 this impressive structure – built on the profits of chain stores selling merchandise for a nickel – was the world's tallest building.

At City Hall I found myself at the west end of Brooklyn Bridge. Crossing the East River by the board footwalk suspended over the bridge I set foot in New York's most populated borough, which held about a third of the city's eight million inhabitants. With another borough under my belt I made my way along the Brooklyn waterfront to the Manhattan Bridge, to cross back to the Lower East Side. Unfortunately the original pedestrian walkway on this bridge had been closed and I found myself dependent on a

nine-inch wide girder, running alongside the carriageway. Trying
to ignore the steady flow of traffic that thundered past me I inched
my way along the girder, fully aware that one false step would
guarantee me a permanent bond with New York City.

The bridge was half a mile wide and it took me an hour to get
across. Unheedingly the cars and trucks rushed by, wafting me to
one side. My only reward was the view of Brooklyn Bridge to the
south, suspended by its tracery of cables and wires between its
elegant, Gothic-arched piers. Beyond it stood the hazy towers of
the Financial District at the tip of the peninsula.

By the time I got off the bridge I was in Chinatown, deep in
the heart of Manhattan. Or should I say the heart of Peking. This
was, after all, centre of the largest population of Chinese people in
the Western hemisphere. Turning away from the oriental bustle of
Canal Street I entered a wider thoroughfare running northwards
that had a quieter sense, almost of desolation. Looking at the signs
I saw that I was in the Bowery.

The Bowery had the reputation of a kind of universal Skid
Row, haunted by down-and-outs and dope addicts. It was a place
you could finish up if you didn't follow The Dream. This image, of
being at the end of the road, gave it a kind of spurious glamour in
the eyes of all except those who lived on it. The guide books made
little reference to the Bowery, but it was still one of the places you
needed to see, along with the Empire State and the rest, just to reassure yourself that there was someone further down the pile than
you.

The denizens of this street, exploited in a thousand photo
essays, had an uncomfortable familiarity. A line of drunks swaying
arm in arm across the sidewalk, one of them with dried blood
on his nose. Another foraging listlessly for cigarette butts in the
windswept litter. But the saddest figure of all was the one doing
nothing. A black man in a long, patched overcoat, standing on the
edge of the kerb. Not drunk, or foraging, or even chewing a butt-
end. Just staring into empty space, the desert of his life.

I thought of the pillars of glass on Park Avenue, inhabited by the
smart ones, and could see that the abuse – much of it hypocritical
– heaped by non-Americans on Americans had some justification.
To coin a cliché, New York *was* a jungle, thriving on a bed of decay.

If you made it to the canopy you received the sunlight, but if you didn't have the growth hormones you languished at the bottom.

West of the Bowery, in Washington Square, I gave Mrs Merrill another call. A youth, identifying himself as Mrs Merrill's son, answered the phone. 'You wanna see Monty? Sure, come around. Mother was kinda expecting you. You know where we are? Number Two, Horatio Street, fourteenth floor. Mother's in the laundry right now. Try there before you come up.'

Horatio Street was at the north-west corner of the village, slanting defiantly away from the right-angle grid of the streets to the north. The apartment building overlooked Jackson Square, in actuality the triangle formed by the convergence of Eighth Avenue, Greenwich Avenue and Horatio Street. When I arrived there I was pretty tired, having covered about five miles in the course of my downtown wanderings.

Mrs Merrill, sure enough, was in the laundry, down in the basement. A passable stand-in for Lauren Bacall, she wore stretch jeans and a Country and Western shirt, open at the neck. As she hauled the mangled clothing from a drier I couldn't help thinking that I might have chosen a better time to call, but then remembered that she'd been the one to make the date.

'Hi! You wanna see Monty?'

The directness of her greeting reassured me. With an armful of laundry I followed her to the elevator and we went up to the fourteenth floor. 'Monty's kinda nervous with visitors,' she said on the way up, 'but once he gets to know you he'll settle down.' Her son Michael, a nineteen-year-old college boy, let us in to the apartment. While Mrs Merrill disposed of the laundry and Michael showed me to a sofa I looked cautiously round the room. Cupboard tops first, and then under the tables. But there was no sign of life, no lurking jungle cat coiled ready to spring.

Relaxing on the leatherette I took in some details. The Merrills lived well, undoubtedly conscious of the role décor played in their lives. Velour drapes, hand-crafted furniture, concealed lighting. The home entertainment centre built discreetly into the corner cabinet, the flameless electric fire set into the colonial-style fireplace. Everything was in its place, but I couldn't help noticing that most of the movable objects, such as the porcelain, were locked away in glass cabinets. I concluded that Mrs Merrill was either a very tidy person, or...

She came back into the room in a cord slack suit, ready for the interview. Sitting beside me on the sofa she apologised for her hair, which looked fine to me. 'The steam in that laundry is a wrecker,' she said. '*Drink*, Michael.'

Michael obliged us with a Bourbon. With the glass in her hand, I could see Mrs Merrill settling into the image of herself that made her comfortable. That made me comfortable, too. We were soon talking inconsequentially about life in New York, the Village and the problems of keeping pets in apartments. The Merrills, I learned, had a very special problem.

'*Mon-ty!*'

Half the Bourbon went down my trouser leg as a tawny shape flashed past me and landed on Mrs Merrill. Not much larger than a domestic cat but with the body of a panther, lithe and heavy-limbed. Marked with decorative blotches and stripes, like an ocelot. And with the most extraordinary eyes, like orbs of obsidian set in the blunt, slanting head. All this I noticed in a few fleeting seconds, before the animal leapt down and scudded across the floor into another room.

With an anguished sigh, Mrs Merrill dropped into a chair. 'That was Montezuma,' she said. 'Montezuma the margay. He always gets excited when we have someone visit. He'll settle down in a while, when he gets used to you.'

The Merrills had seen Montezuma in a pet shop while on holiday in Ecuador. Separated from his mother the little fellow's pitiful squeaks tugged at their heartstrings and it was love at first sight. They had brought him back with them, as a six-week old cub, to New York. For most animals born in the wild such an extreme change of environment might have been fatal, but this did not apply to Montezuma. Unlike most wild cats, margays were adaptable, easily-tamed creatures. The transition from tropical jungle to air-conditioned apartment had not imposed too great a strain on Montezuma: more on the apartment. Since his arrival the Merrills' home had become a playground, hit by intermittent cyclones. The Merrills' two Persian cats, at first resisting the newcomer, had finally acknowledged his superiority, proved in the rough-and-tumbles from which the margay invariably emerged the victor. Mrs Merrill, meanwhile, had become an expert in restoring china.

'I shouldn't think there's a single vase in this place still in one piece,' she said. 'That cat's real wild – and he's the tamest damn creature on earth! You've gotta play with him, that's all. If Monty wants a game, you play. You ignore him, and he jumps on your head.'

At that moment the margay reappeared from behind the sofa and looked at us with his dark, questioning eyes. 'He must have heard us talking about him,' said Mrs Merrill. We watched as he climbed with leisurely deliberation onto the sofa then turned, fixing us with that round-eyed, melancholic gaze.

'Gosh, he's a beauty.' I wanted to stroke him, just to feel that supple feline body, but remembering what Mrs Merrill had said about the margay's reaction to strangers I held back. Instead I asked Mrs Merrill if I could take a picture while there was still light, as I only had daylight film.

Mrs Merrill frowned. 'That's no good for indoors, is it? You want high-speed. Why don't I call my husband? He's got some in his studio, he can bring home with him.'

Before I could tell her not to trouble she'd picked up the phone and dialled a number. 'That you, Si? Look, honey, will you do me a favour? I've got the man here, wants to photograph the cat. You know, the *Animal* man. Well, look, he's only got daylight film. You got any of that *fast* stuff in the studio? You have? Well, be an angel and bring a coupla rolls, will you honey?' Nodding a couple of times, she put the phone down. 'That's OK,' she said to me. 'He's on his way right now.'

Inspecting my camera I saw that I still had some exposures left on my film. Before changing to high-speed, I thought I might as well use them. The only problem was Montezuma, who had just leapt from the sofa onto the top of a bookcase.

It took Mrs Merrill ten minutes to coax him down. And another ten minutes to get him back on the sofa where he sat watching us cautiously, his body tense and quivering. Fearing that he would take off again at any moment I quickly checked my exposure meter. There was now very little light, and I opened the lens right out. The dark reflective eyes, like matching lenses, followed my every movement.

'Hey, how about a bit of extra light?'

I watched hesitantly as Mrs Merrill went and switched on a lamp positioned strategically over the sofa. I was having serious doubts about my credentials as an animal photographer, and wandered how my editor-in-chief, the famous wildlife expert and film maker Armand Denis, would have handled the situation. His equipment, for a start, would have been a little more sophisticated.

The overhead lighting was not too good for the subject, but Monty had been here before and was settled into a suitable pose, his neck regally arched and front legs stretched sphinx-like before him.

Then, before I had a chance to adjust the exposure, the light began to fade. Mrs Merrill cursed and flicked the switch a couple of times.

'Well I'll be –'

It was still fading, slowly but surely. 'That was a new three-hundred I put in there yesterday –'

I watched uneasily as the ceiling lights began to flicker and then dim to a hesitant glow. With a groan Mrs Merrill strode over to the telephone. 'Hold on a moment, I'll get the houseman. They must be playing with the damn fuse-box or something.' Picking up the receiver she rattled the phone rest. 'Hello, is that the lobby?' Shaking her head, she put it down again. 'Busy. Guess there must be other folks with a problem.'

At that moment the lights went out completely. For a few seconds there was total darkness in the room and total silence, as though the apartment had been sealed off from the outside world. Then Merrill Junior, who had been looking out of the window, gave a wild, ecstatic cry.

'Gee, Ma – the Empire State's going out!'

We rushed to the window, for a grandstand view of the most astonishing spectacle Manhattan had ever staged. The tallest building in the world, a mighty beacon of candlepower, gradually fading from sight. Seeing that checkerboard of light, a hundred stories high, growing fainter and fainter until it finally disappeared, I could believe I was witnessing the end of the world.

The giant was twenty blocks to the north. Twenty blocks that had become shadows. The traffic and street lights had gone too and all that marked the course of Eighth Avenue were the headlights of the rush-hour traffic, which was rapidly coalescing into a solid immovable line, blocked by the uncontrolled flow from the intersections. Slowly the impossible truth dawned on us. New York City had a power failure.

At first we kept our calm. Mrs Merrill felt around in the dark for the Bourbon and glasses, her son went into the kitchen for some candles, and I sank onto the sofa. Immediately I began to feel nervous.

Tentatively, I stretched out my hand. But Monty wasn't there. I stared into the darkness of the room, trying to make shapes out of shadows, searching for movement. I wondered how a jungle creature would react in such a situation. Would his domestic upbringing prevail? Would he be cowering fearfully under a chair? Or would he be back in his old home, in the darkness of the tropical jungle?

The thought had, perhaps, occurred to my hostess. The glass of Bourbon pressed into my hand followed the fate of its predecessor, but down the other leg. Mrs Merrill's voice came out of nowhere like a faltering siren. 'Can someone please tell me what is going on?'

The young Merrill provided the answer. In the middle of his search for candles he'd unearthed a transistor radio, the one piece of equipment that did not have to rely on Consolidated Edison. A breathless, edgy voice – enough in itself to trigger a national emergency – gave us the news that ten minutes ago a large part of New York had been blacked out by a power failure. The fault had not yet been traced, but the announcer was confident that within a short time full power would be restored.

'In the meantime, folks, we've rigged up a temporary turntable and microphone, powered by emergency equipment, and will be bringing you reports on the situation as they come in...'

Merrill Junior gave a long, drawn-out sigh of relief. 'Well, at least the Martians haven't taken over the radio stations yet.'

The Armageddon humour was lost on his mother, who was groping around for something in a drawer. 'Where are my pills, Michael? Did you remember where I put my pills, for Chris' sakes?'

The boy didn't answer, and I prayed she'd find them. Then something clawed at my shoulder and I swallowed my breath.

It was Mrs Merrill, grabbing me in the darkness. 'Dear God, if Si's caught in that subway –' Her hand closed tightly on my arm. 'What time did I call him – you remember?'

'About half an hour ago.'

'Half an hour? It takes twenty minutes from his office to Fourteenth Street. Oh, my God –'

'Wow...' Merrill Junior was back at the window, gazing at the dark obelisk of the Empire State. 'How about being stuck in an elevator, or walking down from the ninety-second floor...?'

'Or maybe fetching some goddam candles!' The urgency in his mother's voice connected and he stumbled back into the kitchen.

The voice on the radio had reached a similar pitch.

'This is WCBS, bringing you the latest news on the New York power failure. The cause of the failure has not yet been confirmed, but is thought by officials of the Con-Ed Corporation to have originated somewhere in the upstate system. This failure has affected Manhattan, Bronx and Queens, and parts of Brooklyn. Also parts of Newark, New Jersey and Westchester County. New Haven, Connecticut is out, and Providence, Rhode Island. We'll broadcast reports as they come in, and in between we'll play you some music. The message is: "Stay calm, folks, and stay tuned".'

Thinking of all the places I might have been at this moment – the subway, a stranded elevator, a taxi on Fifth Avenue – I determined to follow the announcer's advice. Here I was, after all, sitting comfortably in a Greenwich Village apartment, insulated from the outside world, while those unfortunate New Yorkers – many of them stranded miles from home – milled about like blind lemmings in the streets below. Gratefully I swigged the remnants of my drink, and nearly fainted as something brushed against my leg.

'WCBS reporting. We've just heard that Providence, Rhode Island, and parts of Connecticut are out –'

My whole body was shaking, my nerves stretched like piano wires. I could already feel the sinewy, smooth pelted body embracing me, the taste of death on its breath...

'Hey, Ma, I just thought – they'd be warming up for the basketball in the Garden round about now –'

'Yeah? In the dark? Where are those goddam candles?'

'WCBS reporting. With the traffic signal failure resulting from the loss of power, New York City traffic is now at a standstill. Mayor Wagner has been summoned back to City Hall, to take overall charge of the emergency. We have reports, however, that the police car sent to fetch him has been lost. If you're listening to me, good luck your honour.'

I could feel the needle-sharp claws stabbing through my shirt, sinking into my flesh...

'Hey, Ma, the light in the ice-box has gone out –'

'Sure it's gone out, but you won't find what you're looking for in there –'

'WCBS reporting. It has now been confirmed that the city of Boston Massachusetts is out.'

I could feel the vice-like jaws closing on my windpipe, the teeth joining in mortal union, the powerful hind legs threshing, raking my viscera...

'Hey, Ma – Sinbad and Shah have gotten into the wall unit – they're sure scared!'

'For God's sake, Michael – you won't find the candles there, either. Try the store cupboard –'

'WCBS reporting the latest on the power shut-down, which has extended to Portsmouth, New Hampshire and Portland, Maine –'

Through my ebbing consciousness I could feel my life-blood draining. Somehow it didn't matter, on the wipe-clean leatherette...

'Hey, Ma – I found them!'

'Thank God. Light them, quick.'

'Parts of Vermont –'

The telephone rang, shocking me back to reality. Mrs Merrill leapt on it.

'Si? Is that really *you*, honey? Where are you, for heaven's sake? In the lobby? I don't believe it. You got off the train then? Oh, my God. The train stopped short of Fourteenth and you had to walk along the tunnel? Oh, God. Now listen here, Si. You got fourteen floors to climb and I want you to take it easy, *real* easy. One at a time. We'll see you when we see you, OK honey?'

As Mrs Merrill put the phone down her son came back into the room with three candles, already lit. 'Three? Is that all we had left from the candlelight party? Hell, we better get some power, and pretty darn soon –' She peered around the apartment. 'Now, where's that damn cat?'

We each took a candle. Cautiously I followed Mrs Merrill, looking in hidden places under furniture and bracing myself for a surprise attack. The candlelight was creepy, more deceptive than the darkness because it made the shadows move. At any moment, I feared, one of those shadows would materialise into a snarling, spitting jungle cat, ready for the kill. My suspense was only relieved by the voice of Mrs Merrill's son, calling from the bedroom.

'It's OK, Ma. Monty's under the bed.'

I returned to the sofa. Mrs Merrill fetched the Bourbon, this time filling my glass with some concentration. 'I should have remembered that,' she said. 'Whenever that cat gets scared, it makes a dive under the bed.'

With Montezuma accounted for, and Mr Merrill out of danger, it seemed we could relax. But that was reckoning without WCBS.

The voice was controlled, but only just. 'Hi, folks. The power failure which has immobilised New York City is now affecting large areas of the state. Cities affected include Albany, Utica, Schenectady, Syracuse, Rochester, Buffalo and Niagara Falls. In Manhattan, where all traffic and street lights have failed, the city is blocked by the worst traffic jam ever. We have reports of a subway train trapped under the East River, and another bound for Jersey City trapped under the Hudson. Flights into La Guardia and Kennedy airports, now in total darkness, are being diverted to Newark. Emergency generators are now supplying power to all New York hospitals –'

The voice cut off and we froze as a key turned in the door. In the flickering light of our candles we beheld the spectral figure of Si Merrill. Ashen-faced, shirt collar torn open, tie hanging loose. He looked around the apartment nervously, as though to convince himself it was still there.

'Fix me a Bourbon, quick.'

While Mrs Merrill helped her husband to a chair and Michael fixed the drink we went through the introductions. But I got the impression that Mr Merrill had other things on his mind at that moment than meeting the man who'd come to photograph his cat.

'WCBS reporting. We've been notified of a blackout in Toronto, Canada –'

At that point, gulping down my third Bourbon, I reckoned it was time to leave. Even if there was a miraculous return of light, and we got Monty out from under the bed, the shoot was definitely kaput.

'Are you sure you have to go?' Mrs Merrill sounded genuinely anxious. 'All those stairs, in the dark – !'

'Give him a candle,' said Mr Merrill.

I accepted the offer. My farewells tendered, I left the three of them standing there in the candlelight like traumatised waxworks and started down the stairs. Very slowly, because I didn't have any matches and the flame would have to keep going till I got to the bottom. Fourteen floors seemed a long way, but at least it was downhill.

Halfway down I met a couple of policemen with flashlights, herding a heavily-blowing procession of tenants determinedly scaling the heights to their apartments. At the bottom of the stairs, groping my way into the lobby, I saw the others. White-faced, talking in whispers and huddled round a flickering oil light. With the elevator out of action they were stranded, unable to face the unknown.

Nervously I went out into the darkened street. It wasn't until I got to the corner of the block that I realised I was still holding the candle aloft. But it had gone out, so nobody was going to arrest me for impersonating a patriotic symbol. Not tonight, anyhow.

Sometime next morning I was sitting in a bar off 52nd Street, drinking my last cup of American coffee and reading the *New York Journal American*. 'The Big Blackout' carried no less than ten pages, with such compelling headlines as 'If Enemy Struck – the Stark Preview for 30,000,000' reflecting the latent paranoia of a city whose lifeline – electric power – had been severed for twelve hours. Most of the stories were about people trapped half the night in a subway tunnel, employees suspended in frozen elevators and commuters sleeping rough in Grand Central Station. Beneath it all, I felt, was this undercurrent of fear, that perhaps the whole thing might be a hideous plot by an enemy power to destroy the United

States. The blackout was therefore an act of sabotage, the prelude to a massive thermo-nuclear attack in which millions of people, caught in the streets in the rush-hour exodus or immobilised in transit, would have perished like blinded rats.

Eighty thousand square miles of pitch darkness had been the nearest thing to judgment day – not only for America but for the world. Within fifty seconds of the failure, North-eastern Military Command had brought itself to 'Condition One', the final stage of war readiness. While the radar scanners had probed the skies, the Minutemen and Titan rockets had been checked for 'ready' and the bombers put on runway alert. For ten long minutes, until the cause of the failure had been identified, the world had been poised on the edge of Armageddon. Such was the derangement of the nuclear age, that the great American nation – and a fair percentage of the rest of the world – had nearly been destroyed by a short circuit in upstate New York.

Here was the central paradox of America. A great country, born out of a quest for individual liberty, achieving its nationhood by the same ideal, directing its limitless energy towards the breaking of frontiers, at first on land and then in space: a country with a vast record of achievement and even vaster potential. And yet painfully aware, as the champion of the modern democratic ideal, of its vulnerability. Not only to the forces that opposed it, but to the forces within, that were questioning the very nature of that ideal. Why this should be I could not attempt, with my limited vision, to explore, but to all those who had watched the agony of America in the last half decade the truth was known. In the midst of its success, America had faltered.

In race relations, in social justice, in the exercise of power abroad. Examples need hardly be quoted, in a country so exposed to the critical gaze of the world. Through the medium of television we had seen – and almost smelt – the fires of Watts, Newark and Detroit. In the context of the Affluent Society the figure of forty million poor seemed an aberration.

At the start of my journey I had wondered how much of the truth I would see with my own eyes. After 12,000 miles I realised that I had seen very little. Mountains, forest and deserts, yes. Bridges, highways and skyscrapers, certainly. Some Old Glory heritage, some space-age ephemera. But how much of the reality that lay beyond those diverting images?

I remembered the glimpses. The black receptionist in the hotel in Washington, resentful of the attitudes of white society. The tomato-pickers of San Jose, an urban underclass on a day-haul to their next meal. Charlie Sunrise of Cedar City, the Comanche Indian whose wanderings in search of work – and acceptance – had taken him across half a continent. And that sad, solitary figure in the Bowery, the black drifter in the patched overcoat who had lost the reason to hope.

'Give me your tired, your poor, your huddled masses yearning to breathe free...' That was how Emma Lazarus had put it. It might have been the motto of the new nation, if John D. Rockefeller hadn't taught his Sunday School about the 'survival of the fittest'. Rockefeller, of course, had been talking about business, but his words might have applied equally to the society that he and his fellow capitalists were creating.

The growing disparity between his kind and the huddled masses could paradoxically be attributed to the 'natural law' enshrined in so many of the constitutional documents drawn up by his forebears. That law, which gave the right to fail the same credence as the right to succeed, perhaps ensured the continued existence of the poverty, the overcrowding and the persecution from which so many had endeavoured to escape by making a new life in America.

If I could make any judgment on this land, after my kaleidoscopic view, it would relate to that strange paradox, of a powerful nation in search of reassurance. Its faith in that power, diminished by the endless war it was fighting in a small Asian country thousands of miles away, had little hope of recovery while that war continued and its people became more and more disenchanted with their nation's cause. Vietnam has not been a topic in this memoir, and I had become aware on my travels of America's deep sensitivity on the subject. It was easy, after all, for our Old World cultures to express their condemnation of America's actions, but we couldn't hope to fathom them until we first accepted that this New World was still making its history, crossing the same frontiers that we Europeans had crossed so heedlessly in our colonial past.

Unlike us, with our beds of tradition to fall back on, America had nothing but those slender three and a half centuries. A cracked bell, an old colonial church and meeting hall, a mission in Texas. Wherever I'd gone, I'd seen America working at its history, as though it were something that could be created with the right amount of brawn and ingenuity. How much easier to build the legacy with a concrete dam, a thousand-mile freeway, or an air-conditioned sports arena!

The memorial temples of Washington DC and the Lamar High School Orientation Day would not seem related. But I realised that they were both part of the same process. The creation of history in those classical marble shrines, the creation of tradition with those bouncing cheerleaders and stirring anthems. Lamar was clearly America's investment in the future. To build more temples the nation would need more heroes.

The question that I'd started out with remained unanswered. Where the Gettysburg address and popcorn came on the scale of priorities was still a mystery. The only declared priority was the image of the Americans themselves: what they stood for, what they were worth and where they and their country stood in the eyes of the world. Such self-awareness, though a little uncomfortable for the stranger, was perhaps the most redeeming characteristic of the American people. They could make more cars than babies and send a chimpanzee into space, and yet they still needed cheerleaders.

Momentarily I imagined that I had company, but then saw the rucksack sitting on the bar stool beside me. After the rigours of three months' travel it looked rather sad: rumpled, tattered and grimy. Strapped on the top was my souvenir copy of the Sunday *New York Times*, which weighed at least ten pounds. And inside was packed the debris of my trip, shortly to be unearthed with the first rush of nostalgia.

Amongst the mountain of clothing, books and film I would discover the mementos: everything from a San Francisco cable-car ticket to that farmworker's card with the holes punched in it. Looking back on the trip I knew that I'd be grateful not only for what I'd seen but what I'd avoided. The hurricane in Florida, the earthquake in California, the blizzard in the Rockies. And that ferocious grizzly, subsequently transformed into a fat and friendly black bear hooked on oatmeal jumble cookies.

The coffee was fifteen cents, the last of the earnings from my day at the Coliseum. If one thing had been proved conclusively by this trip, it was the limitations of my mathematics. Six dollars a day? Even with the Greyhound bus ticket to take care of the travel the whole trip had cost me, per day, six dollars *and thirty cents*.

Camel-like I bent down and strapped on the rucksack, ready for the last hike. An old fellow in a boiler suit sitting further along the counter watched every movement with curiosity. As I straightened up under the weight he grinned and saluted me.

'Have a good trip, feller!'

I smiled. Better late than never. I felt like shaking his hand, the only New Yorker who'd ever wished me anything. Leaving the bar I turned west and headed for Pier 92.

Waiting for me was the RMS *Queen Elizabeth*'s sister ship, the *Queen Mary*. I felt that the two great ladies were making a special effort for me. There was a thick mist on the Hudson and the skyscrapers on the far side of the river were soft, intangible shapes.

From the deck I could see a clutch of people gathered on the pier, umbrellas up to ward off the cold drizzle. In a moment they had disappeared in the mist as the ship cast off. Gliding out into the harbour, Manhattan was scarcely visible to my gaze. In a way I was glad that I wouldn't see that skyline disappear, remembering everything that had happened on the other side of it.

Afterword

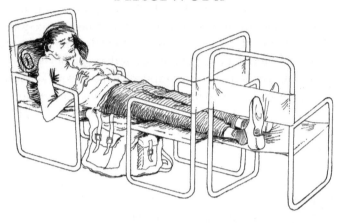

It's been a strange 'out-of-body' experience, returning to the images and words of my younger self. Typed laboriously on yellowing foolscap paper, fifty-five years ago.

When I started re-reading *Go Greyhound, Go!* after all that time it was as if I had discovered – and then reinvented – this innocent and impressionable individual who had lived through a multitude of adventures in a land that, until then, existed only in his imagination. An individual who wasn't me at all but a stranger who was spared, happily, the wisdom and scepticism of those five and a half decades.

This made it easier, when it came to revisiting the story, to utilise the space between us, and the objectivity that it brought to our relationship. Easier, indeed, to negotiate the encounter with a singular 'other' who had thrown himself unwittingly into the seminal, life-changing Sixties in a country so like – and yet so unlike – his own.

I learned from the book that this fearless character had blown about a bit in the streets of New York, revelled in the colonial history of Boston and Philadelphia, gone wild in the West, paddled in the Pacific and flippered in the Atlantic, swung to Dixieland in New Orleans, and shivered in the awesomeness of Yellowstone. And met with some folks who had filled him with joy, and others with sorrow.

I recognised all of my responses to the journey as the playback of my cultural education, certified by my white-British passport. And coupled with this, the privilege of my innocence.

The babe in the woods had, it seemed, coped with it all. He'd even learned the language that made pavements 'sidewalks', a lift an 'elevator' and a chemist a 'drugstore'. He'd learned that the divisions of a common language had their counterpart in the divisions of a common history, as witnessed by the stirring events at Philadelphia and Boston. And regardless of whether he'd been challenged by the sharks of city nightlife, or of the waters of the Florida Keys, he'd maintained a British calm.

That it was all so long ago was evident in every faded page. In 1965 I'd recorded the Great Fire of San Francisco as the worst disaster to hit an American city. With the Twin Towers as yet unbuilt, 9/11 was not even predicted. Similarly the New York blackout had been a cataclysmic event at the time, but since then three more blackouts have extinguished the city. The Empire State Building, dramatically disappearing into the darkness in the final chapter, was noted as the world's tallest building: now a skyscraper in Dubai has elbowed it to forty-eighth.

The Watts riots of 1965, sparked by the arrest of an African American for drunken driving, were then the worst in the history of Los Angeles, only to be eclipsed by the Rodney King riots in 1992. After Watts there were successive anti-police riots in Newark and Detroit in 1967, and all across the country following the shooting of Martin Luther King in 1968. The seeds of the black rebellion that had reached a critical mass in the anti-segregation protests of the Fifties and early Sixties could be traced to those symbols of servitude I'd seen in Charleston's Old Slave Mart Museum.

When considering these unhappy events the question of language came up again. Some definitions had to be changed. In the original text the word 'negro' – acceptable in the Sixties – had been prevalent, but could hardly be recast as the 'African American' unfamiliar at the time. 'Black' had to be the catch-all. The term 'Native American' being similarly unknown I thought it right to stay with the 'Indian' or 'American Indian' in use until the end of the century. And was I not compromised by the name of that famous university football team, the 'Stanford Indians'?

What else did I not know then, that I know now? That Disneyland, Knott's Berry Farm and Miami Seaquarium would still be going strong in the 2020s? That Disney would consume Twentieth Century Fox? That Stanford would become just a small part of the area south of San Francisco known as Silicon Valley? That San Francisco itself would become the mecca of the 'Flower Power' dreamed up by Ginsberg in the mid sixties as a protest against the Vietnam War?

Or how about that meeting with the venerable Ham in Washington Zoo? Who could have foreseen that the first 'chimponaut', launched into space in 1961, would become the trailblazer for the first man on the moon in 1969?

Like Smokey Bear, Ham was a national icon, but during my long haul across the States I got close and personal with several other creatures who though not in the same league of celebrity possessed their own unique personalities. Frances the American Badger, Muffin the perfumed Peke and – most memorable of all – Montezuma the Margay. All since sadly consigned to a desert grave, silk-lined casket or tropical heaven.

Following animals with humans (in the natural order of things) I considered the twenty-first century view of some of the figures I had admired in different places. What price now the Spanish monk Fra Junipero Serra, whose saintly presence I had encountered in the Mission San Carlos Borromeo at Carmel? In 2020, as an act of contrition for the brothers' harsh treatment of the subjugated tribes at this and other missions in the late eighteenth century, California's political activists had removed his statue from the State Capitol Park in Sacramento. Canonised by Pope Francis in 2015, Serra's statue in Washington's Capitol, representing the Golden State, was little more secure, with talk of its replacement by the astronaut Sally Ride.

Following the tragic death of George Floyd at the hands of racist police in Minneapolis in 2020, the statues of all those figures now recognised as white supremacists were getting a bad press. An unfortunate turn of events for General Robert E Lee (1807-1870), commander of the Confederate forces in the American Civil War. A splendid equestrian bronze of the general in Richmond, Virginia, was separated from its plinth in the same year. Remembering my visit to his family mansion, Arlington House in Washington, maintained in his name to honour his memory as a post-war healer of wounds, it seemed paradoxical that his statue in the former capital of the Confederacy should be removed.

The third candidate for reappraisal was Henry Ford. After my visit to his home in Dearborn I came away with the image of a great industrialist, creator of the universally popular Model T Ford and pioneer of the modern assembly line. That there was a darker side to the man was not examined in the memorial displays in the Ford Museum: for example his anti-semitism, well known in his life-time but tolerated by those who were in awe of his prestige and respectful of the acceptance of his beliefs in American society. It was only in the writings of recent historians and journalists that his virulent attitudes to the Jews had been properly condemned.

And what of the intrepid traveller himself, looking back at it all? The trip had been achieved by a much younger man, whose timid and less resourceful older self would never have made it. Imagine humping that rucksack on the desert highway at dead of night, searching for somewhere to lay my sleeping bag! Or diving off a boat into the tropical waters of the Florida Reef (yes, I might still do that, but only with a shark pole).

What of the threats of climate change, greenhouse gases and plastic pollution, then little known? With that knowledge, and of the later devastation of California's forests, could I still have viewed the Firefall as a great tourist attraction?

Final question: would I be up to carrying out the journey again on such limited funds, even with a book of bus tickets and a friendly sponsor? With my immigration credentials I'd been able to bail myself out in the tomato fields of San Jose and the kitchens of New York, but the thought of bending my back again to reach that elusive fruit, or of gagging at those saucepan-loads of fat was inconceivable. I had to remind myself, too, that those helpful documents held a hidden danger. If I'd remained in America for longer than six months they might have spelled my doom.

But looking on the bright side, as a Private First Class in the US Army, parachuted onto Vietnam's Highway One, I would have found new challenges. And with one certain hope to reassure me, that the next Greyhound bus would be along very soon.

On the Bowery

Acknowledgements

With the advent of the transatlantic airliner I was lucky to have been one of the last steamship passengers to America on the two great Cunarders, RMS *Queen Elizabeth* and her sister ship the *Queen Mary*. Sadly the former (retired in 1968) ended her days as a burnt-out hulk in Hong Kong harbour; the latter (retired a year earlier) has happily found new life as a floating luxury hotel at Long Beach, California. Their successor, the more economical QE2, which was successfully operated as both a transatlantic liner and a cruise ship from 1969 to 2008, enjoys a similar retirement as a luxury hotel in the harbour at Dubai.

I have already expressed in these pages my heartfelt gratitude to Greyhound International and the Young Men's Christian Association. They offered a home and a refuge throughout my journey.

The people who helped me on my way – one or two friends but mostly strangers – are safe in my memory. Sadly they're mostly no longer with us, but those who are will hopefully appreciate their inclusion in this tribute.

Robert and Jean Schroeder, Elizabeth Mendell, Mr and Mrs Wilbert T. Mendell and members of their family including the estimable Marsden Blois III, who later joined them as Elizabeth's husband. Lewis Wayne Walker and Mervyn Larson of the Arizona-Sonora Desert Museum, Bernie Crampton, Sarah Harper, Andy Hosack, Al Kolaski, Charlie Sunrise, Mike Noble, Leslie Morris, Charlie Standen, Dee Knapp, Mr and Mrs Si Merrill and their son Michael. The multitude of drivers who helped me along the highway, including that intrepid OshKosh guy.

To those who helped me reclaim my story fifty-five years on, I offer special thanks. Typewritten pages of yesteryear became digital files with the aid of my son Thomas Watkins, and editorial comments were kindly contributed by Persephone Pearl and Kate Belinski. Author and traveller John Mole was kind enough to read the words.

'THEY WAS BUS DRIVERS, ONCE'

ACKNOWLEDGEMENTS

Mrs. Si Merrill

2 HORATIO STREET, NEW YORK 14, N. Y.

August 9, 1965

Letters from Mrs Merrill on my arrival in New York and on my return home following the Blackout

Dear Mr. Watkins:

I will be more than happy to have you visit us and the one I suspect you are most interested in .. Montezuma.

Our phone number is Ch-2-6269. If the weather is marvelous, it is possible that we will be on Fire Island if you arrive on a weekend, but usually by the end of October we are in the city for good. Do try to let me know in advance when you will be in the city.

I have just recently received a copy of Animals from France with Montes picture on the cover. It was a pleasant surprise. He really is as pretty as his pictures but sometimes not quite as angelic as his pictures although he is going on six years old now and doesn't seem to spend as much time looking for mischief as he used to.

We do hope to see you.

Sincerely

Meg Merrill

Mrs. Si Merrill

Dear Paul:

Thank you for your note. We are very happy that you were able to use the film although, as you said, none of it was of Monte.

It certainly was a wild evening and I worried about you constantly because we could see from our window that the busses were worse than cattle cars. I stopped worrying about you, however, when at 11 o'clock I said jokingly to Mike, "Hey, how about running downstairs and getting some ice cream" and he said, "O. K." and did. It is, as you will recall, 13 floors. You have to be young for that sort of caper. He said it was really a night to be out . . it was marvelous and beautiful. I felt that it was also a night for hobgoblins and muggers and wasn't anxious to have him wandering around, but as it turned out, of course, I was quite wrong. The crime rate that night was miraculously low. I suppose every one was in some sort of state of shock. We didn't go to bed until quite late and when I woke up the next morning, Si had the radio on. When it gave the time, I started to set my alarm clock and then said "Oh, you've already set my clock." He hadn't. Our lights had gone on, to the minute, at the exact time 12 hours later that they had gone out.

Best, *Meg*

The author arriving in New York Harbour on August 5, 1965. The view from the boat deck on the *Queen Elizabeth* was glorious but gave little hint of the wonders that lay beyond. After his return from America later in the year, and following the completion of the original text of his book, Paul Watkins moved to Camden Town, London, where he has since lived, writing about travel and editing *The Anglo-Hellenic Review*.